The Twisted Worlds
of Philip K. Dick

LIBRARY OF CONGRESS CATALOGUING-IN-PUBLICATION DATA

Rossi, Umberto, 1960–
    The twisted worlds of Philip K. Dick : a reading of
twenty ontologically uncertain novels / Umberto Rossi.
        p.   cm.
    Includes bibliographical references and index.

    ISBN 978-0-7864-4883-8
    softcover : 50# alkaline paper

    1. Dick, Philip K.—Criticism and interpretation.
    2. Science fiction, American—History and criticism.
    I. Title.
    PS3554.I3Z87   2011
    813'.54—dc22   2011004822

BRITISH LIBRARY CATALOGUING DATA ARE AVAILABLE

Cover illustration by Kim D. French; (inset) Philip K. Dick

Manufactured in the United States of America

*McFarland & Company, Inc., Publishers
    Box 611, Jefferson, North Carolina 28640
    www.mcfarlandpub.com*

The Twisted Worlds of Philip K. Dick

A Reading of Twenty Ontologically Uncertain Novels

UMBERTO ROSSI

McFarland & Company, Inc., Publishers
Jefferson, North Carolina, and London

A mio padre, che comprava gli Urania e i Cosmo Oro

Acknowledgments

I could never have written this book without my 13-year interaction with the people of the PKD list managed by Cal Godot. I also wish to thank Andrew M. Butler, Russell Galen, David Gill, Frank Hollander, Donald Keene, Perry Kinman, Gabriel McKee, Maurizio Nati, and Chris J. Zähller for their help. I should thank Gabriele Frasca and Carlo Pagetti because they showed me how seriously you can read Dick's fiction even if sometimes the author himself did not take it so seriously (yet, being a master of self-contradiction, he took it all too seriously other times). Special thanks to Fredric Jameson and Peter Fitting for the same reason, but in an American context. I thank Luca Briasco, Domenico Caiati, Mattia Carratello, Domenico Gallo, and Paolo Prezzavento for numberless conversations about Dick and his universes that fall apart (not to mention their translations); I thank Antonio Caronia for repeated creative disagreements and for his Dickian encyclopedia entries. Last but not least, I thank my wife, Franca Sinopoli, for her precious and sustained encouragement and manifold support.

Table of Contents

Introduction

...in February of 1974 I saw Christ the new Saviour, but discorporate...
Fat

Took drugs. Saw God. BFD.
Phil

Dick's Twisted World

Maybe the best way to understand Philip K. Dick is by reading Robert Sheckley. This most underrated science-fiction writer once depicted — in his 1966 novel *Mindswap*, one of the neglected masterpieces of both sf and postmodernist fiction — a strange place, maybe a playful allegory of sf (and fiction in general), called the Twisted World. It is described (à la Borges) by three excerpts of imaginary books, the last of which, *The Inexorability of the Specious*, has been written by the villain of the novel, the interplanetary confidence trickster Ze Kraggash, who declares:

> Remember that all rules may lie, in the Twisted World, including this rule which points out the exception ... But also remember that no rule *necessarily* lies; that any rule may be true, including this rule and its exception.
> In the Twisted World, time need not follow your preconceptions. Events may change rapidly (which seems proper), or slowly (which feels better), or not at all (which is hateful).
> It is conceivable that *nothing whatsoever* will happen to you in the Twisted World. It would be unwise to expect this, and equally unwise to be unprepared for it....
> Do not expect to outwit the Twisted World. It is bigger, smaller, longer and shorter than you; it does not prove, it is [Sheckley 174–6].

Sheckley, who evolved from witty (but often chilling) sociological sf to postmodernist metafiction in the 1960s, is obviously referring to the inexhaustible potentialities of the genre he practiced — but I would rather read this as an involuntary prediction of the current state of Dick scholarship,[1] that is, the predicament of critics who are tying to measure a twisted fictional world like Dick's, which is bigger, smaller, longer and shorter than they think. In other words, we have not come to terms with Dick yet, notwithstanding the excellent scholarship devoted to this most beguiling writer by such brilliant critics as Jameson, Suvin, Baudrillard, or Frasca.[2] So far the attempts to find an overall interpretation, a comprehensive assessment of Dick's oeuvre have fallen short of the author. There have been, as I have already said, good readings of single works or groups of works, but whenever critics have tried to tell us — if such a pedestrian idiom is allowed — what Philip Kindred Dick is all about, they have offered unsatisfactory formulations.

The problem is that Dick is a most complex author: one who — like Walt Whitman — used to unashamedly contradict himself. The strangeness of his figure as a writer has been effectively captured by one of his non-academic commentators, Jonathan Lethem:

> There's this writer who works with the pop-culture iconography of science fiction but with such mad originality and verve — and emotional intensity — that he created his own personal genre ... he deserves your serious attention as much as any realist writer ... he also wrote these eight puzzling and unforgettable novels in a dour, lower-middle-class realist mode ... These too, deserve a look (despite, ahem, infelicities in the prose) [Lethem 82–3].

No wonder that Lethem ends this paragraph by admitting that "[t]hat double reverse may simply be too much" (Lethem 83). He is not the only commentator who noticed Dick's strangeness. Douglas A. Mackey, who wrote one of the first overall introductions to Dick's oeuvre, said that his best novels "seem to constitute some kind of topological form as in an Escher drawing, with its own internal logic, completely self-referential, the equivalent of the paradoxical logic loop: 'The following statement is true. The preceding statement is false'" (Mackey 95–6). Besides, the paradoxical character of Dick's fiction had been already highlighted by one of the earliest commentators, Stanislaw Lem, who maintained that "Dick succeeds in changing a circus tent into a temple, and during this process the reader may experience catharsis" and adds "[i]t is extremely difficult to grasp analytically the means that make it possible for him to do so" (Lem 1972, 74).

If grasping what is or are Dick's dominating stylistic and imaginative feature(s) is so hard, one should not be surprised if we have only had partial portraits so far, which only capture glimpses of his oeuvre and world. The only attempts to read Dick's whole oeuvre are Robinson's 1984 monograph *The Novels of Philip K. Dick*, the work of a brilliant PhD student who could not profit from many documents which had not been published yet (some of Dick's non-sf novels, his letters) and appeared when the secondary literature was remarkably smaller than it is today; and Palmer's *Philip K. Dick: Exhilaration and Terror of the Postmodern*, which is a collection of articles — some of which stimulating and rich in precious insights — without an organic plan.

Portraying the whole oeuvre is admittedly a difficult task. Dick is not just a sf writer, but he is also not just a fiction writer. He cannot be canonized as a "simple" postmodernist novelist because he is also a realist, and his sf output is not always a form of postmodernist parody/pastiche or Avantpop[3] hybridization — it was quite often the production of a professional writer who wrote sf to make ends meet. Besides, Dick's relation to sf is also complex and contradictory: his moments of pride in the sf genre notwithstanding (he even proposed the community of sf pro writers as a model of utopian non-competitive society in his essay "Who Is an Sf Writer?"), he — Lawrence Sutin's biography exhaustively proved this — repeatedly tried to escape the ghetto of commercial sf to reach the respectable literary publishing houses as a realist writer. Yet sf is not just a spurious element or a regrettable constraint in the texture of Dick's narratives. Though I do not agree with those critics who, like Patricia Warrick (Warrick xiv), disparage Dick's non-sf novels,[4] I am well aware that some of Dick's most remarkable literary achievements are those works, be they novels or short stories, where the particular fictional devices of sf are used in a most original and usually astonishing way — or those which play a rather different game, deliberately inserting sfnal elements in novels having a substantially realistic texture (this happens for example in *We Can Build You* and *VALIS*).

While the placement of Dick's fictions on the map of late Twentieth Century literature is problematic, it should be said that critics have been mostly interested in the *content* of his novels, if such an old-fashioned term is allowed. Robots/androids, virtual reality, simulation and simulacra, mass-media, late capitalism, schizophrenia/paranoia, Nazism, American imperialism, even post-colonial concerns: interpreters have found these and other issues embodied in this or that figure, scene, or place in Dick's fiction, and have used his works as examples to be discussed according to their political agenda, cultural curiosities, theoretical assumptions, etc. There have undoubtedly been attempts at understanding what is Dick's writing strategy and what sort of a writer he is, to put it bluntly, but also those attempts (Christopher Palmer's, for example) have been marred by some theoretical assumption: often critics who support a certain critical or philosophical theory, be it Marxism, postmodernism, or post-humanism, read Dick looking for a confirmation of those theories, so that they only take into account what chimes in with their theoretical/political agendas. Hence the many partial readings of Dick — some of them brilliant (e.g. Jameson's), some of them not — which do not even try to offer overall picture of his fiction.

Readers should be forewarned that this text will not attempt to cover the whole oeuvre of Philip K. Dick, which includes more than forty novels and a hundred short stories, plus a handful of essays and the cumbersome *Exegesis*, Dick's notes written during his disordered philosophical and religious research in the 1970s, whose publication is imminent. On the other hand it does cover in some detail twenty novels plus several short stories and novelettes, in a reading based on a unifying interpretive hypothesis, and trying to map the intertextual connections which tie these novels to each other and to those I have not dealt with in detail. Though it is not an attempt to discuss everything Dick wrote, it tries to mark off groups of interconnected works and suggest thematic links that may be used by other commentators to work on those texts which are not analyzed here.

A Matter of Style

The issue of Dick's style is one that must be tackled in this preliminary part. Some critics have so far disparaged Dick for the low quality of his prose (a relatively recent example is Adam Gopnik's review of the Library of America publication of a selection of Dick's novels on *The New Yorker*).[5] This approach, which may have contributed to hinder his canonization (especially in the USA), is based on a fundamental misunderstanding of what is a novel. In fact a novel is not just well-crafted prose, possibly with a pyrotechnic display of metaphors and other tropes. Finely wrought prose may often hide a very traditional narrative strategy and a quite primitive textual architecture. The art of the novel is one of telling, and it is in the structuring of the plot, in the architecture of the narrative that we may find Dick's "added value." His prose is not always brilliant (though it may often be) and it is sometimes shoddy (prevalently shoddy, or simply functional, in some of the weakest novels); we should not forget that Dick was a pro writer who had to earn a living and pay alimony to his former wives, unable to escape the sf ghetto and its scanty remunerations — this brought him to produce as much as he could, using amphetamines to write novel after novel.[6] Such a situation sentenced him to frantic hyper-production (between 1963 and 1964 Dick completed nine novels, among which at least four of his most famous ones), which in turn did not always allow him to chisel and polish his sentences.

If we want to focus on microstructures only we will find many unsatisfactory passages and sentences which ask for the intervention of a professional editor; yet we will also find impressive moments of prose like this one from *Do Androids Dream of Electric Sheep?*, not one of the passages that are usually quoted:

> At an oil painting Phil Resch halted, gazed intently. The painting showed a hairless, oppressed creature with ha head like an inverted pear, its hands clapped in horror to its ears, its mouth open in a vast, soundless scream. Twisted ripples of the creature's torment, echoes of its cry, flooded out into the air surrounding it; the man or woman, whichever it was, had become contained by its own howl. It had covered its ears against its own sound. The creature stood on a bridge and no one else was present; the creature screamed in isolation. Cut off by — or despite — its outcry [100].

I have not read many descriptions which managed to capture the lacerating intensity of Edvard Munch's 1893 painting *The Scream* so effectively, in such a terse and compact manner. So, when a critic complained that "[a]t the end of a Dick marathon, you end up admiring every one of his conceits and not a single one of his sentences" (Gopnik 82), I could ask whether the unit that measures prose is the sentence or the paragraph; since there are good reasons to believe it is the latter, Gopnik's criticism seems definitely misplaced, and based on a misconception. Besides, many memorable novels, which are considered now canonized classics, do not contain any admirable sentence, but manage to tell a story with miraculous effectiveness. If a critic is only looking for admirable sentences he should probably read poetry, not fiction.

On the other hand, nobody seems to have tried to understand what were Dick's own ideas about prose, though they are explained in several passages of his letters and interviews. A letter he wrote in 1973 is particularly interesting, because it says that "[t]he entire fundamental basic line of English prose ... makes its great impact not through soaring words — i.e. *poetic* words — but by the strength of prose itself; one must not shift out of prose when one's head soars" (*SL2* 210). Dick's conception of prose derives from Herbert Read, as he admits in the same letter, and it is based on the idea that prose is not poetry in disguise. Uncommon words (including those of the poetic diction) should be avoided; unusual syntax is not advisable as "archaic word-order of a poetic sort" (*SL2* 211) is self-defeating. In his letter Dick presents several examples of the turgid prose that he considers bad prose and bad poetry: from these examples we may understand that he appreciated a linear, essential style. In the letter he mentions Swift, Donne, Hemingway (*SL2* 210) as milestones of English prose; on the other hand he considered Shakespeare "a bore... because of the rhetoric" (Rickman 1988, 212), so the baroque, complex metaphors and luxuriant vocabulary of the Bard did not attract him. Some of his models are not even fiction writers: he appreciated Samuel Pepys, and praised Thomas Paine "for powerful, direct prose" (Rickman 1988, 212).

The fact that Dick loved Joyce and extolled *Finnegans Wake* (Rickman 1988, 212) should not lead us to think he was interested in the linguistic fireworks which characterize the prose of the Irish novelist. A cursory reading of

Dick's more painstakingly written novels of the early 1960s (*Time Out of Joint, The Man in the High Castle, Martian Time-Slip*) shows that what Dick found really interesting in Joyce was the technique of the inner monologue, especially as it is used in the first two chapters of *Ulysses*. In Dick's fiction we often find a peculiar sort of lightweight stream of consciousness like this, mindful of Joyce's rhythm, taken from *The Man in the High Castle*:

> Didn't Diesel throw himself out the window of his stateroom? Commit suicide by drowning himself on an ocean voyage? Maybe I ought to do that. But here there was no ocean. But there is always a way. Like in Shakespeare. A pin stuck through one's shirt front, and good-bye Frink. The girl who need not fear marauding homeless from the desert. Walks upright in consciousness of many pinched-nerve possibilities in grizzled salivating adversary. Death instead by, say, sniffing car exhaust in highway town, perhaps through long hollow straw [35].

In a 1974 letter to his father Dick praises Edgar's style: his parent's letter is "an example for all time of the absolute English prose model, such as they used to have in the great era of simple and direct English, of Swift, of Pope" (*SL3* 32). If we add his appreciation of Thackeray (Rickman 1988, 212) it is clear that Dick's model was the classical 18th-century prose, and it is against such a model that his achievements should be measured. If we are looking for a Don DeLillo or a John Hawkes, we have opened the wrong books.

Jameson's Uncertainty

It may be proved, and this is exactly the aim of my monograph, that at the core of Dick's oeuvre there is something that I propose to call *ontological uncertainty*. Such a condition was already described by one of the earliest academic essays on Dick, Fredric Jameson's "After Armageddon," published on the March 1975 special issue of *Science-Fiction Studies* devoted to the Californian writer.

> Every reader of Dick is familiar with this nightmarish uncertainty, this reality fluctuation, sometimes accounted for by drugs, sometimes by schizophrenia, and sometimes by new SF powers, in which the psychic world as it were goes outside, and reappears in the form of simulacra or of some photographically cunning reproduction of the external [Jameson 1975, 350].

Jameson makes an important distinction about the "nightmarish uncertainty" we find in Dick's works: Dick has a peculiar position in the dilemma "which in one way or another characterizes all modern literature of some consequence" (Jameson 1975, 350), that between a "literature of the self," focused on the subjective dimension, and the "language of impersonal exteriority," which counters subjectivity with some "stable place of common sense and statistics."[7] Dick's peculiarity, according to Jameson, is that he strives to retain and use both dimensions, proposing "subjective and objective explanation systems" at once.

Hence in Dick's fiction there are two forms of *purely* subjective simulation which find no place, and are never used as bases for his narrative architectures: "sheer fantasy and dream narrative" (Jameson 1975, 350), which were typical of symbolism and high modernism (dreams being also a cornerstone of romanticism). This does not mean that Dick's characters do not dream or are never lost in reverie; what Jameson is saying, and my survey of twenty novels by Dick brings me to agree with him, is that neither reverie nor dream are used as the narrative engine which propels the plots of Dick's novels (and short stories). As one can see in the twenty-seventh chapter of *Flow My Tears, The Policeman Said*, Felix Buckman's dream is treated as such (regardless of its meaning in the novel), not taken for a real event; the same may be said for Mr. Baynes' reverie in Chapter 15 of *The Man in the High Castle*.

Hallucinatory experiences in Dick are usually explained with drugs, schizophrenia or half-life, because, in Jameson's opinion, it is

> a way of affirming their reality and rescuing their intolerable experiences from being defused as an unthreatening surrealism: a way of preserving the resistance and the density of the subjective moment, of emphasizing the commitment of his work to this very alternation itself as its basic content [Jameson 1975, 350–1].

If the alternation between subjective and objective is the basic content of Dick's fiction, it should obviously be underscored by critics wherever it is detected; it should be preserved in the interpretive discourse, not explained away. Hence my decision to pursue that alternation, which I have called ontological uncertainty, especially in those novels where it is not merely episodic, but can be said to structure the whole text one way or another.[8]

Jameson's formulation of Dick's ontological uncertainty is particularly important as it was somewhat endorsed by the author himself. A copy of the 1975 special issue of *Science-Fiction Studies* was sent to Dick, who discussed it with Claudia Bush, a student of Idaho State University who was writing her MA thesis. In his March 4, 1975, letter to Bush, Dick quoted several passages of the letter, and commented "this man Jameson who wrote this is brilliant" (*SL4*, 130), and goes on by interpreting Jameson's discussion of the character systems in *Bloodmoney* in a very personal way.[9] The writer quoted Jameson's essay again in his speech "Man, Android and Machine" (1976), where the passage of "After Armageddon" we have quoted, discussing Dick's peculiar inversion of the internal and the external (Jameson 1975, 350), is taken by Dick as validating his idea of external reality as a *dokos*-veil or veil of Maya, hiding the real world—a veil which was, in Dick's opinion at that time, spun by the right hemisphere of the brain (*Shifting Realities* 221). Dick's very personal interpretation of Jameson's solid academic analyses might be easily branded as a misreading, but since Dick's unorthodox use of neurological theories gave us one of his best novels, *A Scanner Darkly*, it should be seen as creative misreading. Moreover, what is at stake both in Jameson's analysis and in Dick's home-made epistemological theories is the difficulty of directly grasping the world (as it is or as it is depicted in fiction) as something immediately meaningful, as something evident in itself. Jameson worked with Marxist and structuralist tools; Dick's approach to the issue was based on a rather unconventional mix of neurosciences, philosophy, theology and sf; both however addressed ontological uncertainty, an issue (or problem) that Dick found at moments more painful than Jameson could imagine when he wrote his essay on *Bloodmoney*.

This is a concept that has often been tackled under different names by different critics: shifting realities, construction of realities, only apparently real worlds, schizoculture, universes falling apart. Brian McHale discussed the issue of "ontological instability" in his fundamental essay on Thomas Pynchon's *Gravity's Rainbow* in 1979, positing this condition as the key feature of postmodernist fiction in general; he subsequently applied this category to Dick's *Ubik* in 1991, though the main focus of his essay "POSTcyberMOD-ERNpunkISM" was cyberpunk, so that no detailed discussion of single Dickian texts can be found in that critical analysis. McHale's reading of Pynchon can however be said to have paved the way for my reading of Dick. Jean Baudrillard's 1980 essay on "Simulacra and Science-Fiction," extolling Dick (and J.G. Ballard) as the narrators of postmodern realities, or better de-realization, is another milestone in the interpretation of Dick's oeuvre:

> Perhaps the SF of this era of cybernetics and hyperreality will only be able to attempt to "artificially" resurrect the "historical" worlds of the past, trying to reconstruct *in vitro* and down to its tiniest details the various episodes of bygone days: events, persons, defunct ideologies—all now empty of meaning and of their original essence, but hypnotic with retrospective truth. Like the Civil War in Philip K. Dick's *The Simulacra*; like a gigantic hologram in three dimensions, where fiction will never again be a mirror held to the future, but rather a desperate rehallucinating of the past [Baudrillard 310].

The simulation of the American Civil War does not actually occur in *The Simulacra* (where an actual civil war takes place, which can however be seen as a resurrection of the historical War Between the States, cf. Ch. 5), but in *We Can Build You* (Ch. 6). However, the reconstruction *in vitro* of the past is something which undeniably characterizes Dick's fiction: we could mention the reproduction of Washington as it was in 1935 in *Now Wait for Last Year* (Ch. 5), the historical characters used as teachers in *Martian Time-Slip* (Ch. 4), the technologically resurrected Abraham Lincoln in *We Can Build You* (Ch. 6), the fake town of the American 1950s in *Time Out of Joint* (Ch. 2), the bogus dictator resembling Mussolini in the short story "If There Were No Benny Cemoli" (1963) and the reconstructed house of 1954 in "Exhibit Piece" (1954). It is, after all, another version of ontological uncertainty, one in which it is the past that can be only apparently real or unreal; and if we take into account counterfactual versions of the past with their events, persons, defunct ideologies, we have other works, such as *The Man in the High Castle* or *The Transmigration of Timothy Archer*, which are undoubtedly hypnotic with retrospective truth.

These insights of the earliest academic interpreters of Dick's oeuvre chime in with Robinson's concept of a "reality breakdown" (35–7), even though here the scope of such a breakdown is somewhat limited by the suggestion that the protagonist's "experience becomes not a reality breakdown, but a breakthrough *to* ... [a] more basic reality," i.e. "the law of entropy, the gradual falling apart of all form" (Robinson 36)—though such a breakdown *to* reality does not always take place in Dick's fictions where reality breaks down. Bukatman is more persuasive in his reading of *The Simulacra*, one of Dick's most destructured postmodernist novels, which leads him to maintain that "Dick constructs a decentered narrative structure wherein multiple characters interact in a futile quest to fix reality, and therefore themselves, in place" (53)—an acceptable formulation, provided we do not forget that the attempt to fix reality may be futile, but the quest may yield something else.

These were the pioneer years of Dick scholarship. It is however interesting that the four axes of ontological uncertainty as hypothesized by Jameson and Baudrillard—drugs, schizophrenia, half-life, history—reappear as entries in Caronia and Gallo's recent Dickian encyclopedia, *La macchina della paranoia*, which—having been published in 2006—aims at summarizing thirty years of critical debate on Dick and his works. The Italian critics felt they had to include entries on *Droga* (drugs), *Follia (schizofrenia)* (schizophrenia), *Vita/Morte* (life/death), and *Storia* (history), plus an encompassing entry on *Realtà/Illusione* (reality/delusion) which proposed an anthropological discussion of the issue, suggesting that "the question of the borderline between reality and delusion in Dick could be the metaphysical disguise (or hypertrophy) of well identifiable material processes, which challenge symbolic structures and social relationships and compel us to redefine them" (Caronia and Gallo 211, translation mine).

Since ontological uncertainty has been repeatedly suggested as one of the fundamental critical issues in Dick's fiction, it is time to use it as a guideline for an intertextual analysis of his oeuvre — which may cover a large sample of his production. This is exactly what you will find in this monograph.[10]

Ontological Uncertainty

The use of the term "ontology" should however be explained. Since it stands for the philosophical meditation on the nature of being, existence or reality in general, as well as the basic categories of being and their relations, one might think that what will be attempted in this book is a philosophical reading of Dick's oeuvre. It is not: this is a monograph of literary criticism. The author does not want to suggest that a philosophical analysis of Dick's works is impossible or unacceptable; provided it is carried out by philosophers (be they academic or not), it is a worthy endeavor which may yield a rich theoretic harvest. I can also accept the idea that some writings by Dick are endowed with a remarkable philosophical value; Dick is neither Hegel nor Derrida, but some of his essays and the *Exegesis* might offer useful insights and a few brilliant ideas. But I am a literary critic, and I do not believe in that muddled form of literary criticism often called "theory," which is all too often either lame literary criticism or incompetent philosophizing (or both, alas!). Hence my decision to stick to the tools of literary analysis, with an eclectic approach drawing from several sources, but never forgetting that even a hybrid form of narrative like the novel, born of the fusion of theatrical dialogue and prose narrative in 18th-century England (plus other components it would take too much time to list), aims at telling a story, after all — which is not the main purpose of philosophy.[11]

Nobody could deny that "ontology" comes from philosophy, but when it is used in the realm of literary criticism it necessarily assumes a different meaning: it is the critical meditation on the nature of being, existence or reality, as well as the basic categories of being and their relations, *as they are found in a piece of fiction*. We might say that it is an ontology *sui generis*, a mutant variety of ontology adapted to the needs of literary criticism when it has to tackle the works of some writers, among which there is Philip K. Dick. The use of a philosophical term to explain what happens in novels which were originally marketed as cheap entertainment fiction seems to be particularly appropriate as it chimes in with Lem's remark that "Dick seems to foresee a future in which abstract and highbrow dilemmas of academic philosophy will descend into the street so that every pedestrian will be forced to solve for himself such contradictory problems as 'objectivity' or 'subjectivity,' because his life will depend upon the result" (Lem 1972, 79).

In Dick's oeuvre the narration is mostly based on a special ontology, that is, a condition in which characters (and readers) do not know what is real and what is not *in the text*, and must frantically search for the fictional reality behind the fictional simulation, often aware that behind the simulation there may well be another simulation (a sort of succession or procession of simulacra, which is unsurprisingly the key feature of *The Simulacra*). Yet in Dick's narratives there must be a distinction between fake and real, even though reality (or truth) is often out of reach. Reality has to be there, if only to be given the lie, denied, or involved in some bewildering metamorphosis where all that is real turns out to be bogus and *vice versa*. The uncertainty is so radical that we might even find out that what looks only apparently real is *actually* real, after all—a supremely paradoxical form of denouement, we might say (it is what happens at the end of *The Transmigration of Timothy Archer*). The use of this term is not casual, as the fundamental scene of Dick's narrative is indeed that of *denouement*. One of the possible forms of denouement may also consist in a character living in an alternate universe where Germany and Japan won the Second World War who visits for a few minutes a strange world where the Axis powers were defeated (ours), while another is told by the *I Ching* that the world dominated by Nazism and Japanese imperialism is not real—this is what happens in *The Man in the High Castle*.

In Dick's fiction truth is not a state of things, something stable and fixed: truth is an event. In fact Dick's most famous definition of reality declares: "Reality is that which, when you stop believing in it, doesn't go away" (*Shifting Realities* 261). Dick first enunciated this strange form of ontology in an arguably never-delivered speech whose title is "How to Build a Universe That Doesn't Fall Apart Two Days Later," posthumously published in 1985 (as the introduction to the short story collection *I Hope I Shall Arrive Soon*). Dick downplays the importance of his saying, telling us that it is just what he answered a girl college student in Canada who had asked him to define reality for her (the girl, according to him, was writing a paper for a philosophy class). It sounds more like a joke or a paradox than a meditated philosophical aphorism, yet Dick maintained in the essay that "[s]ince then [he hadn't] been able to define reality any more lucidly" (*Shifting Realities* 261). I think this is a deeper definition of reality than it seems. Reality is something that does not go away, regardless of our illusions, expectations, and wishes. Reality stubbornly remains; but above all it does not disappear, even when we stop believing in it. Reality is something that refuses to humor us. And we know it is real only when there is a disappointment, when things do not happen or work as we expect them to. Reality is not a full, glowing presence, an undoubted certainty; it is more a nuisance, a trouble, an annoyance. Something which refuses to agree, to go along. It is a dissonance, a gap, a swerve. It is a rip in the fabric of the veil of Maja; it is a small accident which upsets all the num-

berless routines of our predictable daily life, like the one which Dick chose
as an example of his ability (or compulsion) "to see the most improbable possibility in every situation" (*Shifting Realities*, 92) — in itself a handy definition
of ontological uncertainty — namely, that for him "a flat tire on [his] car is (a)
the End of the World; and (b) An Indication of Monsters (although I forget
why)" (92).

In *Time Out of Joint* one of the characters realizes that there is something
wrong in his world because in his bathroom the light switch is not where he
expects it to be (25). Reality gives the lie to his expectations; it refuses to clear
the field of its disquieting presence, to play up to the mental map of the world
that the character unconsciously uses to navigate his world. It is a moment
of bewilderment, but it is also a moment of truth; it is one of those brief
moments in which reality leaves a trace in our mind, gleaming through a rent
in the fabric of our ceaseless projections. Such moments are the hallmark of
Dick's fiction, and they are moments of radical ontological uncertainty.

However, the fact that in *Time Out of Joint* the apparently real world
turns out to be faked does not imply that the denouement is always a revelation, moving from false to authentic. The most improbable possibility in
certain fictional situations created by Dick is not that we are actually living
in another world which — its unlikeliness notwithstanding — is true; or that
it is impossible to decide which world is authentic; sometimes the story dizzy-
ingly shows us that both (or several) worlds can be authentic. This is what
happens in some neglected novels like *The Crack in Space*, where explorers
from an overpopulated future Earth discover a parallel universe where Earth
seems to be depopulated: there the two worlds coexist. Not to mention the
multiple realities visited in *Eye in the Sky* (Ch. 2), none of which is the "authentic" world where the group of protagonists comes from, not even the one they
reach at the end of the story (they have to content themselves with a *slightly*
unauthentic world in the end). A further possibility is the one explored in
The Penultimate Truth, where the war-torn world of the Americans imprisoned
in the underground shelters is bogus, while the world of the privileged elite
living in luxuriant mansions on the surface is authentic; yet both worlds coexist, and none is dismantled at the end of the novel (Ch. 5). It may be that we
have to keep living in a bogus world for the time being (an idea also present
in *Ubik* and *VALIS*).

In Dick's fiction what seems real may be imaginary; individuals may
seem sane while they are deranged; on the other hand, madmen may be wiser
than purportedly sane individuals; a realistic novel can turn into a sf novel
(*Time Out of Joint*), and a potentially fantastic story may turn into an absolutely
realistic one (*The Transmigration of Timothy Archer*); men are actually androids
and androids are more human than us; and so on. We may discover that the

world conjured up by the Californian writer is bogus, or that it is real though it seems bogus, or that it is as real as another world which seems to be in opposition to it. The category of simulation does not help to sort out all these possibilities. This is why I propose to talk about ontological uncertainty, a wider and more open-ended category which may accommodate the whole gamut of narrative solutions devised by Dick in his short stories and novels.

Dick's ontological uncertainty could be useful in the philosophical discourse; maybe it might lead to a new form of ontology proper, or to a revision of some existing ontologies. This will not be discussed in this book. We will try instead to understand to what extent ontological uncertainty shapes the narrative architectures of twenty novels written by Dick. Readers are in any case free to use my conclusions for philosophical purposes, for literary theory, for political analyses, for sociological surveys, or simply to understand what Dick is all about, provided they take responsibility for their usage of my modest proposal.

Todorov Reconsidered

The concept of ontological uncertainty is actually a development (hopefully an improvement) of one of the most contested definitions of the fantastic in literature, the one introduced by Tzvetan Todorov in his 1970 essay *The Fantastic*. Here is a detailed description:

> The fantastic requires the fulfillment of three conditions. First, the text must oblige the reader to consider the world of the characters as a world of living persons and to hesitate between a natural and a supernatural explanation of the events described. Second, this hesitation may also be experienced by a character; thus the reader's role is so to speak entrusted to a character, and at the same time the hesitation is represented, it becomes one of the themes of the work — in the case of naïve reading, the actual reader identifies himself with the character. Third, the reader must adopt a certain attitude with regard to the text: he will reject allegorical as well as "poetic" interpretations. These three requirements do not have an equal value. The first and the third actually constitute the genre; the second may not be fulfilled. Nonetheless, most examples satisfy all three conditions [Todorov 33].

Todorov's definition has been repeatedly criticized,[12] and it is difficult to deny that its greatest limit is that it is so narrow that it only covers very few literary works, such as Guy de Maupassant's story *The Horla* [*La horla*] (1887) and Henry James' novella *The Turn of the Screw* (1898). To accommodate the most important non-realistic genres of the 20th century, science-fiction and fantasy, Todorov must introduce two other categories, the uncanny and the marvelous. The latter should explain science-fiction, but it does this in a very unsatisfactory manner (cf. Lem 1974).

Yet Todorov's idea of pure fantastic as a hesitation between two different explanations of a certain event could be quite useful if we applied it to Dick's oeuvre. It should be changed, however, because the alternative between a natural and a supernatural explanation is just one among those that Dick's novels present us with (it is the one that *The Transmigration of Timothy Archer* and *VALIS* are pivoted upon). If we substitute factual for natural and counterfactual for supernatural, we will have what is at stake in *The Man in the High Castle*: we are presented with a parallel universe where Germany and Japan won World War II. But there is a doubt about that alternate history: a novel-within-the-novel is set in a world where the USA and the British Empire won the war (which is not exactly *our* world, where the USA and the USSR were the winners). Here the hesitation is between two counterfactual realities. In *The Three Stigmata of Palmer Eldritch*, those who use the hallucinogenic drug CHEW-Z enter pocket universes which may appear real but are not, and may have visions related to those universes even after they have exited them (so that they are not sure that they are really out of Palmer Eldritch's pocket realities); thus we have an uncertainty about several realities, not just two, which are all different from ours. In two novels, *Ubik* and *A Maze of Death*, a group of people witness weird events and gradually discover that they are not living in the real world, but in a virtual reality (more precisely a *post mortem* collective hallucination in *Ubik*): here, after an explanation that — in Todorov's terms — would take us to the territory of the scientific marvelous, something happens which makes us hesitate again (the apparition of the coins with the face of Joe Chip in *Ubik*, the manifestation of the Intercessor in *A Maze of Death*). Uncertainty remains, but between two supernatural realities.

Uncertainty is however not necessarily applied to whole worlds: we are often uncertain about the ontological status of single beings or objects in Dick's counterfactual, sfnal, or realistic worlds. There are forged Colt guns and the Zippo lighter in *The Man in the High Castle*; an android president in *The Simulacra* (where the first lady is actually an actress who impersonates an immensely popular First Lady); a forged Neanderthal skull in *The Man Whose Teeth Were All Exactly Alike*; fake human beings in *Do Androids Dream of Electric Sheep?*; ersatz animals can be found in the same novel; bogus documentaries play a key role in *The Penultimate Truth*.

What should be clear is that we are not simply talking about suspense here. It may be that ontological uncertainty was used by Dick to achieve suspense, but it is quite different from what we have in a thriller: there suspense is caused by a psychological uncertainty (what are the real intentions of this or that character, who is the murderer, or — as in many noir novels and movies—will the culprit manage to get away with it?), while in Dick the uncertainty is ontological, because it is about what worlds, people, objects *are*. A classical example is the short story "Imposter," where the plot is pivoted on the uncertainty about the real nature of Olham: is he a man or an android who perfectly simulates a man? An android, moreover, who does not know that he is an artificial human being? This is quite different from asking whether a certain character is guilty or innocent, friend or foe.

The Game of the Rat

However, ontological uncertainty can also be used to produce suspense. This is mostly done through a series of twists or coups de théâtre which make us hesitate about the ontological status of the reality that the characters inhabit, or some element(s) of it. Thomas M. Disch already noticed this interrupted narrative strategy adopted by Dick. He called it the Game of the Rat:

> There is a form of the board game Monopoly called Rat in which the Banker, instead of just sitting there and watching, gets to be the Rat. The Rat can alter all the rules of the game at his discretion, like Idi Amin. The players elect the person they consider the slyest and nastiest among them to be the Rat. The trick in being a good Rat is in graduating the torment of the players, in moving away from the usual experience of Monopoly, by the minutest calibrations, into, finally, an utter delirium of lawlessness. If you think you might enjoy Rat a bit more than a standard game of Monopoly then you should probably try reading Philip Dick [Disch 16].

Changing the rules of a game while playing is quite similar to changing the ontological status of the/a world, a place, a character, an object while telling a story. The game of the Rat may be a useful model of Dick's approach to science-fiction (actually to fiction in general), surely more interesting than the one proposed by John Huntington; that is, the 800-words rule of putting in the story a new idea (a twist or coup de théâtre) every 800 words. Huntington maintains that "the 800-word rule is an explicitly acknowledged device for van Vogt," and though he admits that he does not know "of any such explicit acknowledgement on Dick's part," he thinks that such a technique can explain Dick's fiction because of "the central importance of van Vogt's practice for Dick's sense of SF is easily documented" (Huntington 172). Huntington's hypothesis was then uncritically adopted by Suvin (Suvin 2002, 393). The connection between Dick (especially his earlier fiction) and A.E. van Vogt, one of the most popular sf writers of the 1940s and early 1950s is made by Huntington due to the simple fact that Dick admired van Vogt: his novel *The World of Null-A* was one of Phil's favorite SF classics (Sutin 82); Dick's first novel, *Solar Lottery* is heavily indebted with van Vogt's fiction (to put it in Thomas M. Disch's words, "*Solar Lottery* is van Vogt's best novel" [Disch 20]), and the same might be said of other works of the same decade. Dick met the older Canadian writer at the SF Worldcon in 1954; ten years later he respectfully portrayed the Canadian writer in his short story "Waterspider" (1964).

There *could* be some relation between Dick's shunts and what van Vogt *might* have told him at the SF Worldcon in 1954. The modal verbs are necessary inasmuch as we do not know what van Vogt actually told Dick — we just know what the *fictional character* of van Vogt tells the fan (who *might* be a fictional avatar of Philip K. Dick) in Dick's short story: "I start out with a plot and then the plot sort of folds up. So then I have to have another plot to finish the rest of the story" (224). This is van Vogt's method in Dick's own words; however, what is interesting is the idea of a *discontinuity*, of an interrupted plot that must be superseded by another in order to complete a story. Did Dick faithfully — albeit not literally — report van Vogt's words, or did he put in the character's mouth a statement that reflected his own modus operandi?

My analysis of Dick's fiction (Rossi 2004), proves that the game played by Dick is more complex than the mechanical application of the 800-word rule suggested by Huntington, which is in any case something Van Vogt recommended to apprentice writers, not something that has been found in a detailed analysis of his science fiction. Yet it is true that the game of the Rat works by means of discontinuities (some of them radically affecting narrative conventions) that are deliberately inserted in the plot, what I have called shunts (Ch. 1), as these often — though not always — shunt the narrative from one genre to another (it happens in *Time Out of Joint, The Cosmic Puppets, VALIS*, and in several short stories).

We might say that the Game of the Rat, which is a radicalization of the ordinary techniques and strategies used by genre writers to heighten the suspense of a story, necessarily complements the idea of ontological uncertainty. A succession of twists or shunts creates that condition of ontological uncertainty, of radical doubt that is the hallmark of Dick's most valuable fiction.

How to Produce Ontological Uncertainty: Towards a Map of Dickian Uncertainty

Ontological uncertainty is achieved through different narrative devices, and is found in Dick's fantasy, sf and realistic fiction. In the works we are going to discuss ontological uncertainty is generated by different devices,

many of which belong to the tradition of sf. By showing how Dick achieved
ontological uncertainty by using different devices, or by using the same device
in different ways, I also propose an intertextual network which should hopefully organize Dick's oeuvre in small groups of interrelated works.

A typical device is that of the alternate worlds, also known as alternate
realities/histories, or parallel universes, that is paramount in many of Dick's
works, such as *The Cosmic Puppets* (where its treatment is particularly interesting
as it occurs within the genre of fantasy, not science-fiction), *The Man in the
High Castle, The Divine Invasion, Flow My Tears, The Policeman Said*. A subtler
variety of this device has been used in *The Transmigration of Timothy Archer*,
where the Zadokite scrolls might totally change the religious history of the
West. Surely this device was not invented by Dick, because its sfnal applications
ultimately derive from historians' mental experiments about alternative out-
comes of decisive historical events. Alternate worlds in Dick sometimes belong
to the old historical counterfactual variety, like *The Man in the High Castle*,
where a different world stems from the murder of F.D. Roosevelt by Giuseppe
Zangara well before the outbreak of WWII. In other novels like *Flow* or *Invasion*, the event which should explain the difference between the alternate world
and ours (or the one depicted as the "normal" world at the beginning of the
story) is not indicated. This device is discussed in chapters 1, 3, 7, 9 and 10.

Another fictional device which may create ontological uncertainty is a
peculiar form of alternate reality which Dick elaborated by drawing from several psychiatric and psychoanalytical theories (Freud and Jung, but also Binswanger, Luria, Laing, etc.), which was called "Finite Subjective Reality" by
one of Dick's pupils, Jonathan Lethem (who based his novel *Amnesia Moon*
on this device [Rossi, "From Dick to Lethem"]). FSRs may be (a) pocket parallel universes who are projected by the minds of single individuals thanks to
drugs or VR technologies (usually these pocket worlds are much smaller and
less permanent than the alternate words described above), and/or (b) delusional realities which are projected by the deranged minds (be they paranoid,
schizoid, etc.) of one or more characters in a novel or short stories. FSRs are
present in such novels as *Eye in the Sky, The Three Stigmata of Palmer Eldritch,
Ubik, Clans of the Alphane Moon*, etc. The difference between parallel uni-
verses/alternate worlds and FSRs is that world/universes are forms of *koinos
kosmos*, or "common universe" (to quote a Greek phrase that Dick often used),
while the FSRs are a form of *idios kosmos*, or "private universe."[13] FSRs are
threatened by solipsism and madness, as we can see in one of Dick's bleakest
short stories, "I Hope I Shall Arrive Soon" (first published in *Playboy* in 1980
as "Frozen Journey"). Here the use or abuse of virtual reality makes a man
become so desensitized during an interstellar trip that, once he has reached
his destination, he believes reality to be just another loop of his memories

projected by the AI of the starship. Solipsism and madness also threaten the characters who are trapped in the FSRs created by Palmer Eldritch hallucinogenic drug CHEW-Z in *Stigmata*, as they are never sure that they have really exited the drug-created pocket worlds, and are only dreaming that they are again in the real world. Moreover, the idea of a delusional world projected by a deranged mind may be combined to that of a parallel universe, as one of the characters of *The Man in the High Castle* suspects that the Nazi-dominated world depicted in the novel is a projection of Hitler's insane mind. FSRs will be especially discussed in chapters 2, 4 and 7.

Sometimes the situation of ontological uncertainty derives from another sfnal device which may in any case lead to the creation of an alternate history: in *Dr. Futurity*, as well as in relatively more celebrated novels like *The Penultimate Truth* or *The Simulacra*, or short stories like "A Little Something for Us Tempunauts" (1975), time travel may allow individual or governments to alter the outcome of certain key historical events so that the subsequent historical development may be changed and humankind can find itself in a different world. In *The Simulacra*, for example, a future American government (the USEA, which also include West Germany) wants to contact Nazi party bosses to negotiate the survival of the Jews so that the Holocaust may be avoided. I have tackled Dick's highly idiosyncratic use of time travel in chapter 6.

Ontological uncertainty may also be embodied in the figure of the robot/android which looks human but is not (and sometimes may even believe it is human), an element of Dick's fictional worlds that has often been discussed and interpreted by connecting it with Baudrillard's concept of simulacra (a word he probably took from the title of Dick's novel *The Simulacra*). Here the uncertainty might be defined regional or local, as it is not a whole world or reality which is suspected to be fake, or only apparently real: here characters are uncertain about the real nature of other human beings, or themselves. This device plays a pivotal role in *We Can Build You* and *Do Androids Dream of Electric Sheep*, analyzed in chapter 6.

Another form of ontological uncertainty is the presence of faked objects, such as the Colt pistols in *The Man in the High Castle*, or the bogus Neanderthal skull in *The Man Whose Teeth Were All Exactly Alike*, or Gottlieb Fischer's historical documentaries in *The Penultimate Truth*, the regrooved tires in *Confessions of a Crap Artist*, the fake police station in *Do Androids Dream of Electric Sheep?*, the counterfeit typewriters in *In Milton Lumky Territory*, etc. Sometimes these objects have a great importance for the events told in the novels, so that their authenticity or falseness can change the sense of what is happening. This device is so widespread in Dick's oeuvre that it is discussed in all chapters.

Ontological uncertainty can also be produced by the use/abuse of drugs, as in *Now Wait for Last Year*, *Flow My Tears, The Policeman Said*, or *A Scanner*

Darkly. The sfnal drug in *Wait* (Ch. 5) allows characters to access alternate realities (something which connects this novel to those dealing with alternate worlds); in *Tears*, the use of another imaginary drug, KR-3 (Ch. 7), does not only alter the perceptions of the drug user, but also "objectively" changes the world she lives in, trapping one of the characters, TV star Jason Taverner, in an alternate reality where he does not exist; on the other hand, *Scanner* presents us with a drug addict, Bob Arctor, who is also an undercover nark, S.A. Fred, because the SD drug he is using gradually separates the two brain hemispheres, thus generating a split personality. Here identity itself is uncertain, and this is a form of doubt which is more radical than that suggested by Descartes in his 1634 *Discourse on the Method*.[14] Drugs as generators of ontological uncertainty are discussed in chapters 5 and 7.

Obviously, since we are talking about a writer who mostly practiced science-fiction, two more devices that may generate ontological uncertainty are typically technological ones: virtual reality, which is found in some novels and stories by Dick, such as "I Hope I Shall Arrive Soon," but also *Androids*, with the Mercer machine (Ch. 6), *Maze*, with the polyencephalic fusion (Ch. 7), or the scenes of Herb Asher's life that he has to re-live while in cryonic suspension in *The Divine Invasion* (Ch. 9), or the delusional realities that may be produced by electric/electronic media such as radio, television, cinema: e.g. the android presidents in *Simulacra* and *The Penultimate Truth* (Ch. 5) are broadcast via TV waves or cable. A remarkable example of theatrical fake reality can be found in *Time Out of Joint* (Ch. 2).

Another device that creates ontological uncertainty is amnesia, something that Dick surely derived from an older sf writer, A.E. Van Vogt; loss of memory often hides crucial knowledge, thus beguiling the amnesiac characters (and readers), as in *Time Out of Joint*, *The Game-Players of Titan*, "We Can Remember It for You Wholesale, Inc.," or *The Divine Invasion*, where God himself suffers from amnesia. This device has been discussed in chapters 2 and 9.

All these devices can be used by Dick to achieve the condition of ontological uncertainty enabling him to play what we have called the Game of the Rat. It should be added that such a narrative game may be played with one or more of these devices, as Dick often achieves the most bewildering narrative effects by associating different sfnal or non-sfnal uncertainty-generating devices; in *Now Wait for Last Year*, for example, the drug JJ-180 apparently allows characters to travel back and forward in time and alter the course of history, an alteration which could obviously cause massive ontological uncertainty (the same may be said for *The Three Stigmata of Palmer Eldritch* where FSRs are complicated by time travel and its consequences).

Dick's Game of the Rat also asks for certain narrative techniques. Surely one of these is strictly connected to the idea of finite subjective realities, that is, that each individual lives in a different world, or *idios kosmos*: it is the multiple plot technique (possibly derived from Dos Passos), where a third person narrative is coupled with multiple narrative foci. This is what we have e.g. in *Time Out of Joint, The Man in the High Castle, Martian Time-Slip, The Simulacra, The Penultimate Truth, Dr. Bloodmoney, Ubik, The Three Stigmata of Palmer Eldritch, Flow My Tears, The Policeman Said*, but above all in his realistic fiction, e.g. in *The Man Whose Teeth Were All Exactly Alike, Puttering About in a Small Land, Mary and the Giant*.

There is something to be said about the realistic novels, which should not be taken as an assessment in terms of lesser literary value. In these novels we have the multiple plots and multiple narrative foci which, according to some critics (e.g., Suvin and Robinson) were the hallmark of Dick's most important achievements (Ch. 4); yet these novels have received scant critical attention so far, with few exceptions (cf. Carratello's). From our perspective these novels must necessarily be considered as peripheral works, because they show a weaker form of uncertainty — we might call it a relational uncertainty which is basically limited to interpersonal relations, something which can be also found in other authors, even in the realistic novelists of the 19th century. There are a few exceptions, such as *Confessions of a Crap Artist*, where the unreliable narrator does generate a condition of ontological uncertainty — in fact this novel will be discussed and quoted in some parts of this monograph. Then we have some interesting occurrences of what I have called regional ontological uncertainty, that is the presence of meaningful fake objects, such as the counterfeit skulls in *The Man Whose Teeth Were All Exactly Alike*, which will be also mentioned. However, I have mostly left out the realistic works out of the picture, though I think that there are other approaches to Dick's fiction where his sf output and the realistic works should be read together, such as the treatment of mass media (cf. Rossi 2010).

However, the technique of multiple plots/foci is not at all exclusive; the only realistic novel where we have a form of ontological uncertainty (generated by insanity), *Confessions*, features a first-person narrative: Dick also used this technique in such major sf novels as *We Can Build You, VALIS*, and *The Transmigration of Timothy Archer*, where the presence of a single narrative voice with a single point of view does not prevent the author from achieving his characteristic condition of ontological uncertainty.

The Map

The chapter structure of this essay bears relation to the interpretive hypothesis I have tried to argue. The first chapter presents two case studies focusing on two relatively obscure novels by Dick, *The Cosmic Puppets* and *The Game-Players of Titan*. The former shows ontological uncertainty at work, an uncertainty which besets both the main character of the novel and the world surrounding him (a microcosm, actually, embodied in a small provincial town); the latter shows the workings of Dick's Game of the Rat with a blow-by-blow analysis of the plot, showing how uncertainty may move (or shunt) the text from one subgenre to another. The unifying element of this chapter is the idea of Dick's fiction as a rigged game, where the "master game-player," namely the author, can change the narrative rules while playing with the readers.

The second chapter aims at discussing two novels of the 1950s where Dick shows a higher mastery of his game, *Eye in the Sky* and *Time Out of Joint*; the former introduces the device of FSR, and works with alternate realities, but it also deals with the hallucinations that may be generated by mental derangement, thus complicating what we have found in the first two texts. The latter reuses the idea of *Puppets*, with the main character calling in doubt the reality of his world (a nameless small town), but here the setting is absolutely ordinary, without the preternatural events occurring in *Puppets'* Millgate; the town will be however unmasked as a peculiar sort of FSR, not generated by hallucinations but by a large-scale theatrical simulation. Here we can also see how Dick could move from one genre to another in *Joint*, and what are the relations between the different textual levels (and alternate worlds) in Dick's novels and the koinos kosmos of his readers—*our* shared world, whose reality is covertly called in doubt by these texts.

The third chapter discusses Dick's most celebrated specimen of alternate history, that is, *The Man in the High Castle*, a novel which asks for a detailed discussion due to his complexities but also the wealth of scholarly analyses of its labyrinthine structure. This chapter deepens the discussion of the relation between the worlds inside the novel, and its readers' understanding of the world they live in.

The fourth chapter reads *Martian Time-Slip*, *Dr. Bloodmoney* and *Clans of the Alphane Moon*, three novels where the technique of multiple plots and narrative foci is connected with the device of madness as a generator of idioi kosmoi, and allows us to see how a plurality of points of view and the FSRs generated by insanity may produce bewildering effects of ontological uncertainty.

The fifth chapter deals with three novels, *The Simulacra*, *Now Wait for Last Year*, and *The Penultimate Truth*, which achieve ontological uncertainty also by means of time travel, considered as a device which may led to an alteration of what is usually considered unchangeable, the past (and history). These three novels are also characterized by a strong political content.

The sixth chapter discusses the issue of "limited" ontological uncertainty by focusing on two novels, namely *We Can Build You* and *Do Androids Dream of Electric Sheep?* where some characters have an onytologically uncertain status: the androids, or simulacra, as opposed to real human beings.

The seventh chapter, possibly the core of this monograph, explores three of Dick's most important novels — *The Three Stigmata of Palmer Eldritch*, *Ubik*, and *Flow My Tears, the Policeman Said*— and a purportedly minor novel —*A Maze of Death*— highlighting how the use of FSRs/alternate realities, be they generated by drugs (*Stigmata*, *Flow*) or virtual reality technologies (*Ubik*, *Maze*), is underpinned by a metafictional subtext: the creators of the FSRs are narrative archons which conjure up imperfect worlds, and can be read as portraits of the artist as a sfnal demiurge.

The three final chapters are devoted to a detailed discussion of the VALIS Trilogy, where the three novels are structured according to new applications of narrative devices Dick had already used: *VALIS* oscillates between realistic fiction and religious sf, *The Divine Invasion* reinvents alternate realities and half-life (the post-mortem virtual reality in *Ubik*), *The Transmigration of Timothy Archer* oscillates between realism and fantasy, but also destabilizes our koinos kosmos with an alternate history of Christianity.

Discussing Dick's novels in this or that chapter, since each chapter discusses a different narrative device, means suggesting an intertextual network which might help future interpreters to somewhat organize Dick's oeuvre not just based on genre borders (science-fiction, realism, fantasy), but along thematic faultlines. This is precisely what this monograph aimed at, and it is plain to see that those works which have not been listed above could be linked to those which have. Some novels, though not analyzed in detail, have been discussed in this essay: for example *Solar Lottery* (Ch. 1), *The World Jones Made* (Ch. 9), or *Dr. Futurity* (Ch. 5). On the other hand, *Counter-Clock World* being based on a temporal inversion (dead people resurrect, life flows from the tomb to the womb), achieves ontological uncertainty by reversing our temporal coordinates; it is thus close to the time-travel novels in chapter 6 (and *Martian Time-Slip*, if we privilege the aspect of narrative time manipulation). *The Crack in Space* surely belongs to the group of alternate worlds/histories novels, discussed in Chapter 3 and 9[15]; *Lies Inc.*, being characterized by drugs-induced hallucination, bears relation to the novels in chapter 7[16]; the same may be said for a much stronger novel like *A Scanner Darkly*, where the protagonist, an undercover police officer, hallucinates another person who is actually his assumed bogus identity as drug-addict Bob Arctor.[17] Similar relations of derivation or kinship can be found for the remaining minor works.

Then we have *Galactic Pot-Healer*, occupying a somewhat isolated position, as it is the novel where Dick tried to anatomize artistic creation with a complex symbolic and psychoanalytical allegory. The attempt was not successful, but this does not mean that it does not deserve more critical attention than it has received so far.

Some Fallacies

There are two reviews — not of Dick's works, but of two monographs on Dick's fiction — that must be mentioned inasmuch as their authors, Gary K. Wolfe and Peter Fitting respectively, pointed out two serious issues in Dick scholarship. Wolfe, who reviewed Warrick's *Mind in Motion*, politely rebukes her because "she does not want to deal with Dick *as an SF writer*" (Wolfe 238). Her intent is noble, as "she wants to achieve for Dick what he could never achieve for himself— namely, to liberate him from the stigma of SF" (238), but it is faulty criticism. We might call this the Ennoblement Fallacy, which often plagues Dick scholarship; it happens when commentators think they have to demonstrate Dick's literary value by showing he is a respectable writer, and comparing him to the classics. Two recent contributions on Dick fall prey of this fallacy, that is Kucukalic's *Philip K. Dick: Canonical Writer of the Digital Age*, and Vest's *The Postmodern Humanism of Philip K. Dick*.

On the other hand Fitting, who reviewed Mackey's *Philip K. Dick*, criticized the attitude of those commentators, including Mackey, "for whom the work — particularly in the last years — is the expression of conscious vision, one which has moral consequences and which even ... contains something akin to religious truth" (Fitting 1989, 243). This could be called the Prophetic Fallacy, which then bifurcates in two questionable critical approaches: believing that Dick's fiction can only be understood by delving into his letters and interviews (244), and looking for "some message that Dick was anxious to transmit" (245); Fitting evidently meant the ethical/religious message purportedly vehiculated by Dick's last works, especially the VALIS Trilogy.

I hope I have escaped the Ennoblement Fallacy by discussing Dick's fiction as science-fiction when it was written for that market, and by acknowledging Dick's complex dialogue with other sf authors (Fitting 1989, 244), "his relations with other SF and fantasy writers and editors" (Wolfe 238). As for the Prophetic Fallacy, my initial warning that this is a work of literary criticism, neither theory nor philosophy nor theology, should show that I am well aware of the problem.

However, there are two more fallacies which have plagued PKD scholarship, which could be seen as the twins of those denounced by Wolfe and Fitting. I shall call them the Hack Writer Fallacy and the Crackpot Novelist Fallacy. The latter is easier to explain: it is the stance of those critics who, like Eric Rabkin, think that Dick "did go insane" (Rabkin 186), so that they may elegantly solve any interpretive problem we encounter in reading any of his works, especially those of the last phase of his activity. As for the Hack Writer Fallacy, it turns the Ennoblement Fallacy upside-down: while those who wish to nobilitate tend to forget that Dick was a commercial fantasy and above all sf writer, those who resent the ennoblement tend to forget that Dick had undoubtedly read Van Vogt, Hubbard, and Ballard, but also Vaughan, von Hofmannstahl, and Beckett — just to quote six authors whose names occur (some not just once) in the first volume of Dick's *Selected Letters*.

To avoid these four fallacies that have struck several critics I have adopted a comparative approach derived from comparative literature studies. I have tried to read Dick's works by connecting them to each other (something Jameson has already done, but only for a few novels), and to other writers' works, regardless of national or genre boundaries. I have tried to read Dick's oeuvre as a constellation of texts where Dick used the same devices and tackled the same quandaries in different ways; a constellation which does not shine in the sky alone, but among many others, against the background of that textual milky way we call literature.

Moreover, I have linked Dick's works with music (his lifelong passion) and the electric/electronic media, because his (and ours) is a multimedia culture, where writers are not always inspired by other writers, but by films, TV and radio programs, even comics.[18] But the comparative approach also asks for a careful examination of Dick's historical context, because numberless hints at what was happening or had happened in the koinos kosmos around him can be found in his fiction. I have tried to put Dick in the context of the 1960s, following Freedman's brief but insightful reconstruction of his deep connections with that decade (Freedman 1988, 147–52); but, since I do not share Freedman's belief that Dick's "essential masterpieces ... are all products of the most eventful decade in postwar American history [i.e. the 1960s]" (Freedman 1988, 147), I have linked his subsequent fiction to the different historical background of the 1970s and early 1980s.

History did not stop in 1982, of course. But Dick's interrelation with American (and world) history continues, as we can see thanks to one of Dick's commentators, Aaron Barlow, who decided to end his uneven but passionate monograph, *How Much Does Chaos Scare You?*, with a chapter whose programmatic title is: "What's Going Down: Lessons of Philip K. Dick's Short Fiction for the Post-9/11 World." This is not to say that we should read Dick's sf as the prediction of things to come: I am all too aware of the dangers of the Prophetic Fallacy. But I do believe that writers somewhat manage to see the seeds of the future in the folds of the present; and it takes a maker of twisted worlds like Philip Kindred Dick to tell us how twisted this world we live in really is.

Chapter 1

The Game of the Rat
(and Its Players):
The Cosmic Puppets and
The Game-Players of Titan

> "'Sblood, do you think I am
> easier to be played on than a pipe?"
> William Shakespeare

Our discussion of ontological uncertainty in the fiction of Philip K. Dick will start from a novel which has not been considered very important in the Dickian canon so far. In fact *The Cosmic Puppets* (1957) has been rated quite low by Dick's biographer, Lawrence Sutin, who gave it just three points out of ten (Sutin 292); while Andrew M. Butler deemed it barely sufficient, rating it 3/5 (Butler 2007, 28).[1] There is no doubt that such ratings, subjective as they may be — though expressed by authors with an exhaustive knowledge of Dick's oeuvre — cannot be taken as the ultimate scholarly assessment; yet they somewhat mirror a widespread lack of interest of literary critics towards this novel. Sometimes it is lack of knowledge, something that could explain Kim Stanley Robinson's idea that "the appearance of evil aliens" (Robinson 20) in this and other works by Dick is the "sign of a weak book," a rather puzzling statement because there are no aliens in this novel, as we shall see. All in all, browsing the bibliography of this volume one will not find monographs or essays specifically devoted to *The Cosmic Puppets*, and critics who tried to offer a comprehensive view of Dick's fiction, like Patricia S. Warrick, contented themselves with a passing mention (Warrick 120).[2] Mackey, the only commentator who devotes a few pages to this work, finds several faults in the novel, and considers it interesting only because it "stands as a remarkably clear paradigm of the essential Dick myth" (Mackey 16) of a fundamental cosmic dualism which will take more successfully form in the novels of the 1960s (Mackey 15).

The explanation of such neglect is quite easy for anyone who is knowledgeable with the history of Dick scholarship: the first wave of Dick criticism was written by scholars who were interested in science-fiction as a literary genre and a form of imagination (possibly with a strongly utopian/dystopian component, and/or a remarkable political subtext), and those critics, be they those tied to *Science-Fiction Studies* or others, were busy reading science-fiction as allegories or critiques of sociopolitical realities and definitely not interested in fantasy novels; while *The Cosmic Puppets* is correctly described by Butler as "a contemporary fantasy which shows a cosmic battle over reality being fought out in a mundane present day" (Butler 2007, 28).

When the first Marxist — or however politically engaged — pioneering critics were followed by the postmodern wave (in the mid-eighties), there was a change in the appreciation of Dick's fiction, but not one that could rehabilitate *Puppets*. Critics who read Dick through the lenses of Baudrillard or Jameson looked for simulacra, virtual realities, posthuman or android identities; the fight between two ancient godheads belonging to Zoroastrianism/Mazdaism, a relatively obscure religion in the West at that time, was surely not in the agenda of any critic interested in the quandaries of the postmodern age. The situation has not improved till today.

Yet there are good reasons to pay attention to this hitherto neglected novel. First of all, though Dick's first published novel is *Solar Lottery* (1955), we know that *Puppets* had been completed in 1953, almost a year before *Lottery*[3]; so *Puppets* should not be considered as an occasional and unimportant foray into fantasy of a science-fiction writer, but the beginning of Dick's activity as a genre writer. The only surviving novels written by Dick before *Puppets* are two posthumously published realistic works, *Gather Yourselves Together* (1994, but written in 1949–53) and *Voices from the Street* (2007, written in 1952–53), and this tells us that in 1953 he was trying different genres and had not concentrated on science-fiction yet. After the success of his first sf novel, *Solar Lottery*, Dick still kept writing realistic fiction that his literary agent regularly sent to respectable publishing houses, and these attempts continued till the early 1960s.

As I have already argued in the Introduction, we cannot read Dick's sf output if we overlook those works of his that do not belong to sf: his realistic fiction, and his only fantasy novel. We should never forget that he was a writer who managed to express himself in different genres, and often he managed to do that by crossbreeding them (something which is particularly important in works like *Do Androids Dream of Electric Sheep?*, *Martian Time-Slip*, or *VALIS*); in any case, Dick did not consider fantasy something extraneous or marginal in his oeuvre. In 1957, writing to his literary mentor Tony Boucher, he said that *Puppets* was "its pure fantasy, which as you know has always been my favorite" (*SL1* 35). External factors seem to have prevented him from writing other fantasy works, as he tells one Mr. Haas in another letter: "As you know, my own private love is fantasy, but fantasy is disappearing from the marketplace. Boucher tells me that he does not dare print a long fantasy; only a long science fiction is tolerated by his readers.... Gradually, I and other fantasy writers, have been discouraged from continuing" (*SL1* 32–3). In the same letter he said that he called Kafka's works "fantasies," and Kafka was a writer he identified with (in a 1973 letter Dick maintained that the middle initial of his name should stand for Kafka [*SL2* 126]); in 1960 he stated that he had been influenced by "the fantasy writers such as Kafka" (*SL1* 56) and that "fantasy was once [his] field." Moreover, Dick also affirmed in 1970 that he was still writing "psychological fantasies" (*SL1* 269). Surely not everything Dick wrote in his letters can be taken at its face value, yet these statements should be read in connection with the undisputable fact that Dick wrote a fantasy novel and several fantasy stories in the early 1950s. Among the pure fantasy stories we have "The King of Elves," "The Cookie Lady," "Beyond the Door" and "Out in the Garden" (all completed in 1952), plus "Of Withered Apples" and "Small Town" (both completed in 1953); then we have "The Preserving Machine" and "The Short Happy Life of the Brown Oxford" (published in 1953 and 1954 respectively), two fantasy stories barely disguised as science-fiction, and "Expendable" (1953) which might be read as science-fiction, but was considered a "short fantasy story" by Dick (*CS1* 403). Another short story, "The Great C" (completed in 1952), has a stronger science-fictional component, but is undeniably a rewriting of the Biblical narrative (or better hints at the narrative) of the god Moloch and the human sacrifices it required (as in e.g., Leviticus 18:21): it is thus endowed with a powerful mythical/religious subtext, which is a typical feature of fantasy fiction.

Dick clearly told Gregg Rickman that when he wrote *Puppets* he had the sort of fantasy fiction published on *Unknown Worlds* in his mind (Rickman 1988, 115). Though *Unknown*, which had started in 1939 and was directed by John W. Campbell, had ceased to exist in 1943 — probably due to wartime paper shortage — Dick wrote his novel in such a way that it could have been published by the extinct pulp magazine; the models he quotes are Cleve Cartmill, Heinlein, Lewis Padgett (Rickman 1988, 116) — all of them authors who had written stories published on *Unknown*. In particular Lewis Padgett — which actually was the pseudonym of Henry Kuttner and C.L. Moore — was one of the most famous fantasy writers of the 1940s. When he was asked about *Puppets* by Rickman, Dick replied: "I enjoyed writing it, and I enjoy reading it" (Rickman 1988, 116). He did not disown his fantasy novel, and proved to be well aware (and knowledgeable) of the genre it belongs to.

Besides, Dick did not consider fantasy very different from science-fiction. In one of his last letters (May 14, 1981), he explained:

> ... to separate science fiction from fantasy ... is impossible to do.... Take Psionics; take mutants such as we find in Ted Sturgeon's wonderful MORE THAN HUMAN. If the reader believes that such mutants could exist, then he will view Sturgeon's novel as science fiction. If, however, he believes that such mutants are, like wizards and dragons, not possible, nor will ever be possible, then he is reading a fantasy novel. Fantasy involves that which general opinion regards as impossible; science fiction involves that which general opinion regards as possible under the right circumstances. This is in essence a judgment-call, since what is possible and what is not possible is not objectively known but is, rather, a subjective belief on the part of the author and the reader [SL6 153].

Dick is not speaking as a scientist or a philosopher, but as a professional writer who knows the workings of a narrative text from the inside.[4] It is not a matter, as in such critics as Suvin, of defining an objective criterion to discriminate between those imaginary worlds that belong to fantasy and those belonging to science fiction proper; it is a matter of what may be found in a text which tells readers that they are reading fantasy or science fiction — provided they care. In other words, it is a matter of literary genre as a reading protocol.

There is a difference, says Dick, but it is very thin. The borderline between fantasy and science-fiction may be blurred; that barrier may be highly permeable. Moreover, there may be an uncertainty about the genre a narrative belongs to: it may be fantasy to some readers and science-fiction to others. No wonder then if Dick moved so quickly and easily from fantasy to science-fiction after finishing *The Cosmic Puppets*: in fact his next novel, *Solar Lottery*, is unmistakably a work of science-fiction, which respects many of the clichés of the genre, and can be even said to be derivative (Thomas M. Disch ironically called it "Van Vogt's best novel" [Disch 20]).

However, fantasy offered Dick one of his most important narrative tools, which he subsequently applied to his science-fictional works: the parallel universe or alternate reality. It is one of the narrative devices which he used with a dazzling originality, like probably no other writer inside science-fiction. Before we try to understand how fantasy fiction (and cinema, as we shall see) offered Dick such a powerful narrative tool, we should see how it is used in *Puppets*.

The novel is pivoted upon the bewildering experience of Ted Barton, an ordinary man who visits Millgate, the small Virginian town where he was born and grew up, with his wife Peggy. It is an ordinary trip of ordinary people visiting a town in the heart of the Appalachians which is "sleepy and ordinary like a hundred other little towns" (8); Ted is simply driven by nostalgia, as he has not visited Millgate for eighteen years. But when Barton reaches the ordinary small town he finds out that it is not the one he remembers, being totally different from the Millgate he grew up in (10). It is not just that the town has changed: it is another town. Besides, Ted soon discovers, browsing old issues of the local newspaper, the *Millgate Times* (whose name is not *Millgate Weekly*, the one he remembers [15]), that there is a substantial reason why nobody seems to know him: in the 9 October 1935 issue he finds an article about the death of Theodore Barton, 9 years old, due to scarlet fever (16).

This discovery casts Barton in an abyss of radical uncertainty. His memory tells him the Millgate he grew up in is not the town he is in now; his memory also tells him he left the town with his parents. But documents (the newspaper) tell him Ted Burton never left Millgate, and died in 1935. "Maybe he wasn't Ted Barton. False memories.... The whole content of his mind — everything. Falsified, by someone or something.... But if he wasn't Ted Barton — then who was he?" (17).

This is already a typical Dickian situation. The protagonist is not sure of his very memories; he is not even sure he is Ted Burton: the uncertainty about his personal history brings about a radical uncertainty about his identity. This is what we will find in Dick's subsequent major works: uncertainty about reality dominates *Eye in the Sky* and *Time Out of Joint* (Ch. 2), *The Three Stigmata of Palmer Eldritch*, *Ubik* and *A Maze of Death* (Ch. 7), *The Penultimate Truth* (Ch. 5); uncertainty about one's memories is paramount in *Time Out of Joint*, *A Scanner Darkly* (Ch. 8), *Do Androids Dream of Electric Sheep?* (Ch. 6), "We Can Remember It for You Wholesale Inc." The rest of the novel stages Barton's quest for his own identity and past, his thwarted attempts to understand why he remembers a different town and how he can be at the same time dead when he was 9 and still alive and 27 years old. If something has been falsified, what is it? The whole content of his mind (which should mean Ted is insane) or the town around him (which should mean that something very strange is going on in that only apparently ordinary town)?

In a short sf story Dick sent to his agent in February 1953 (that he may have written while he was working on *Puppets*, as the novel was completed in August 1953; or after finishing *Puppets*, if we trust Dick when he says that his fantasy novel was ready in 1952), "Imposter," a similar problem of uncertain identity is treated in a different context: the protagonist, Olham, might not be a human being but an android, a perfect replica of the real Olham, who might have been killed by the aliens at war with Earth, and replaced with an intelligent weapon. The android simulacrum of Olham in fact contains a powerful bomb which will detonate at the end of the story, when it will be all too clear that if Olham is dead (his corpse is ultimately found) then the protagonist must be bogus.

However, there is a fundamental difference between the short story and *Puppets*. The former remains a science-fiction story whether Olham is a real human being or an android[5]; while the authenticity or falsity of Barton's memories in the novel changes the genre of the text itself. If Barton's memories are false, and the real Ted Barton really died when he was 9, the novel could be the description of a case of insanity; Barton might well be a madman who persuaded himself that he is somebody else, and the solution of the mystery should be psychiatric. This would bring the novel and its readers into the field of realistic fiction, maybe close to a novelette that had strongly impressed Dick, Ron L. Hubbard's *Fear* (1940). Dick mentions this work twice in his letters, in 1954 (*SL1* 33), when he compares it to *Puppets*, and in 1970,[6] when he says "*Fear* ... impressed me very much, and still does. Without *Fear* I would never have come up with what I do" (*SL1* 269).

Hubbard's novelette tells the story of an anthropologist, James Lowry,[7] who has published an article on a magazine which rationally explains demons and other supernatural entities as delusions. This leads to his being fired by the president of the college where he teaches, because his denunciation of pagan religions might ultimately pave the way to an attack on Christianity (Hubbard, 107–8). After being expelled by the college, Lowry suffers from temporary amnesia and forgets four hours of his life; this episode is followed by a series of hallucinations which might be interpreted by readers as the demons' revenge on Lowry for his denial of their existence. *Fear* thus reads until the last few pages as a fantasy novelette where a man who has denied the existence of supernatural beings must face the wrath of those very beings, but it is ultimately revealed to be a crime narrative when we discover what really happened in the four lost hours: Lowry killed his wife Mary and his best friend Tommy Williams in a fit of homicidal mania (possibly triggered by the stress of his expulsion plus jealousy). His hallucinations are actually distorted memories of moments of the slaughter and the subsequent hiding of the corpses in a cellar; when Lowry confesses his crime to a policeman, we are also told the real meaning of an enigmatic message he has repeatedly received from the shadows: "*if you find your hat you'll find your four hours, and if you find your four hours then you will die*" (Hubbard 129). The hat was left by Lowry in the cellar where he hid the two corpses; to find it he should get back to that place and discover his crime; but by discovering it he might easily expose it, and be subsequently sentenced to death for murder. Hubbard wrote in the Author's Note that "this story is wholly logical, for all that will appear to the contrary" (Hubbard 100): it is a crime novelette disguised as a fantasy tale, and the demons are no more than metaphors of the destructive, murderous drives in the main character's mind.

Dick was impressed by this "psychological fantasy" (we should interpret this phrase as meaning that whatever is fantastic in Hubbard's *Fear* is actually caused by psychological processes, however deranged those may be), but he turned it upside down in *Puppets*. Though, as we have already said, the psychiatric explanation of Barton's plight in Millgate is at least suggested in the second chapter of the novel ("Maybe he wasn't Ted Barton" [17] implies that the protagonist might be somebody else who only believes he is Burton, maybe a madman), as the story proceeds the fantastic elements prevail, so that if *Fear* moves from fantasy to crime fiction,[8] *Puppets* moves from mystery to fantasy.

The novel decidedly enters the field of fantasy at the end of chapter 6, when Barton finally finds someone who remembers the old Millgate, the same town that the protagonist remembers, and can confirm that the town has been replaced (61). But we have already discovered at the end of chapter 4 that the Millgate Barton has not recognized is not at all an ordinary town: it happens when, in the porch of Dr. Meade's house, "two shapes, faintly luminous, emerged" (39); two shapes of a man and a woman, walking together and apparently talking, though no sound is heard. The shapes are indifferently met by the people on the porch, until they disappear, stirring no attention or curiosity. Dr. Meade comments: "Seems to me there've always been Wanderers.... But it's perfectly natural. What's so strange about it?" (39). This tells us that Millgate is not a normal place, after all.

After Ted Barton meets a bum called William Christopher who remembers Pine and Central Street, the streets of the old Millgate (61), his memories are confirmed. To use a terminology that Dick derived from existential psychoanalysis (which in turn took it from Heraclitus), Barton's *idios kosmos*, his individual world, is different from the *koinos kosmos*, the world where all the inhabitants of Millgate live; until his idios kosmos remains private, personal, it may be easily explained as the product of a delusional syndrome, caused by trauma or psychosis. But when Ted and William Christopher meet and are thus able to compare notes, and realize that they share the memories of the disappeared Millgate, they have an alternative koinos kosmos, no more an idios kosmos.

It is then a matter of alternate realities, and we are well inside the territory of fantasy fiction. In fact Dick probably took the idea of two alternative Millgates from a famous American fantasy film, Frank Capra's *It's a Wonderful Life* (1946). That this film may have had an impact (direct or indirect) on Dick's fiction is a hypothesis that was already proposed by an Italian scholar, Gabriele Frasca, in his 2007 monograph *L'oscuro scrutare di Philip K. Dick*, where he connects Dick's presentation of ordinary life in provincial America as hiding something alien, uncanny, possibly threatening, to Orson Welles' *The Stranger* (another film which premiered in 1946) and Capra's comedy (Frasca 40–1).

Frasca does not overtly suggest that Dick saw Capra's movie and was struck by it, but this is what may have happened if we take into account some interesting similarities between *Puppets* and *It's a Wonderful Life* (which Dick might have seen when it was originally shown in movie theatres in January 1947; at that time he was eighteen and not yet suffering from agoraphobia [*SL1* 64–5]).[9]

Capra's film tells, through a series of flashbacks, the life of George Bailey, an ordinary (we might say even representative) middle-class American man who has spent his whole life in the provincial town of Bedford Falls. He has missed several opportunities to leave his home town and travel to exotic places (he is an avid reader of *National Geographic* and dreams to visit Africa and Asia); he has devoted his whole life to the Bailey Building and Loan Association, the little building society which has allowed many citizens of Bedford Falls to have a house of their own. But on December 24 George, due to an omission by his uncle Billy, finds himself on the verge of bankruptcy, and suffers a nervous breakdown which makes him almost commit suicide; he is saved (and this places this mostly realistic film well inside the territory of fantasy) by the intervention of a well-meaning — albeit bungling — angel second class, Clarence Odbody, who subsequently shows George Bailey what the world would have been if he had never been born.

Bailey is thus brought to an alternate reality, a parallel world which is similar to the one he comes from, with the only difference that he was never born. And the alternate reality is visually materialized by Capra as a different town, which is no more called Bedford Falls but Pottersville, after the name of the wealthiest man in town, Henry Potter, an avid and ruthless banker and slum lord. The alternate town where capitalist greed is unrestrained is shown as a dismal place: it is mostly a slum, with its Main Street dominated by pawn shops and sleazy bars. Bailey Park, the tidy model neighborhood financed by George's loans, was never built. There is no doubt that the world where George never existed is remarkably worse than the one we have been presented with in the first part of the film. In Pottersville all the characters surrounding George live a miserable life; some of them are not even alive (George's brother, Harry, died when he was a little boy because his brother was not there to save him after he fell in a pond through the ice; he didn't grow up to become a fighter pilot and save the crew of a US cargo ship in W.W.II, so also the sailors' lives have been lost due to George's non-existence); people are generally unfriendly, selfish, often hostile; the only place where some lame form of socialization takes place is the sleazy bar where George meets Mr. Gower, who is an alcoholic in the alternate reality because George couldn't prevent him from accidentally poisoning a boy.[10]

After visiting Pottersville, George comes to understand the numberless relations which tie him to other people and ultimately to the world, and realizes how important he has been to others; this brings him to beg Clarence (and God) to let him live again. He is granted this second wish, and can thus get back to Bedford Falls, where he will manage to save his building society thanks to the gratitude of all those he has helped, directly or indirectly, in his life. Thus we have a happy ending which puts the film in the tradition of Christmas edifying tales, whose most famous representative is probably Charles Dickens' *A Christmas Carol* (1843). This novella may have influenced Philip Van Doren Stern, the historian and writer who wrote "The Greatest Gift," the 1943 short story which was turned into the screenplay of Capra's *It's a Wonderful Life* by a pool of screenwriters which also included Capra himself. In fact when George Bailey is shown what the world might have been had he never been born, we are presented with an alternative present: a parallel universe, we might say, which is not so different from the possible future that Ebenezer Scrooge is shown by the Ghost of Christmas Yet to Come in Dickens' novella. In both Capra's film and Dickens' tale showing an alternative reality (be it a possible future or a parallel present) is a way to teach a lesson about the meaning of life, a narrative device through which the main characters may understand what could be or have been the ultimate consequences of their choices. In Dickens, Scrooge is shown what will be the effects of his insensitivity, selfishness and greed; in Capra, George must understand that his generosity, unselfishness and socially responsible attitude have changed the world around him.

We might say that in both works the projection of an alternate reality is a thought experiment, a what-if which allows characters and readers/watchers to meditate on the interconnectedness of human lives. This is not very far from what Brian Stableford quoted as one of the earliest examples of alternate worlds in the homonymous entry of *The Encyclopedia of Science-Fiction*, that is, "If Napoleon Had Won the Battle of Waterloo" (1907), a short essay written by G.M. Trevelyan, one of the most prestigious historians of the Twentieth Century. Alternate histories or "what ifs" have often been used by historians as thought experiments, but they — as we have seen — have also been used by popular genres, be they fantasy or science-fiction.

In Dick's case the presence of two alternate realities (the Millgate Ted Burton remembers and the one he finds when he visits the town where he was born) also provides an opposition between two genres: fantasy and realism. Such a peculiar articulation of his narrative will become more evident in another novel of the fifties that will be discussed in the next chapter, *Time Out of Joint*, and will be developed into one of Dick's last literary achievements, *VALIS* (Ch. 9), but there is no doubt that its testing ground was this obscure and neglected fantasy novel. There is a striking difference, though, between

Dick's novel and the two other previous works, *A Christmas Carol* and *It's a Wonderful World*; while the novella and the film are clearly aimed at teaching a moral truth, extolling the virtues of generosity and solidarity, it is more difficult to pinpoint an overt moral in Dick's novel.

There's no doubt that the Millgate where Ted Burton died in 1935, the town we are presented with at the beginning of the novel, is worse than the town Ted remembers. As soon as he arrives, he enters a hardware store to ask for information, and the description of the business is quite eloquent:

> It was old, an ancient wood building, leaning and sagging, its yellow paint peeled off. He could make out a dim interior, ... faded calendars on the walls. Behind the fly-speckled window was a display of fertilizers and chemical sprays. Dead insects lay in heaps in the corners. Spider webs. Warped cardboard signs. It was an old store — old as hell [11].

Later on, when Ted talks with Will Christopher, he is told that Pine Street was replaced by Fairmount, and that "Pine Street was a nice place. A lot nicer than Fairmount" (61). Christopher reveals that the town was "replaced" abruptly, overnight, eighteen years before, and complains that "[e]verything is worse" (63); we might doubt this, since this judgment is uttered by a drunkard, yet also Ted realizes that the part of the town where Will lives is more decayed than the one he remembers. Surely the change has worsened Will's life: "I wasn't all run-down like this. I was hard-working. Had my shop and my ability. Led a good clean life" (65). Now he must live like a bum in a "packing crate" which took the place of his "nice little three-room cabin" (64). His plight is quite similar to that of the characters in *It's a Wonderful Life* whose life depends on George Bailey's intervention: I have already quoted Mr. Gower, the druggist, but one might also mention Mr. Martini (who does not own the bar in Pottersville) or Violet (who is reduced to be a pickpocket and possibly a prostitute). Another example of how the "new" Millgate is worse than the Millgate Ted and Will remember is the park, which has been replaced by Dudley Street, that is, "a row of drooping, decayed old shacks. Ancient stores, no longer used. Missing boards. Windows broken. A few tattered rags fluttering in the night wind. Shabby, rotting shapes in which birds nested, rats and mice scampered" (79).

Other examples might be quoted, but what is important here is to understand that the qualitative difference between the two alternate realities (here two alternative towns) has another meaning from the Bedford Falls vs. Pottersville opposition in Capra's film. It could be in fact easily argued that behind the two alternative towns in *It's a Wonderful Life* there are two different political and economical visions of the United States (Frasca 146): Bedford Falls is the America of the New Deal, where social solidarity prevails and the third of President F.D. Roosevelt's four freedoms, the freedom from want, has been achieved; Pottersville is obviously the projection of the mentality of Henry Potter, the local banker and slum lord, the embodiment of unrestrained laissez-faire capitalism, a place of alienation and ruthless exploitation. Capra's film is thus a cautionary tale that should teach both an ethical and a political lesson.

In *The Cosmic Puppets* the lesson to be learned seems to be metaphysical: once Ted discovers that there are greater powers at work in Millgate than it may seem, and is told who the two "cosmic towers of being" (49) are who loom large over the town (104), it is quite clear that behind the strange events, the replacement of the town with a degraded version of it (and its original inhabitants), the isolation of the place by means of uncanny barriers (52–7), the acts of witchcraft performed by Peter, a weird and hostile boy, there is the struggle between two ancient and mysterious godheads, Ormazd and Ahriman (104). Millgate was invaded by Ahriman, the god of "darkness, filth and death," who replaced the real town with its distorted replica; obviously worse than the original Millgate, as Ahriman is the wrecker (104), forever struggling to undo what has been created by Ormazd. A psychological reading of these "cosmic polarities" is not very difficult: behind these two godheads, which Dick derived from Zoroastrianism, there are two conflicting principles that are quite familiar even to those who ignore the 2,500-years-old Persian religion. In Dick's novel Ormazd is life and Ahriman is death, not just from a biological point of view, but also psychologically. In his 1954 letter to Mr. Haas Dick explained that the novel started with a "natural, factual, normal" (*SLI*, 33) situation and then progressed "into greater and deeper levels of fantasy; a trip into the dream-region of symbolism, the unconscious, etc. as one finds in Alice in Wonderland" (*SLI*, 33). Dick then adds that "all human minds, sick or well, have regions of dream-symbolism," and this means that *Puppets* was meant to be an exploration of this symbolism, and that the godheads in the novel should be explained as psychic symbols. One might then wonder whether behind Ahriman and Ormazd there are the Zoroastrian godheads Angra Mainyu and Ahura Mazda, or the Freudian concepts of Eros and Thanatos.

Surely Dick's version of Zoroastrianism is quite original. While it is true that a certain interpretation of the relation between Angra Mainyu and Ahura Mazda posits them as peers, dialectical forces whose contrast animates the universe (they are even considered twins by the Zurvanite branch of Zoroastrianism), so that Dick's bi-theistic system can be said to be faithful to at least one tradition of the ancient Persian religion, it should be also said that the writer only chose to include in his novel those figures which somewhat fit his own psychological symbolism. Armaiti, for example, who first appears in the novel as Mary, the daughter of Dr. Meade (who is actually Ormazd's "cosmic puppet"), is the daughter of Ahura Mazda also in the Zoroastrian tradition, but she is not just "the essence of generation. The bursting power of woman, of all life ... the energy behind all growing things ... an unbelievably potent aliveness that vibrated and pulsed in radiant, shimmering waves" (136); in Zoroastrianism Armaiti is associated to earth, so she is the goddess of both fertility and the dead, who are buried in the earth. This second association was omitted by Dick; besides, he does not say that Armaiti is one of the seven Amesha Spentas, divine beings that belong to Ormazd's retinue, nor are any of the other Amesha Spentas mentioned; and while Ormazd fights against Ahriman, first through the two human embodiments or puppets (Peter and Dr. Meade), then directly (132), in the novel there is no trace of Nanghaithya, the archfiend which is the usual opponent of Armaiti in the Zoroastrian tradition.

It is safe to say that here Dick is *using* Zoroastrianism, including in his narrative only those figures which may symbolize the psychological drives he was really interested in; it is quite different from the anxious interrogation of religious ideas, narratives and figures which will take place in his final works, from *A Scanner Darkly* (Ch. 8) to the VALIS Trilogy (Ch. 8–10), when Dick was frantically trying to make sense of the strange experiences he had or declared to have had in February–March 1974 (the so-called 2–3–47 experiences).[11] Behind the decaying Millgate there is the real Millgate of Ted Barton's memories; the whole novel is pivoted upon the protagonist's struggle to recover the aliveness of his childhood memories against the pernicious, deadening entropic process of ageing. When Barton manages to rescue the real Millgate, he also manages to get free from his dead and deadening marriage (when he leaves Millgate at the end of the novel we are not told that he is going back to his wife Peg). It is true that Ted cannot live with the attractive and fascinating Armaiti, as she belongs to a different ontological level; but once he has seen her, he will never forget her.

> Armaiti wasn't gone. She was everywhere. In all the trees, in the green fields and lakes and forest lands. The fertile valleys and mountains on all sides of him. She was below and around him. She filled up the whole world. She lived there. Belonged there.... He'd be seeing reminders of her just about everywhere [143].

So, though the embodiment of aliveness disappears as a person (or character), Ted Barton does not lose contact with the vital force that she represents. We should not underestimate the fact that the god of light, life and order, Ormazd, lives in Millagate, under the domination of Peter/Ahriman, disguised as a doctor. If the decayed Millgate is "cured" by Ted and Will (who act on behalf of Ormazd, even if they are not aware of this, as Ted has been "manipulated" by Armaiti [134] since the beginning of the novel), and restored to its pristine condition, it is difficult to deny that a parallel process of healing takes place in Ted's mind, who is cured by the alienation and despair which strikes him at the beginning of the story, when he discovers that he is actually dead (a death which can be read as a symbol of emotional paralysis and/or mental derangement).[12] Maybe the full psychological implications of *Puppets* can only be understood if we take into account those psychoanalytical essays Dick recommends to his literary mentor Tony Boucher in his long April 25, 1960 letter, among which there is the collection of essays *Existence*, edited by the American psychiatrist Rollo May (*SL1* 64), which introduced existential psychology in the United States.[13] It is in the essays of *Existence* that Dick first met the concepts of idios kosmos and koinos kosmos,[14] which are equivalent to *Eigenwelt* (individual psychological dimension) and *Mitwelt* (social dimension) in existential psychology; these are the concepts that Dick nonchalantly applies to the description of a personal experience in the same 1960 letter (*SL1* 66), and that I have applied to Ted Burton's situation in *Puppets*. Other key concepts of existential psychology, such as the tomb-world (which will reappear in *Do Androids Dream of Electric Sheep?* [Ch. 6]),[15] play an important role in this psychological fantasy; the false, decaying Millgate created by Ahriman might be an example of such a tomb- or grave-world.

But there is another aspect of *The Cosmic Puppets* that should be analyzed in this opening chapter of our exploration of Dick's fiction, as it sheds light on the literary workings of this and other, more celebrated works of the Californian writer. It is the role played by the two Zoroastrian godheads in the overall structure of the novel, which is illuminated by some remarks that Dick wrote in a letter dated October 26, 1967. At that time he was discussing the possible plot of a novel he wanted to write with another sf author, Roger Zelazny. Since we only have a fragment of this letter, and what Dick describes in it is quite different from the novel he and Zelazny actually published in 1976, *Deus Irae*, it is not easy to outline what the proposed plot should have been; but it is quite clear that it involved a game in which a group of characters was placed on a sort of board and subsequently manipulated by unspecified "Cosmic Game-Players" (*SL1* 226). In the novel the humans should then have been unaware pawns (or puppets) of these Game-Players, though Dick suggests that the two levels (the one of the pawns and that of the Game-Players) "could merge in several ways." The characters could ally with one of the Game-Players; the Game-Players might manifest themselves, directly or indirectly; one or more of the pawns might "catch a transcendental glimpse of a Game-Player" (*SL1* 226). But from our point of view the last kind of interference between the two plans (human and cosmic) is the most interesting: "one of the characters could change progressively until he becomes unhuman — reveals himself as one of the Game-Players, rather than a "pawn." (Vide my Ace book, THE COSMIC PUPPETS)" (*SL1* 226).

The connection between the hypothetical plot Dick was sketching and *Puppets* is undeniable. There are three characters in the 1957 novel that reveal themselves as cosmic Game-Players: Mary, who actually is Armaiti, who has pushed Ted to enter Millgate to sabotage Peter/Ahriman's domination of the town; Peter, who is actually Ahriman (and is well aware of his real identity); Dr. Meade, who is actually Ormazd, and seems to have been struck by a cosmic amnesia, as he is unaware of being one of the two Zoroastrian godheads (a situation that will return with a vengeance in one of the last novels, *The Divine Invasion* [Ch. 10]). But what is more important is that whatever happens in the novel is part of a game, the "eternal struggle" between "the cosmic polarities" (104). All the characters in the story are ultimately cosmic puppets, pawns manipulated by the cosmic forces of light and darkness embodied in Ahura Mazda and Angra Mainyu. No wonder then that one of the first displays of Peter's magic powers is the creation of small clay golems at the beginning of the third chapter (19): the cosmic polarities fight by proxies in *Puppets*, and the story ends soon after they strip themselves of their human husks (Dr. Meade and Peter) to resume a struggle that is "much bigger than anything [we] can experience" (135), as Armaiti explains to Ted.

Besides, the novel begins with a scene of children playing while Peter watches them; they are "carefully kneading and shaping brown lumps of clay into vague shapes" (5), something that Peter will do much better and with startling results. This innocent scene of daily life can be said to metonymically represent, *pars pro toto*, the whole novel, where humans are no more than clay figurines in the hands of angry gods. The initial scene ends with the beginning of the game, when Peter says "I'll play" (6) and starts reshaping the clay animals molded by Mary. Here we actually have Ahriman declaring that he'll play the game of deceit and simulation which will involve Ted Barton and the other characters of the novel: the game he is going to play is nothing more and nothing less than the novel itself.

It is quite interesting that in an earlier version of this short novel, "A Glass of Darkness" (published on *Satellite* in December 1956) the beginning was different, as the story started with Ted's arrival in the secluded Appalachian valley where Millgate lies, a scene which in the 1957 paperback edition follows immediately the passage where the children play with clay figurines. In this first version of the novel the plot begins when Ted enters the valley and ends when he leaves it. If readers are expected to identify with the protagonist and his gradual discovery of the cosmic game played in the enchanted valley of Millgate, it is clear that entering and exiting the space where magic forces are at work is equivalent to entering and exiting the text itself, crossing the border between the real koinos kosmos where we all live and the space of narration, an idios kosmos created not by Zoroastrian godheads, but, in a Blakean fashion, by a much lesser god, or creator: the writer Philip Kindred Dick.

Then there is a metatextual dimension in *Puppets*: if the plot is the manipulative game played by the two Zoroastrian godheads of light and darkness (symbolizing eros and thanatos, but also perhaps the whiteness of paper and the blackness of ink), it is also, undeniably, a game of telling where the creator (Dick) manipulates fictional events, places and characters to play with readers and their expectations. Behind the glass of darkness of the false Millgate (a place of sorcery) lies the real town where Ted was born (a place of real life); the interplay of the two towns, which metonymically stand for two alternative realities, is the game readers have to play, being manipulated by Dick. One might then suspect that Dick was inspired by *Typewriter in the Sky* (1940), another novella written by Ron L. Hubbard, the text that admittedly inspired *Puppets*. Since *Typewriter* was often published with Fear on pulp paperbacks, Dick cold easily have read them both.

Typewriter is a rather odd fantasy novella where a 20th-century pianist, Mike de Wolf, ends up in "Blood and Loot," a swashbuckling buccaneer story set in 17th-century Caribbean which is being written by his friend Horace Hackett, a hack writer (the pun is surely intentional) who must quickly finish his book to respect the terms of a contract he has signed with a pulp fiction publisher. In the novel Mike becomes a Spanish admiral, Miguel Saint Raoul de Lobo (an approximate translation of his real English name), the villain of a story that must necessarily end with his defeat and death at the hands of the protagonist, Tom Bristol. Mike is well aware of being a character in a cheap fiction, also because he now and then hears the noise of Horace's typewriter coming from the sky; he knows that the author is now the god who creates and governs the world he is living in. Horace may also be a shoddy god, given all the historical inconsistencies which litter the botched 17th century where "Blood and Loot" is set (including Steinway pianos and 18th-century buildings), but he is omnipotent, as Mike finds out when he tries to change the plot of the novel in order to avoid his dire fate, or at least to postpone it as much as he can.

Hubbard's novella is a parody, clearly meant to poke fun at the world of hack writers, who have to concoct stereotyped narratives to pay the bills and satisfy the needs of easy-going readers. It was the same world that Dick belonged to in the 1950s, by the way, and he could easily identify with Horace, the hack writer typing his implausible yarn in a dirty bathrobe, but also with Mike, the sophisticated artist (in real life he is a gifted classical pianist) who is sufficiently learned to spot all the inconsistencies in Horace's story, which adds to the ironic atmosphere of the novella. When Dick wrote *Puppets* he was at the same time Horace and Mike: he had to write fantasy and science-fiction to pay the bills, but he yearned to become a "serious" writer, as he tells Anthony Boucher in his June 3, 1957 letter (the year *Puppets* was published as part of an Ace Double, a pulp paperback not so different from the ones presumably written by Horace Hackett [*SL1* 35–7]).

It is then likely that Dick the fantasy writer was influenced by Hubbard's *Fear*, but also by the metafictional game played in *Typewriter in the Sky*. Both texts had been republished together in a paperback edition in 1951, a year before Dick managed to publish his first short story, "Beyond Lies the Wub," while he was busy writing *The Cosmic Puppets*. Besides, his first published story has been read as a metaphor of the relation between writer and reader (Barlow 2005, 3–5), embodied in a human who eats an intelligent alien, the wub, who subsequently manages to emerge within the man who has ingested him — continuing, by the way, a discourse on Odysseus, who has been for a long time considered as the protagonist of the founding narrative of Western Civilization.

If game and players, to be read as a metaphor of narrative, play an important role in *Puppets* — and there are excellent reasons to say they do[16] — there is a strong thematic connection between Dick's only fantasy novel and a sf novel he wrote in 1962–1963, *The Game-Players of Titan* (1963), which features game-players in its very title. Like *Puppets*, this is one of Dick's neglected novels: already in 1975 Darko Suvin branded it as an unimportant work, as "up to Palmer Eldritch ... the novels by Dick which are not primarily dystopian (*The Cosmic Puppets, Dr. Futurity, The Game-Players of Titan*) are best forgotten" (Suvin 1975, 7). Unsurprisingly, the fundamental collection of essays *On Philip K. Dick*, which contains all the PKD-related articles that were published on *Science-Fiction Studies* from 1975 to 1992, simply ignores it. Sutin gave *Game-Players* a rating of 6/10, that is the mark of mediocrity (Sutin 301); an even worse rating is Andrew M. Butler's, who gave *Game-Players* 2 points out of 5 (Butler 2007, 41). Robinson sees it as a weak novel due to the presence of evil aliens (Robinson 28), because he believes that in Dick's most successful works "aliens are usually sages in disguise" (Robinson 28); Warrick thinks that *Game-Players* "does not succeed in synthesizing all the parts with dramatic economy" (Warrick 101). Such judgments undoubtedly tell us that the novel I am going to deal with is definitely not considered one of Dick's major works: even Dick himself told Gregg Rickman he had "not a thing" (Rickman 1988, 146) to say about it.

Yet something in the title, i.e. the term "game," hints at the textual strategy Dick had already used in *Puppets* and then in his major works: a game based on the uncertainty of the rules — a deliberate, purposeful uncertainty, one should add, which is also ontological. *Game-Players* might then be endowed with a somewhat "programmatic" value which has been "divined" (and sometime outlined) by some critics, but not expressed at length yet. I have already carried out a detailed analysis of the plot (Rossi 2004) that will be summarized here, which could help us to better understand what is really at stake in Dick's fictional game (Bluff) and in his textual game (the novel itself).

Unlike *Puppets*, *The Game Players of Titan* is a science-fiction novel. After the Vugs, aliens from Saturn's moon Titan, take over an Earth ravaged by nuclear war, the surviving humans are governed by Bluff, a Titanian board game that determines not only the land they own but also whom they will sleep with. Since the war between America and China left most of the survivors sterile, the Vugs have imposed Bluff to foster population growth by mating humans randomly. The game is based on wagering deeds on the spin of a wheel; luck is the principle that governs post-war, Vug-ruled Earth. Pete Garden, the protagonist of the novel, discovers that the Vug dominion is not as benign as everybody thinks, and that among his fellow humans there might be metamorphosed Vugs which look like human beings. After a series of twists, conspiracies and counter-conspiracies there is a big final game on Titan, where a human team plays against the Vugs, using alcohol and amphetamines to thwart the telepathy of the aliens and increase their own psi faculties. Terrans win, but their victory is held back; at the end of the novel a breakaway faction of the Vugs contacts Freya, former wife of Pete and team member, to ask for her help in a rematch. This means the plot is left open, as in many other novels by Dick.

Let us now see how the narrative is structured from the point of view of genre conventions. The first five chapters of the novel describe the future society ruled by the Bluff (and the Vugs who have imposed the Bluff) by showing how Pete Garden loses Berkeley and his wife in a night and strives to win them both back. Here the plot is on the whole rather linear. The only twist might be the moment that Pete discovers that Berkeley does not belong anymore to Walt Remington, the man who defeated him, but has been sold to Matt Pendleton Associates (15), a firm who operates on behalf of the strongest (and luckiest) Bluff player in the world, Jerome Luckman. This is however a twist which does not impact on the genre conventions of the text.

The novel in fact begins as a typical narrative of the sociological science-fiction of the 1950s (Luckhurst 110–11, 115–6), something that might have been written by the young Sheckley[17] or Pohl & Kornbluth. We obviously know that Dick's apprentice period as a novelist lies in that decade, roughly speaking 1955 to 1960; his first published novel, *Solar Lottery* (1955) does belong to sociological sf. The most illustrious example of this trend is arguably the 1952 novel *The Space Merchants* by Pohl & Kornbluth, which — like other works of the sociological sf— presented the readers with a "potentiated present": the beginning of the *Game-Players* is not much different. The readers of 1963 were well aware that they were going to be served a satire on the U.S. middle class moved to a more or less imminent future, with futuristic gadgets (talking handles, flying cars, etc.) set against the background of a way of life which disquietingly resembles the "real life" in Eisenhower's *America Felix*, with its life in the suburbia, Peyton Place sociality, conformism, the consumeristic obsession of status-symbols, etc.

That Dick was interested in this form of science-fiction (especially in the 1950s) should not surprise us. We know that while he was writing his sociological sf, which includes the novels *Solar Lottery* (1955), *The World Jones Made*, *The Man Who Japed* (both 1956) and *Vulcan's Hammer* (1960), plus many of the short stories he published from 1952 to 1963 (approximately 80% of his short fiction), he was also working on several realistic novels that his agents failed to sell: *Gather Yourselves Together, Voices From the Street, Mary and the Giant, The Broken Bubble, Puttering About in a Small Land, In Milton Lumky Territory, Confessions of a Crap Artist, The Man Whose Teeth Were All Exactly Alike, Humpty Dumpty in Oakland* (all posthumously published with the exception of *Confessions*: Dick managed to have it published in 1975 by a small press). There are recurring issues in both his sf and fantasy texts of the 1950s and the unpublished realistic novels: troubled marriages, threatening female characters, little men and businesses struggling to preserve their dignity in the world of corporate economy, consumerism and status symbols, conformism and massification, life in the suburbs, the impact of the electronic media on US society (TV first and foremost), the fear of the looming nuclear holocaust, the changing roles in nuclear families. These are also some of the most relevant issues in the USA after the Second World War, and characterize the decade called "The Fifties." Since his sf and realistic novels were written on the same typewriter, in the same one-man literary workshop, characters, themes, motifs, places that were originally created for realistic fictions were recycled for science-fiction. Whole scenes may have been moved from lost realistic novels to science fiction ones; characters which appeared in *The Broken Bubble* and *Voices from the Street* reappear in *Dr. Bloodmoney* (Butler 2007, 61); no wonder then that Dick was interested in the sociological form of science-fiction, which allowed him to depict the ordinary American reality he was interested in through a glass of darkness which might transmogrify the Northern California of the 1950s into Mars or some other planet — or a future America, as in *The Game-Players of Titan*.

Sociological sf is however suddenly abandoned when Peter Garden finds himself in his car, flying high over the Utah desert, without any knowledge of how he got there (62). The protagonist's interruption of consciousness and mysterious amnesia lead us to a different kind of narrative, the fast-paced, surrealistic sf of Alfred E. van Vogt, whose heroes have fractured or lost identities, and usually strive to recover their own past (such as the protagonist of *Null-A* [1948], Gilbert Gosseyn).[18] This hurls us from the reasonable sociological sf into a frantic and intricate adventure typical of the 1940s — a more "pulpish" sort of fiction. This discontinuity of the genre frame is coupled with a discontinuity of the text: after Peter exits Patricia's house, there is a blank space and then he is in his car over Eastern Utah. What happens after the moment when "Pete turn[s] and str[ides] out of the apartment, away from her" (62) has disappeared, leaving a gap in the text. Here we have the first, serious twist of the plot that makes Pete and us readers lose our bearings.

Such a strange interruption of the textual and fictional continuum might make us ask what is the narrative game Dick is playing here. Previous critics have asked another question instead, that is: "who are the *game-players* of Titan?" This seems to be a question about the content of the novel, but we shall see that it concerns its narrative strategies as well. We shall also see that the question about the identity of the players turns into the one about the nature of the game.

The first question to be asked is *who* are the game-players of Titan. The group of Vugs which play against the Pretty Blue Fox team? The powerful Vug extremists that cheat Terrans out of their victory in the end? The Earthmen and -women who have been carried on Titan? Somebody/thing else? The last is no idle question, since it drew the attention of those critics who — unlike the ones I have quoted at the beginning of my discussion of *Game Players*— deemed this novel worth discussing. We have then Pierce who wonders whether there isn't "a Master Game-player [who] operates the game according to rules they [the characters] do not come close to understanding" (Pierce 118). And she is quoting Dick, because at least once in the novel "The Master Game-Player" is mentioned by one of the characters (93).

Trying to identify the game-players just by focusing on this or that group of characters might be totally misleading: in Dick's novels the Master Game-player is often Dick himself, according to Haylos, because: "[Dick], like the Queen of Hearts, is changing the rules halfway through the game" (Hayles 53). And changing the rules in a novel is equivalent to changing the genre (or sub-genre) it belongs to. In his Introduction to the latest Italian translation of the novel, Carlo Pagetti wholeheartedly agrees with Hayles; he maintains that Dick is a postmodernist writer who plays with the conventions of the (sub)genre:

> A parodic meta-narrative, *The Game-Players of Titan* is also the story of a science-fiction writer who manipulates science-fiction's most predictable formulas, who uses his characters as puppets, who thinks he is allowed to

call in doubt his own ending with the tricks and the sleights of hand of a juggler, a *game player* [Pagetti 2000, 14, translation mine].

So Dick's novel is an exhibition of sf conventions, icons (and what is more stereotypically sfnal than the alien, malignant blob?), rules and techniques. The Game is science-fiction, and the game-player, or better, the Master Game-Player is Dick himself.

This is also true for *The Cosmic Puppets*. The ontological uncertainty that we have found at the beginning of that novel — when it is unclear whether Ted Barton's memories or the "new" Millgate are fake — is possibly stronger than the uncertainty in *The Game-Players of Titan*: in *Puppets* the alternative is between two very different genres, fantasy and realism, while here we have moved from a form of science fiction to another, but always remaining well inside the area of non-realistic fiction. We will however see that there are other games Dick plays in this novel; other form of ontological uncertainty will impact on the story of Peter Garden and his companions.

However, Dick's game is here overtly rigged, we might say: the writer repeatedly and deliberately thwarts the expectations of the readers, as we shall see, and this is mirrored by the role played by *cheating* in the whole plot. Both human and Vug characters cheat as much as they can. A fundamental passage of the text might be quoted here:

> In the center of the table he saw what appeared to be a glass ball, the size of a paperweight. Something complex and shiny and alive flickered within the globe and he bent to scrutinize it. A city, in miniature. Buildings and streets, houses, factories...
> It was Detroit.
> *We want that next*, the Vugs told him.
> Reaching out, Joe Schilling moved his piece back one square. "I really landed on that," he said.
> The Game exploded.
> "I cheated, Joe Schilling said. "Now it's impossible to play. Do you grant that? I've wrecked the Game" [156].

Cheating is in fact an integral part of the Game of Bluff:

> "You certainly broke up The Game," Doctor Philipson chuckled. "It never occurred to them that you'd cheat."
> "They cheated first. They changed the value of the card!"
> "To them, that's legitimate, a basic move in The Game. It's a favorite play by the Titanian Game-players to exert their extra sensory faculties on the card; ... You see, the Titanian Game-players believe in following the rules.... Their rules, yes; but rules nonetheless" [157–8].

Playing a rigged game is what Dick deliberately does in his fiction, and this is explained quite clearly by Thomas M. Disch with his Game of the Rat (cf. Introduction), a form of Monopoly where the Banker can arbitrarily change the rules in the midst of the game. If the Game of the Rat is a reliable model of Dick's approach to fiction in general, we might suspect that here the Game metafictionally embodies literature, or at least Dick's own version of it. Thus, as I have already stated, *The Game-Players of Titan* is representative of Dick's narrative strategies, perhaps in a more blatant fashion than "deeper" and more celebrated works, such as *The Three Stigmata of Palmer Eldritch* or *Dr. Bloodmoney.*

We should then focus on the points where Dick, our narrative Rat, changes or sabotages the narrative rules; points like the one in chapter six that we have already described, with its triple discontinuity.[19] That seems to be one of Dick's favorite tricks: (sub)genre short-circuit, something that places him close to postmodernist fiction.[20] This shifting to one genre from another has already been noticed by Christopher Palmer, who said that "Dick often seems restless with the assumptions of sf as a genre and with the delicate negotiations of reason and fantasy characteristic of sf at its best" (Palmer 173–4); such restlessness may push him to move to crime, horror, or realistic fiction.

I propose to call sub-genre *switches*, or *shunts* those crucial points where genres or subgenres are shifted. The use of these nouns coming from railway terminology seems appropriate to me since Bluff is clearly based on Monopoly (cf. Dossena) whose original U.S. board features four railway stations, Reading, B. & O., Pennsylvania, and Short Line (we might say that by referring to Monopoly, Dick opened an intertextual link that is available to readers as well as critics).[21] The shunts Dick has placed in his narrative switch the plot to another sub-genre, thus changing what is both in the foreground (characters, events and their meaning) and in the background (the sub-genre and its conventions which consciously or subconsciously affect the reader's expectations, and the way s/he deciphers the text).

Dick operates one of such sub-genre shunts when, at the end of the seventh chapter (69), the corpse of Jerome Luckman is found, and the story is switched to a non–Sfnal track. We are led in a proper detective story, relying on all the conventions of the genre,[22] good cop/bad cop couple included (97). What makes this couple different from those we often meet in Hollywood products is that one of them is human (Wade Hawthorne),[23] the other is a Vug (E.B. Black).

We have barely enough time to readjust our expectations, tuning to this odd whodunit, before Dick operates his shunts again, routing us in van Vogt's territory once more. This happens when a twist in the plot suddenly changes our understanding of the facts: because "six persons in this group show similar lapses of memory. Mrs. Remington, Mr. Gaines, Mr. Angst, Mrs. Angst,

Mrs. Calumine, and Mr. Garden. None of them have intact memories" (77). This takes us back to the frantic Vanvogtian adventures where no identity (and memory) is certain.

We are right in the middle of the novel when the plot is twisted again. This time it is not an event but a revelation, when Dr. Philipson tells Pete Garden: "You're involved in an intricate, sustained illusion-system of massive proportion. You and half your Game-playing friends. Do you want to escape from it?" (105). Thus reality is not what the characters (and the readers) have been living in till now. Dick ups the ante: the question is neither "who will win the Bluff game?" nor "who killed Luckman?" but "what is real?"—or its more paranoid version "are we being duped?" (cf. Ch. 2). These are—needless to say—the fundamental Dickian questions.

Dick has thus led us, shunt after shunt, to his own, totally recognizable version of sf, a maze of simulacra, beguiling realities and shocking revelations. We are now close to *The Three Stigmata of Palmer Eldritch*,[24] *Martian Time-Slip*, *Ubik*, what we might call his psychedelic sf, if we did not know Dick was actually addicted to amphetamines when he wrote those novels; we might then call it metaphysical sf, as ontological uncertainty dominates. The climax of this segment of the novel is when Mary Anne McClain turns into a Vug (that is, in a B-movie blob of the 50s): we don't have the girl endangered by the alien, malignant monster anymore, but the girl who doesn't know she *is* a monster, the girl transubstantiated into an alien blob (110). We are not far from the Christian symbology of the Eucharist, often quoted by Dick (cf. Ch. 7 and 11), though this is undoubtedly a sfnal narrative sleight-of-hand.

But Dick gets out of his territory when Peter Garden is kidnapped at the beginning of the eleventh chapter (121). We are thus led well into a plot of competing supermen which is classically Vanvogtian (cf. Suvin 2002, 374, 384). A new conspiracy, a new reversal; the vision of Mary Anne who turns into a Vug is given the lie, the conspiracy against the alien invaders comes back (129). Then there is a counter-reversal which takes us back to Dick's own metaphysical sf, when we discover that nothing is what it seems to be and the conspirators are Vugs without their knowing it. Here is the moment of the discovery, told by Dick in his usual deadpan tone:

> He opened his eyes.
> In the motel room, discoursing in shrill, chattery voices, sat nine vugs. And one human being besides himself. Dave Mutreaux.
> He and Dave Mutreaux, standing in opposition to the rest of them. Hopeless and impossible. He did not stir; he simply stared at the nine vugs [143].

Fredric Jameson posited an "android cogito" which equates real humans and artificial human beings in Dick's fiction due to a radical uncertainty (Ch.

6), expressed by the syllogism "I think therefore I am an android" (Jameson 2005, 373–4); an alternative version we find in several novels and short stories might be "I think, therefore I am an alien." Soon after another revelation makes clear that the survival of the human race is at stake: "The Titanians ... are tinkering with our birth rate. On some technological level ... they're responsible for holding out birth rate down" (150). This further twist does not anyway take us to another sub-genre: we remain in Dick's metaphysical sf, or better, in a field without rules, where everything may happen. We are "trapped" in the Game of the Rat: all the twists of the plot after the revelation in chapter 12 (the real nature of the nine conspirators) will not send us to another fictional turf, but will maintain the atmosphere of uncertainty and frantic struggle to understand what is actually going on and why.

We might say that Dick brought us into his deranged world, starting from a familiar Sfnal territory, by means of a careful use of sub-genre shunts. Once he has us where he wants, he can manipulate whatever element he likes to propel his narrative. The following list of plot twists (that I distinguish from genre shunts inasmuch as they do not lead us to a different subgenre frame of reference) occurring after chapter 12 gives an idea of the intensification of the narrative rhythm:

1. Dr. Philipson is a Vug (152)
2. Joe Schilling is abruptly carried to Titan to play against the moderate Vugs (153)
3. Shilling wins by cheating and is immediately brought back to Earth (156)
4. The bogus conspirators are exterminated by Mary Anne McClain (159)
5. The Pretty Blue Fox team gets back into being, to play against the Titanian Game-players (164)
6. Pete Garden leaves the team because he mistrusts Nats Katz, and attempts suicide (174)
7. Mutreux has crossed over and joined the extremist Titanian fraction; he tells Pete that Nats Katz is a Vug disguised as a human (177)
8. Patricia is forced to commit suicide by her daughter Mary Ann, Pete is set free, Mutreux captured (184)
9. The Pretty Blue Fox team plays against a team of simulacra of the Terran players (188)
10. The game is instantly moved to Titan, the simulacra crumble revealing the Vugs inside (192)

After this barrage of *coups de théâtre* we have the sequence (192–201) of the Bluff game which is finally won by the Earth team: this is obviously the final climax of the novel. It might be argued that when we get into this sequence there is another genre shunt, because in these pages the rules that structure readers' expectations and understanding are those of the Bluff, a game invented by Dick — albeit largely based on Monopoly. So here the frame is not a literary subgenre, a variety of science fiction or detective story, but a board game, one so world-famous that it has been elevated to a part of our collective imagery. (It might be objected that Bluff's rules, however resembling those of Monopoly, are ruthlessly manipulated by Dick whenever he likes or needs to, so that this is just another instance of Disch's Game of the Rat. I leave the matter open, and will insert this shunt in my table just as a proposal to be discussed by critics and readers.)

However, the end of the game does not end the sequence of twists. Three more should be mentioned, that is:

1. After the victory the team is abruptly returned to Earth and scattered (200)
2. In a moment of supreme clarity Mary Anne McClain sees humans through Vug eyes, thus understanding the prejudices of the aliens (205)
3. Freya Garden Gaines is contacted by Dr. Philipson (an undercover extremist Vug) who proposes her to work for his fraction against other Terrans (214)

The last twist of the tale leaves the ending open, something which, as I have already said, is typically Dickian. But what is really important is the intensification of the reversals, the acceleration of the plot which can be easily understood by confronting the previous lists with the following table of sub-genre shunts:

Table 1.1
Dick's sub-genre shunts

	from	*to*	*page*
1	sociological sf à la Pohl & Kornbluth (sf as social satire)	VanVogtian surrealistic adventurous sf (amnesia)	62
2	VanVogtian surrealistic adventurous sf	Detective story	69
3	Detective story	VanVogtian surrealistic adventurous sf (fractured identities)	77
4	VanVogtian surrealistic adventurous sf	Dick's own simulacra sf	105
5	Dick's own simulacra sf	VanVogtian surrealistic adventurous sf (conspiracy, competing supermen)	121

6	VanVogtian surrealistic adventurous sf	Dick's own metaphysical sf	136
(7)	Dick's sf	Bluff (a Sfnal mutation of Monopoly)	192

What we have is a vortex-shaped architecture, where twists are less frequent in the first three quarters of the text, with a sudden increase of frequency in the last quarter. Moreover, there is a change: while the shunts or switches listed in the table (those occurring in the first, longer part of the novel) lead, as we have seen, from one sub-genre to another, those occurring in the last, shorter part of *Game-Players* keep the action going but remain well inside the same textual territory, where all expectations based on genre are suspended (and that is probably why Dick does not need genre reference frames any more): a fictional space where everything may happen, where the Rat (i.e. the Author) rules.

As I have already said, I derived the term "shunt" (or switch) from Monopoly, one of the "texts" Dick has phagocytized to build his novel. There is also another reason: *shunt* appealed to me since trains and railroads appear in an early short story by Dick which is endowed with a paradigmatic value: "Small Town," written in 1953 and published on *Amazing* in May 1954.

In this story we have a trodden-upon little man, Verne Haskel, who has been disappointed by his job, his adulterous wife Madge, and Woodland, "the rich, expensive little suburb of San Francisco" (*CS2* 432) he unhappily lives in. His only consolation is the model town he has built in the basement over years. It is a faithful scale replica of Woodland: every building, street, park, house, facility has been painstakingly reproduced and carefully placed so that the layout perfectly maps the territory.

At the beginning of the story it might seem that what is really important are the trains that travel around and through the miniature town. Verne "had always loved trains, model engines and signals and buildings" (*CS2* 431). It is not just trains that appeal to him: it is the idea of reproduction, of simulacra, of things made smaller but resembling the original. Dr. Tyler, Madge's lover, has a reasonable explanation for such a fascination, which starts with the impact of trains upon infantile imagination.

> Power ... that's why it appeals to boys. Trains are big things. Huge and noisy. Power-sex symbols. The boy sees the train rushing along the track. It's so huge and ruthless it scares him. Then he gets a toy train. A model, like these. He controls it. Makes it start, stop. Go slow. Fast. He runs it. It responds to him [*CS2* 434].

But Verne has extended his model to Woodland in its entirety. And, since this is a fantasy story, the power on the simulacrum becomes a (magic) power on the original: when Verne, utterly disgusted by his job at the Larson's

Pump and Valve Works, destroys the scale model of the factory, he triggers a reversal of the relationship between town and layout. The model is no more a passive representation of Woodland, but becomes the active tool of Verne's reprisal. He discovers he can change the world outside the basement by discarding everything he hates from his model town and replacing it with something he likes. It is the application of something already found in *Puppets*, where it is called M-Kinetics: "the symbolic representation is identical with the object it represents" (115), which is actually the basic operating principle of magic (Mackey 15). So he starts rebuilding Woodland according to his own tastes:

> The new Woodland looked pretty good. Clean and neat — and simple.
> The rich district had been toned down. The poor district had been
> improved. Glaring ads, signs, displays, had all been changed or removed.
> The business community was smaller. Parks and countryside took the place
> of factories. The civic center was lovely [*CS2* 441].

What we have at the end is a one-man utopia: Verne's ideal town comes true. But what is utopian to one may well be dystopian to others. Because, as Verne tells to himself, "the new Woodland was going to be moral. Extremely moral. Few bars, no billiards, no red light district. And there was an especially fine jail for undesirables." Of course the undesirables include Madge, Verne's wife, and her lover, Dr. Tyler. After having witnessed (and misinterpreted) Verne's disappearance, the couple of adulterers gets out of the house to discover that the Woodland they knew has disappeared, and that they live in the reformed Woodland Vernon has built in the basement. The territory has mapped the scale model; and the adulterous couple is arrested by the Woodland police (*CS2* 444), because now Vernon R. Haskel is the town mayor.

All in all, this story is an elaborate self-portrait of Dick and his literary activity. He played with science-fiction and fantasy (at that time childish genres), like Verne plays with his trains and model town. His fiction can create a faithful reproduction, a simulacrum of the "real" world (Woodland before Verne's intervention; or the "real" Millgate), but he can also build a model which does not coincide with the real world of 1953, that is, the more or less estranged, twisted, distorted USA we find in the sociological sf of the 50s (or the Millgate with wanderers and golems). Verne substitutes a park for the "sprawling business district" (*CS2* 440), substitutes two bedroom, one-story dwellings for the ostentatious upper class mansions. Dick substituted flying, talking autonomic vehicles for cars, rockets for jetliners, Mars for California (that's what happens in *Martian Time-Slip*, basically a realistic novel with a more or less thin sf paint layer to camouflage it [Ch. 4]). Besides, the first name of the protagonist hints at the origins of sf: we know that "Verne" was one of Dick's favorite names (we have the character of Verne Tildon in *Gather*

Yourselves Together), but could not it refer to Jules Verne the author of *From the Earth to the Moon* and *Twenty Thousand Leagues under the Sea,* one of Dick's (and sf's) literary forefathers?

However, what is important is the idea of the Sfnal fictional space as a trap where readers may be snared. What happens to Madge and Dr. Tyler is what happens to us readers. We get lost in the model town modified by Verne/Dick; we get lost in the secluded valley there the replaced town, Millgate, lies; we get lost in the Bluff game. Maybe this happens because there is a power fantasy behind these narratives: Dick is the boy who gets a toy train, controls it, makes it start, stop, go slow, go fast. Dick runs it, and the toy responds to him. And the toy train is the narrative itself.

The idea that trains and/or railways may be metaphors of fiction (in particular of plots) is not new (cf. Ceserani). It is hidden in the opening scene of Thomas Pynchon's *Gravity's Rainbow,* "Pirate" Prentice's dream of the railway station full of refugees. The railway track hints at the linear plot; but it may hint at the postmodernist multidimensional, non-linear plot too, if we take into account the railway network as a whole (or Pynchon's railway station, since it is a knot of several tracks). That is what may be found in such an experimental work as Geoff Ryman's web-based hypertext *253,* where the London Underground becomes a model of the network structure of the hypertext and of a non-linear plot made of hundreds of interconnected character descriptions. More recently the idea of train as symbols of narratives has been extensively exploited by Richard Powers in his avant-pop novel *Galatea 2.2* (1995), a text with noteworthy Sfnal elements.

Like Verne Haskell, Dick may operate the switches, or shunts, so that the train of his narrative may change direction whenever he likes. And that's what Verne does in a scene at the beginning of "Small Town," which expresses all the frustration of the protagonist:

> Haskel turned up the power. The train gained speed. Its whistle sounded. It turned a sharp curve and grated across a cross-track. More speed. Haskel's hands jerked convulsively at the transformer. The train leaped and shot ahead. It swayed and bucked as it shot around a curve. The transformer was turned up to maximum. The train was a clattering blur of speed, rushing along the track, across bridges and switches, behind the big pipes of the floor furnace.
>
> It disappeared into the coal bin. A moment later it swept out the other side, rocking wildly.
>
> Haskel slowed the train. He was breathing hard, his chest rising painfully. He sat down on the stool by the workbench and lit a cigarette with shaking fingers [*CS2* 431].

Isn't this, after all a scene of power fantasy with striking sexual undertones? Increasing speed, hands jerking (Dick did know how to use *double-*

entendres when he wished to!), a climax of excitement, and then the penetration of the dust bin, an orgasmic moment followed by the traditional cigarette. This adds another layer of meaning to the character (sexual frustration), but let us not forget that the climaxing rhythm of the passage reflects Dick's own climaxing narrative rhythm, the acceleration of twists we have previously analyzed.

Verne maneuvers the trains and the narrative paths of the characters in the story, but he also alters the miniature town, i.e. the setting of the story, just like Dick: as we have already seen, his twists are very often not only changes in the foreground (the characters, their actions, their aims), but huge transformations of the background. Time travel stories, for example, are based on abrupt changes of background, and this is a narrative sf device (also found in fantasy)[25] that Dick used e.g., in *Dr. Futurity* and *Now Wait for Last Year* (Ch. 5), *The Three Stigmata of Palmer Eldritch* (Ch. 7) and in one of his best short stories, "A Little Something About Us Tempunauts" (Ch. 5); this is exactly what happens in *Game-Players* too when the Pretty Blue Fox team is transferred to Titan during the final Bluff game.

Now, if we wished to summarize Dick's literary Game of the Rat we might say that basically it all boils down to putting a bunch of characters in a familiar or alien setting, and then operating plot shunts and unexpectedly changing the background (or the reference frame) at an increasing speed. That's the way most Dickian novels work: *Ubik*, *The Three Stigmata of Palmer Eldritch*, *A Maze of Death*, *The Simulacra*, but also such later works as *Valis* and *The Divine Invasion*. Obviously this is what is normally found in most popular genre novels or stories, be they sf, fantasy, crime, romance, etc. Twists are what propels a narrative only meant to entertain, to keep readers' boredom at bay. Of course Dick started from genre fiction, and published most of his short stories on pulp magazines, and several of his novels on pulp paperbacks, the notorious Ace Double, which sold two compact novels together in dos-à-dos binding, often nonchalantly cutting them to fit the size of the book. Some of Dick's novels underwent this brutal editing (even if it was carried out by the author), among them *The Man Who Japed* (*SL1*, 35–6).[26] But Dick managed to turn plot twists into something else: the tool which allowed him to achieve a condition of ontological uncertainty — an uncertainty that another writer was able to create and sustain, though he never published on pulp magazines or paperback. We are talking about a highly prestigious European author, whose fiction has never been considered as merely aiming at entertainment, the creator of such modern classics as *The Trial* and *Amerika*.

It is in fact easy to prove that Franz Kafka, a writer often mentioned in Dick's letters, one whose surname, as we have seen, Dick would have adopted as his middle name, structured (or better, destructured) his novels by means of a barrage of twists. One might consider the beginning of *The Castle* (1922): late at night K., a land surveyor, arrives at the inn of a village. The innkeeper tells him he cannot stay there without the Count's authorization. K. replies that he came at the Count's command. A lackey of the Count comes to the inn an threatens to throw K. out, in the icy winter night. K. tells him to phone the Castle and check that he has been invited by the Count. The lackey calls the Castle, but he is told that nobody knows K. The land surveyor is going to be thrown out, but the telephone rings. The order is countermanded: K. may stay for the night, the matter will be settled the next morning. It is a tourbillion of interrupted actions, frustrated intentions, small coups de théâtre — not as stunning (and sometime lurid) as Dick's, but surely as bewildering.

Thus this unsettling technique was not only used by literary hacks, but also by respected (and imitated) masters of modernist fiction. It should be added that Dick did not always manage to use it as more than a useful tool to keep readers' attention awake; but when he did, he could achieve impressing results, even from an aesthetic point of view. What is in any case more important is that the Game of the Rat might put readers in such a position as to question some fundamental concepts of their culture, or history, or society — concepts which may still apply.

In *The Cosmic Puppets* the effect of the alternate reality which hides the real Millgate, and the struggle to dispel it, is a gigantic metaphor for the passing of time. Ted, in a wholly realistic fiction, might get back to his town and find it changed, and say "it looks like another town altogether." This would be a metaphor, and it could be acceptable to realistic conventions. But by literalizing the metaphor, or better, by *materializing* it (something which characterizes fantastic literature, as Todorov surmised in 1970 [Todorov 113–14]) we end up in fantasy or science fiction. Ted doesn't find a changed Millgate: he finds another town. Hence his dismay, because what he finds is an ageing, decayed, wizened place, and that decay suggests that the passing of time is deadly, that it takes you nearer to death (something that took Marcel Proust a bigger textual apparatus to visualize; but, coming after Proust, Dick could use a sort of textual shorthand). Retrieving the lost Millgate is something that asks for a painful *recherche du temps perdu* which is surely shorter than Marcel's in Proust's gigantic novel, a search which ends up when Ted gets in touch with the principle of aliveness, a vitality which is always accessible (even for elderly people like Will Christopher). Here any uncertainty is wiped out in the end: the ending is indisputably happy, and may also be said to be consolatory (though it is poetic enough not to serve up a guy-gets-girl ending). The dismal world of Ahriman is dissolved, and we are left with the happily ordinary Millgate of Ted's childhood.

Things are rather different in *The Game-Players of Titan*. Here it is no matter of alternate realities but metamorphoses: most of the shunts in the tale deal with the opposition human vs. alien and characters who are able to move from one term of it to the other; the girl turning into an alien blob, as we have seen. This series of twists may be said to prepare the climactic moment when Mary Anne McClain can see humankind through Vug eyes, one of the most impressive — and unexpected — moments of literary grace in Dick's fiction:

> Stunted, alien creatures, warped by enormous forces into miserably mal-formed, distorted shapes. Crushed down until they were blinded and tiny.... the waning light of a huge, dying sun lit and relit the scene and then, even as she watched, it faded into dark red and at last utter blackness snuffed it out once more.
> Faintly luminous, like organisms inhabiting a vast depth, the stunted creatures continued to live, after a fashion. But it was not pleasant.
> She recognized them.
> That's us. Terrans, as the vugs see us. Close to the sun, subject to immense gravitational forces [205].

Thanks to the series of shunts, which keep identities instable, we may ultimately *become Vugs* and see a defamiliarized image of our species; and we know that defamiliarization is — at least according to the Russian formalist critics such as Shklovsky (who called it *otstranenie*) — the main purpose of lit-erature. Surely the ability to make us adopt such a different point of view is a remarkable feature of Dick's fiction, and it can be said to be his main added literary value.

This is something that was already surmised by Huntington in the article we have already quoted, when he realizes that Dick's fiction cannot be simply dismissed even *if* we explain it — as Huntington tried to do — by means of the mechanical workings of the 800-word rule that Dick might have been taught by A.E. Van Vogt. Huntington then detected an open problem for critics:

> [Dick's work's] contradictions are as often as not the result of arbitrary and random reversals as of any conscious critique of bourgeois culture. But the absence of conscious intent does not thereby render the thought of the narrative trivial. In fact, it may well be argued that it is precisely this free-dom from controlling rational structures ... that gives Dick's writings their value. This is not to say that the arbitrary is free: free association is enlight-ening because it subtly responds to deep necessities of the author's psyche and of the culture. It reveals unknown structures not because it is free, but precisely because it is determined [Huntington 176].

After having analyzed Dick's Game of the Rat, I might rephrase some of Huntington's statements. In fact we might say that it is precisely the ability to short-circuit controlling rational structures (such as sub-genre reference frames) that gives Dick's writings their value. And what Huntington calls "free association" should be read as metaphorical association, thematic interplay, symbolic manipulation, something that has always existed in literature. Thus we should ask ourselves if the matter of consciousness is so important: Huntington himself says that "the absence of conscious intent does not ... render the thought of the narrative trivial"; I might as well add that the presence or absence of conscious intent is difficult to ascertain in most literary achievements, inside and outside sf.

Then Huntington admits that

> Dick's approach to narrative renders conventional modes of evaluating art and thought problematic. It would be inadequate simply to celebrate him as a hack and therefore promote him as authentic. By the same token, we cannot just denounce him as a fraud. Like something in one of his novels, he is always on the other side of whatever posture or value we choose [Huntington 176].

In fact the authentic/faked opposition is one that is ceaselessly questioned and deconstructed in Dick's opus (crammed as it is with forgers, simulacra, dummies, stage props, con-men, conspiracies, etc.); we might as well say that Dick's fake-obsessed fiction is a form of metafiction (which is nothing new, since Carlo Pagetti has been telling us that for about twenty years, and with a huge amount of evidence), just because *all fiction lies on the borderline between authenticity and fakery*. We might as well say that Dick's fiction is postmodernist (it depends on what is meant by that term, cf. Rossi, "From Dick to Lethem"); but in his being always "on the other side of whatever posture or value we choose," Dick is also close to some canonized modernist novelists, from Louis-Ferdinand Céline to Franz Kafka.

So, is Dick a hack who casually stages the contradictions of late modernity thanks to arbitrary and random reversals, or a respectable Author capable of a conscious critique of bourgeois culture? Is his game based on luck or on deliberate, planned programming? Is he like Jerome Luckman, the Bluff champion who wins simply because he is lucky, or like Joe Schilling, whose skills are as big as Luckman's luck (28)? Curiously enough, the matter discussed by Huntington — that is, the difficulty to ascertain whether Dick is just a lucky hack or a skilled artist/artisan — is present in the novel itself. Does not Shilling say that "Bluff's a fascinating game. Like poker, it combines chance and skill equally; you can win by either, or lose by either" (28)? We might also say that the Game of the Rat (Dick's own fictional strategy) equally combines arbitrary, random reversals and conscious critique of bourgeois culture; or perhaps it can criticize late capitalist culture by means of a system of *apparently* arbitrary and random reversals, or reversals which are sometime instinctive, but never totally random.

We might now ask ourselves whether a writer who shows in all these strategic parts of his works such insights can be considered a hack who stages a naïve show of narrative fireworks, or an insightful novelist whose sophistication has not been fathomed yet, who was compelled to work as a hack writer to make ends meet, but could never stop being the complex, learned, sometime absolutely brilliant writer he was. But one might wonder whether this is a legitimate question. In fact, we should not forget an important lesson of a past master, Northrop Frye, who warned us that

> the assertion that the critic should confine himself to "getting out" of a poem exactly what the poet may vaguely be assumed to have been aware of "putting in," is one of the many slovenly illiteracies that the absence of systematic criticism has allowed to grow up [Frye 17].

I suspect that if we keep on asking ourselves whether Dick was a hack who hurriedly concocted his novels without being fully aware of their theoretical implications, we are guilty of that Frye called the fallacy of premature teleology. It is a form of blindness that prevents us from understanding that meaning in literary works is not simply something which "is there," buried under a variable number of layers of textual dirt, but something that *happens* when the text is read, no matter where and when and by whom.

The potentialities of Dick's Game of the Rat will be perhaps better understood when we read two more important works in the next chapter, *Eye in the Sky* and *Time Out of Joint*. Here alternate realities will not be applied to psychological realms, but to a more complex and troublesome maze, Flaubert's multicolored nightmare, which is the same nightmare from which Stephen Dedalus was desperately trying to awake: history.

Chapter 2

"The Enemy That's Everywhere Around Us": Alternate Worlds in *Eye in the Sky* and *Time Out of Joint*

> "The paranoid style is not confined to our own country and time; it is an international phenomenon."
> Richard Hofstadter

In his essay *Science Fiction* Roger Luckhurst summarizes his assessment of Dick's oeuvre by placing it in the area of sociological sf. In fact he maintains that

> Although Dick wrote a number of novels within ... Realist conventions, he perceived himself as a genre writer ... To lift two or three Dick novels into the 'literate' New Wave or into a separate tradition of SF-as-critical-theory is to canonize by isolating those works from the confusing and confused avalanche of SF he produced in the 1960s. The later phases of Dick's career deepened the resonances with structures of technological paranoia ... but Dick's vision remained absolutely continuous with the satirical and psychological fictions typically associated with the works of Pohl, Kornbluth and Sheckley in the 1950s. Dick did not substantially depart from that tradition [Luckhurst 163].

This is a questionable reading of Dick's oeuvre: saying that Dick "perceived himself as a genre writer" is an untenable oversimplification, and this chapter and the next should prove it; as for departing from sociological sf, one cannot imagine a more straightforward departure than *The Man in the High Castle*, the subject of the next chapter. Yet we cannot deny that Dick started his career as a sf writer in the decade that was dominated by sociological sf: his fantasy novel *The Cosmic Puppets* is an *unicum*, after all; and though

Dick wrote both fantasy and sf stories in the early fifties, the works he published in the first decade of his activity as a professional writer mostly belong to the second genre. From 1955 to 1960 Dick managed to publish eight novels, and six definitely belonged to science-fiction; as we shall see, one of them, *Time Out of Joint* (1959), starts as a realistic novel set in a nondescript town of the 1950s (just like *Puppets*), but then moves to a sfnal futuristic setting. And there is no doubt that the six purely sfnal novels are typical representatives of sociological science-fiction.

This area of science-fiction has been painstakingly and persuasively analyzed by Luckhurst in a sub-chapter whose title is "Science Fiction as Social Criticism" (109–19); its features are still clearly recognizable in the initial chapters of a novel written and published in the early 1960s like *The Game-Players of Titan* (Ch. 1). If this variety of sf aimed at "envisioning transformation … through the lenses of sociology, psychology and political economy" (Luckhurst 110), and if its tone is fundamentally satirical, as in its most representative novel (Scholes & Rabkin 66), Pohl & Kornbluth's *The Space Merchants* (1952), then it is easy to read Dick's purely sfnal novels of the 1950s as specimens of this trend.

His first published novel, *Solar Lottery* (1955) replaces elective democracy with the random selection of the Quizmaster, i.e., the president of the Solar System, and depicts a world where people belong to corporations and social status has turned into a caste system; surely the plot derives from the adventurous sf of the 1940s, especially from A.E. Van Vogt's narratives of intrigue and amnesiac supermen (Disch 19–20), but the numerous hints at the status obsessed U.S. society of the Eisenhower Era are easy to detect. Dick's subsequent works of this decade are even easier to place in the sociological trend: *The World Jones Made* (1956), by depicting a future Earth falling under the rule of a theocratic, intolerant dictatorship, satirizes the intolerance and xenophobia of the years of senator McCarthy, HUAC and black lists against the background of Cold War; *The Man Who Japed* (1956) presents us with a world dominated by Moral Reclamation, where any deviation from moral behavior is immediately repressed and everybody is under strict surveillance (also thanks to spying robots), a situation which may remind us of Orwell's *1984*, but is strongly connected to the atmosphere of conformism and paranoia that dominated Eisenhower's America; *Dr. Futurity* (1960) is a tangled time travel story whose complicated plot is pivoted upon the issue of the colonization of North-America by Europeans and the subjugation of Native Americans, that is, a matter of race or ethnicity which was published only five years after the Montgomery Bus Boycott and three years after the bombings in the Alabama town; *Vulcan's Hammer* (1960) shows another repressive and regimented society, ruled by a computer, Vulcan 3, and an elite of men-in-grey-flannel-suits which can be said to embody the outer-directed individual theorized by David Riesman and other sociologists of the post–World War II years.

All these stories might be somewhat summarized by the title of Dick's 1953 novella "The Variable Man": they all set independent and nonconformist characters against a technocratic society which strives to enforce total control. The protagonists of these novels — from *Solary Lottery*'s little man Leon Cartwright (and space expansion prophet John Preston) to unconscious japer Allen Purcell (in *The Man Who Japed*), from open-minded and tolerant Fedgov agent Doug Cussick to technicians Jim Barris and Jason Dill — are all Variable Men, struggling to overthrow a system which turns humans into predictable quantities or cogs. Once again, it is the opposition theorized in such classics of U.S. sociology as Riesman's *The Lonely Crowd* (1950), between inner-directed and outer-directed individuals.[1] They are also Little Men, like the protagonist of a German novel published in 1932 that Dick loved (*SL1* 64, 79), Hans Fallada's *Little Man, What Now?*, where a young couple strives to survive in Berlin during the difficult years of the economic crisis triggered by the Wall Street Crash.[2]

However, these novels are fundamentally aimed at entertainment and, as Dick complains in some of his letters (Ch. 1), they were often drastically shortened in such a way that their convoluted plots could be barely followed (this is especially true for *The World Jones Made* [*SL1* 40]). Unlike other classics of sociological sf, Dick's main aim was, to put it in Andrew Butler's words, write adventure novels which "paid the rent" (Butler 2007, 51). We know that in those years Dick devoted most of his creative energies and resources to the writing of those realistic novels that publishers invariably rejected: from 1949 to 1960 Dick completed nine manuscripts that have survived and have been posthumously published, plus others which have been lost. Dick was well aware of the limits of the sf novels that were published in DAW's Ace Doubles: he wrote that *Vulcan* was a "botched job ... one of the worst of [his] efforts" (*SL1*, 51); in the same letter he explains that *Dr. Futurity* was basically an expansion of a short story ("Time Pawn" [1954]). We have a letter to James Blish where Dick praises *The Man Who Japed*, saying that "it has genuine literary worth" (*SL1* 41), but Blish had written a positive review of the novel, and Dick usually tended to humor the addressees of his letters. Besides, he did not seem to have much to say on these novels in the following years.

There are, however, two more novels of the fifties that can compare favorably to *Puppets*, and they are *Eye in the Sky* and *Time Out of Joint*. These two novels were both already discussed in one of the most important articles on Dick's sf output published in the pioneer years of PKD scholarship, Peter Fitting's 1983 article "Reality as Ideological Construct," and this shows that critics detected their higher quality and maturity quite soon. Also Dick indirectly told us that those two novels were different from the rest of his early production, because he kept finding new meanings in them in his *Exegesis* (*Pursuit* 177, 186), where — at least in the published parts — he does not bother to mention, say, *Vulcan's Hammer* or *Dr. Futurity*.

The higher quality can be easily explained for *Time*, which was sold to Lippincott, a more respectable publishing house than DAW, and printed in hardback edition in 1959 not to be sold as sf, but as a "novel of menace"; we should think that Dick wrote it more carefully than the other genre novels, and it shows. On the other hand, *Eye* was hastily written in two weeks in 1955 (Butler 2007, 32), and was published on one of the notorious Ace Doubles. However, it was an ambitious work, as it should have been preceded by a prologue where the characters of the novel commented on it, which was subsequently edited out (Butler 2007, 32–3). In both novels, however, Dick develops his narrative techniques to achieve ontological uncertainty, and shows a greater mastery of the Game of the Rat.

This is easy to prove if we compare those two works to *Puppets*. In fact the 1957 fantasy novel features a *limited* ontological uncertainty. As I have already said in the previous chapter, we are unsure if this is a realistic or a fantasy novel until Ted meets Will Christopher; then the novel solidifies as full-blown fantasy, which ends when Ahriman leaves Millgate (and Earth) and the original Millgate returns once and for all. This is the moment when the world of fantasy dissolves so that Ted (and us readers) may get back to the ordinary world, to our shared world where there are no wanderers and no golems. The interplay between these textual levels (each standing for a different reality) can be then schematized by means of this table (Rossi "Fourfold Symmetry," 405):

Table 2.1

Fictional levels	*"Real" (Historical) Level*	
PRIMARY TEXT: Millgate I (Ted's — and Ormazd's — town)	ZERO TEXT (historical reality of 1957)	*"accepted" levels*
SECONDARY TEXT: Millgate II (Peter/Ahriman's town)		*alternative levels*

The terminology I am using here (Primary, Secondary and Zero Text) is taken by Carlo Pagetti's introduction to the Italian translation of *The Man in the High Castle* (Pagetti 1977, 139), which will be discussed at length in the next chapter. Such a terminology can be nonetheless applied to other works by Dick, and it will be done wherever possible in this essay. We could then say that *Puppets* takes us readers from a normal world (Millgate I) and realistic fiction to an abnormal reality (Millgate II) and fantasy, but ultimately takes us back to the primary text, to the Millgate Ted expected and remembered, and this means that after our visit to the world of fantasy we may safely get back to our familiar world: the zero text is not called in doubt.

We cannot say that this is the case in *Eye*. The novel begins in a slightly futuristic setting, as its first sentence declares that "The Proton Beam Deflector of the Belmont Bevatron betrayed its inventors at four o' clock in the afternoon of October 2, 1959" (5). The Bevatron was not a fictional machine (it was a particle accelerator at Lawrence Berkeley National Laboratory which began operating in 1954, the year before Dick wrote the novel), and it did accelerate protons, though its location was not Belmont but Berkeley (a place Dick knew well, as he had attended the University of California there). However, the particle accelerator is no more than a device Dick uses to conjure up not just one secondary text (and alternative reality) but four. The accident described in the first chapter involves eight persons, including the main character of the novel, Jack Hamilton, who has been just fired from a missile manufacturing plant because of his wife Marsha's leftist leanings (6–14). Marsha is another victim of the accident; on the platform incinerated by the six billion volt beam there are also Charley McFeyffe, head of the security at the missile plant, Arthur Silvester, a former Army officer, Edith Pritchet, a middle class matron with her eight-years-old son David, Joan Reiss, a withdrawn spinster, and Bill Laws, an Afro-American physics student who works as a guide to the Bevatron plant.

After the accident the eight characters soon find out that they are no more in the normal world where the story started, which is basically the world of the 1950s with the Cold War and witch-hunting (Jack and Marsha are victims of the latter, and Jack's position in a missile plant directly connects them to the former), plus the sfnal Belmont Bevatron and the accident it causes. The world they find themselves in is one where God exists and blatantly intervenes in everyday matters: the angels of the Lord suggest the correct answers to the faithful (63) and confound the heathens (62); engineers "are mainly preoccupied with the job of piping grace for every Babite community the world over" (53); those who build mosques, temples, altars are struck by lightning if they make mistakes (53–4); God can be reached flying with an umbrella (it just takes the right prayer) and he is an immense eye in the sky (90–6); "big, brutish, masculine angels" (120) emerge from television screens to punish those who express heretic opinions. But the first alternative reality that we visit in *Eye* is not, like the secondary text in *Puppets*, the embodiment of a historical religion (be it Zoroastrianism or Christianity). This strange world is dominated by a fictional religion, whose sacred text is the *Bayan of the Second Bab* (49); this imaginary cult is loosely based on the Bahá'í Faith, founded in 19th-century Persia, and the version which is shown at work in the first secondary text of *Eye* is the superstitious and mean one projected by the mind of Arthur Silvester, one of the victims of the Bevatron accident, "a crackpot old soldier who believes in his religious cult and his stereotyped ideas" (110).

In his biography of Dick, Lawrence Sutin explains that A.A. Wyn (the founder of Ace Books) forced Dick to call Silvester's God "(Tetragrammaton)" and to mould his religion as a small and non-existent crackpot cult based on Islam, not Christianity, because he did not want to offend "the American Legion and fundamentalist Christians" (Sutin 92; see also Rickman 1989, 196).[3] This tells us that the world of Arthur Silvester could easily be read as a satire of Fundamentalist Christianity, which already was a powerful force in U.S. society; no doubt then that the interplay between primary and secondary text remained within the scope of sociological science-fiction. What Dick did in this novel was to take the idios kosmos of a typical fundamentalist (righteous, bigot, narrow-minded, superstitious) and turn it into the limited koinos kosmos where the eight characters are trapped. We might also say that Silvester's Babite world is a Finite Subjective Reality.[4]

This is the name that Jonathan Lethem gave the pocket worlds in his 1995 novel *Amnesia Moon*, a deliberately Dickian pastiche. There the United States are fragmented in a myriad of small cities or even neighborhoods, each one surviving by itself, and bearing the signs of an enigmatic catastrophe (shattered buildings, abandoned cars, lack of communications, no functioning radio or TV, etc.) which has not only erased all individual and/or collective memories of the past, but has also torn apart the fabric of reality itself. Each city visited by Chaos, the protagonist, in his journey form Hatfork, Wyoming, to California is a Finite Subjective Reality (Lethem, 200). People in different places experience a post-catastrophic reality, but each place seems to have been stricken by a *different* catastrophe. The differences are explained once we discover that each Finite Subjective Reality is subjective inasmuch as it is the projection of an individual mind, a dreamer who creates and controls it to a certain extent.

Amnesia Moon is a brilliant rewriting of *Eye*, so that we may apply the concept of FSR to the worlds projected by Dick's characters in his novel.[5] The most relevant difference between the two novels is that in *Eye* the FSRs do not coexist; the characters (and the readers) can only visit a new FSR once they have neutralized the individual who is projecting (or dreaming) the pocket world they are in. Moreover, while there is no more "normal" reality in *Amnesia Moon* (the catastrophe has made it disappear just by fragmenting it into a myriad of FSRs), in *Eye* there is a real world which is repeatedly glimpsed by the characters, as at the beginning of the ninth chapter, where we are shown the eight victims "strewn across the floor of the Bevatron" while "like snails, medical workers crept cautiously down ladders into the chamber" (125). The eight characters are living not only in a sort of virtual reality, a shared FSR, but also in an accelerated time, because they are actually lying in a state of unconsciousness where they fell due to the annihilation of the platform.

The problem is that getting back to the genuine koinos kosmos is definitely not easy. Even if they manage to knock down Silvester and interrupt the projection of the FSR of the Bab, they move to another FSR, this time projected by Mrs. Pritchet. It is a puritanical world where women are sexless and all tasteless things have been removed; it is a world where "Sigmund Freud developed the psychoanalytic concept of sex as sublimation of the artistic drive" (134), in an ironic reversal of sublimation according to the founder of psychoanalysis. A world where electronics industries "continue the search for the *ultimate communication medium*, the device ... by which all living humans will be faced with civilization's cultural and artistic heritage" (135). If the first FSR was the projection of a religious fanatic, the second is the creation of a sex phobic mind, with the aggravating circumstance of a philistine (and ultimately snobbish) conception of art (and life). Mrs. Pritchet is prudish, gluttonous, posh, but what is important is that she is as intolerant as Silvester; but while Silvester does not tolerate those who do not conform to his bigoted morality (though in his world some venial sins are tolerated, as we are told and shown in the hilarious scene in the bar [72]), Mrs. Pritchet does not accept all those things and people who annoy her — and she is quite easily annoyed. She eliminates Silky because she is a prostitute (153), all snakes so that her son cannot set out his snake trap (168), "old farmhouses with tottering windmills" (169) because they spoil the landscape, seagulls (176) because they are "evil-minded birds" and cows (177) because one of them "did something unmentionable," that is, defecated. Other categories are wiped out of existence due to Mrs. Pritchet's dislike, until, in a frenzy of annihilation, she makes chemical elements disappear one by one (183), causing her FSR to collapse.

This moves the eight characters to another world, the one devised by Joan Reiss, who suffers from paranoia: "everything she sees has some significance, part of the plot directed against hers" (192), we are thus plunged into a nightmarish display of "predatory horrors" (200), like the transformation of Silky in a horrible spider-like creature in the basement of Hamilton's house (195–99) or Joan Reiss' house which turns into "a house-creature ... ready to feed" (210) on the group of characters, in a remarkably horrific and surrealistic sequence (208–12) which stands comparison with Dick's more celebrated psychedelic phantasmagorias in *Ubik* and *The Three Stigmata of Palmer Eldritch*.

After Joan is brutally slaughtered by Silvester, Bill Laws and David

Pritchet, turned into monstrous (and obviously predatory) insect-like creatures by her hallucinatory paranoid syndrome (214–7), the narrative moves to another secondary text (we might call it a quaternary text, but probably this complication is not necessary) or FSR, which is this time believed to be projected by Marsha Hamilton, because it is a caricature of the world as it might be seen by a tremendously dull and fanatic Communist militant: a place where capitalists are robber barons, protected by merciless thugs, and workers must defend themselves with any possible means, including violence. It is "the Communist idea of America — gangster cities, full of vice and crime" (229). Such a black-and-white (actually black-and-red) FSR is however too crude, too simple, too moronic to have been projected by a sophisticated woman like Marsha, but Hamilton discovers this only after having knocked his wife unconscious. Then McFeyffe undergoes a miraculous and grotesque metamorphosis, turning into a heroic, god-like figure (241). Dick's ironic comment is that "the resemblance to (Tetragrammaton) was startling. McFeyffe had clearly not been able to shed all his religious convictions" (241).

It is interesting to notice that Hamilton has been fired because McFeyffe reported on Marsha's political activism (described in the first chapter [10–1]); the "rabid patriot and ... reactionary" which Marsha calls "a dangerous fascist" is actually a closet Communist (30). Dick's explanation for his behavior is voiced by McFeyffe himself, when he says that "People like [Marsha] — they're more of a menace to the Party discipline than any other bunch. The cult of individualism. The idealist with his own law, his own ethics. Refusing to accept authority" (243). Once again, this is a fictional embodiment of the opposition between the inner-directed and the outer-directed individual; the former can be represented by the homogenized men-in-grey-flannel-suit like colonel T.E. Edwards (one of the managers of the missile plant) or the submissive member of the Communist Party (or, in the Soviet regimes, the so-called *apparatchik*) like Charley McFeyffe. However, whether they work for the Military-Industrial complex of the United States or the Cominform they are both not specimens of what Herbert Marcuse called the One-Dimensional Man in his homonymous 1964 essay, a stark criticism of both capitalist and Soviet societies. Once again, the world projected by one of the characters can be easily interpreted in sociological terms.

This has been done by Fitting, who reads the "four subjective realities" as "ideologies," totalizing views of the world that reject consensus, "the U.S. as a harmonious blend of differing cultures, beliefs, and philosophies which is governed by the will of the majority" (Fitting 1991, 96). But that consensual democracy, Fitting warns us, hailed in the 1950s as "the end of ideology" cannot be said to be embodied in the "normal" world we are presented with at the beginning of the novel, where Hamilton is fired because of his wife's political activism (1–26). When Hamilton gets back to the koinos kosmos after his (and his companions') travel through the four versions of idios kosmos, he desperately tries to unmask McFeyffe (246–9), but fails because in that only apparently consensual world, "a group of extremists attempts to impose their construction of reality on others, *and they succeed*" (Fitting 1991, 97)—those extremists being symbolized by McFeyffe and the management of the missile plant, who stand for Senator McCarthy and the various witch-hunting committees then in action (one of them, HUAC, also included the man who will become Dick's political nemesis, Richard Nixon). Thus Hamilton and Laws have to "reject a *koinos kosmos* that before their terrifying experience seemed reasonable" (Robinson 16) and invent a new job, which in a typical Dickian fashion will be a small business building hi-fi equipment (252–6).[6]

But there is more to be said about the ending of *Eye*. The return to the "normal" world of 1957—its disquieting ideological implications notwithstanding—might look similar to what we have at the end of *The Cosmic Puppets*, according to this scheme (which may help readers to grasp the overall architecture of *Eye*):

Table 2.2

Fictional Worlds	*Projected by*	*Pages*
Objective reality		
The World of Eisenhower (political intolerance)	Consensual	1–26
Finite Subjective Realities		
The World of the Bab (religious fundamentalism)	Arthur Silvester	26–122
The World of Puritanism (sexual intolerance) and Philistinism (class discrimination)	Mrs. Pritchet	122–182
The World of Fear (paranoia)	Joan Reiss	182–217
The World of Class Warfare (political intolerance)	Charles McFeyffe	217–245
Objective reality (?)		
The world of 1959 (?)	Consensual (?)	245–256

Yet some commentators questioned the reality of the world where the characters live at the end of the novel. Butler suggests that "the ending is ambiguous: they assume they are back in the real world, but there is no evidence for this," and pinpoints an asymmetry between the number of the victims of the Bevatron accident and the FSRs that are visited in the novel: "after all, they haven't been in eight hallucinated universes yet" (Butler 2007, 34). Fitting had already noticed this in his 1983 essay, but he explained it in another way, consistent with his Marxist interpretation of the novel, saying that "there are three ... characters who ... are excluded *by definition* from participation in the elaboration of a consensus" (Fitting 1991, 97): Marsha, because she is a woman; David Pritchet, because he is a boy; and Bill Laws, as he is black. The underprivileged are not entitled to their own FSRs, to show us their *weltanschauung*.[7] But Butler reads this asymmetry as a clue to a different interpretation: why should we believe that the final world is the same where the characters live at the beginning of *Eye*?

Maurizio Nati noticed another tell-tale detail in the ending, that is, the earwig which stings Laws when he tells Mrs. Pritchet that she will get back the money she is lending him and Hamilton for their small hi-fi business (255–6). Hamilton rushes to correct Bill: "We *hope* you'll get your money back" (256), as if the sting were a punishment for what Bill has said. In fact Hamilton had said, a few pages before, "From now on I'm going to be perfectly honest with everybody, say exactly what I think" (252). If somebody is stung just because he was not perfectly honest with somebody, could it be that the world at the end of *Eye* is just another FSR, this time projected by Hamilton, the sensible and open-minded protagonist (Nati 139–40)? Also Nati notices that four worlds are missing, and the small accident at the very end of the story may be Dick's indirect way to tell us that the odyssey of the characters is not over yet.

If the stable and consensual koinos kosmos is not reached in the ending (even though Hamitlon's world seems to be less oppressive and unpleasant than the previous ones), we should read this novel as the first full-blown occurrence of ontological uncertainty in Dick's fiction. As in other major works, the ending is open (maybe not overtly, but, as we have seen, other interpreters have noticed this, and that should mean that the openness is not so difficult to be perceived); it is the same situation that we have in the last pages of Dick's "canonical" novels of the sixties, from *The Man in the High Castle* to *Ubik*.

However, there is another element which should be highlighted. Though sociological readings like Nati's or political interpretations like Fitting's are not to be discarded, as this novel does belong to the current of sociological science-fiction after all, a socio-political framework cannot account for all the FSRs listed in the table above. It is quite interesting that when Fitting lists the "contents" of the FSRs visited in the novel, he mentions only three: "Silvester's religion, Mrs. Pritchet's moralism, McFeyffe's politics" (Fitting 1991, 96). What about Joan Reiss? In the table I have called her FSR "The World of Fear"—being well aware that, unlike other categories in the table, fear is not *per se* political. The problem with Ms Reiss is that she suffers from a paranoid syndrome, which forces her to see the world as a conspiracy of "predatory horrors." This may be the reason why while other FSRs are basically funny or grotesque, Joan's world is scary (already Nati has noticed that *Eye* is "science fantasy with some trespassing on horror" [Nati 131, translation mine]); satire works quite well with political contents, but when Dick stages the fears and delusions of a deranged mind we enter a different genre, and the atmosphere is one of fright, not irony — closer to the gloomiest scenes of *Ubik*.

This should tell us that *Eye in the Sky*, though belonging to sociological science-fiction, is also indebted to fantasy; and that it can be read politically or sociologically, but its architecture based on a series of FSRs also lends itself to a psychoanalytical reading, where the existentialist concept of *Eigenwelt* (one's own world) which Dick had surely found in Rollo May's collection of essays (as we have seen in the previous chapter) is sfnally embodied in the FSRs projected by the characters.[8] We should not then forget that the phrase comes from Heraclitus' Fragment B89, "The waking have one common world, but the sleeping turn aside each into a world of his own." That fragment is quoted by Ludwig Binswanger in the essay "The Existential Analysis School of Thought" which was included in May's collection (Binswanger, 196) — a book Dick had read. For the ancient Greek philosopher the moment where the idios kosmos is fully revealed is that of dreaming; and this adds a further element to our reading of *Eye*, because there is probably no word in the English dictionary which connects the political, collective dimension and the private sphere like *dream*, especially when used in the phrase "American dream." The three FSRs projected by Silvester, Pritchet and McFeyffe are undoubtedly American dreams, or better nightmares; but Reiss' dream could be dreamt also elsewhere — unless we accept Richard J. Hofstadter's idea of a peculiarly paranoid style in American politics (Hofstadter 1964).[9] One should in any case acknowledge that the paranoid discourses analyzed by Hofstadter are quite different from the surrealistic visions conjured up by Dick in the third FSR visited by his characters.

All in all, while in *Puppets* there is a koinos kosmos that the protagonist and readers can get back to, *Eye* is closer to *The Game-Players of Titan*, inasmuch as the return to shared reality is at least problematic — though ontological uncertainty casts its shadow on the ending of *Eye* in a less flamboyant fashion than it does in *Game-Players*. *Time Out of Joint*, on the other hand, can be said to be placed in a middle position between those two novels: the ending does not seem to be uncertain, as the familiar reality of the 1950s is unambiguously given the lie, and the story reveals itself as sheer science-fiction.

The story begins in a nondescript U.S. small town in 1958. Ragle Gumm, the protagonist, is a forty-year-old idler who has no job, no family and no house of his own. He lives with his sister, Margo, who is married to the owner of a supermarket, Vic Nielsen. Ragle's only occupation, apart from attempting to seduce his neighbor's wife, Junie Black, is solving the quizzes published every day by the local newspaper, the *Gazette*. The name of the contest is *Where Will the Little Green Man Be Next?*, and it consists in locating, on a map divided in 1,208 squares, where and at what time will the little green man be: the players have to decide what is the right square on the basis of a semi-logical procedure involving deciphering some sibylline sentences and taking into account the answers of previous weeks. Ragle has been the undisputed champion of the contest for years: he keeps finding the right answer day after day, month after month, something that makes him and the editorial staff of the *Gazette* quite happy. He wins, it must be added, thanks to his records, his charts, his deductive abilities, but above all thanks to an almost inexplicable intuitive talent.

Ragle is quite famous on a local scale. Every day the newspaper publishes his picture above the contest grid. He is so popular that readers have grown a bit fond of him: he's like a family member, and they expect him to keep winning week after week. This is the reason why the editorial staff exceptionally allow him to submit more than one solution for each day's puzzle, provided he indicates their order of value, i.e., which is the most probable solution, then the second most probable, etc.

Surely the secret compact between Ragle and the people of the *Gazette* is a bit odd, but it should be said that the nameless town he lives in is even odder. In what should be an ordinary town of the United States in the late fifties Marylin Monroe is totally unknown (63), *Uncle Tom's Cabin* is a book that Vic has never heard of (8), there are no radios but only TV sets (20–1), etc. All characters remember small details of their life, their homes, their workplaces, that turn out to be false, or inconsistent: a switch that should be there is not there, a step you remember is missing, and so on. And when we are presented with the disappearing of a soft-drink stand in a public park, a vanishing that leaves an astonished Ragle with a slip of paper in his hand, with block letters saying SOFT-DRINK STAND on it, we cannot help thinking that there is something definitely rotten in that nondescript, would-be ordinary town.

In fact there is a conspiracy going on. Ragle is not the man he thinks he is, Vic and Margo are not his relatives, all the world we have been shown in the first 50 pages of the novel is totally, bogus. The story takes place in year 1998, but not *our* 1998; Dick has imagined his 1998 in 1958, envisioning it through the lenses of the SF of the fifties. Earth is ruled by a totalitarian planet-wide government (called One Happy World) that has decided to ban space exploration, the Moon has been colonized, the lunar colonies have resented the domination of Earth and eventually revolted against it,[10] subsequently adopting an attrition tactics to compel Terra to acknowledge the independence of the Moon. Every day they launch a nuclear missile on a city of

Terra, choosing it on the basis of a randomized, unpredictable method. We should say a *would-be* unpredictable method, because there is at least one person who can foresee where the big H-bomb-carrying missiles will fall next.

That person is Ragle Gumm himself: thanks to his partly deductive, partly aesthetic technique, Ragle can detect a pattern in the previous strikes and locate the next target — with a certain degree of approximation — and that explains why he is allowed to provide alternative solutions. While he thinks he is following in the green man's footsteps, he is actually following in the missiles' tracks.

There is not much to be said about why Ragle is imprisoned in a faked town of the 50s and can solve his ballistic problems only if disguised as harmless prize contests: the government decided that, due his moral doubts about the war, Ragle was too unreliable to be left free; then Ragle's retreat syndrome, triggered by excessive strain, helped the One Happy World to put him into an artificial urban setting which reproduced the world of his childhood.

Ragle's psychological problems contribute to the atmosphere of radical uncertainty that dominates till he and Vic manage to hijack a truck and leave the nameless town in chapter 12. In the first three fourths of the novel Ragle asks himself what is wrong in his world — but he is *not* sure that there really is something wrong. He oscillates between the feeling that a vast organization is busy around him to cheat him and his relatives, and the atrocious suspicion that the conspiracy is no more than the creation of a deranged mind: his. Until the eventual denouement, *Time* might well be a realistic novel realistically describing a case of paranoid syndrome (and that might also be what Dick was originally aiming at, since another, almost contemporary novel of his, *Confessions of a Crap Artist*[11] is pivoted upon a character who is really deranged and only imagines aliens, flying saucers, etc. [Robinson 20–2]).

Fitting reads this novel as a denouement of ideology (the peaceful, happy, and fake 1958 town) as opposed to a reality of conflict, militarism and fear; Ragle's amnesia should be then read as "ideology's efforts to erase its own traces, as it were, to 'naturalize' its own historical and class-based origins" (Fitting 1991, 98). Here Fitting is using the idea of naturalization as it is presented in Roland Barthes' *Mythologies* (Barthes 140, 144), where the French semiologist discusses cultural constructs that are universally (and erroneously) considered natural, hence undisputable and unchangeable. If the quiet and drowsy reality of an American suburb as Dick depicts it, "a sunny universe. Kids romping, cows mooing, dogs wagging. Men clipping lawns on Sunday afternoon, while listening to the ball game of TV" (80) is *the* reality, why question it? Why worry?

But the America Felix depicted in the novel is bogus. Behind it there is an estranged future, a threatening world of totalitarian oppression and war.

I have suggested (Rossi "Fourfold Symmetry," 405–6) that when Dick exposes the archetypal small town of the fifties as a simulacrum, he is also saying something about the decade which was ending at the time the novel was published. As in *Puppets*, there are two towns here, the one where Ragle Gumm lives in the fake fifties and the one he visits after he has escaped, and they stand for two different worlds: but those two alternative textual levels in turn stand for two very different images of the historical 1950s.

Table 2.3

Fictional Levels	*"Real" (Historical) Levels*	
PRIMARY TEXT: 1959 America Felix Peace — Unity Mainstream literature Ragle is a dropout and (probably) a "lunatic"	ZERO TEXT (1): Eisenhower's America, Earth's richest and most powerful country, the core of the *Free World*	"accepted" levels
SECONDARY TEXT: 1998 One Happy World vs. loonies War — Secession SF literature Ragle is the saviour of humanity and then its (heroic) traitor: he becomes a *loonie*	ZERO TEXT (2): America is ruled by the industrial-military complex, in a continuous state of (cold) war, doomed to nuclear destruction.	alternative levels

This fourfold scheme provides a symmetry that allows for several effects of signification (*effect de sense*).[12] At the end of this novel we have two parallel movements: Ragle, no more insane, gets "back" from the accepted—albeit fake—1959 to the hidden—albeit real—1998[13]; the reader reaches the alternative zero text of the U.S. in the 1950s, hidden behind the facade of nationalistic Cold War rhetoric, i.e., the daily life of a country which is already at war, dominated by the industrial-military complex, divided by a conformist and xenophobic conservatism on the one hand and those forces which challenged the status quo (e.g., the Civil Rights movement) on the other hand. Ragle's discovery that he is not living in 1959 but in the "future" (actually, a psychologically removed present) corresponds to the denouement of the simulacral essence of U.S. daily (and historical) reality of 1959.

Such a reading might seem to counter Jameson's interpretation of *Time*, which stresses the positive capacity of the novel to show us the historicity of the fifties by turning them into the past of a "conditional" future, what Jameson calls "a trope of the future anterior" (Jameson 1991, 285). This allows Dick to capture "the stifling Eisenhower realities of the happy family in the small town, of normalcy and nondeviant everyday life" (Jameson 1991, 280), something that "high art" cannot deal with. Jameson seems then to suggest that the device of the fake town enables Dick to achieve a surprising and paradoxical "authenticity," moreover infusing historicity in his contemporary reality, that is, "the perception of the present as history" (Jameson 1991, 284). This may be true for the two climactic epiphanies which take place at the end of chapter 14, when two italicized paragraphs show us two key moments in Ragle's childhood, and show us in an estranged way the "present-as-past" (or "future anterior") of the U.S. fifties (180–1, 182–3).

Can such an authenticity be reconciled with our reading of the alternative reality as a denouement of the normal and nondeviant daily life of the 1950s as ideological construction? It should be said first that Jameson is using *Time* to devise a theoretical framework which allows him to analyze two films of the 1980s based on a postmodern representation of that decade. The critic is well aware of the complexities of Dick's novel, because he acknowledges that "a twofold determination plays across the main character" (Jameson 1991, 282): the fake village is at the same time the result of Ragles' infantile regression, to be read then as "a collective wish fulfillment" (Jameson 1991, 283) and a deceptive manipulation, which may be interpreted as "the expression of deep, unconscious, collective fears about our social life" (Jameson 1991, 282). The nameless town is then a synecdoche for "the United States surrounded by the implacable menace of world communism" (Jameson 1991, 283) or any other external threat (which makes this novel so interesting in our current age of terrorism paranoia). Even little Sammy knows that if something is wrong in the small town where he lives with his family, it must be because someone is trying to dupe them; and that someone is obviously "the enemy that's everywhere around us" (63), possibly armed with "dupe-guns." Of course Sammy's guess is that "they're the Reds" (63).

Besides, if the issue is what the fifties were really like, we may accept Jameson's remarks but never forget that our shared image of that decade is more *Happy Days* and Fonzie, or *Grease*, than the fifties themselves, or better, that decade as it was daily experienced by those who lived through it (we have then to acknowledge, and this is something that also Jameson is implicitly doing, that there may be many different visions of that period, because — to put it into Heraclitus' terms — there are many idioi kosmoi in a complex relation to the koinos kosmos).

A more troublesome aspect of the novel is the unexplained episode in the park, that I have already discussed in an article on this and other components of the novel (Rossi 1996, 200–8). This episode was already quoted by Fitting in his 1983 article, who did not suggest a detailed explanation (Fitting 1991, 224). This scene begins as a rather realistic depiction of what could become an adulterous affair, but then turns into a supernatural event. What is remarkable is the series of overt literary references in this episode: in a novel whose title quotes Shakespeare's *Hamlet*, and might have the story of the Danish prince as a subtext (Pagetti 2003, 15–6), literary quotations are undoubtedly worth considering.

It all begins when Ragle takes Junie Black to the public park; while they are sunbathing, Ragle feels both Junie's attractiveness and her disarming immaturity. He asks himself: "Could I fall in love with a little trollopy, giggly ex-high school girl ... who still prefers a banana split with all the trimmings to a good wine or a good whisky or even a good dark beer?" (36). The difference of tastes marks a clearly defined semic opposition between Ragle and Junie: he is characterized by the semes of maturity, age, manhood, experience, moral awareness as contrasted to Junie's immaturity, youth (or teenage), womanhood, inexperience, moral irresponsibility. It could be argued that this is a rather conventional sort of characterization (with a distasteful flavor of sexism), but we must always remember that the episode is seen through Ragle's eyes, so these semic oppositions are part of Ragle's weltanschauung; we are presented with how *he* experiences his relation to the attractive younger woman or, better, how he *would like* to experience it. Moreover, Ragle's cultural pattern is not just a manifestation of some (American) Male Ideology defining Real Men on the basis of virile tastes (whether in wine, whisky, beer, or whatever else): there is something alchemical in this irrational "meeting and mating of opposites" (36). No wonder then that Ragle suddenly wears the ancient robe of a Renaissance magician, turning his small affair in a scene of magical rejuvenation: "The old Doctor Faust sees the peasant girl sweeping off the front walk, and there go his books, his knowledge, his philosophies" (36).

Ragle/Faust could become young again by mating with Junie/Gretchen; the "trollopy, giggly ex-high school girl" then turns into something loftier, an embodiment of the *Ewigweibliche* (Goethe's ideal of transcendent womanhood as it appears in the last lines of his poem); and such a quotation of Goethian terminology is not out of place. Junie/Gretchen possesses a peculiar kind of pre-human innocence that lets her remain unspoiled by time and human intercourses; Ragle/Faust sees her as a female archetype of sorts:

> No matter how deeply she got involved with men ... she probably remained physically untouched. Still as she had been. Sweater and saddle-shoes. Even when she got to thirty, thirty-five, forty. Her hair-style would alter through the years; she would use more make-up, probably diet. But otherwise, eternal [37].

That is why Ragle quotes Goethe's poem, first in English — "in the beginning was the deed" (36) — then in German, *Im Anfang war die Tat*: it only seems that he is just seducing his neighbor's wife, but the deed he is so interested in is presented as the philosophic principle of action, the noble *Streben* that plays such an important role in Goethe's masterpiece. Yet poetry must be explained to the eternal woman: "That was poetry.... I was trying to make love to you" (37), which is something Faust did not have to do; moreover she refuses to kiss him — but this does not deter Ragle/Faust: "He knew that one day he could have her. Chance circumstances, a certain mood; and it would be worth it, he decided" (37).

But as soon as Ragle walks away toward the soft-drink stand, he muses over the possible consequences of his deed: will Bill Black take his revenge on him, "the trespasser of that most sacred of all a man's preserves, that Elysian field where only the lord and master dares to graze" (39)? He begins to understand the moral and, more than that, practical implications of adultery. And when he reaches the soft-drink stand, where children are "buying hot dogs and popsicles and Eskimo Pies and orange drink" (39), the ordinariness and banality of the scene completely changes his mood:

> Stunning desolation washed over him. What a waste his life had been. Here he was, forty-six, fiddling around in the living room with a newspaper contest. No gainful, legitimate employment. No kids. No wife. No home of his own. Fooling around with a neighbor's wife. A worthless life [39].

The Goethian *Streben* and *Ewigweibliche* seem definitely out of tune with the ordinary life of U.S. suburbia in the 1950s: Ragles realizes that he is attracted to an immature woman because he himself is immature, notwithstanding his virile tastes. Junie is not Gretchen: she is just the ideal partner for a man who is living in a protracted childhood, and by conquering her he is looking for a reconfirmation of his manhood. But the deed (*Tat*) Ragle/Faust is striving to accomplish is no metamorphosis or rejuvenation; it is just irresponsible (and ordinary) "fooling around with a neighbor's wife."

After these realistic pages, their insisted literary allusions notwithstanding, Dick introduces a coup de theatre that unleashes ontological uncertainty. The soft-drink stand fades away. And, what is even stranger, Ragle is not very much shocked by this uncanny event, because he thinks: "It's happening to me again" (40). Once the stand has disappeared, Ragle picks up a "slip of paper. On it was printing, block letters. SOFT-DRINK STAND" (40). Ragle can just put the small sheet in a metal box, where there are already six slips of paper with the names of other, already vanished objects: "DOOR FACTORY BUILDING HIGHWAY DRINKING FOUNTAIN BOWL OF FLOWERS" (44).

The episode in the park may make us suspect that Ragle is not sane after all (Vest 93), and the world of 1998 is a delusional construct; if we pursued such an interpretation, we would have a more radical form of ontological uncertainty than that suggested by the novel in a reading that simply accepts the sfnal world of 1998 (as it is depicted in the novel) as the real one, and the nameless town as a materialization of Ragle's idios kosmos. If we may suspect that Ragle's final flight to the Moon is a psychotic delusion, then the liberating ending becomes dubious at least (such an interpretation has been suggested *ad absurdum* by Rispoli [Rispoli 35]).

Yet a cursory survey of the text tells us that this is a 3rd-person narrative whose focus is not always Ragle Gumm: episodes where he is not present which confirm the falsity of the town are Bill Black's visit to the Municipal Utility District Office where he talks to Mr. Lowery about the danger that Ragle is becoming sane again at the beginning of chapter 5 (54–6); Bill's phone call to Mr. Lowery, where he complains that a phone book of 1998 has been left in the ruins next to the Nielsons' house at the end of chapter 5 (66–8); Vic Nielsen's mental experiment which allows him to realize that the town around him is mere scenery at he end of chapter 6 (81–2); the scene at the beginning of chapter 8 where a young man is getting ready to play the part of a highway policeman, and rehearses his lines (96–100); Margo's final conversation with Bill Black where the woman discovers that Bill, not Vic, is her husband (173–8).

All these small scenes are there to persuade us beyond doubt that the world of the 1950s is fake and the war between Earth and Moon is true. But what is the meaning of the slips of paper, then? In the interview that Charles Platt Dick mentions this scene and maintains that he was trying "to account for the diversity of worlds that people live in" (Platt 151). Dick adds that he did not know Heraclitus at that time, and his distinction between koinos and idios kosmos, but that is what should explain the disappearing of the soft-drink stand. This does not really explain much: does it imply that the soft-drink stand and the other disappeared objects are just figments in Ragle's mind? Since he is suffering from hallucinations this fits into the plot, but what about the slips of paper?

An easy way (maybe too easy) to solve the riddle could be a metafictional reading. But if we read Ragle's "word is reality" as "my reality is made of words, because I'm the character of a novel, and I know it," all the complex game of mirrors between *Time* and Eisenhower's (and today's) America gets lost — we are left with a game with words which defuses itself by reminding us that it has no substantial reality.

If we understand the original value of *word* in a Ragle's meditation on the slips of paper he has found (in the park and elsewhere), that is, "Words don't represent reality. Word is reality. For us, anyhow" (44), we can see that Ragle is not the metafictive character realizing he is just a character. Reality is not denied. What is denied is the possibility of a naïve, irresponsible, immediate access to the "Deed": Ragle can't have Junie, he can't simply enjoy his small world because it keeps turning into "printing, block letters" (44). In other words, there is no naked truth (that is why the naked body of Junie is ultimately not available); there is no immediate intuition of the world, of himself, of anything. Everything Ragle is and will be is mediated by and into the all-pervading speech, the Word.[14] To reach his real identity, Ragle will be forced to rediscover his (and the world's) real history, deconstructing the scientifically organized fakery surrounding him.

Word — considered as the sense-creating *logos* mentioned by John in his Gospel — is reality. Sense is shared reality: the reality Ragle shares with Vic, Margo, Sammy, Junie. To set himself free Ragle must regain his lost (both personal and national) history. He has to renounce the illusory Faustian identity, he has to feel like Alexander Selkirk, a.k.a. Robinson Crusoe (nonchalantly mentioned by Ragle, but then recognized as a literary quotation with an act of anamnesis [62]). The slips of paper he is left with are made of the same substance (paper, from the scientific point of view; language, from the philosophic and literary point of view) of the copies of *Time* from 1997 he finds at the Keitelbein's (119–20), where he begins to discover who he really is. Ragle's process of deconstruction of the fake reality includes a talk with his brother-in-law Vic in which he reveals what the slips of paper really are:

> Reality, ... I give you the real. ... Under everything else, ... The Word. Maybe it's the word of God. The logos. 'In the beginning was the Word.' I can't figure it out. ... I think we're living in some other world than what we see, and I think for a while I knew exactly what that other world is [138].

The "other world" is reached when — after Ragle's and Vic's escape from the nameless town — other people tell them the history of the world (and America) after 1959; it is Ragle's discussion with Vic that allows us to reach reality, the shared history. We could also say that *Time Out of Joint* is the story of the discovery of a hidden text; that text is the *logos*, the removed history/reality (while the fakery is a not-really-living, ineffective word).

All in all, Dick's novel tells us that our real world is made of words; and that words are necessary to give sense to it. Words have a strange substantiality, which is particularly evident in some recent historical events. If the world of the 1950s is made of words, and this may hint at the undeniable fact that the fifties are also a *myth* of the fifties (cf. Jameson 1991), made of words, images, icons, such as Montgomery Clift maybe, or Marilyn Monroe (quoted in the novel), James Dean, saddle-shoes and soda fountains, souped-up cars and rock-and-roll, we might well ask ourselves what is the substantiality of the world we live in. What is the substantiality of those Weapons of Mass Destruction which started a substantial invasion of a substantial country, and the loss of thousands of substantial lives, both American and Iraqi (with the occasional

Italian)? Is not Dick telling us that words may be as substantial as things, in our world of vicarious experience through the media? Even if a novel is made of words, after all, it may play such games with words that we become aware of the stories, myths, urban legends that we are relentlessly told to persuade us that the large part of the world we cannot directly access means this or that; and that even what we think we can "directly" access has this or that meaning.

And those whose job is building texts (e.g., fiction writers) are well aware of the verbal nature of the common world we live in. Ragle Gumm can be seen as a self-portrait of the author as a sf writer (Robinson 20–2; Rossi 1996, 208); Mr. Lowery's description of how he solves the riddles of the *Little Green Man* contest hints at artistic creation:

> You work from an aesthetic, not a rational, standpoint. Those scanners you constructed. You view a pattern in space, a pattern in time. You try to fill. Complete the pattern. Anticipate where it goes if extended one more point. That's not rational; .... That's how ... vasemakers work [30].

The title of the contest itself, with the Green Man that may be easily interpreted as a stereotyped alien, hints at cheap sf. *Time Out of Joint* could be read as a vindication of sf, but it is above all the vindication of an unlucky, underpaid sf writer who was trying to escape the sf ghetto. Is not Ragle Gumm, losing time with a childish game, an alter ego of Phil Dick, wasting his time with a literary form that had almost no cultural dignity at that time? Is not the final condemnation of the 1959 reality the revenge of the *loony* Phil Dick? Here is a short but poignant description of the status of sf writers in the 1950s and 1960s,[15] part of a never-delivered speech about science-fiction:

> A few years ago, no college or university would ever have considered inviting one of us to speak. We were mercifully confined to lurid pulp magazines, impressing no one. In those days, friends would say to me, "But are you writing anything serious?" meaning "Are you writing anything other than SF?" We longed to be accepted. We yearned to be noticed [*Shifting Realities* 259–60].

If the contest of the *Gazette* is a childish version of sf, like Sammy's "Robot Rocket Blaster from the 23rd century, Capable of Destroying Mountains" (84), then Ragle's escape from the game and the fake world containing it may be seen as an anamorphic image of a movement towards a more mature form of fiction, where the devices of sf can be taken seriously as complex metaphors of real concerns, maybe not capable of destroying mountains, but capable of debunking the artificial image of Eisenhower's America Felix (and our current dreams of the 1950s as happy days). We know today that Dick's escape was not successful, that his realistic novels remained unsold in his lifetime, that *Time* in its respectable Lippincott edition was a commercial failure so that it was reprinted in 1965 as a garish Belmont sf paperback "with an SF cover depicting spacemen and the moon falling out of the sky" (Sutin 94). Dick had to stick to Sf to make ends meet.

Yet the complexity of this novel was not lost on another, more prestigious American novelist: we know today (Rossi 2003) that Thomas Pynchon took several elements from *Time* (Ragle's ability to predict where missiles are going to fall, his map, his paranoid state of mind, the conspiracy surrounding him) to build "Beyond the Zero," the first part of his postmodernist masterpiece *Gravity's Rainbow* (1973). Of course this could not be a consolation for Dick in January 1963, when he witnessed the ultimate failure of his escape from the sf ghetto (Sutin 118) embodied in a big package with all his unsold non-sf manuscripts returned by his literary agent — but it is further proof of the vitality of this novel and its ability to produce ever new and bewildering effects of signification.

Chapter 3

Obscure Admixtures:
The Man in the High Castle
Considered as a (Cold) War Novel

"A screaming comes across the sky."
Thomas Pynchon

There is at least one unambiguously realistic novel among those Dick wrote in the late fifties that was published in the author's lifetime, and that is *Confessions of a Crap Artist* (1975). The crap artist is Jack Isidore, a slightly retarded young man who believes in UFO, ESP and whatever pseudo-scientific body of knowledge we can imagine. His opinion on almost everything is quite odd, yet, like other literary fools, he may see some truths better than ordinary people. He may be a crap artist, but in his own very peculiar way he is an artist like Ragle Gumm (we have already seen that *Confessions* is a companion piece of *Time Out of Joint* in Chapter 2), who may be wasting time in an apparently unimportant activity but can see things others cannot.

The novel starts with Jack's rambling monologue about the problems that beset humankind. The first is that we are made of water, and water can be absorbed by the ground (3), a very original way to muse on mortality; but there is a greater problem: "We don't feel at home everywhere we go" (3). It is a rather existentialist statement, but the explanation of that sense of homelessness is not based on Heidegger's philosophy, but on an all-too-solid historical event: "The Answer is World War Two."

After this Jack tells us about the climactic moment when he heard the news about Pearl Harbor on his home-made radio and called his schoolmate Hermann Hauck to inform him about the startling event. Their subsequent conversation immediately turns in an overexcited display of ruthless racism. Here are Hermann's opinions about the Japanese: "... they have no culture of their own. Their whole civilization, they stole it from the Chinese. You know, they're actually descended more from the apes; they're not actually human beings. It's not like fighting real humans" (4). To this racist rant, Jack adds: "Today we know that the Chinese don't have any culture either" (5).

Traces of World War II can be found also in other realistic novels: we have Leo Runcible, one the protagonists of *The Man Whose Teeth Were All Exactly Alike* (published in 1984 though written in 1960, the year before Dick wrote *The Man in the High Castle*), who is proud to be "the only Jew in the world to sink a Jap sub on Yom Kippur" (15); in an earlier realistic novel, *Puttering About in a Small Land* (published in 1984 but written in 1957), Virginia and Roger Lindahl move to California in the winter of 1944 to work in the aircraft plants that ceaselessly produce airplanes for the war.

Dick's relation to the war was necessarily indirect. He was only 12 when Pearl Harbor was attacked and 16 when nuclear bombs were dropped on Hiroshima and Nagasaki. Unlike other post-war U.S. writers (Norman Mailer, Joseph Heller, Kurt Vonnegut), he could not take part in the war; while J.G. Ballard, another, slightly younger sf writer who has often been compared to him — all their remarkable differences notwithstanding — was imprisoned in a Japanese concentration camp in Shanghai with his parents, Dick's experience of the war was totally mediated by the available media — newspapers, radio, cinema.[1] Moreover, Dick was a pacifist and intensely disliked the military. Maybe this can also be explained with his indirect exposition to the horrors of World War I, thorough the stories his father Edgar — a veteran of the 5th Marine Regiment[2] — told him; Dick, then a boy, "felt a lot of anxiety listening to [his] father's war stories and looking at and playing with gasmask and helmet" (Sutin 14), culminating in the notorious moments when Edgar Dick put on his gasmask and turned into a threatening alien creature in his son's eyes.

Though the details of actual fighting were intensely disliked by Philip, and he repeatedly expressed his anti-war opinions in interviews, letters and his own fiction, he could not deny the overwhelming importance of World War II in shaping the world he grew up in (the war took place in the years of his adolescence) and the virtual war in which he lived as an adult and a professional writer; not just World War II but the threatening World War III — aka Cold War — plus the historical, albeit geographically removed, Korean and Vietnam War.

However, even the most superficial survey of Dick's short fiction of the 1950s might easily prove that one of his most common themes or motifs is the Third World War. Jameson already noticed this in his 1975 article on *Dr. Bloodmoney*, when he wrote that it "serves in one way or another as the precondition and the premise of other books" (Jameson 2005, 349). If this is true, it is also difficult to deny that *The Man in the High Castle*, placed after the huge corpus of short stories featuring World War III as precondition and premise (two extremely interesting examples being "The Defenders" [1953][3] and "Autofac" [1955]) and before *Dr. Bloodmoney*, Dick's most sustained and original treatment of the nuclear holocaust (possibly the only text where World War III is directly described and not just remembered or mentioned by the characters), is strongly related to the Third World War because it deals with the conflict which originated the bipolar world Dick lived in, torn by the not-completely-virtual Cold War between USA and USSR. Questioning World War II and its outcome meant questioning the post-war world with its competing superpowers.

So, even if Dick disliked war, he was somewhat fascinated by World War II; it appears in those realistic novels written before *The Man in the High Castle*, and is the main issue of his 1962 novel. But Dick tackled the war quite differently from other writers of the 1960s, such as Mailer (whose popular 1948 novel *The Naked and the Dead* is based on personal experience and belongs to a tradition of fictionalized memoirs or autobiographic novels dealing with war and/or combat which started with Stendhal's *The Red and the Black* [1830]) or Heller (whose postmodernist novel *Catch-22* was published in 1961, when Dick was writing *Castle*). Mailer and Heller had fought in the war (the former in a cavalry regiment in the Pacific, the latter in a bomber squadron in Italy); Dick, whose involvement was mediated, did not directly depict the war, but devised an alternative present in which the war is remembered by those characters which took part in it.

In *Castle* Germany and Japan won World War II, with little help from Fascist Italy. After defeating and invading Britain, the two powers attacked the USA and divided them in three states: the eastern seaboard under German influence; the West Coast, a satellite of Imperial Japan (called Pacific States of America); and what lies in between turned into a buffer, the Rocky Mountain States. Life in California (where most of the action takes place) and in the Rocky Mountain States (where one of the plot lines is set) is totally determined by the outcome of the war; some of the characters took part in it (Joe Cinnadella, Frank Frink, Mr. Baynes). To define this novel as a war novel[4] would not stretch that definition too much. By showing how different the world would be if the winners had been other than the USA and the USSR, Dick somewhat subscribes to Jack Isidore's belief that our existential inquietude is rooted in that macro-event who shaped the world we live in.

Dick's decision to tackle World War II may well explain the success of the novel in the science-fiction community, sanctioned by the Hugo Award it won in 1963. This should not make us forget, however, that Dick had not written this novel for the science-fiction market, but that it was sold to Putnam (another respectable publishing house)[5] and advertised as a political thriller closer to Peter George's *Red Alert* (1958) or Eugene Burdick's *Fail-Safe* (1962) than to the hack novels Dick had been publishing on Ace Doubles (Sutin 118). Besides, there was at least one important literary forerunner of Dick's depiction of the USA under Nazism or Japanese imperialism, and that was a novel written by a Nobel Prize winner, Sinclair Lewis, whose *It Can't Happen Here* (1935) describes the rise of a fascist regime in the U.S., whose leader Berzelius "Buzz" Windrip has striking similarities to Mussolini and Hitler.[6] Anyway, it should be said that—positive reviews notwithstanding (Sutin 118)—*The Man in the High Castle* was not very successful in terms of sales outside the science-fiction ghetto. Like *Time Out of Joint*, it was the paperback reprint in the Science Fiction Book Club that was commercially successful, and paved the way to the Hugo Award.

So another failed escape from the science fiction ghetto, but one which produced such a dense and striking novel that critics began to discuss it quite soon; few novels by Dick have been read in so many different ways. Already in the 1975 *Science-Fiction Studies* Darko Suvin praised *Castle* because here "it is to be found for the first time the full Dickian narrative articulation" (Suvin 1975, 4): "MHC divides into two parallel plots with these narrative foci," namely, Mr. Tagomi, Robert Childan, Frank Frink and Juliana Frink, plus four less important foci, Baynes/Wegener, Reiss, Kreuz von Meere and Wyndham-Matson. Those foci are also grouped in terms of what social class or group they belong to, that is, an upper level of Axis officials, a middle level of collaborationists (Childan and Wyndham-Matson) and a lower level of humble Americans. Suvin's reading is then interested both in narrative technique (multi-plot, multi-foci) and in socio-political stratifications.

Other critics followed soon. In 1977 Carlo Pagetti wrote a scholarly Introduction to the Italian translation of the novel, stressing the symbolic identification of Nazi Germany and American imperialism, and highlighting the interplay of "external" historical reality and the two internal textual level of the alternative defeated America and the novel-within-the-novel *The Grasshopper Lies Heavy* (Pagetti 1977, 139) which will be further discussed in this chapter. Patricia Warrick's 1980 essay on Taoism and Fascism in *Castle* underscores the mix of Eastern and Western cultural materials in Dick's novel, pointing out the moment of choice that each major character endowed with a narrative focus must face; her reading is thus similar to Pagetti's interpretation, which outlines a threefold process of inner change of the main characters (Tagomi, Juliana, Frink, Childan, Baynes/Wegener and Cinnadella), who can reach an inner truth only by crossing the borderline between sanity and insanity, authenticity and simulation (Pagetti 1977, 141–3). Robinson devotes the fourth chapter of his monograph to this novel, pointing out the weakness of the ending but praising its overall structure. Lorenzo DiTommaso's 1999 article also deals with inner changes in the main characters, by persuasively suggesting that each of them must experience a symbolic travel which reaches a final redemption with strong Christian undertones (Di Tommaso is not so persuasive, however, when he tries to argue that this redemption is a state of grace and not a *moment* of grace).

These approaches are implicitly challenged by John Rieder's 1988 article on the metafictive world of *Castle*, a typical example of the deconstructionist approach which was fashionable in the eighties, which sets aside the powerful political subtexts of the novel in order to illustrate and explore the aporia between cognition and ethics in the text (purportedly depicting a "collectivity without a center or a goal" [Rieder 231]); an aporia which does not really appear to be specific to Dick's novel. Laura Campbell examined Dick's use of time in the novel three years later, discovering a series of not-so-evident inconsistencies which might be a mere effect of careless plotting, but could also be read as meaningful distortions of time flux aimed at controlling the pace of the narrative regardless of internal consistency. Cassie Carter's 1995 essay focuses on "Mimicry, Parasitism and Americanism in the PSA," by applying Said's interpretive framework to racial/ethnic relations in the novels, with mixed results; I have tried to correct some weak aspects of Carter's reading in my 1997 essay "All Around the High Castle," where I have connected the narrative technique of multiple points of view with the strong racial theme developed in the novel. Carl Freedman focused on the issue of the novel-within-the-novel, *The Grasshopper Lies Heavily*, which is a sf novel in its own right and gives Dick and readers a chance to meditate on "the fundamental conceptual structure of the genre" (Freedman 2000, 180). Christopher Palmer discussed the irrationality of history and the difficulty to reconnect individual actions and the collective dimension in *Castle* in the sixth chapter of his 2003 essay[7] on Dick, *Exhilaration and Terror of the Postmodern*, whose title "The Reasonableness and Madness of History" tells us how it addresses the problem of history in the novel based on postmodern theories typical of the 1980s. To these contributions we should necessarily add the first chapter of Gabriele Frasca's monograph *L'oscuro scrutare di Philip K. Dick* (2007), "Su un fondo nero" (On a Black Background), which reads *Castle* based on a complex analysis of the presence and importance of media in the novel, also attempting an economic interpretation (which can be said to be a huge development of Suvin's original insights).

This brief (and far from complete) survey of the critical readings of *The Man in the High Castle* should show what a knot of issues and ideas can be and has been found in this novel; *vital* issues and ideas, one should add, because all these essays read our reality by superimposing Dick's alternate realities to it. Our world, where the USA and USSR won World War II (with the British Empire as a junior partner, similar to Italy in *Castle*) seems to be fully readable only thanks to its negative image as a world where the losers have actually won, and Nazism and Japanese Imperialism have shaped our reality. But this is not at all something specific of Dick's novel; all alternate histories have aimed at better understanding the world as it is by showing how it might have been, since G.M. Trevelyan's "If Napoleon Had Won the Battle of Waterloo" (1907), one of the first specimens of alternate history. No wonder that it was written by a British historian, and dealt with the results of a decisive battle which gave Britain world supremacy for about a century. Thus the title of Dick's novel might well be read as "If Hitler Had Won the Battle of England," though there is more to be found in a 250-page novel than in a short essay.

Dick never mentioned Trevelyan's essay in the novel or the letters he wrote before the publication of *Castle*; he tapped another literary model, implicitly acknowledged by the name of his character Hawthorne Abendsen. Dick expressed his admiration for Nathaniel Hawthorne at least once, in 1960, when he included *The Scarlet Letter* in a list of works exemplifying his "idea of great novel" (*SL1* 56). Valerio Massimo de Angelis (De Angelis 169–70) has persuasively shown that alternate versions of historical events can be already found in Hawthorne's short story collection *Twice-Told Tales* (1837); events endowed with a highly symbolic value, as they all belong to the early years of the American colonies, that is to say to the genesis of the United States. Like Hawthorne's *Scarlet Letter*, "The May-Pole of Merry Mount" (one of the *Twice-Told Tales*) is a foundational story, whose slight differences from historical accounts allow Hawthorne to express a judgment on the origins of his own nation (De Angelis 170).

Hawthorne also wrote "P.'s Correspondence" (1845), where P., an American would-be writer in London, talks about his occasional meetings with British poets and politicians (but also Napoleon Bonaparte) who should be long time dead in the year when the tale was published. It could be read as the depiction of an alternate reality, even though the famous people P. meets "have long ceased to be visible to any eye save his own" (Hawthorne 287), and could just be the product of an intermittent form of insanity. What can be already found in this story, and will be later typical of alternate histories, is that whenever P. meets someone who should not be alive in 1845, such as Byron, Shelley, or Keats, he discusses in detail what happened in their alternative life, usually depicting remarkable changes in their personality, opinions and creative powers; in other words, the story may record the ravings of a madman, but those ravings build up a whole alternate history of Britain from 1815 to 1845.[8]

However, Dick was aware of another, more mature specimen of alternate history fiction: he mentioned a classic of alternate history, Ward Moore's *Bring the Jubilee* (1952), in his October 29, 1952 letter to Francis McComas (*SL1* 24–7), a science-fiction editor and writer. Moore's novel depicts what the United States might have been if the Confederation had won the War Between the States; Dick criticizes the novel because the alternate historical line it presents is too unlikely, but he is subsequently persuaded by McComas (as he admits in his November 22 letter [*SL1* 27]) that Ward Moore had good reasons to hypothesize a world where the Confederate States are a world power and the United States are a poor and underdeveloped country. Ten years before the publication of *Castle*, Dick was already speculating on the outcome of a decisive war (and the decisive Battle of Gettysburg) which had determined the history of the country he lived in; in his 1962 novel Dick upped the ante, by tackling a war whose outcome had determined the history of the world.

But Dick's novel is also different from Ward Moore's (and Trevelyan's) speculations inasmuch as it does not content itself with conjuring up another history (meaning both what Romans called *res gestae*, the historical events themselves, and *historia rerum gestarum*, the narration of those events), but two. A very important feature of *Castle* is the novel-within-the-novel *The Grasshopper Lies Heavily*, written by Hawthorne Abendsen, a scandalous work of fiction (forbidden in Nazi-controlled East Coast) describing the world as it would be if the USA and the British Empire had won World War II — a world which is *not*, and Dick takes pains to make this clear, coincident with his and our world where USA, USSR and Britain were the winners.

Carlo Pagetti already noticed this in his 1977 Introduction to the novel, by distinguishing three textual levels: the *fictional* reality described (or built) in the novel, the *hyper-fictional* reality that is alternative to that fictional reality, and the reality of the reader — or, in Pagetti's terms, primary text, secondary text, and zero text (Pagetti 1977, 139). The first and second texts are such because they are parts of a literary text; the zero text is virtual, and it is quite close to Barthes' Referential Code as it is introduced in his essay *S/Z*. Of the five codes which, according to Barthes, structure a narrative text, the Referential code is that which refers to common bodies of knowledge, one of them being the knowledge of the main events of world history.[9]

Pagetti's model should be in any case enhanced.[10] In its 3-level version it does not take into account the process through which the duplication of reality levels inside the literary text can trigger a scission of the zero text, something which we have already postulated for *Time Out of Joint* (Ch. 2). Let us get back to the three textual levels suggested by Pagetti for *The Man in the High Castle*. The primary text is the one where Germany and Japan won the Second World War; the secondary text is the hyper-fictional novel *The Grasshopper Lies Heavy* which tells how the Third Reich and Japan were defeated by the British Empire and the U.S. Since the hyper-fictional world where the Western capitalist powers (not including the USSR) are the winners is revealed as the real world in the ending, when Juliana Frink asks the *I Ching* (which Abendsen used to write *Grasshopper*) why it wrote that novel and what its readers are supposed to learn (246). The answer is hexagram 61, Chung Fu, "Inner Truth," which Hawthorne angrily questions thus: "my book is true? ... Germany and Japan lost the war?" (247). Both questions are answered by Juliana's peremptory yes.

I have already suggested (Rossi "Fourfold Symmetry," 406–8) that the three texts might be thus tied by a sort of "veritative ratio": $A : B = B : C$, where A = zero text, B = primary text, C = secondary text. If *The Grasshopper Lies Heavy* is true and *Castle* is false, Dick might be suggesting that our world is false, and that his book is true. This would lead to a splitting of the zero text: we would have an "accepted" zero text which tells us that USA e USSR won the war and evil was defeated, so that a new age of peace and prosperity has begun, with the USA as the leading power of the so-called "Free World"; but this would be nothing more than an ideological construct hiding an alternative, disquieting zero text where the world lives under the menace of nuclear war, USA and USSR waste their resources due to militaristic politics, Third World countries are exploited and ultimately destroyed, and — notwithstanding the apparent decolonization process — indirectly controlled by the great powers, Nazi techniques of mass-indoctrination are widely used both in the West and in the East (Rispoli 57; Proietti 35).

The relationship between the four texts or textual levels can be represented by this table:

Table 3.1

Fictional Levels	*"Real" (Historical) Levels*	
PRIMARY TEXT: *The Man in the High Castle* Japan and Germany won the war; total destruction of Africa; possibility of a nuclear war between the former allied powers.	ZERO TEXT (1) USA and USSR won the war, and destroyed Nazism (evil) If and when Soviet Communism will be eventually defeated there will be an unprecedented age of peace and prosperity.*	*"accepted" levels*
SECONDARY TEXT: *The Grasshopper Lies Heavy* England and USA won the war; economical and cultural exploitation and colonisation of Third World countries (China); possibility of a nuclear war between the former allied powers.	ZERO TEXT (2) Japan and Germany are going to be major economical powers; USA and USSR still use Nazi military technologies, mass media strategies, domination policies and hypertrophied militarism; Third World countries are on the verge of destruction; a	*alternative levels* (cont. next page)

Table 3.1 (continued)

	nuclear war is still possible (the novel was written shortly before the Cuban crisis). **"Inner truth"**: if Nazism is a collective psychosis, the world is anyway trapped in Hitler's nightmare of mass destruction and technological hypertrophy

*Other elements of the "accepted" text zero in this novel could be the same we found in the scheme in *Time Out of Joint*. Basically, the "accepted" zero text is always the same for the novels Dick wrote in the late 1950s-early 1960s, because it is based on the same shared history (here one could venture to use a more compromised term as *ideology*). The difference among the alternative zero texts might well be that different components of the virtual History Book are used (or, in more structuralism-tainted terms, "made pertinent"). For example, the historical figure of Dwight D. Eisenhower is more important in *The Penultimate Truth* while social life in the suburbia of the 1950s is more important for *Time Out of Joint* though both are relevant parts of the complex historical (zero) text whose title could be "Postwar America."

Such a reading may have its attractive symmetry,[11] yet it would not have been accepted by Dick. In his August 7, 1978 letter to Joseph Milicia he overtly said: "I have never meant MITHC to be deconstructed to indicate that the Axis "really" won the war. This is a favorite interpretation. It is not one I intended" (*SL5* 182–3). This indicates that Dick was well aware of the effect of meaning which the textual levels present in his novel could generate, an effect which Robinson already analyzed in his 1984 dissertation, where he maintains that also the zero text (our koinos kosmos) is dystopian for readers who have traveled through the primary and secondary texts (Robinson 43–4).

We might object that by refusing that interpretation of his novel as one he had not intended, Dick falls prey of Northrop Frye's fallacy of premature teleology: it is a widespread but questionable idea that an interpreter (even a non-professional one, such as someone who reads a novel "just for fun") should confine him/herself to extract from a literary text what its author may be assumed to have been aware of putting in it (Frye 17). Moreover, in this letter Dick seems to have forgotten that the world described in *Grasshopper* is quite different from the zero text where he and his readers lived (the survival of the British Empire after World War II and the humane and well-meaning American colonization of China being its most glaring counterfactual elements). Dick corrected himself in a subsequent letter (August 21) evidently written to answer Milicia's objections; there he says that what is true are "all worlds in which the Axis lost" (*SL5* 183). According to Dick, Abendsen's novel "got the one essential idea correctly," i.e., the defeat of the Axis, but "the vague manner of the I CHING would never make possible accuracy in detail." This should mean that the final revelation is valid even if Abendsen's book is not set in our world; the writer-within-the-novel managed to glimpse the real world *in speculum, per aenigmata* (to quote St. Paul, one of Dick's favorite writers), and offered his readers a blurred image: an ontologically uncertain one. A typical Dickian situation indeed, which however does not simplify the task of the critic.

If the world where most of *Castle* takes place is false or unreal, what is it then? A collective hallucination? A vast FSR, projected by the deranged mind of Adolph Hitler? Madness does play an important role in the symbolic structure of the novel: after all, Hawthorne used madness to justify his alternate history in his "P.'s Correspondence." Madness is somewhat suggested by Juliana's inner monologue, when she envisions her world as the projection of Hitler's mind: "And the horrible part was that the present-day German Empire was a product of that brain. First a political party, then a nation, then half the world" (40). This is echoed by Baynes/Wegener's musings about the "psychotic world" he lives in, where "the madmen are in power" (44); the German secret agent wonders whether the broad masses "guess, glimpse, the truth" (45). And this is what Juliana and Abendsen are offered in the ending scene; no more than a glimpse at the truth. A truth which is as ambiguous and elusive as the *I Ching* hexagrams that have guided Abendsen while he was writing *Grasshopper*, a procedure Dick knew quite well because he repeatedly declared that he too had written *Castle* by interrogating the Chinese oracle (another element which encouraged several interpreters to identify Dick with Abendsen, though Dick told Milicia in his August 7 letter that he did not intend Abendsen to resemble himself [*SL5* 182]).[12]

If the world where Germany and Japan won is simply an illusion, and the real world is the one where the Axis is defeated, we are back to *The Cosmic Puppets*. The alternate reality depicted in the novel is as unsubstantial as the Millgate where Ted Barton died at nine. Dick's parallel universe is a self-denying or self-erasing fictional construct, whose evaporation takes us back to our reality, to the history we know: it is an universe falling apart whose stabilization, according to Rispoli, is doomed to failure, like the other megalomaniac enterprises attempted by the Nazi in the novel (Rispoli 63). If we accept this interpretation of the novel, its narrative core is quite similar to that of *Bring the Jubilee*. In that alternate history novel Ward Moore wipes out the world where the Confederates won the War Between the States by having the protagonist, historian Hodge Backmaker, travel backwards in time and reach the battlefield of Gettysburg, thus involuntarily triggering a small accident which will change that course of the decisive battle and history. The Southern army will be defeated at Gettysburg; the ancestor of Barbara Haggerswell, the physicist who invented the time machine, will be killed in that epochal battle; the alternate world will inexorably disappear — or better, seen from the final perspective of our 1877 (the year in which Hodge writes his memoir), will never be.

But in *Puppets* the ending unambiguously shows us the original Millgate replacing once and for all the illusory town conjured up by Peter/Ahriman; in *Bring the Jubilee* there is a detailed final explanation of the temporal paradox which causes the alternate history to be totally erased by somebody who was born and grew up in that world. On the other hand the ending of *The Man in the Castle* may well announce a truth, but the fact it is only glimpsed makes it quite uncertain. Ontologically uncertain, we should add, as this is a matter of what world really exists, and what is only apparently real. Dick himself was not satisfied with the ending, as he wrote in his letter to Joe Milicia "I really would have liked to have finished MITHC with a stronger, better ending, but even now, so many years later, I am mystified as to what should have been done to it that I didn't do. One reader said charitably that it was 'Open ended,' which is true in a sense, because I wanted to go on with a sequel" (*SL5* 182). Dick even wrote two chapters of the projected sequel in 1964, which were posthumously published in *The Shifting Realities of Philip K. Dick*, a collection of essays and other non-narrative materials, but never really tried to complete the novel.

So we are left with an open ending and a masterful example of what Dick's strategy of ontological uncertainty can accomplish. Because it should be clearly said that this extreme form of uncertainty operates here on so many levels that the overall effect is almost disturbing. The interplay among the three textual levels (four if my interpretive hypothesis is acceptable, Dick's opinion notwithstanding) already creates a suspension of our certainties, forcing us to ask ourselves to what extent our world is real, and who was really defeated in World War II. But there is ontological uncertainty also due to the fake objects which circulate in the plot, such as the "original" 19th-century American revolvers bought by collectors like Tagomi and sold by antiquarians like Childan — weapons which are actually manufactured by the artisans working for Wyndam-Matson, a mix of entrepreneur and con-man. "Is it possible, sir, that you, dealer in such items, *cannot distinguish the forgeries from the real?*" (59) is the overwhelming question Frank Frink asks Childan, and the consequences of forgery are devastating if one thinks how much of our ability to reconstruct the past (and to write history) is a matter of authenticity of documents and objects. This is the argument of an important conversation between Wyndam-Matson and his mistress Rita (64–7), where the historicity of two Zippo lighters, only one of which belonged to F.D. Roosevelt, is questioned. It is highly ironic that the shady businessman declares of the authenticity of one of the two lighters based on a certificate of the Smithsonian Institution which might be faked as well (66).

But antiques are not the only elements of the novel which obey the maxim "[t]hings are seldom what they seem/Skim milk masquerades as cream" (26), actually two lines from Gilbert & Sullivan's *HMS Pinafore* remembered by Mr. Tagomi when the first line reaches him as a coded cable from Tokyo. Coded messages do not mean what their literal sense proclaims; they are masquerading, as the skim milk in the maxim, or the characters of *Castle*.

In this novel Caucasians masquerade as Japanese (like Mr. Ramsey, Tagomi's secretary, who darkens his skin [24]); Frink is a bogus Caucasian, as he is a Jew under false pretences, who in a scene of hyper-simulation also pretends to be a representative of a non-existent Japanese admiral commanding an aircraft carrier which was actually sunk during the war (57); Joe Cinnadella pretends to be Italian, but he is actually a German SS (maybe Swiss) who dyed his hair black[13]; Mr. Baynes is not a Swede and a businessman, but actually a German, captain Wegener of the Abwehr; Mr. Yatabe, the elderly retired gentleman who meets Baynes/Wegener in the climatic scene of Chapter 12 is actually general Tedeki, the former Imperial Chief of Staff (179). We might also add Wyndam-Matson to this list, as he pretends to be a respectable businessman, but is actually a hoodlum; Robert Childan who wants to be accepted by the Japanese and imitates their lifestyle[14]; and Hawthorne Abendsen, because everybody believes he lives as a recluse in a sort of fortress while actually Juliana finds him in a rather ordinary suburban house, surrounded by his guests.

Uncertainty also rules on a collective level. There is a secret plan of the Nazi regime to wipe Japan out with a massive nuclear attack, Operation Dandelion; opposing factions in the regime may hinder or favor the plan. Doctor Goebbels, apparently the most sensible Nazi hierarch, is an advocate of the plan; S.S. General Heydrich, head of "the most malignant portion of German society" (183), opposes Operation Dandelion, so that he has to be supported by those who want to avoid World War III. Also here things (and people) are not what they seem. The atmosphere of intrigue is heightened by Joe Cinnadella's mission aimed at eliminating Hawthorne Abendsen.

This might answer an objection raised by Christopher Palmer to a purported "lack of fit between the local, the sphere of individual actions by unimportant people, and the epochal" (Palmer 131), that is the great historical events which are dominated by the Nazis, "that element of evil and irrationality in global history which shocks the mind into uncertainty" (Palmer 131). The opposition between the world of little men and women in the foreground (Tagomi, Frink, Juliana and the other characters endowed with a narrative focus in the novel) and the great events in the background (the death of Chancellor Bormann and the ensuing struggle in the Nazi Party; the threat of a nuclear attack against Japan) has been noticed by other critics, and Palmer is right in underscoring it as one of the key architectural elements of the novel; but his examination of how Dick tried to bridge the gap between daily life and history[15] does not tackle a structural feature of the novel, the most important textual device that keeps those two spheres or realms together, that is intrigue — or better paranoia.

It is easy to show how intrigue is typical of spy stories and a certain sort of science-fiction, namely Van Vogt's narratives about competing supermen, clashes of empires and almost superhuman conspiracies; we have already seen how Van Vogt was an important and acknowledged model for Dick. Intrigue, conspiracies, secret identities, more or less hidden power struggles abound in Dick's fiction before *The Man in the High Castle*; one might mention accomplished works like *Time Out of Joint*, but also novels that are completely inside the conventions of commercial science-fiction, books Dick wrote to make ends meet like *Solar Lottery* and *Vulcan's Hammer*.[16] In *Time Out of Joint* (Ch. 2) an only apparently realistic depiction of ordinary U.S. suburban life in the 1950s is actually the result of a complex conspiracy set in a disquieting future of interplanetary warfare; the apparently unimportant life of an idler, Ragle Gumm, is actually the most important life in the word. Individual life and history are connected by intrigue, and this is something that may be found in different forms in other novels and stories by Dick; we might also say that they are always connected by paranoia. Dick once wrote that for him "a flat tire on [his] car is (a) The End of the World; and (b) An Indication of Monsters (although I forget why)" (*Shifting Realities* 92); surely the remark is a fine specimen of his deadpan humor, yet it is hints at a poetics of sorts. Small events are actually cosmic; God is in the gutter; trash (be it science fiction, or any other mass product of cultural industry, or actual rubbish) is actually the most precious thing in the world: such sudden reversals have been endlessly highlighted as the hallmarks of Dick's fiction, and sound a bit too much like critical commonplace. Yet paranoia as a poetics is something critics cannot get rid of, also because this is possibly the most important common feature which links Dick with at least one of the major postmodernist novelists, that is, Thomas Pynchon.

We have already dealt with complex but quite visible recycling of *Time Out of Joint* in the first part of *Gravity's Rainbow* (Ch. 2). However, paranoia plays an important role in both *Time* and *Castle*, and it is an important theme in *Gravity* as well. The connection between paranoia, history and individual life is quite clear in *Time*: Ragle can be an ordinary person who hallucinates a conspiracy (and only has an *indirect* connection to the great historical events), or an extraordinary person whose private life (the typical space of "the local" in Palmer's terms) is *directly* determined by larger historical events (the war between the One Happy World and the Lunar rebels). If paranoia is just a mental disease, the former interpretation applies; but if it is turned into a gnoseologic method, by which small anomalies in daily life may be read as the direct effect of much greater (and threatening) events, the latter applies. In *Gravity* the alternatives are the same: Tyrone Slothrop may be the victim of a conspiracy started when Laszlo Jamf subjected him to a Pavlovian conditioning, he may be able to predict where V–2s will fall, and there may be a secret plot pivoted upon the special 00000 V–2 missile, masterminded by Captain Blicero; or he is simply paranoid. *Castle*, on the other hand, is not interested in paranoia as a mental condition, but paranoia as an interpreting device: there is no doubt that the lives and actions of little men and women are directly connected to the greater momentous historical events through intrigue (or conspiracy).

The harmless business meeting of Mr. Yatabe and Mr. Baynes is suddenly unveiled as a momentous contact between agents of the Japanese Imperial Staff and a faction in the power struggle taking place in Berlin. The absolutely unimportant trip of Joe Cinnadella and Juliana to Cheyenne turns into a secret mission aimed at eliminating a famous and troublesome intellectual. One might wonder where is the gap between the local and the epochal if the vast impersonal forces of history burst into ordinary daily life with devastating violence; it is true that Juliana manages to survive almost unscathed[17] and Frank Frink is released, but Tagomi's death tells us that intrigue cuts both ways, that small acts of courage and integrity may jam the deadly engine of history, but individual lives may also get lost.

The atmosphere of intrigue is in any case necessary, and fitting, once we read *Castle* as a war novel; but — like *Gravity's Rainbow* — it is only partially about World War II. Dick's novel, like Pynchon's, is mostly about the Cold War. This undeclared war was mostly a matter of secret agents, secret strategic and tactical planning, secret research and development of deadly and then deadlier secret weapons, often a conflict by proxy (Vietnam, Angola, Korea, Afghanistan, and other "small" wars), always on the verge of the ultimate clash. The Cuban missile crisis took place a year after the publication of *Castle*, but the Bay of Pigs invasion was attempted and failed in April 1961; the building of the notorious Berlin Wall started on August 13, 1961; both events took place when Dick was writing his novel, which was completed in November of the same year. We have already said that intrigue is a key element of spy stories; and much of what takes place in *Castle* is a spy story, inasmuch as Wegener is a member of the German military intelligence, Kreuz vom Meere is the chief of the Sicherheitsdienst in the West Coast, and Joe Cinnadella is a secret agent and killer sent by the S.S. Robert Childan may complain that he is stuck on "the West Coast, where nothing is happening" and that "[h]istory is passing [him] by" (118), but it is difficult to deny that a lot of extraordinary events take place in this novel, though most of the action takes place in the last chapters.

The very ontological uncertainty which operates in this novel has much to do with Cold War and the ensuing obsession with secrecy, but we should not forget the situation of uncertainty caused by witch-hunting, carried out by senator McCarthy in the Tydings Committee in 1950 and the Senate Permanent Subcommittee on Investigations in 1953–54, plus the investigations into Communist influence on the motion picture industry in 1947. Uncertainty about personal identities dominates in *Castle*, as it had dominated the U.S. media in the preceding decade; one might just mention the 1951 trial of Julius and Ethel Rosenberg,[18] or the persecution of the Hollywood Ten, a group of movie industry professionals whose affiliation to the Communist party was proof enough — according to HUAC — that they were Soviet agents or propagandists. The atmosphere of intrigue and conspiracy had directly touched Dick at least once in 1953–4, when two friendly FBI agents contacted him and his wife Kleo Mini, offering them the opportunity to study at the University of Mexico "all expenses paid, if they would spy upon students activities there" (Sutin 83–4).

Intrigue and paranoia dominate the American fifties; no wonder that Richard Hofstadter published his "The Paranoid Style in American Politics" in 1964, just two years after the publication of *Castle*. One might object that there is no paranoia in Dick's novel as the momentous events that occur in the plot (the attack of the Nazi commando, Joe Cinnadella's mission, the arrest of Frank Frink and his threatened deportation) are real, at least in that fictional space; but such an objection fails to acknowledge that the plot was developed with the help of the *I Ching*, but above all by Dick's paranoid narrative imagination, which had produced such a masterpiece of paranoid creativity as *Time Out of Joint* just three years before.

However, though both *Gravity's Rainbow* and *Time Out of Joint* are (non-realistic) Cold War narratives, they articulate in a quite different fashion the relationship between the virtual Third World War and the already-happened Second World War, and this allows them to offer different interpretations of the conflict which never took place: by setting his novel in 1944–1945, Pynchon wants to show that the Cold War and the threat of mass extermination by means of nuclear weapons carried by intercontinental missiles have their roots in Nazi Germany, so that its science and technology are somewhat tainted by the collective madness which seized that country between 1933 and 1945. *Gravity* can thus be read as a giant analepsis which ends in the final scene,[19] when the CONELRAD signal is heard on the radio, and missiles fall on Los Angeles (and the cinema where the fictional film *Gravity's Rainbow*, the "content" of the novel, has been shown); in a bewildering narrative short-circuit the missile aimed at the movie theatre is the same 00000 missile fired by Captain Blicero in the penultimate scene of the novel, so that it is clear that the inhuman and murderous technology devised by Nazi scientists and technicians (among which Wernher von Braun, the father of the A-4, aka V-2, and the Saturn missile which brought Americans on the Moon) could destroy the USA and the rest of the world if World War III actually broke loose.

On the other hand Dick, who was not a historical novelist like Pynchon,[20] tackled the relationship between the fearful present of Cold War and the dreadful past of World War II in a sfnal fashion by imagining a different outcome for that war and an alternative present whose origins in the war were as evident as possible; the original sin of nuclear warfare technologies is made evident by the fact that both missiles and the Bomb are developed by Nazi Germany, governed by the same criminal leaders which ruled it during the war. It is in fact curious that, when Tagomi and other Japanese officials in California meet at the embassy to be informed about the power struggle in Germany after the death of Chancellor Bormann, they listen to a series of profiles of the notables (93–6) which only presents the readers with those Nazi hierarchs (Göring, Heydrich, Goebbels, von Schirach, etc.) which were already in power before May 1945; no new figure is introduced. Continuity between pre-war and post-war leadership is thus highlighted.

Yet the alternative present dominated by the Nazis seems to lead to the same dead end which faces Dick's own world of 1961. Nuclear war looms large on the reality of 1962, in the real world where both USA and USSR are well equipped with H bombs, and in the two alternate realities of *The Man in the High Castle* and *The Grasshopper Lies Heavy*, where only one of the two competing superpowers is endowed with nuclear armament. All its ontological uncertainty notwithstanding, all the three textual levels of the novel seem to be doomed to the same global catastrophe of mass holocaust. The destructive madness of Nazism could easily destroy the "mad" alternate reality conjured up by Dick, but also the "real" world where he and his readers lived in 1962. Though Nazism has been defeated, its cosmic death drive is still active, still threatening to wipe out humankind. Thus the Game of the Rat here seems aimed at telling us that behind all beguiling appearances, behind all masks and intrigues, there is something hard and solid and heavy, "like cement," thinks Tagomi: "There is evil!" (97).

We might end this discussion of *The Man in the High Castle* by pointing out that this novel is a sort of postmodernist theodicy. If theodicy is that part of theology and philosophy which strives to reconcile belief in God with the perceived existence of evil, then Dick's novel tries to reconcile the solid presence of evil, which is experienced by all the main characters (Tagomi, but also Juliana, who finds out who Cinnadella really is, and Frink, who is imprisoned and faces deportation to a concentration camp), with something that may counter evil and justify hope. No wonder then that there are so many meditations about the philosophical and psychological nature of Nazism, which is the fictional embodiment of evil in the novel; no wonder if one of the parallel plots ends with Wegener/Baynes' musing which is on the impossibility to have "clear good and evil alternatives" (236), particularly meaningful in a novel where alternative realities determine the overall architecture of the text, and the necessity to face "obscure admixtures, ... blends, with no proper tool by which to untangle the components" (236) — this being a form of ethical uncertainty, after all.

Reading *Castle* as a sort of theodicy is also authorized by the meaningful quotation of Nathanael West's novelette *Mrs. Lonelyhearts* (1933),[21] read by Paul Kasoura, who asks Childan help to understand its Christian symbolism. In West's novel, a young writer wastes his life working for a New York newspaper, answering the letters sent by desperate readers to the advice column entitled "Miss Lonelyhearts," which is also the nickname his feature editor has assigned him. The protagonist of the novel is exposed to the suffering and despair of humankind (the novel was written and published during the Great Depression), and feels terribly burdened by the letters he receives; he falls into a cycle of depression, accompanied by heavy drinking and occasional barfights. Miss Lonelyhearts develops an identification with Christ, and this is the aspect of the novel which baffles Kasoura; Childan, who has not even heard of the novel, is totally unable to explain it. It is quite clear, on the other hand, that Dick used this small episode to suggest his readers how they should read his novel: if Miss Lonelyhearts is exposed, through the letters of his readers (which West deliberately inserted in his novel, with all their ramshackle English), to the concrete suffering of humankind that no pietist rhetoric can assuage, the characters of *Castle* must discover evil by direct contact, realizing that they live in a hellish world where madmen are in power. A world beset with horrors that resemble those of the zero text: Cold War, the nuclear threat, the extermination of African peoples, racism, witch-hunting.

West's theodicy is such only in a metaphoric sense; unlike Leibniz's, which optimistically posited our world as the best of all possible worlds, *Miss Lonelyhearts* ends with a scene where the protagonist might be accidentally killed by one of his readers (West wrote the scene in such a way that readers cannot be sure of the outcome of the tussle). Dick is not as pessimistic as his predecessor: Tagomi manages to stop the Nazi commando and has Frank Frink released, Juliana thwarts the Nazi plot to eliminate Abendsen. Evil cannot be defeated once and for all, but it can be kept at bay, at least temporarily. The ending, with the revelation of the defeat of Germany and Japan, may also be part of this postmodernist theodicy: it hints at St. Augustine's idea of evil as *privatio boni*, or absence of good, which proposes evil as something insubstantial. In Dick's own version, evil is something fake; something which is not endowed with inner truth. In the very last pages of the novel, evil is implicitly defeated.

Dick thought the ending was not open; in his opinion, as we have seen, it was simply not very good. If evil (the world threatened by nuclear death and plagued by violence and oppression) is insubstantial, or bogus, why do we live in this only apparently real nightmare (an idea which ultimately derives from the second chapter of Joyce's *Ulysses*, where Stephen Dedalus says that history is a nightmare from which he is trying to awake — and we know Joyce was one of Dick's favorite authors)? If Germany and Japan lost World War II, why do the characters of the novel live in a world dominated by those powers? Dick was not satisfied because he did not have a solution to this aporia. No wonder then that it will come back in the rest of Dick's oeuvre, always coupled with ontological uncertainty. Which is at the same time a game Dick loved to play, but also a nightmare from which he was trying to awake.

Chapter 4

A Maze of Lives: *Martian Time-Slip*, *Dr. Bloodmoney*, and *Clans of the Alphane Moon*

"No man is an island entire of itself; every man
is a piece of the continent, a part of the main"
John Donne

In his groundbreaking essay on Dick's oeuvre, Darko Suvin divided his
fiction up to 1974 in three phases, one of apprenticeship, then another which
he called "a high plateau" (Suvin 1975, 2), which included Dick's masterpieces
and a third phase of decadence.[1] Suvin's periodization was updated in another
article, published in 2002, where he also covered the works Dick wrote and
published after 1974, positing a second plateau which included the VALIS
Trilogy and *A Scanner Darkly*. His first article is however relevant to our discussion inasmuch as he pointed out *Martian Time-Slip* and *Dr. Bloodmoney*
as Dick's masterpieces, preceded by *The Man in the High Castle* as Dick's "creative breakthrough" (Suvin 1975, 2), which could be considered as the cul-
mination of his apprenticeship or the beginning of that climactic phase which
culminates in the two masterpieces. What characterized these three novels is
Dick's polyphony, that is, the fact that his third-person narrative does not
feature "the old-fashioned, all knowing, neutral and superior narrator" (Suvin
1975, 3).

Multiple internal focalization was not invented by Dick; there are several
examples already in the second half of the 19th century. Nor were multiple
plots, which Dick used in their purest version in *Castle*, invented by him;
such a technique may already be found in one of John Dos Passos' earliest
novels, *Three Soldiers* (1921), and is typically associated to his USA Trilogy

(1930–36). In his February 10, 1958 letter to sf writer James Blish, Dick stated that he was interested in Joyce's "technique of starting with more than one thread and drawing these threads together at some nexus later in the book" (*SL1* 40); he is evidently referring to *Ulysses*, where the shorter plot focused on Stephen Dedalus and the longer one whose focus is Leopold Bloom ultimately converge in the third and last part of the novel. In the same letter Dick also mentions Dos Passos' USA trilogy, where "there are a multitude of threads, finally drawn together" (*SL1* 40). Then he says that the same feature may be found in modern Japanese novel, which are "of course, based on French novels."

Dick discussed again the issue of multiple plots and narrative foci in *The Man in the High Castle* and other novels of the 1960s, but he dropped Joyce and Dos Passos as models; in his April 29, 1969 letter he says he was inspired by "the novels of the students of Tokyo University, who were themselves in the French Department, and hence influenced by the French" (*SL1*, 246). In two letters written in 1978[2] Dick talks again about these novels, and in one of them he adds that their authors were active after the Second World War; moreover, following Japanese models is what could be expected of Abendsen, as he wrote his *The Grasshopper Lies Heavy* in a world where the Japanese had won and their culture was dominant (*SL5* 8). He repeated this claim in Gregg Rickman's interview (Rickman 1988, 140), which was carried out in late 1981 and early 1982, just before Dick's death (Rickman 1988, xvii–xviii).[3]

Though Dick insisted on his having drawn inspiration from Japanese novelists, he never specified who those novelists were. There are indeed important Japanese writers who earned a degree in French literature at the University of Tokyo (Kenzaburo Oe, Osamu Dazai, Hideo Kobayashi), while others studied French literature at the University of Kyoto (Hiroshi Noma and Shohei Ooka), but the works of these authors which were available in English translations before the publication of *The Man in the High Castle* do not have a multiple plot structure, though one of them, Hiroshi Noma's war novel *Zone of Emptiness* (1952, translated into English in 1956) does have multiple points of view. It is however difficult to see it as a narrative model to Dick's 1962 novel because there is only one plot, pivoted on the tragic story of a Japanese soldier who is imprisoned for two years in a military penitentiary for a crime he has not committed and then sent to fight (and probably die) in a faraway Pacific island; and this novel has only two narrative foci, unlike *Castle*. Moreover, while Dick's novel presents the reader with a rather positive image of the Japanese domination in California, which is depicted as stern but substantially fair, Noma's novel denounces the corruption of the Imperial Japanese Army and the hypocrite and narrow-minded militarism which dominated the country in World War II years. It is in any case true that private Soda's desperate efforts to save the doomed protagonist, Kitani, from the deadly bureaucratic machine of the army may bear resemblance to the rebellion of the little man Nobosuke Tagomi, which instead manages to save Frank Frink from the deadly machine of Nazi racial warfare. But this is not enough to prove that Dick had read *Zone of Emptiness*, as the overall architecture of the two novels is too different.[4]

If we want to point out more credible candidates as models for Dick's multi-plot and -foci narratives we should perhaps get back to his 1958 letter, and look at the tenth chapter of Joyce's *Ulysses*, the so-called "Wandering Rocks," where the cavalcade of the Lord Lieutenant through the streets of Dublin is witnessed by 19 different characters, whose wanderings are told in nineteen short vignettes from each characters' point of view. It is then interesting that Dick did not only mention Dos Passos' celebrated trilogy; in a 1960 letter he cites another work by Dos Passos, *The Prospect Before Us* (1950), surely not one of his most famous achievements, which might indicate a sustained interest in the oeuvre of the American novelist (*SL1* 56). However, Dick does not mention Dos Passos in the letters written after 1971, and one must notice that the full-blown multi-plot technique was not used after that year (we only have a simplified version of it in *The Divine Invasion*).

Regardless of what sources of inspiration Dick tapped, one thing is sure: the multiple plot/point of view narrative technique dominates his fiction in the early 1960s. It is the approach he adopted in the most important novels published in this decade, maybe also for the simple reason that it was functional to Dick's strategy of ontological uncertainty. Having multiple points of view on multiple plotlines fictionally embodies the dichotomy of koinos kosmos vs. idios kosmos Dick had derived from the existentialist psychoanalysts. Seeing events unfold through the eyes of different characters allows the reader to perceive how different individual takes on reality may be, how conditioned by highly subjective drives, fears, expectations, obsessions, etc. Above all it generates a condition of general uncertainty, because what readers are shown might not be a reliable representation of a fictional koinos kosmos, but a very deformed *perception* of that common world, as seen from a very odd and twisted private world. According to Dick, "any given person ... cannot tell what part of that which he experiences is the *idios kosmos* and which the *koinos*" (Gillespie 32). Besides, we should not forget that the dichotomy of koinos vs. idios kosmos is a simplification of what Dick found in existentialist psychoanalysis, where idios kosmos (*Eigenwelt*, or private world) is opposed to koinos kosmos (*Mitwelt*, or shared world), but both are the human counterpart of the *Umwelt* or environment, the natural world: the world as it is. This explains something that Dick wrote in the same 8 June 1969 letter we have already quoted: "In all my books ... the protagonist is suffering from a breakdown of his *idios kosmos*— at least we hope that's what's breaking down, not the *koinos kosmos*" (Gillespie 32). Dick's remark is more than a shaft of wit; it is true that the subjective point of view of single characters may be unreliable (and this is something novelists already knew well before Dick, at least since Conrad and Henry James), but the shared world is just another human construction, a cultural artifact, one might say, the product of the interaction of individuals, and also the shared world or koinos kosmos could break down, in Dick's terms, revealing an *Umwelt* or natural world that we are not equipped to directly cope with. This might explain why Dick, in the same letter, felt he had to quote "Kant's concept of the *Dinge-an-sich* [*sic*]": he could misspell the German phase (should be *Ding-an-sich*, "thing-in-itself"), but he was aware that the non-human *Umwelt* is something difficult or almost impossible to experience directly, something which is always mediated by human and cultural categories or conditions of possibility, in Kantian terms (such as causality or necessity). If both the idios kosmos and the koinos kosmos break down, we are left with the *Umwelt*, but this might be a deadly experience, if we may call it thus.

Dick depicted such a double collapse in one of his most philosophical short stories, "The Electric Ant" (1969), where the protagonist discovers that he is not a man but an "electric ant" or organic robot, and then tinkers with its sensory apparatus, with the tape from which "all sense stimuli received from [its] central neurological system emanate" (*CS5* 295). Garson Poole, the electric ant, ultimately cuts the tape, because it thinks that this is the only way to know his personal secretary "completely"; to know if she really exists or if she is just "a stimulus factor on [its] reality tape" (*CS5* 305). In other terms, Poole wants to know where his private world (the illusory sensory stimuli recorded on the tape) ends and what is really there, beyond the tape. When the tape ends and the photoelectric beam directly hits the scanner, a sort of psychedelic experience takes place, described in an impressive paragraph (*CS5* 307) where Dick manages to convey a surreal compresence of everything with everything else. But this ultimate experience of the unknowable and unexperienceable thing-in-itself brings Poole to death, or better, to burning its brain circuits. Dick commented: "Again the theme: How much of what we call 'reality' is actually out there or rather within our own head?" (*CS5* 489); the borderline between the private world, the shared world, and the natural world or environment (the *Umwelt*) is quite difficult to pinpoint. This difficulty leads to ontological uncertainty; no wonder then that, at the end of "The Electric Ant" Sarah Benton, Poole's secretary discovers that she and the world surrounding her are part of the artificial reality emanated from Poole's "reality tape," which is quickly fading away. This is one of Dick's typical bewildering endings which is not only aimed at surprising readers with final fireworks, but at reminding us that nothing can be taken for granted.

Private worlds, shared world and environment all play an important role in a novel that Dick wrote just after *The Man in the High Castle*, that is, *Martian Time-Slip* (1964).[5] Dick told Gregg Rickman that the latter was an attempt "to escalate from *Man in the High Castle* to the next level of quality, complexity, and value" (Rickman 1988, 146). He felt confident as he thought he had found his own structure (the "multi-foci structure"); moreover, he had won the Hugo Award for *High Castle*, and he had sold his two previous novels to hardcover publishers. Dick felt he was headed to success or at least respectability, and he could finally forsake the pulp paperback market. No wonder then that he used again the multi-plot, multi-foci architecture in this novel, and tried to reach new depths. The multi-foci structure of the novel allows Dick to show us several private worlds, those of the eight characters endowed with a narrative focus,[6] thus retaining and deepening "the *MHC* narrative polyphony" (Suvin 1975, 5); the web of human relations — be they personal, economical, familial, political — ties the characters in a "maledictory web," to put it in Brian Aldiss' terms (Aldiss 37), which is of course the shared world[7]; and the environment — threatening, hostile, bleak, alien — is planet Mars, where the novel takes place in its entirety.[8]

Ontological uncertainty is thus not based on the competition of alternative histories or parallel universes; it is rather based on the narrative polyphony which allows readers to enter the idioi kosmoi of the characters, that are quite different from each other. Suffice it to say that one of the narrative foci is Jack Bohlen, who suffers from schizophrenia, while another, Manfred Steiner, is an autistic boy. This offers Dick the opportunity to conjure up highly different private worlds — a deliberate move, explained in an interview with Paul Williams (Rickman 1989, 206–7), where he says that "it is more striking ... if I use a more exaggerated discrepancy between people's viewpoints, like in *Martian Time Slip*" (207).

The discrepancy is temporal: the title is quite clear about this. Whether it was devised by Dick or chosen by the publisher, it is rather felicitous, as it hints at the non-linear plot of the novel, where prolexes abound, especially in the long sequence of Jack Bohlen's bout of schizophrenia (chapters 10 to 12, according to Warrick "the most bizarre and dramatically original section of the novel" [73] and I tend to agree), but also at the core of Manfred's autism. This mental condition is explained by Dr. Glaub as "a derangement in the interior time-sense" (92), an acceleration of the inner sense of time which forces Manfred's mind to be out of tune with the shared world; his private world is tuned to a moment in a more or less remote future, which grants the boy the power of precognition. But the time-slip that allows Manfred to see what will happen also prevents him from communicating with others in the present; moreover, the future he can see is one of alienation, imprisonment in a mental institution, a nightmarish vision of an exceedingly long life (124–5) which is actually an overlong agony — a death-in-life. Hence the plot of the novel where the ruthless labor union leader Arnie Kott asks Jack Bohlen to design a device that may allow him to communicate with Manfred. Arnie's involvement with the autistic boy is definitely not altruistic; the chief of the Water Workers Union wants to use Manfred's precognitive ability to ward off any threat to his power over the Martian colony.

Manfred's schizophrenic time-slip allows Dick to show Mars and the events taking place there from a very different perspective from what we are accustomed to, forcing us to adopt the point of view of what we usually consider as a defective mind. This creates a condition of ontological uncertainty, because since the boy's mind is out of phase with the koinos kosmos of other characters we may have serious difficulties to understand what belongs to the present of the novel and what lies in the future. It is something definitely more sophisticated than what can be found in a later novel, *Counter-Clock World* (1967), where the so-called Hobart Phase has inverted the time flux, and people get younger day by day, while the dead resurrect[9]: the linearity of the inversion in Counter-Clock does not create a real condition of ontological uncertainty.

Manfred's perception of people is also strongly deformed by his schizoid condition. Here is how he sees Arnie Kott: "Inside Mr. Kott's skin were dead bones, shiny and wet. Mr. Kott was a sack of bones, dirty and yet shiny-wet. His head was a skull that took in greens and bit them; inside him the greens became rotten things as something ate them to make them dead" (126). This description returns twice (133, 141), because it is part of a prolexis caused by Manfred's precognitive powers: the scene of the meeting between Arnie and Jack Bohlen in chapters 10 and 11 is shown in three prolexes and then it is nonchalantly bypassed by the main narrative line (168), with another crucial time-slip; no wonder that Kim Stanley Robinson considers these chapters as central, since they manage to capture also readers in this nightmarish time-slip (Robinson 57).[10]

But it is not Manfred's point of view alone that causes the ontological uncertainty dominating the novel; though it is the most interesting focus, endowed with a somewhat emblematic role in the character system (something which has been acknowledged by most commentators, from Suvin to Warrick, from Pagetti[11] to Vallorani,[12] not to mention Brian Aldiss), also Jack Bohlen's point of view questions the distinction between objective and subjective realities, as we can see in this passage where we are shown Dr. Glaub as seen by Jack, "a thing composed of cold wires and switches, not a human at all, not made of flesh. The fleshy trappings melted and became transparent and Jack Bohlen saw the mechanical device beyond" (94). Is this just the effect of madness, hence a purely subjective vision which blurs objective, shared reality? Warrick calls it an "intuitive vision" (72), because it unveils a hideous aspect of the psychiatrist's personality (whose manipulative and sordid character is subsequently shown during his confrontation with Anne Esterhazy [148–51]). Jack, who suffers from schizophrenia (and is thus both closer to Manfred and at risk of being absorbed by his autism, as Glaub correctly diagnoses [156]) may be imprisoned in his own idios kosmos, but he (like Manfred) may see something other characters are blind to; in this case, something even Dr. Glaub does not seem to be wholly aware of. We might quote a famous proverb by William Blake, which also applies to Manfred: "If the fool would persist in his folly he would become wise."

This does not mean that what Jack sees or hears should be always taken at its face value. When he hears all the teaching androids[13] at Camp Ben-Gurion (the school for autistic children in the Israeli settlement) utter unintelligible words, rendered as "Gubble gubble" (153–4), he concludes that "his own psyche ... had not misinformed him: it was happening, what he heard and saw" (154); but we soon discover (and the narrative shifts to Dr. Glaub's point of view to make this clear) that Jack is "in a state of catatonic stupor" (155), and that, as Jack realizes when he recovers, the "gubble" were Manfred's words apparently coming from the android teachers (156). A mental short circuit caused Jack's private world to be invaded by Manfred's, something which had already happened in a previous episode (143), though then Jack had managed to realize that "[h]e had imbibed ... of Manfred's world-view."

This invasion leads readers to see Manfred as a threatening, possibly destructive presence; but this happens because in these last chapters we mostly see the autistic boy's private world through Jack's idios kosmos, suffused with fear and anguish. When we "directly" access Manfred's private world (e.g., in a short sequence in chapter 12 [165–7]) we see that the boy is not threatening, but threatened by the looming future of solitude, deprivation and decay in the bleak AM-WEB building (167). Thus he is quite different from another figure of psi-empowered child, Jory in *Ubik*, who can and does impose his world-view on others (Ch. 7).

The early commentators of the novel underscored its negative depiction of the Martian society; Suvin posits the dismal AM-WEB building as its symbol, and then interprets the acronym as the "*American Web* of big business, corrupt labor aristocracy and big state" (Suvin 1975, 8), drawing from Brian Aldiss' idea of a maledictory web which imprisons the Terran settlements on Mars, though in Aldiss' essay the negative web is not a sociopolitical system but the entrapment of psychosis (Aldiss 40), represented by Manfred's autism (which in Aldiss' opinion is the epitome of the uneasy mental condition of all the characters, a stasis which "means death, spiritual if not actual" [40]). Also

Carlo Pagetti sees Mars as a place torn by "the ruthless struggle for power" (Pagetti 1975, 21), reading it as "another of the many images of the Waste Land that 20th-century culture proposes us with obsessive repetitiousness."[14] Both Pagetti and Suvin interpret Mars as an anamorphic image of the United States,[15] an image that is at the same time defamiliarized and insightful, a group portrait of very real characters (Butler 2007, 61) on a science-fictional background. Kim Stanley Robinson suggests that Dick's Mars is "an American suburb of 1963 simplified in order to make certain processes in it clearer" (Robinson 55). Another critic, Fredric Jameson, quoted a line by Marianne Moore to summarize the results of his interpretive method applied to this and other Dickian novels of the sixties: "real toads in imaginary gardens" (Jameson 2005, 379); this line also applies to the uncanny effect of Dick's peculiar approach to fiction in this novel.

The real toads are not only the characters of *Time-Slip*,[16] a fully persuading group of Americans displaced on the Red Planet. One should also mention another achievement, that is the depiction of California seen through a science-fictional mirror, darkly. Mars *is* California, in a way that only Dick's fiction allows. The barren Martian landscape is quite similar to that of the state where Dick lived for most of his life, as depicted in the first chapter of his realistic novel *Puttering About in a Small Land*:

> The hills ... were so bleak, so lacking in life.... The hills in the East; before the present generation other people had lived there, and before them others. It was clear that someone had always lived there. Before the English the Indians. Before the Indians — nobody knew, but certainly some race, some form of life, intelligent, responsible.... Here, the hills were like refuse heaps, without color; the ground was only dirt, the plants were patches of weeds separated from one another, holding beer cans and paper that had blown down the canyons. This was a canyon ... not a cleft. And the wind roared... [7].

Like California, Mars is a dry, desolate land, kept alive by complex and precarious water works, anamorphic images of the complex system of aqueducts supervised by William Mulholland which allowed the fast growth of Los Angeles at the beginning of the Twentieth century; the real estate speculation organized by Jack Bohlen's father Leo (which will lead to the building of the dreadful AM-WEB building) resembles the speculations described in Dick's non-sf novels, such as *The Man Whose Teeth Were All Exactly Alike* or *Humpty Dumpty in Oakland*, set in California, where real estate development has always played an important role; and the Bleekmen are evidently the Martian equivalents of the Native Americans or Mexicans which lived on the west coast before it was colonized by European Americans. All in all, the whole novel puts the readers in a situation of ontological uncertainty: is the alien world really alien, or does it look suspiciously like California? We might say that here we have the reverse of what Dick did in *Time Out of Joint*: there an apparently familiar world turned out to be completely alien, while here the Red Planet is bewilderingly similar to the West Coast.[17] This might add another meaning to the "terrible sincerity" that Patricia Warrick finds in this novel (Warrick 78).

If Mars is a bleak place, dominated by "violence, deceit, and, finally, the spiritual aridity of man" (Pagetti, 1975, 21), California, this synecdoche of the United States, fares no better. Yet we cannot say that this is a dystopian novel like *A Scanner Darkly* or *Radio Free Albemuth*. Fredric Jameson has located a strong utopian element in *Martian Time-Slip*, and that is undoubtedly the final apparition of Manfred (218–9), getting back from a far future and turned into a cyborg, which presents us with

> the collective, the primitive communism of the aboriginals, who have also become the helpers and the rescuers of the schizophrenic Manfred, himself now a new kind of prosthetic being who has emerged from out of the future of his own past, immobilized in gubbish, and about to escape, with his friends around him bearing him away, all tubes and hoses trailing behind, into the alternate dreamtime of another History and another present [Jameson 2005, 383].

Though the apparition of Manfred scares both his mother and Jack's wife Silvia, it is undoubtedly an apotheosis (which according to Jameson unites the four main semic clusters which structure the textual space in this and the other novels Dick published in the 1960s); it is also the climactic moment when Manfred may communicate with another human being. Manfred came back from the future not just "to say goodbye to [his] mother" (219), but to thank Jack Bohlen: "You tried to communicate with me, many years ago. I appreciate that."

We are also told that Manfred managed to escape *am-web*, which may be read, in this final scene, as both the dismal building and the socioeconomic wasteland which built (and also, thanks to the time-slip, *will* build) it. "I am with my friends," says Manfred, and they are the Bleekmen. Salvation can be reached if one can escape the American Web and get in touch with the defeated, the marginalized people, or, as another postmodernist writer called them in his *Gravity's Rainbow*, the Preterite. If madmen were in power in *The Man in the High Castle*, and were busy bringing the world(s) to nuclear holocaust, here madmen are the only hope left: madmen who can forsake the dismal logic of exploitation and deception and drop out of the American Web. Christopher Palmer defined this novel as "anti-psichiatric" (Palmer 146), and connected it to the theories of Thomas Szasz and R.D. Laing; it should also be connected to its countercultural context, as represented e.g., in Ken Kesey's

One Flew Over the Cuckoo's Nest (a connection also made by Link [27–8]). While in Dick the autistic boy Manfred manages to escape the American Web,[18] in Kesey's novel only "Chief" Bromden, a half-Indian, ultimately manages to escape the totalitarian mental hospital dominated by Nurse Ratched (another anamorphic image of the United States) and find shelter in his tribe's lands. If in Dick's novel we are ultimately uncertain about who is really insane and who is not (as the purported sanity of characters like Arnie Kott and Otto Zitte brings to exploitation and murder), the title of the 1963 novella "All We Marsmen"— that Dick expanded into the novel — might also suggest that it is a story about "All We Madmen (and Women)"; and the protagonists of Kesey's novel are mostly madmen, oppressed by sane people who (like the domineering and sadistic nurse) are probably not so sane as they think or say they are.[19]

Having been completed just four months after *Time-Slip*, *Dr. Blood-money, or How We Got Along After the Bomb*, though published in 1965, is strictly connected to the previous novel. Suvin noticed that there were structural similarities, such as the multiple plots and the presence of several narrative foci,[20] and consequently included it in the so-called Plateau Period. It did not take Dick a long time to complete the novel because he usually wrote them in a very short time (he repeatedly explained in his letters and interviews that he thought about the plots of novels for a long time, sometimes writing notes and outlines of plots, but it generally took him less than a month to type the first draft of his novels), but also because he had already written a story "about Hoppy Harrington on his cart ... a novelette version of *Dr. Blood-money*" (Rickman 1988, 71); Dick had been invited to submit a story for an ambitious anthology of experimental sf which was cancelled for lack of suitable materials (something which, according to Dick, could have anticipated Harlan Ellison's *Dangerous Visions*). Moreover, according to Patricia Warrick, Dick drew on the manuscript of the then unpublished realistic novel *Voices from the Street*, especially for the initial chapters (Warrick 80).[21]

Though Dick's expectations about *Martian Time-Slip* were great, as we have seen, the novel had not been sold yet when he started working on *Blood-money*, and he knew all too well that if he was not paid much for his novels he had to compensate with a huge output. In 1963 and 1964 he wrote or completed eleven novels plus several stories, in what was the most productive time of his life. Hyper-production was also an answer to the disappointments that he had to face in those months. In January 1963 his literary agent sent back all his non-sf manuscripts, having been unable to sell them to any publisher.[22] After this failure, Dick felt "completely deflated" (Rickman 1988, 146) when his most ambitious novel so far, *Martian Time-Slip*, could find no hard cover publisher, and had to be ultimately sold to Ballantine for a meager $2,000, to be published as a cheap sf paperback; moreover, the novel did not sell well at all. "It went unnoticed, it went unreviewed, unnoticed by the critics, by the publishers, and by the readers" (Rickman 1988, 146): maybe it was not as great a disaster for U.S. and world literature as the commercial failure of Herman Melville's *Moby-Dick*, but it was surely a terrible blow for the 35-years-old writer who had thought to be on the verge of fame and success.[23]

No wonder then that Dick went back to science-fiction for good, first with *Dr. Bloodmoney*, then with the following ten novels he completed in 1963–64. It was a compromise solution: "it was not exactly what I wanted to write, and it was marketable, and it had enough of what I wanted to do in it to make it worth my interest" (Rickman 1988, 147). *Dr. Bloodmoney* was in fact first published as an Ace paperback.

However, it is quite clear that the new novel could not be that different from *Time-Slip*. The narrative architecture with multiple plots and narrative foci is similar; we also have a group of well-differentiated characters, among which there are two individuals characterized by mental derangement, Bruno Bluthgeld and Hoppy Harrington (though the mental problems of the latter are less evident and somewhat lighter than those of Bluthgeld and the two schizophrenics — Jack and Manfred — in the previous novel). Hoppy is endowed with psi powers like Manfred, and he is also physically different from other characters, being a phocomelus; but he is as greedy and violent as Arnie Kott, maybe even more.

However, if a web of human relations tied all the characters of *Time-Slip*, the same may be said of those in *Dr. Bloodmoney*. The novel is set in a small community of survivors in Marin County, and it tells their daily life, remarkably quiet and bucolic, after the disaster of World War III which wiped away the United States and most national governments. The web in this novel is purely local, though there is another thin, precarious web connecting the small community with the others scattered on the rest of the world: the orbital DJ Walt Dangerfield, an astronaut who should have reached Mars with his wife, but remained in orbit due to the war and then used the powerful radio transmitter of the space capsule to contact the survivors and keep them in touch with each other. The small bucolic society, daily listening to Dangerfield's wise and ironic pacifist comments, has definitely countercultural and utopian undertones; after all, Dick had lived for years in the bohemian, anti-establishment community of Berkeley, and the novel was written less than two years before the beginning of the Free Speech Movement.[24] Maybe the war is no more than a device allowing Dick to depict a utopian community; besides, he overtly said that he thought it was an excellent book above all because the society he portrayed was "not what you'd expect to find after a Holocaust" (Rickman 1988, 155): it was a fusion of the rural Point Reyes Station community with the urban Berkeley milieu, confirmed by Anne Dick (Warrick 83–4). The result of such a fusion is, and Jameson's analysis convincingly proves this, "a genuinely Jeffersonian commonwealth beyond the bomb" (Jameson 1975, 362), a reestablished utopian collectivity.

Yet it is difficult to read the nuclear war in *Bloodmoney* as nothing more than a narrative device. Fredric Jameson noticed that nuclear war can be found in most of the short stories and several novels Dick had written before *Dr. Bloodmoney*, but that it is not usually shown; it is mentioned by the characters or the 3rd-person narrator as something lying in the past, which should explain the difference between the science-fictional world Dick has conjured up and the world of his readers (Jameson 2005, 349). In these earlier works World War III is indeed a fictional device "in which [his near-futures] find their historical sustenance" (349). There are exceptions that Jameson does not mentions, such as *The Man in the High Castle*, where nuclear war looms large on the three alternate worlds intersecting in the novel, or *Time Out of Joint*, where a "serialized" nuclear war is going on; but Jameson is right in underscoring the fact that the moment when the bombs actually detonate is only shown in *Bloodmoney*. Here the nuclear holocaust manifests itself; it is not just an antecedent, or a possibility. Though enclosed in an analepsis in chapters 5 and 6, it is staged in a giant 38-page flashback introduced by Bonny Keller's musings at the end of chapter 4, when she comes to think, by association, of "the day, seven years ago, when the bombs began to fall on things" (57).[25]

According to Jameson, the two chapters showing the war posit "artistic problems unlike any other" (Jameson 1975, 350); the critic notices, as we have already seen in the Introduction, that the power of Dick's fiction lies in his ability to keep together and somewhat integrate (though it is a rather troublesome integration) "subjective and objective explanation systems" (350); what I have called ontological uncertainty. But can Dick's own literary solution accommodate such a cumbersome object as nuclear war? In Jameson's words: "Dick's narrative ambiguity can accommodate individual experience, but runs greater risks in evoking the materials of world history, the flat yes and no of the mushroom cloud" (351). And this contradiction, or tension, or fault is well present in *Bloodmoney*, not just because the author felt somewhat compelled to show something that had been just implied in former novels and short stories, but because readers "are less and less able to distinguish between ... 'real' explosions and those that take place within the psyche" (350). This remark is preceded by a hint at the fact that one of the characters, nuclear physicist Bruno Bluthgeld, "takes [the nuclear war] to be a projection of his own psychic powers" (350), something which Jameson does not see as a major interpretive problem, however not as great as the second; the two remarks point to two very important episodes which should be discussed at length, because here our interpretive hypothesis of ontological uncertainty may unearth something that Jameson has briefly hinted at but other interpreters seem to have overlooked.

Actually Patricia Warrick paid attention to the character of Bluthgeld (whose surname may sound German, like that of other nuclear scientists such as Oppenheimer or Fuchs, but was actually invented by Dick by putting together the German words *Blut*, "blood" and *Geld*, "money," hence the title of the novel)[26]: she suggests that Bluthgeld is "a thinly disguised" (Warrick, 81) Edward Teller, the Hungarian physicist who had migrated to the USA in the 1930s, worked under Enrico Fermi, and subsequently became the father of the hydrogen bomb. Like most Americans in the postwar years Dick was quite well informed about Cold War and the threat of a Third World War; in addition to all his short stories and novels set in a post–World War III world, we should mention the Minimax, repeatedly mentioned in *Solar Lottery*, one of the games studied by Hungarian-born mathematician John von Neumann, a friend of Teller and another key figure of Project Manhattan and subsequently U.S. defense strategy (Poundstone 52–5); several details of Bluthgeld's life are taken from the real life of Teller, such as the fact that he worked at the Lawrence Livermore National Laboratory (54), or the fact he was born in Budapest (7), though 34 years after the real scientist.

When the nuclear bombs fall, Bluthgeld's reaction seems to be simply dictated by his mental disease: a little before the war breaks out, Dick has the scientist visited by a psychoanalyst, Dr. Stockstill (another narrative focus in the novel), to make it clear that he suffers from a paranoid syndrome (4–10); the psychoanalyst also remembers Richard Nixon's[27] distrust of Bluthgeld (8), due to the latter's growing mental problems. No wonder then if Bluthgeld believes he made the nuclear war happen: in a powerful sequence of Chapter 6 (80–7), Dick shows us the catastrophic aftermath of the nuclear attack on the San Francisco Bay Area through the paranoid delirium of this deranged character (whose madness is now fully manifest), who first gloats over the devastating effects of "the almost limitless potency of [his] reactive psychic energy" (80–1), then moves his hands to heal the damage done in a demented act of forgiveness (83–4). Bluthgeld has moved from taking responsibility for a failed nuclear experiment in 1972 which caused malformations in many children (5, 14) to taking liability for something he cannot have caused, and the mental stress caused by the 1972 disaster may well explain his psychotic reaction to the nuclear war.

This first episode is not a major problem because everything we read before the episode in chapter 6 authorizes readers to see Bluthgeld as a madman entrapped by his paranoia: he only believes that he is the cause of World War III. But a major problem rises when, in chapter 12, Bluthgeld, now living in West Marin some years after the war, under the false identity of Jack Tree, meets Stuart McConchie, the same man he had met before being visited by Dr. Stockstill, and immediately thinks that the war will start again (208). He is scared by this at first, but then he decides to unleash nuclear destruction again as a punishment to the small community (213), which has gathered in the Foresters' Hall to listen to Dangerfield's radio broadcast. Megalomaniac delirium again, we might say, but something happens which calls everything in doubt, because after Bluthgeld has decided to eliminate Dangerfield, whose radio-broadcast voice annoys him, with high-altitude hydrogen blasts (215–6), the voice of the orbital DJ ceases (216). Bluthgeld is then so excited that he stands up and addresses the community, announcing that "[t]he demolition of existence has begun. Everyone present will be spared by special consideration long enough to confess sins and repent if it is sincere" (218), in a mix of megalomania and religious mania, then revealing his true identity.

This could obviously be no more than a coincidence; we also know that Dangerfield is the victim of his difficult condition (living alone in a small space for years), the grief for the death of his wife (who committed suicide [111]), and the psi powers of Hoppy Harrington. When Dangerfield's voice is heard again (218–9), the people in the hall and the readers may well be reassured that Bluthgeld is mad, not endowed with supernatural powers. But another fact is much more difficult to explain, and that is the explosions in the sky which take place soon after the scene in the Foresters' Hall (212–9): they are seen by Bonny Keller and Mr. Barnes (231), but also by many other members of the West Marin community (239).

The night explosions, two over West Marin, another over San Francisco, are not explained in the novel. Since they resemble the enigmatic scene in the park in *Time Out of Joint* we have discussed in chapter 2, we could ascribe them to Dick's poor control of his texts, also because we know that this novel was definitely not written as carefully (and/or properly edited) as *The Man in the High Castle* or *Martian Time-Slip*, and ignore them.

There is however at least a critic, Patricia Warrick, who takes them at their face value, and believes that Bluthgeld is endowed with "mental powers" allowing him to "begin another atomic war" (Warrick 87). If this is true, he might also have caused the first nuclear war.[28] Such a reading might justify Jameson's discomfort: ascribing the nuclear holocaust to the evil powers of a single deranged individual may be something childish, something "unconvincing and ineffectual" (Jameson 1975, 351), because America and its institutions (including that fearful American creation, the nuclear Bomb, Dick's equivalent or complement of Thomas Pynchon's threatening Rocket, and the vast apparatus managing it during and after the Cold War) are too massive and unchangeable for Dick's typical approach to fiction: "to prevent the reestablishment of the reality principle and the reconstitution of experience into the twin airtight domains of the objective and the subjective" (Jameson 1975, 351)—in other words, one of the forms of ontological uncertainty.

It is indeed a matter of being objective or subjective; if the power to trigger the nuclear holocaust is merely subjective, then Bluthgeld is just a pathetic case of madness. But those explosions seem to be something objective, belonging to the koinos kosmos of the characters, not just to Bluthgeld's deformed idios kosmos. Bonny Keller thinks that we are well in the domain of the objective, as she says: "It's an evil god ... who gave him that power, whatever it is. I know it's him .... We've seen a lot of strange things over the years, so why not this? The ability to recreate the war, to bring it back, like he said last night. Maybe he's got us snared in time" (231).[29]

Actually the explosions might be also explained in another way. Since Hoppy Harrington is going to kill Bluthgeld in order to become the hero of the community (thus reinforcing the unity of the society with the old trick of sacrificing a scapegoat), and Hoppy does have psi powers (including telekinesis and precognition), plus amazing technical skills to repair and build electric and electronic devices, the explosions might well be something conjured up by him by supernatural or technological means in order to persuade the members of the West Marin community that Bluthgeld is not somebody to be pitied (and possibly cured), but a real threat.

Dick does not tell us this overtly, but it is a possibility which is left open. Besides, it is not the only issue left open in the novel. Dick does not explain what are the causes of the nuclear catastrophe which wipes out the United States as we know them: was it a Soviet attack, or an accident? Dr. Stockstill thinks that "something had gone wrong with the automatic defense system out in space" so that "it was Washington that was dropping bombs on them, not the Chinese or the Russian" (66). He ends this overexcited meditation by concluding that "The impersonal ... has attacked us" (67). This may mean, as the doctor himself does, that the war has caused the break-up of society; but it also means that ascertaining individual responsibilities after such a catastrophe is practically impossible and possibly pointless. The multiple narrative foci are there because they make us understand that such an enormous event is beyond the human faculty to perceive, and maybe even mentally picture it; such a difficulty of telling, representing or picturing has been repeatedly discussed in connection with the experience of modern warfare,[30] so that it is not surprising that we only have fragmented views of the nuclear attack, as Warrick has noticed (Warrick 84–5).

Ontological uncertainty is thus at work also in this novel, maybe in a less pyrotechnic and blatant way than in *The Three Stigmata of Palmer Eldritch* and the other novels discussed in chapter 7, but it is there, not just in the greater issue of the nuclear war (the big one of 1981 and the much smaller one of 1988), but also in other episodes of the novel. We have the many lies and falsifications of Hoppy Harrington (whose fake id is just the first of a long series, possibly including the explosions in the sky), up to the imitation and replacement of Walt Dangerfield (266) facilitated by the invisibility of the orbital DJ; we have Billy Keller's uncanny imitations of dead people's voices which terrify Hoppy and bring him to his eventual defeat (271–5); the musing of Andrew Gill about Stuart's authenticity as a salesman, and then the discussion about real coffee and the substitute that Andrew must offer Stuart (193–4, 197); Hoppy's vision of the afterlife in chapter 3 which is only revealed as a fraud when Stuart realizes that what Hoppy was really seeing was the wrecked world after the nuclear catastrophe (81). Ontological uncertainty is generated because the story is told through a web of points of view, each one with a very different conception of what is subjective and what is objective in the shared world — a shared world that Dick's narrative technique in this novel shows us as something remarkably shifting and undetermined.

Any discussion of Dick's novels where the collective dimension is paramount must necessarily include another text, completed in January 1964 and published in the same year: *Clans of the Alphane Moon*. Neither Jameson nor Warrick have connected this novel to *Dr. Bloodmoney*: conversely, they see *The Simulacra* as its "less successful companion piece" (Jameson 1975, 349) or "twin" (Warrick 88), based on its having been completed only six months later. Surely there are reasons for grouping these novels together, as it is not difficult to find similarities between works written by the same author in a relatively short period; but in my opinion the elements with tie *Simulacra* with *Now Wait for Last Year* (the third novel completed in 1963) are much stronger than those that connect it to *Dr. Bloodmoney*, as we shall see in Chapter 5.

On the other hand, *Clans* is a close relative of *Time-Slip* and *Bloodmoney* for more than one reason. Warrick noticed that two themes, "mental illness and domestic disharmony" (Warrick 65), are pivotal both in *Time-Slip* and *Clans*; these issues are also present also in *Bloodmoney*, and they do not play a secondary role.[31] Multi-plot and multi-focal architecture are a common feature of these three novels; they are used to provide ontological uncertainty, as we shall see; they are meant to analyze the workings of a community, considered as a complex web of interacting private worlds. Moreover, madness plays a vital role, though this time it is not just a pair of characters who suffer from mental disease (be they positive, as Jack Bohlen and Manfred Steiner in *Time-Slip*, or negative, as Hoppy Harrington and Bruno Bluthgeld in *Bloodmoney*): in *Clans* all the inhabitants of the Alpha Centauri moon Alpha III M2, where a large part of the action takes place, are insane.

But insanity here is not at all something dangerous, as it is in *Bloodmoney*, or a social stigma. The inhabitants of the Alphane moon are the former inmates of the Harry Stack Sullivan[32] Neuropsychiatric Hospital (95), which was cut off from Earth during the war between humans and the Alphanes; once set free, the madmen (and women) organized themselves in a clan system according to their mental disorder, which I have tried to describe in the following table (based on Mary Rittersdorf's analysis in chapter 7 [77–9]):

Table 4.1

Clan	Mental disorder	Town	Vocation	Character
Pares	Paranoia	Adolfville	Leaders, statesmen	Gabriel Baines
Mans	Manic-depressive	Da Vinci Heights	Warriors	Howard Straw
Polys	Polymorphic schizophrenia	Hamlet Hamlet	Creative individuals, producers of new ideas	Annette Golding
Heebs	Hebephrenia	Gandhitown	Untouchables, saints, ascetics	Sarah Apostles, Ignatz Ledebur, Jacob Simion
Ob-Coms	Obsessive-compulsive neuroses	-	Clerks, office holders	Miss Hibbler
Deps	Depression	Cotton Mather Estates	-	Dino Walters
Skitzes	Schizophrenia	-	Poets, religious visionaries, dogmatists	Omar Diamond

The table is incomplete because Dick did not bother to describe everything in detail. In fact we should not forget that only a half of the novel is devoted to the Alphane moon with its clans, a utopian or quasi-utopian society; another half is set on Earth, and is pivoted upon the troublesome marriage of Chuck and Mary Rittersdorf, and the mission they have been assigned by the CIA—to persuade the members of the clans to undergo a psychiatric therapy "to put them actually in the position which, by accident, they now improperly hold" (81). A rather paradoxical mission, because the autonomous community which lives on the Alphane moon should renounce its independence in order to enter a program which will allow them to "govern themselves. As legitimate settlers on [that] moon, eventually" (81); the program is actually utter nonsense, as it is no more than a cover for the machination of the Terran authorities who only want to subjugate the lost colony. A complex web of intrigue surrounds Alpha III M2, but it is much less serious than what we have found in *The Man in the High Castle*; the simple fact that in the far future of interstellar travel and interplanetary wars the CIA still exists and is still plotting to overthrow foreign governments tells us that Dick was poking fun at the USA and its imperialistic policies.

What is really important if we want to fully understand *Wait* is that this novel is based on the opposition of two worlds: Earth and the Alphane moon. The former is the world as it was in 1964 and still is, dominated by competition, intrigue, power struggle, conspiracies: it is a world where everybody spies on everybody else; even the benevolent Lord Running Clam, one of Dick's most sympathetic aliens, regularly reads Chuck's thoughts (51–2). Everybody on Earth is busy scheming against somebody else: no wonder that several characters in this part of the novel are or are suspected to be spies, secret agents, or double-crossers. The symbol of this world of mistrust, resentment and unease is the teetering marriage of Chuck and Mary, whose reciprocal hostility brings the former to devise an elaborate plan to eliminate his wife, reminiscent of the plot in *Solar Lottery*, where another murder by android is described. All in all, the Terran part of the novel has all the elements of a noir, inasmuch as readers already know who wants to kill the potential victim and only have to wait and see if the plot will be successful, or will be hindered by the freaks who know about it (Lord Running Clam, Joan Trieste, RBX303); we even have a dark lady, that is, Mary Rittersdorf, scheming against her husband with a bunch of hoodlums.

If this is the "real" world, the Alphane moon is evidently the place of an alternative society where cooperation, not destructive competition, is the rule. The opposition between the two worlds has already been analyzed by Christopher Palmer, who sees *Clans* as "a satiric novel contrasting the sanity of the 'mad' and the insanity of the 'sane'" (Palmer 150), though Dick's animosity towards Mary Rittersdorf unbalances the novel, as the writer "does not maintain the necessary detachment." Here Palmer is evidently influenced by Dick's life as it has been reconstructed by Lawrence Sutin, who describes in detail the crisis of Dick's marriage with Anne Rubinstein, which reached its climax at the end of summer 1963 and ended with their separation in March 1964; since the novel was written in that stormy period, Palmer reads it as mirroring Dick's real life feelings and worries. Mary Rittersdorf is then a fictional portrait of Anne, and this reading seems to be strengthened by the fact that on the Alphane moon Mary is first believed to be a manic (197), but then, after being accurately tested, is diagnosed as a Dep (198–9), that is, suffering from depression. This bears a strong connection with an unpleasant episode of Dick's own marital crisis, when a psychiatrist diagnosed Anne as manic-depressive

(Sutin 123) and then filed involuntary commitment papers which led to Anne's internment at Ross Psychiatric Hospital for seventy-two hours and then at Langley-Porter Clinic for two weeks of further evaluation. Anne was eventually released, but the psychiatrist (whose name Sutin tactfully omitted) insisted on his diagnosis and prescribed the use of Stelazine, a powerful tranquilizer which turned Anne "into a zombie" (Sutin 124) for three months.

Dick was certainly not proud of the at least acquiescent role he had played in this episode, and "never alluded publicly to the commitment" (Sutin 124), even though, as the biographer duly observes, it is mirrored by the fate of Mary Rittersdorf in *Clans* and Kathy Sweetscent in *Now Wait for Last Year*. This may explain Palmer's remarks about Clans being a "deranged novel," "a return of Philip K. Dick's repressed" (Palmer 150); evidently the critic is annoyed by Dick's treatment of female characters, in connection to the injustice suffered by Anne Dick (whose responsibility, however, mainly falls upon the anonymous Marin County psychiatrist), which explains this remark: "the brew thickens, and also goes sour, in the opinion of many, if we add to it Dick's feelings about women" (Palmer 154).

Such generalizations may be dangerous, and a bit too much black-and-white, especially if one realizes that female commentators of Dick's fiction are not so annoyed by his portrayals of women (I might quote Warrick[33] and Vallorani, but there are others, such as Dillon and N. Katherine Hayles). But let us accept a biographical reading like the one underpinning Palmer's interpretation of *Clans* (though I cannot honestly say that all his interpretation can be reduced to this, as his analysis of Lord Running Clam is insightful and adds much to our understanding of the novel): if Mary is Anne *sub specie* science-fiction, we will have to admit that Chuck — unlike the historical Philip K. Dick — does not eventually divorce her, but gets back to her after having discarded two possible substitutes (Joan Trieste and Annette Golding [Palmer 151]). Moreover, Palmer maintains that sterility is one of the main themes in the novel (154), the embodiment of the entropy which threatens the human society on Earth; "women ought to offer nurture, kindliness, fertility" but "they have turned aside from this potential in them" (Palmer 154). I suspect that the Australian critic is reading female characters' failure to counter socioeconomic sterility as ultimately related to the abortion Anne Dick had in 1960 (Sutin 108–9), one of the indirect reasons of Dick's real-life marital crisis. But this is Dick's own biography, which is not so faithfully mirrored in the novel. In fact once Chuck and Mary are reconciled, she suggests that "maybe we'll have more children ... like the slime moulds ... we arrived and we'll increase in numbers until we become legion" (204). The reference to slime moulds, the alien race that Lord Running Clam belongs to, is quite clear if one keeps in mind Palmer's argument that if women have forsaken their capacity to generate and nurture, "males have to assume the role: Chuck as midwife-gardener, assisted by Annette, and Lord Running Clam reproduces himself" (153). But the novel ends when Mary proposes to have more children, who will grow up on the Alphane moon, and Chuck sees this offer as "a good omen, one that could not be overlooked" (204).

The point that Palmer seems to have missed is that biographic readings are a risky business because they can and will never explain how readers can enjoy the reading of literary texts even if they do not know anything about the life of their authors (be they long time dead like Homer or living like Thomas Pynchon). But this objection is not as important as his having apparently overlooked the fact that sterility (and social entropy) dominates *one* of the two worlds depicted in the novel, that is, Earth. Until Chuck and Mary are on planet Earth their marriage, "perverted into ruthless competition" (Palmer 149), is reduced to a sterile, maddened struggle which may predictably end in merciless exploitation or murder. But once the couple moves to the Alphane moon, a sort of harmony is regained, and fertility counters sterility.

Mary is indeed diagnosed as depressive, but this does not mean that she is humbled and punished (150). In fact we should not forget that she is a psychologist specialized in "marriage counseling" (18), who is sent to the Alphane moon to negotiate with the clans; this negotiation, masterminded by Earth authorities (including the CIA), is not political but medical, hence not based on parity. The Alphane clans are not recognized as peers when Mary tells them "*You are, individually and collectively, mentally ill*" (134)—which, from the point of view of Terran authorities, justifies the landing on the moon without any attempt at securing permission (135), a point which the Clans delegation immediately raises.

In other words, Mary is not just Chuck's wife. She is a psychologist who "used to think that [she] was ... completely different from [her] patients" (202–3). This radical difference between sane and insane individuals has heavy political consequences: the allegedly (or self-proclaimed) sane world considers itself to be entitled to the tutelage of the insane world of Alpha III M2. A radical inequality between the two planets is suggested, which is parallel to the inequality between therapist and patient (e.g., between Anne Dick and the anonymous psychiatrist who had her committed); this inequality is used by Earth to legitimate its claims on the Alphane moon and its inhabitants— who can be elegantly ignored as political subjects. Thus Palmer's idea that "the come-uppance Mary Rittersdorf receives is a matter between Philip K. Dick and his feelings about women" (Palmer 158) is totally untenable.

The diagnosis of Mary's psychosis (performed by members of the clans [198]) is not a punishment, but a political act; its purpose is to show that those who claim to be sane may well be as insane as the madmen and -women of the Alphane moon. It is a denunciation of Earth's attempt to subjugate the Alphane moon, which represents too different a model of society from the one existing on Earth. It should then be clear that Robinson's interpretation that the Alphane moon is a sort of mirror image of Earth, "a satiric microcosm of the world at large" (Robinson 73) fails to grasp the opposition between the two worlds, one where purportedly sane people struggle for power (even in the marital context), the other where the alleged madmen are able to cooperate.

Once Mary is diagnosed as depressive, she is not humiliated and discriminated (as she would surely be on Earth), but becomes part of one of the clans, that of the Deps. Even Chuck, who is diagnosed normal, admits that "suicidal impulses had motivated him, and after that hostile, murderous impulses towards [Mary]" (203). Being normal is not a matter of "complete difference," one that may justify inequality, discrimination, dispossession or exploitation (like the seizing of Alpha III M2, somewhat legitimized by a psychologist); it is, in Chuck's words, just a matter of *degree*, and "[w]hat a slight degree it was" (203). No wonder then if Chuck, having to settle on the Alphane moon, plans to found a new clan once he is diagnosed as normal, that of the Norms, which will live in a new settlement called Thomas Jeffersonburg (199).

The name of the Norm settlement to be is revealing, from a political point of view, and reminds us that a biographical reading of the novel may hinder our understanding of the political apologue it contains (including, among other things, memorable scenes of marital disharmony).

To summarize these three novels we should focus on mental disorders again. If the multiple point of view technique allows for a fragmented image of the koinos kosmos, which in itself fosters ontological uncertainty, as we have seen, it is evident that the insertion of mentally deranged characters among the narrative foci allows Dick to conjure up highly twisted worlds, such as Manfred's one, invaded by *gubbish*, or the apocalyptic world hallucinated by Bruno Bluthgeld, or the strange perspectives that the members of the Alphane moon clans (lunatics, after all, because Luna is indisputably a moon) project. Seeing the world from the point of view of madmen and -women, however, may be a way to understand that we all are madmen and -women, at least to a certain degree; that the borderline between sanity and insanity is rather thin and difficult to locate, notwithstanding the pronouncements of psychiatric (or political) authorities.

Dick was well aware of this. One day, while driving with his daughters to visit Anne, who was residing in the locked ward of Langley-Porter Clinic at Berkeley, he said he was going to talk with the doctors, and added "I'm sure they're going to tell me that I'm the one who should be in there, not your mother" (Sutin 124). If we want to read *Clans* on the basis of biography, we should keep also this in mind.

Surely the issue of mental disease is one that ties all these novels together. Dick somewhat minimized it as a transitory interest while talking about *Clans* in 1981, when he said that "the world of the psychotic is no longer of any interest to me" (Rickman 1988, 152); yet this is a powerful intertextual bridge among *Clans, Martian Time-Slip* and *Bloodmoney*. But there is another common theme, suggested by Dick himself when he says that *Clans* is "[t]he story of the survival value of various forms of psychosis" and then asks "[d]id they have any utilitarian utility?" (Rickman 1988, 153). According to Dick they did, and the proof that psychoses may be useful is the fact that, at least "in other cultures" (including those Dick conjured up), psychotics may work together — and, to quote Gabriel Baines, one of the members of the clans delegation, "if we can work together *we are not sick*" (134). Working or living together is the other important issue of these three novels: not just because the multi-foci technique allows Dick to render the complexities of a maze of individual lives seen as a web of human relations, but because salvation and community go hand in hand in these novels. Manfred may escape the dire Am-Web building which looms large on his future by joining the Bleekmen, who are presented as his friends in his final apparition; Walt Dangerfield is saved by establishing a two-way relation (a human bondage, we might say, using the title of the Somerset Maugham novel he reads to his listeners) with Dr. Stockstill, thus rejoining the human community; Chuck and Mary can save their marriage moving to Alpha III M2 and joining the local clans (Chuck, as we have seen, goes one step beyond and founds a new clan).

Besides, all this may have its roots in Dick's own life. At the end of *Bloodmoney*, Bonny Keller, Andrew Gill and Stuart McConchie leave the isolated West Marin community and get back to San Francisco, which is definitely not as bad as the survivors in the countryside thought: "We heard the awful stories, — muses Bonny — that it was only ruins, with predators creeping about, derelicts and opportunists and nappers, the dregs of what it had once been ... and we had fled from that too, before the war. We had already become too afraid to live here" (288). Is this the ending of a post-nuclear holocaust sf novel, or a meditation on what pushed millions of Americans to abandon the residential areas in city centers and move to the suburbs? The opposition of alienated individuals vs. cooperative community may then have also a socioeconomic and historical dimension, which is undoubtedly developed in different fashions in the three novels that we have discussed.

Chapter 5

Time Travels and Historical Manipulation: *The Simulacra, Now Wait for Last Year* and *The Penultimate Truth*

"Time present and time past
Are both perhaps present in time future,
And time future contained in time past."
T.S. Eliot

This chapter deals with three novels written in 1963–64 which have generally been considered as minor works, compared to those we have discussed in the previous chapter or will discuss in the next two. Dick himself plus some commentators might disagree, yet it is true that these three works have received scant critical attention so far, compared to those of the first Plateau period and the final trilogy (with the exception of *The Divine Invasion*). Besides, Butler considers *The Simulacra* a book which lacks coherence (Butler 2007, 66), while Palmer objects to how Dick challenges "the reader's capacity for belief" in that novel, in a game where the author is "embroiled, risking disorientation, if not humiliation" (Palmer 234). As for *Now Wait for Last Year* and *The Penultimate Truth*, these novels rank higher in Butler's appreciation, but other interpreters mention them occasionally and never deemed them worth a sustained and detailed critical examination: Warrick just mentions *Penultimate* and *Wait*, while she deems *Simulacra* worth discussing as a sort of prequel to *Bloodmoney* (Warrick 88–93). Palmer finds "the manufacture of the news" in *Simulacra* worth discussing (Palmer 20–1), but only hints at the *Wait* in a few pages. The only critic who has covered all the three novels so far is Robinson, who considers *Wait* underrated (Robinson 80), *Penultimate* flawed in the second part (Robinson 73) and *Simulacra* "one of Dick's best books ... but ... seriously flawed" because of "extravagant inclusion": there is just too much in it (Robinson 72).

Even Dick thought that *Simulacra* was somewhat overloaded, as its different plots of do not hang together: he told Rickman he had tried to draw a chart of the plotlines "to see if by any chance it all cohered," but had to admit that some characters "just don't have any relation with some of the other people in that group" (Rickman 1988, 152). Yet he thought that this was not necessarily a fault, because heterogeneity and multiplicity were to him a form of richness: "[m]y idea is to put as much into the book as I can put in. In other words I want to give the reader as much as I can give him" (Rickman, 1988, 152). Suvin and Robinson might undoubtedly object that sometimes what Dick can put in a novel is simply too much, but I wonder whether measuring Dick's novels based on some criterion or rule of classical elegance and simplicity is an acceptable critical move. I cannot see why the proliferating imagination of a novelist like Thomas Pynchon is praised by interpreters as an impressive example of postmodernist complexity, while it should be a fault in Dick's novels.

Besides, there may be a less evident form of coherence in *Simulacra*: in my first critical attempt I tried to apply to this novel the same fourfold scheme of fictional levels that I have used in the previous discussion of *The Cosmic Puppets, Time Out of Joint* and *The Man in the High Castle* (Rossi "Fourfold Symmetry"); the scheme worked quite well when applied to *The Penultimate Truth*, as we shall see, but was not satisfactory when I used it to analyze *Simulacra*. It is difficult to say that there are two or more alternate worlds in that novel, so I had to shift to a diachronic opposition, different from the synchronic alternance I had found in *Puppets* and *High Castle*. The two poles of that antithesis should have been on the one hand the scientifically and technologically managed political system we are presented based on at the beginning of the novel, based on the dual *Ge/Be* communication system (with a future society divided into two castes, those who know certain political secrets — the *Ge*, the ruling elite — and those who do not — the *Be*, the ruled masses), plus the TV charisma of Nicole Thibodeaux which supports the power system (that also includes an android president); on the other hand, the destruction of social structures (and oppositions) which takes place at the end of the novel, when we have discovered that all the political leaders (android and human) were simulacra, and the USEA are ravaged by civil war (Rossi "Fourfold Symmetry," 409–11). My hypothesis was that the whole novel is articulated along a diachronic opposition: the series of events which leads from the initial state of relative order and functionality to the final state of mayhem and destructuration is an entropic process leading from the primary to the secondary text, and it coincides with the very plot of the novel.

I have also attempted a more detailed discussion of *The Simulacra* as a peculiar sort of disaster novel, not a natural disaster like many other famous science-fiction texts (especially in the British tradition, from Wyndham's *The Day of the Triffids*, to John Christopher's *The Death of Grass* up to Ballard's catastrophic tetralogy of the 1960s), but a *political* disaster, which brings the future USA (or better USEA) depicted in the novel to civil war and nuclear destruction (Rossi, "The Great National Disaster").

The novel could then be read as another chapter of the American jeremiad. All in all, Dick's vision of the future United States of Europe and America (West Germany has been admitted to the Union), ruled by an android president whose forever young and attractive dark-haired wife is the real charismatic figure, while Washington cabals ruthlessly struggle for real power, was a way to poke fun at the Kennedy administration and its myth of a new Frontier. This novel — published in 1964 but written in the summer of 1963, well before the Dallas assassination — is indeed deeply rooted in the historical moment Dick found himself in. Once civil war breaks loose one of the characters muses on the rampaging destruction: "The destruction, the great national disaster, was still there. That was the terrible thing about civil war; no matter how it came out it was still bad. Still a catastrophe. And for everyone" (216). The reference to the historical civil war should not surprise us, because Dick wrote this novel during the Civil War centenary (1961–1965); unmistakable traces of that event can also be found in *We Can Build You* (Ch. 6).

Besides, reference to the hottest political issues in the early 1960s abound in this novel. Dick's anamorphic rendering of the Civil War (triggered by an attempt to change history by means of a time machine, helping Nazi Germany to win the war in exchange for the life of the Jews in concentration camps) creates a short circuit between racism and Nazism, between the limits of American democracy and the manipulation of mass unconscious, between Goebbels' scientifically managed propaganda and PR in the age of TV politics; and, last but not least, it connects the past of the United States with its imminent future. *The Simulacra* was published in 1964; can one pretend not to foresee the Watts race riot that would blow up just a year later? The racist bombing in Birmingham, Alabama, had occurred in September 1963; Vietnam was raging, year after year, sending more and more images of destruction to the screens of American TV sets; those were, to quote Todd Gitlin's history of the sixties, years of discord. Before the ghettos of major U.S. metropolises blew up, before Vietnam became a national emergency, before political figures such as Malcom X, Martin Luther King, Robert Kennedy were slaughtered, before Chicago and four dead students in Ohio, before the conspiracies and counter-conspiracies of the Nixon era, Dick perceived the oncoming destruction, the great national disaster ahead.

The political aspect is also quite important in *The Penultimate Truth*, completed in March 1964: Andrew Butler summarized this novel as "Cold War paranoia at its height" (Butler 2007, 78) and it is a felicitous description. Though we tend to associate Cold War to the 1950s, we should not forget that the confrontation between the two superpowers who had won World War II lasted till 1989; besides, the Cuban Missile Crisis and the building of the Berlin Wall were recent events. The future world depicted in *Penultimate* is divided in two different realities by the ground line which separates the world of the *tankers* from that of the *Yance-men*: the former are the vast majority of U.S. citizens who live underground because they believe that an apocalyptic nuclear/biological warfare is raging on the uninhabitable surface; the latter is the elite of PR professionals which live in vast luxurious country demesnes, because the war actually ended years before and the surface has been reclaimed by the military-political ruling class. The dividing line structures all the text with a binary opposition which gives it a rather symmetrical structure (Rossi "Fourfold Symmetry")[1]:

Table 5.1

Fictional levels	*"Real" (historical) levels*	
PRIMARY TEXT: underground (morlocks)* Yancy, the charismatic President, and the war are real; Americans are dispossessed due to the war	ZERO TEXT (1) history is a faithful and verifiable narrative of reality in its objective progress Cold War is an objective, undisputable menace	*"Accepted" levels*
SECONDARY TEXT: surface (ehloi) Yancy is a simulacrum; the war is a mass media simulation. Americans are exploited by the *Yance-men*, who are ultimately in cahoots with the Eastern Bloc	ZERO TEXT (2) history is a technically reproducible product, a regulative device of textual practises, the instrument of governments and cliques Cold War is a power system which legitimizes business, control, repression, etc.	*Alternative levels*

*Here it is necessary to indicate the textual references to H.G. Wells' *The Time Machine* which are quite important in shaping the narrative fictional levels and the topography of *The Penultimate Truth*; Dick inverted Wells' opposition between the morlocks — the subhuman and predatory descendants of the working class — living and proliferating underground, and the ehloi — the effete offspring of the upper and middle classes — who graze on the garden-like surface, waiting to be hunted by the morlocks. The inversion turns the lower classes in their underground shelters into powerless subjects, exploited and cheated by the greedy and cynical inhabitants of the georgic surface.

The issue of history-manufacturing, embodied in the activity of Gottlieb Fischer and the Yance-men (whose scientifically organized and "authorized" forging of historical evidences clearly derives from Orwell's *Nineteen Eighty-Four*) is coupled in this novel with the issue of one-way communication, of the modality of the circulation of historical discourses and consciousness in the U.S. mass-media civilization of the sixties, as already discussed in Boorstin's 1962 essay *The Image*, especially with reference to the 1960 presidential elections (51–3).[2] Here Dick issues (not in an overt way, but without the ambiguities of *The Man in the High Castle*) a remarkably negative judgment on America: his deconstruction of the mass-media circulation of discourse ends up with the bitter awareness that all the government tells people is just a lie, or better, an irredeemably penultimate truth. The U.S. political system is called in doubt well before the Watergate scandal: Cold War is an useful threat which may scare Americans and force them to accept whatever is convenient to the industrial-military complex.

Also the third novel of the trio, *Now Wait for Last Year*, has a strong political content, though it does not seem to be directly related to the current U.S. affairs of 1963, the year it was written; it was completed by the beginning of December, not many days after the assassination of John F. Kennedy, but no elements of the story seem to refer to the Dallas event. Yet Robinson proposed a historical reading of the novel by putting it in connection with the Vietnam war (Robinson 78–9); it is true that Wait depicts "the grim world of war economy in service of conquest" (Robinson 79), but the historical-political subtext is not contemporary, as the critic suggests. It actually refers to a then recent past, as Dick himself explained to Rickman:

> In some ways I was quite an admirer of Mussolini. He's the basis for Gino Molinari in *Now Wait for Last Year* .... I think Mussolini was a very, very great man. But the tragedy for Mussolini was he fell under Hitler's spell. But then so did many others. In a way you can't blame Mussolini for that ... [Rickman 1988, 142].

The plot of the novel — albeit set in 2055 — parallels the history of Italy and Germany during World War II, moving it to a sfnal future with aliens and space travel. In the novel Gino Molinari, aka The Mole, is the leader of Earth, unified by the UNO; the Mole is a charismatic (and rather authoritarian) ruler who allies himself with the first alien visitors, the Lilistarians, who are at war with another race, the insect-like Reegs. Molinari's choice, biased by the similarity between humans and the people from Lilistar (explained with Earth being an ancient colony of Lilistar which lost contact with the mother planet and then memory of its real origins), turns out to be a terrible mistake: the Lilistarians are cold and cruel imperialists, and the Reegs just want to defend themselves; moreover, notwithstanding what war propaganda tells people on Earth and Lilistar, the Reegs are winning the war. Molinari desperately tries to stave off Lilistar's increasing demands, and to negotiate a separate peace with the Reegs: a very dangerous situation, as the Lilistarians could easily liquidate Molinari, occupy Earth and then use humans as forced labor in their industries.

Though there is a striking similarity with the plight of Italy in the Second World War, Dick's reference to Mussolini is actually mixed up. It is true that the Duce made a fatal mistake when he decided to declare war on France and the British Empire in June 1940, having allied himself with Nazi Germany in May 1939; Mussolini mistakenly thought that after the defeat of France, the victory of Germany was a matter of days or weeks, and that Italy could reap much with little effort. The cynical comment of the Duce about his decision was: "I only need a few thousand dead so that I can sit at the peace conference as a man who has fought" (Badoglio 37, translation mine). When it was clear that the war would not be short and painless (especially after 1942, when things got remarkably worse for the Axis powers), Mussolini did not change his mind, and remained faithful to Nazi Germany and his disciple Adolph Hitler till his death in April 1945; the alliance with Germany only ended when the King, Victor Emanuel III, seeing that the war was lost, decided to switch sides in summer 1943; Mussolini was dismissed as prime minister (his formal role in the Italian state), and immediately arrested, while the King negotiated an armistice with the Allies, who had already landed in Sicily. The fact that Mussolini subsequently accepted to become the head of a Quisling government in Northern Italy (the Repubblica Sociale di Salò) proves that he never changed his mind about the alliance with the Nazi regime.[3]

However, the history of Italy in World War II offered Dick a complex and tragic historical background that allowed him to write a story of intrigue and tragedy, which also included a religious subtext where Molinari is a Christ-like figure ready to sacrifice his own life to save humankind (quite different from the historical Benito Mussolini). The novel however does not only deal with political issues, but with a troubled marriage, that of the protagonist, Eric Sweetscent, and his estranged wife Kathy (something which is quite common in Dick's oeuvre but is remarkably absent in the other two novels); with a deadly synthetic drug, JJ-180, which causes addiction and moves people back and forward in time; with nostalgia, as Kathy's job is to reproduce Washington as it was in 1935 for Eric's employer, Virgil Ackerman (who, like Leo Bulero in *Stigmata*, also produces JJ-180).[4]

One might criticize Dick's idea of a good ruler, either by showing how his perception of Mussolini was blurred (and not very detailed), or by pointing out that all the characters who belong to that category (Molinari in *Now Wait for Last Year*, Leo Bulero in *Stigmata*, Glen Runciter in *Ubik*, etc.) ultimately derive from Dick's substitute paternal figure, Herb Hollis (Sutin, 50–5), the owner and manager of the record and radio shop where the writer worked in the late 1940s. One thing is portraying the decent and humane employer that treated adolescent Phil like a son (something he badly needed in that phase of his life), another thing is believing that the owner of a multinational corporation or the autocratic ruler of a whole planet may behave as a father; paternalism is a dangerous option in politics. Darko Suvin criticized this when he wrote that this is "Dick's permanent ideological type that I would call 'the good ruler,' or finding the good in the bad ruler" and complained that this attitude is "illusory and misleading" (Suvin 2002, 377; cf. also 393). One cannot escape the feeling that this problem is connected with another issue Suvin raised in the same article, that is, Dick's "taboo on large industry, industrial workers, and the workings of high finance" (Suvin 2002, 392), because Dick lacked the experience of working in a big industry or corporation; he derived his depiction of leadership from his personal experience in a shop and a repair laboratory.

Yet what Dick lacked in direct experience of the powerful and their environment, he could compensate by reading history books; and we know that *historia* may be, as Cicero said, *magistra vitae*, but in postmodernist fiction it may be *magistra artium* as well. Much of the description of power struggle in *Simulacra* comes from the history books Dick had read while researching *The Man in the High Castle*. The history of Hitler's rise to power was surely in his mind when he conjured up the character of Bertold Goltz in *Simulacra*, a demagogue who apparently opposes the USEA government with his paramilitary organization The Sons of Job (clearly inspired by Fascist Blackshirts, or MVSN, and Nazi SA, or Brownshirts), but actually is part of a secret council that controls the First Lady, Nicole Thibodeaux (actually a young actress chosen because she resembles the long-dead First Lady).

However, the common element of these three novels which is really relevant to our discussion is not the issue of political power in general. What will be discussed in the remainder of this chapter is another key element that plays such an important role in the three novels that we are allowed to read them as variations on a theme, that of time travel; a narrative device which is another important application of the principle of ontological uncertainty, with conspicuous and so far uncharted political underpinnings. Creating hallucinations through drugs or virtual realities or mass-media simulation may alter the present; but Dick envisioned a future in which it is the past that may be changed.

Walter Benjamin's "Theses on the Philosophy of History" were written in early 1940, when the German philosopher and critic was in Vichy France, and could be handed over to the Gestapo because he was a German political refugee, a Marxist, and a Jew. When he wrote in his Theses that "[o]nly that historian will have the gift of fanning the spark of hope in the past who is firmly convinced that *even the dead* will not be safe from the enemy if he wins" (Benjamin 257), he was not just presenting his readers (of whose existence Benjamin was not sure, as the text was only published well after his death) with a striking hyperbole to make his abstract theoretical point; he was talking about his threatened life, which ended abruptly only a few months later. Benjamin was well aware that if there is a spark of hope in the past, the expectation of a Messianic regeneration to end the evils of history (Benjamin 256), that spark must be totally extinguished by those who aim at totalitarian power. Totalitarianism is not just a form of total control on the present; as another leftist writer knew, totalitarian power means also the ability to rewrite the past, because "who controls the past controls the future, who controls the present controls the past" (Orwell 197).

In these three novels the control of the past is not something that is achieved, as in *Nineteen Eighty-Four*, by retroactively altering the traces of the past, be they letters or newspapers, documents or records, as Winston Smith does in the Minitrue; Dick ups the ante by showing how the traditional science-fictional device of the time machine may be applied to a radical remaking of the past, so that neither the living nor the dead will be safe. This is what happens in the first novel of the trio in chronological order of completion, *The Simulacra*.

One of the narrative threads of this multiple-plot and -foci narrative is pivoted upon a daring hi-tech military project to be carried out by means of the von Lessinger time machine, which should enable the *Ge* élite to correct such historical mistakes as the extermination of the Jews in Nazi Germany, a stain on the otherwise spotless façade of the USEA. "Days of Barbarism –that was the sweet-talk for the Nazi period of the middle part of the previous century, now gone nearly a century but still vividly, if distortedly, recalled" (27); once Germany has been phagocyted by the U.S., the ruling élite feels that those (not presentable) days must be erased by changing the course of history, as we can infer from Nicole's conversation with the Prime Minister of Israel (44–50). The time machine brings Hermann Goering back from the past, so that the *Ges* may put a proposition to him (45): the USEA will exchange the military technology of 2050 which will allow the Nazi armies to defeat the Allies for the life of all the Jews imprisoned in the extermination camps (48). If the operation will succeed, the *Ge* will add a total control on the past to the total control on reality assured by the mass media technology (including the management of such simulacra as *der Alte* or Nicole).

The operation is opposed by Bertold Goltz, who is a Jew, because he thinks that the Nazis will exterminate the Jews anyway. One cannot negotiate the life of the Jews with the creators of Auschwitz, because "...the objective in the war for the Nazis was the extermination of World Jewry; it was not merely a by-product" (124). I have already argued that the *Ge* oligarchy in the novel cannot understand that the irrational element in Nazism is not a secondary aspect, but is deeply ingrained in Hitler's Reich, because the ruling class of the USEA has been infected from the start by inequalitarianism, authoritarianism, and an intellectual arrogance preventing it from perceiving the deep nature of Nazism, something Dick had already grasped in *The Man in the High Castle*. Bringing back Goering from the past will unleash a contagious form of insanity which will in turn unleash the final slaughter; this is Dick's own way to tell us (as he had already done in *High Castle*) that the winners of World War II have come to resemble the losers. Something quite similar to the "Nazi thuggery" Dick had described in *Castle* will wipe out the ruling élite of the USEA, so that the Nazi regime can be said to play the role of a distorted mirror image of the rulers of the futuristic America: both are enthralled by a morbid fascination with violence, murder, and death.

The *Ges* had been forewarned, though, by the inventor of the time machine: "Von Lessinger was right in his final summation: *no one should go near the Third Reich*. When you deal with psychotics you're drawn in; you become mentally ill yourself" (46). This warning might be read as something more than the recommendation to avoid a quarantined area of the past, infected by madness, violence and irrational destructive drives; it may be read as a warning about the incontrollable ontological uncertainty that may be unleashed once the past may be changed, thus altering the chains of causes and effects which tie it to the present — and the future. What is metaphorical in Orwell becomes literal here, as it often happens in science-fiction. When Wilder Pembroke, one of the commanders of the National Police suggests to bring an *Einsatzgruppe* (one of the Nazi commando) to the present, so that they can dispose of the management of a German corporation which is opposing the government (88), Dick seems to be suggesting us (even if Pembroke's plan will not be carried out) that the consequences of time (and history) manipulation may easily get out of control; destruction from a barbaric past may infect the purportedly civilized present. Nicole objects that "we're too modern, too civilized for massacres now" (88), but her words assume a bitterly ironic flavor when we think that a massacre ends the novel, and that the modern and civilized Americans of the USEA will use nuclear weapons against their fellow countrymen (209), in a final large-scale outburst of "Nazi thuggery."

Time travel and its paradoxes had been explored and exploited by other science-fiction writers before Dick; one might mention one of the most virtuosic examples of this sub-genre, Fritz Leiber's novelette *The Big Time* (1958) and other short stories included in the cycle of the Change Wars, where a temporal conflict rages between two factions, the Snakes and the Spiders; each faction strives to change the outcome of certain key historical events according to a plan which is so vast and complex that the soldiers never know what the ultimate purpose of their actions will be. In one of the stories in the cycle, "No Great Magic" (1963), a group of actors belonging to the Snakes is sent to Elizabethan England to perform *Macbeth* for Queen Elizabeth I, apparently to persuade her not to have Mary Stuart executed; but Elizabeth is then revealed to be a substitute of the real queen, who has been replaced several times by look-alikes sent by the Snakes or the Spiders. Such was the instability that the idea of time-travel used as a weapon could bring to, that Leiber felt he had to somewhat curb this principle of ontological uncertainty, by introducing the Law of the Conservation of Reality in *The Big Time*, which is so enunciated by one of the characters at the beginning of the novelette: "when the past is changed, the future changes barely enough to adjust, barely enough to admit the new data" (Leiber 23).[5]

Unsurprisingly, Dick's first novel to extensively deal with time travel and the manipulation of history (meaning *res gestae*, not *historia rerum gestarum*) was written in 1959 and published in 1960[6]; it is *Dr. Futurity*, a hastily written expansion of a 1954 novelette, "Time Pawn." The expansion was radical, because Dick told his literary agent in a letter that he had "put in ideas not already there" (*SL1* 51), and he may have been influenced by Leiber's novelette. The complicated plot is pivoted upon a 22nd-century physician who is kidnapped via time travel and brought to the 25th century, where his medical competence and tools (lost in the intervening centuries) may save a dying woman. Summarizing the rest of the plot would take too much time; suffice it to say that in the 25th-century society non-white people hold the power, and a political leader of Native American descent, Corith, wants to prevent the genocide of American Indians by getting back to the 16th century and killing Francis Drake during his expedition to Nova Albion in 1579.[7] This should discourage England from colonizing North America; but Corith is killed before he can hit Drake, and this is the effect of a counter-plot organized by another leader of 25th-century America, Stenog, who reached the place of Drake's landing before Corith thanks to the time-travel device. We might add that Drake himself might be Stenog or have been replaced by Stenog just to convey how baroque is the plot of this "neat but dull time paradox history" (Butler 2007, 47).

However, the idea of a direct manipulation of history resurfaced just four years later in *The Simulacra*, as we have seen, in the subplot to save the Jews by negotiating with the Nazi regime, though the plan fails in the end, and Goering must be executed (190). But something else ties *Simulacra* to

Futurity; like Corith and Stenog, Bertold Goltz uses time travel to play his game of political intrigue (156–9). He appears wherever and whenever he wants thanks to the Von Lessinger principle, achieving a sort of ubiquity.

> We ought to get back, Nicole thought, to Goltz's babyhood and destroy him. But Goltz had anticipated them. He was long since back there, at the time of his birth and onward into childhood. Guarding himself, training himself, crooning over his child-self; through the von Lessinger principle Bertold Goltz had become, in effect, his own parent. He was his own constant companion, his own Aristotle, for the initial fifteen years of his life, and for that reason the younger Goltz could not be surprised [158].

Actually Goltz is killed by Wilder Pembroke (198–9), who will in turn be killed by psi-empowered pianist Kongrosian in the final massacre, so what Goltz told Nicole in an earlier episode, "you have *nothing* under control" (157), applies to him too. Direct manipulation of past events via time travel is a metaphor of absolute, unrestrained power, also symbolized by the image of a man who is "his own parent"; such an absolute power should ensure total control (and an absolute patriarchal domination, one should add),[8] but the dream of total control (which is the aim of the USEA as the hyper-technological state) fails due to the irrational element of destruction (which is often self-destruction, as in Kongrosian's case) that cannot be eliminated or controlled. Goltz, the man who could not be surprised, the master game-player, is surprised in the end, and this is not just a cheap trick to entertain readers[9]; it is Dick's own way to suggest that no dream of total control can be successful. Thuggery leads to more thuggery, manipulation leads to more manipulation, and there is no law of the Conservation of Reality to protect Dickian characters from the consequences of their plots and conspiracies tampering with the past. Where ontological uncertainty reigns, the conservation of reality is only wishful thinking.

On the other hand, since it is unattractive power-hungry characters that dream of total control on space and time, the failure of their plans is good news to the little men who do not aim at absolute power, but at staying alive in the chaos unleashed by great power struggles. This happens in a counter-historical context in *The Man in the High Castle*, with Juliana, Frank, and Baynes/Wegener surviving the two conspiracies to kill general Tedeki and to liquidate Hawthorne Abendsen; it happens again in a science-fictional futuristic context with the group of little men and women watching the civil war raging on TV screens in the last pages of *Simulacra* (218–20). Maybe humankind will be ultimately wiped out and the Chuppers — the Neanderthalians who reappeared in Northern California possibly due to nuclear fallout — have good reasons to rejoice in the last pages of the novel; they are forefathers, but if *Homo sapiens* manages to commit a collective suicide, they may as well be our progeny, as Nat Flieger suggests (220). However, this is only a possibility, because "time will tell us which it is" (220): the little men could survive the massacre of their leaders and build a different society on the ruins of the USEA. The ending of *The Simulacra* is cautiously open.

Time manipulation returns in *Now Wait For Last Year*, surely not one of Dick's most linear novels. Completed four months after *The Simulacra*, it could have been written immediately before or after *The Three Stigmata of Palmer Eldritch*,[10] another novel where time-slips turn the plot into a diegetic maze, with a complex interplay of prolepses and analepses which are fictionally materialized by the sfnal device of the hallucinogenic drug Chew-Z, which also allows a ghostly form of time-travel (Ch. 7). The title itself of *Wait* tells us that the ordinary chronological succession has been radically subverted in this narrative.

Here we have a sfnal drug, JJ-180, which is first introduced in the third chapter by Christian Plout, a taxi driver (and drug dealer) in Tijuana. JJ-180 is a new, unknown drug, and the nonchalant attitude of Plout and his customers (including Kathy Sweetscent) to it reminds us of the reckless and enthusiastic experimentation with mind-altering drugs which was taking place in the early 1960s (one might mention Timothy Leary's and Richard Alpert's Harvard Psilocybin Project, which started in 1960). The drug in the novel is described as "tempogogic," inasmuch as "it alters your perception of time in particular" (33).

The experiences caused by JJ-180 could be travels to a more or less far future, or hallucinatory FSRs: I have in any case mapped them in the following table.

Table 5.2

JJ-180 experience	*Character involved*	*Pages*	*Chapter(s)*
Kathy disappears, but her experience with the drug is not described	Kathy Sweetscent, Chris Plout, Bruce Himmel, Marm Hastings	41–2	4
Kathy goes back to the United States in 1935	Kathy Sweetscent	95–103	7–8
Eric goes to 2065, ten years in the future, and is almost cheated by Don Festenburg	Eric Sweetscent	131–5	10
Eric travels to a future time, but then he discovers that it is an alternate future, the future of a different present where Molinari did not enter	Eric Sweetscent	146–170	11–1

(cont. next page)

Table 5.2 (continued)

into an alliance with the Lilistar Empire; he has troubles in getting back to his year (2055)2			
Eric goes to 2065 to check that his wife cannot recover from the brain-damaging effects of JJ-180	Eric Sweetscent	195–203	14

Much of the complication of the novel lies in the fact that readers are first told that JJ-180 causes hallucinations (which explains why Chris Plout cannot see the other people in the apartment after he has taken the drug, while the others can see him [41]), as the alteration of Kant's "categories of perception" (33) mentioned by one of the characters does not necessarily entail a modification of objective reality. But things change when we are shown what Kathy Sweetscent sees in her trip to the past in chapters 7 and 8, during her second experience with JJ-180, and a regressive movement back to the past starts (95–9) until the radio of the flying cab she is traveling on receives an old soap opera, *The Story of Mary Marlin* (99), broadcast from 1935 to 1952, and she understands that the drug actually brought her to the 1930s, so that it is not just a tempogogic drug, but a substance which allows time travel.

Having seen what Dick's treatment of time travel and the manipulation of history had been in *The Simulacra*, it is not surprising that Kathy immediately sees her trip to the past as an opportunity to manipulate history. She considers setting up a savings account with a small sum which would become huge by 2055; to call President Roosevelt and warn him about Pearl Harbor; to talk him out of building the atom bomb (100). Then she realizes that her future boss, Virgil Ackerman, the owner of the corporation she and Eric work for, is just a small boy in 1935, and this "gives [her] enormous power over him" (100). She considers sending information about the future that may make him richer and more powerful than he already is; she settles on sending Virgil a transistor taken from the cab via mail, enclosing this message in the envelope: "This is a radio part from the future, Virgil Ackerman. Show it to no one but save it until the early 1940s. Then take it to Westinghouse Corp. or to General Electric or any electronics (radio) firm. It will make you rich. I am Katherine Sweetscent. Remember me for this, later on" (102). Kathy thinks that this move will insure (or determine) Virgil's "economic future and therefore her own" (102); it is a crude attempt to alter the past to control the future and achieve economic power (because Virgil should reward Kathy for revealing the secret of a future technology ahead of its time).

It is not important that her attempt ultimately fails because when the effect of the drug is over everything which was brought from the future gets back there, so that Virgil received only an empty envelope in 1935. It is the impulse to manipulate the past in order to control the future that connects this sequence of the novel to *The Simulacra*.

The same should be said about Eric's trips to the future, also caused by JJ-180; but in his first, involuntary time-slip (he has been given the drug behind his back by his wife, who wishes to addict him too; the two are the typical Dickian couple torn by marital struggle) Eric does not try to manipulate the future. On the contrary, Dan Festenburg, one of the Mole's consultants, tries to manipulate him, by offering him an antidote to JJ-180 (the drug immediately addicts its users and has huge damaging effects on the brain) in exchange for something which remains unspecified because Eric rejects the deal (132). Festenburg tries to make Eric believe that now he is the UN Secretary by showing him a copy of *The Times* (133) and wearing a uniform similar to the one usually donned by Molinari; it is interesting that he tries to cheat Eric by using a fake copy of the same newspaper which was altered by Winston Smith in Orwell's *Nineteen Eighty-Four*.

Though we are not told what Festenburg wants from Eric, it is quite simple to understand that — since Eric comes from what Festenburg thinks *the* past — the ruthless and power-hungry consultant wants to manipulate that past through Eric, who is the surgeon assisting the Mole in his periodic health crises. Eric could easily kill Molinari, thus paving the way for Festenburg's rise to power.[11] Once again, by manipulating the past (even by proxy) one can control the present — and the future.

But in his third and longest JJ-180-induced travel, Eric discovers that the future that he has visited is not *his* future; in fact, it does not really stem from the events taking place in the 2055 that is his present. A history lesson delivered by an employee of Hazeltine Corporation (the firm, owned by Virgil Ackerman, which produces JJ-180) in the "future" (150) makes it clear that the past of the world Eric is visiting is not the one he has lived: The Mole signed "the Era of Common Understanding Protocols with the reegs" (150) and then Earth and the reegs defeated the Lilistar empire. Molinari was subsequently killed by a racist fanatic, because he let the reegs immigrate and settle on Terra (151).[12]

This explains one of the mysteries of the novel, the corpses that Molinari keeps in refrigerated caskets under the White House, which look exactly like the UN secretary (106): they are not robants, that is, android simulacra of the politician, but alter-egos of the Mole coming from parallel universes (152) that he reached thanks to JJ-180, as Willy K., an alien from Betelgeuse, tells Eric (154).[13] In Eric's final meeting with Molinari (183–6), the world leader explains that he is the third Mole, because the original Gino was killed and replaced by another, coming from a different alternate world; the second Mole dies at the end of chapter 12 due to a heart attack, and is replaced by the younger and healthier Molinari that Eric meets at the end of the novel. The Mole takes advantage of the fact that JJ-180 does not really transfer its users to their past or future, but to parallel universes with alternate histories; this enables the Mole to recruit his less successful alter-egos, the Molinaris who did not manage to become UN secretary or were ousted. Since the parallel universes are not synchronous, Molinari can always find some unsuccessful and younger version of himself that can replace him and resist the crushing psychophysical pressure put on him by the unfortunate alliance with Lilistar; moreover, by recruiting his failed alter-egos, the Mole does not risk altering the course of history in other universes.

Two remarks should be made now. First, the revelation that JJ-180 does not allow "vertical" time travel, but "horizontal" trips to alternate histories, eliminates the risk of those paradoxes that may easily be generated by visiting the future or the past (those paradoxes curbed by Leiber's Law of the Conservation of Reality); but this "stabilizing" effect is countered, in the architecture of the novel, by its strengthening characters' and readers' uncertainty about what is really going on — once again, we have ontological uncertainty, or the Game of the Rat. There are many coups de théâtre in this novel, which was aimed at the sf paperback market, after all; we should mention one connected with the dynamics of the apparent time-slips generated by the drug, that is, the moment when, in the middle of his second experience with JJ-180, Eric thinks to be back to his own year, 2055 (157), only to discover that he "failed to make it to his own time" (158); he is in 2056, after Gino Molinari has broken off his alliance with Lilistar. This twist in the tale reminds us of the difficulty to get back to one's own world in *Eye in the Sky* (Ch. 2), or the deceptive returns to normality experienced by Leo Bulero while under Chew-Z in *Stigmata* (Ch. 7); it is indeed part of Dick's game of the Rat. Uncertainty is then heightened by the discovery that the 2056 where Eric is stranded is not the future of *his* present.[14]

Second, if JJ-180 takes its users to alternate histories, not to their "real" future or past, Molinari, who has been using it for a long time, has thus acquired an extensive knowledge of a series of "what-ifs"; he can *see* — not just conjecture — what the consequences might be of certain choices he or others made or will make, as if he was shown the materialization of those thought experiments so often practiced by historians. Visiting the alternate histories of universes where his alter-ego failed, for example, warned him about the negative consequences of his decisions. Molinari cannot change the past or foretell his future, but he may figure what the right course of action should be based on the alternate histories he visits. Though he is no time-traveling superman like Bertolt Goltz in *Simulacra*, his abnormally wide knowledge of historical possibilities allows him a certain power of "indirect foreknowledge," so that he may tell Eric "I had it all worked out. Nothing by accident" (183).

The Mole's ability to access other worlds differentiates him from Goltz and makes him similar to Palmer Eldritch; his ability to predict future events and prepare plans in advance can also be found both in Goltz and in Eldritch, but while Goltz and Eldritch fail to prevent their assassination, Molinari manages to stave off crises and to thwart Lilistar's attempts to totally subjugate Earth. It is not simply a matter of sloppy writing (how could Goltz miss Pembroke's raid if he had already dodged countless attempt to liquidate him?) or fatalism (Eldritch seems to have resigned to his death in his last conversation with Barney): the destiny of those two characters is determined by a moral judgment. Eldritch and Goltz ultimately fail because Dick sees them as villains, while Molinari, with all his faults, is a positive character. Suvin's mistrust of Dick's "good rulers" is understandable, but such figures exist in this and other novels that we are going to read (*Ubik*, *Sigmata*, but also *Flow My Tears, The Policeman Said*) and must be interpreted as such.

Dick actually saw Molinari as a mythical figure; when he compares his troubles to Eric's, he uses a meaningful image: "One of us ... suffering unbearably on the private level, hidden from the public, small and unimportant. The other suffering in the grand Roman public manner, like a speared and dying god.... The microcosm and the macro" (51). The "small and unimportant individual" is Eric with his marital agony — the typical Dickian little man; while the other is Molinari, ruler of Earth, suffering from a heart condition (which may seem bogus but ultimately kills him in chapter 12). The hint at a speared and dying god is explained later in the novel, when Eric meets himself in his second JJ-180 experience (actually his alter-ego in an alternate universe), and his 2056 counterpart says "Molinari is Arthur with the spear wound in his side" (168), thus equating the Mole with the archetypal good king of the Arthurian legends.

This is not enough to say that *Wait* is a rewriting of the Parsifal/Perceval legend, though some elements could be read as hinting at that legend: Eric is a sort of not-very-competent Parsifal (he is a doctor, hence a healer, and Parsifal's aim is to heal the dying king) looking for the grail that may cure he and his wife (the antidote) and the truth that may explain the mystery of the corpses in cryogenic suspension under the White House; Freneksy could be an avatar of Klingsor, the evil enemy of Amfortas (the equivalent of Arthur in Wagner's *Parsifal*, an opera that Dick was surely familiar with); Molinari's replacement by his younger selves after his death(s) may be a science-fictional anamorphic image of the symbolism of death and regeneration which underpins the Arthurian legend, especially in the part about Parsifal/Perceval and the quest for the grail, according to the anthropological interpretation made famous by Frazer's *The Golden Bough*.

Though *The Three Stigmata of Palmer Eldritch* will be analyzed in Chapter 7, a comparison between a scene in *Wait* and another in *Stigmata* may help us to understand a fundamental difference between the Mole and Palmer Eldritch. The similarities between these two scenes seem to have escaped commentators so far, but they are blatant. In Chapter 4 of *Wait* (46–51) Eric is forced to live again an unpleasant scene of his marriage with Kathy; it is a sort of mental time-slip which brings him back to the moment when his wife deliberately erased one of the tapes in his collection to set up a particularly nasty form of emotional blackmail. Unlike the other time-slips we have found in this novel, this one is not produced by JJ-180, neither it is caused by some psi-power that the Mole may be endowed with (Dick takes care to rule out this explanation [46]); it seems to be simply triggered by Molinari's sheer will-power, and his deep understanding of Eric's personality.

This scene, focused on marital struggle, is quite similar to what happens to Barney Mayerson, one of the main characters in *Stigmata*, once he takes Chew-Z in chapter 10 (150–7): the drug brings him back to two episodes of his past, a quarrel with his wife Emily (which Barney has divorced, though he regrets this decision) and a meeting with Emily and her new husband Richard Hnatt. That the latter episode is placed in the past is evident inasmuch as Barney wakes up in Roni Fugate's apartment (153), the same scene described at the beginning of the novel (7); Dick even repeated Roni's description almost verbatim ("He saw an unfamiliar girl who slept on, breathing lightly through her mouth, her hair a tumble of cottonlike white, shoulders bare and smooth" [153]).

In both novels the protagonist is brought back to his past. But the attitude of the two characters who supervise this time-slip (or materialized analepsis) in each novel are quite different. The Mole wants to know the reason why Eric almost committed suicide in a critical moment of his life, the quarrel which is then lived again under Molinari's control (45–6). He does not want to change Eric's past, nor wants Eric to change his own past. He is much like a self-taught psychoanalyst: while Eric relives his painful confrontation with his wife, Molinari comments on it, sympathizing with Eric in a crucial moment (49). He subsequently analyses Eric's and Kathy's behavior, and then suggests a possible therapy: a new job. "How would you like to be attached to my staff? ... You wouldn't be running into her all the time. This might be a beginning. A start toward prying the two of you apart" (51).

On the other hand, when Palmer Eldritch intervenes in Barney Mayerson's disheartening repetition of past experiences, his attitude is quite different.

When Barney fails to interact with his wife and expresses once again his discontent with her and her job (vase-making), Eldritch chides him: "Mayerson, you're using your time badly. You're doing nothing but repeating the past. What's the use of my selling you Chew-Z? ... I'll give you ten more minutes ... So you better figure out very damn fast what you want and if you understand anything finally" (152).

In the second part of Barney's experience with Chew-Z he goes to Emily and Richard Hnatt's apartment, and pointlessly tries to persuade her to divorce Richard and remarry him. When this attempt fails, Eldritch reappears, superimposing his features on Richard's face (and hand), and he coaxes Barney into trying again, though he cannot persuade Emily to get back to her former husband. What Eldritch says at the end of the experience, when the effects of Chew-Z are almost over, is revealing: "Don't give up ... Remember: this is only the initial time you've made use of Chew-Z; you'll have other times later. You can keep chipping away until eventually you get it" (157).

Eldritch — unlike Molinari — wants Barney to believe that the past can be changed. Molinari's approach to the matter is quite different, and it is expressed in a straightforward fashion in his last meeting with Eric: "Has using that time-travel drug scrambled your wits, you don't know you've got only one tiny life and that lies ahead of you, not sideways or back? Are you waiting for last year to come by again or something?" (186). The importance of these words is underscored by the fact that they provide the title to the novel (one which does not seem to have had a working title, so that *Now Wait for Last Year* should be Dick's own choice); and its main argument is that the dreams of omnipotence fostered by Golden Age science-fiction, including the idea of changing the past to improve the present, are sterile forms of wish-fulfillment, which somewhat betray science-fiction's mission to envision a possible, viable, sustainable future.

Molinari tries to persuade Eric to live his own life by looking at the future (not regretting his childhood, like Virgil Ackerman, whose yearning for the past is embodied in Wash-35, the maniacally painstaking reproduction of Washington as it was in 1935 [27-9]), and this is more or less confirmed by the final opinion of the cab whose advice has been asked by Eric; after describing his plight, the possibility to remain with Kathy even if there is no hope of recovery for her, or to leave her because staying "would mean no other life for [him] beyond caring for her" (205), the cab answers that it would stay with her. "To abandon her would be to say, I can't endure reality as such. I have to have uniquely special easier conditions" (205). The final message of the novel is that one has to face the difficulties of life, whatever they are, not to escape them, possibly helped by drugs or dreams of a different past leading to a different and more pleasant present, one under "uniquely special easier conditions."

Behind this scene we may see Dick's marital crisis with Anne, his third wife. That he could not follow the advice of the cab and eventually divorced Anne in 1966 is only one of the many contradictions of a most contradictory man and artist. What is important for us readers and commentators is the fact that the dream of changing the past is always fostered by negative characters, such as Palmer Eldritch; hence, time travel and the direct manipulation of the past to gain something or to strengthen one's power is a typical activity of Dick's villains, from Goltz to the USEA government, to David Lantano.

We cannot say that Lantano is one of the main characters in *The Penultimate Truth*. In this novel the multi-foci and multi-plot narrative approach is streamlined, so that there are only two main points of view, each belonging to one of the two coexisting worlds: Nicholas St James is the one of the tankers who live underground, while Joseph Adams belongs to the yance-men who have sequestered the surface. We never see through Lantano's eyes, and we never partake his inner monologue; yet he is a more important character than previous interpreters (including myself) have realized so far.

Even a very perceptive reader like Robinson does not see Lantano as a key character, but as an interpretive nuisance, betraying a structural fault of the novel:

> The interesting setting that I have described as a political metaphor made literal [i.e., the two worlds of the underground and the surface], becomes in the second half of the novel nothing more than the background for an adventure concerning the character of David Lantano, a Cherokee Indian chief who (like Goerring [*sic!*] in *The Simulacra*) has been scooped out of the past by a time machine [Robinson 72–3].

Suvin, quoted by Robinson, backs up this judgment as he sees the plot in the second half of the novel, pivoted upon Lantano and his intrigue, as a Van Vogtian residual which mars "one of Dick's potentially most interesting books" (Suvin 1975, 17).

The first part of the novel is the one that depicts the system of mass media simulation allowing the ruling elites to control the majority of the population, forced to live underground and build combat robots (the "leadies") that are actually used as servants by the upper classes living in their vast surface demesnes. It is a rather transparent anamorphic image of a system of social classes: the exploited lower classes under the exploiting upper classes is the materialization of a traditional metaphor born in sociological analyses. According to Suvin and Robinson, Dick had set up a promising background for his novel, but when he focused on Lantano and his machinations we have no more than an adventure story — possibly something whose only purpose is to entertain readers with the usual fireworks of turn-ups for the book.

But Lantano becomes a much more interesting figure if we connect him with the direct manipulation of past events, one of Dick's strategies to foster ontological uncertainty, which goes beyond Orwell — who contented himself with the manipulation of the records and traces of past events carried out in the Ministry of Truth. That kind of manipulation is introduced in the first half of *The Penultimate Truth*, when Stanton Brose, the Minister of the Interior,[15] hatches a plot to incriminate a wealthy and powerful builder, Louis Runcible, suspected of tipping the people in the underground shelters off about the end of the war on the surface (43–50). Runcible does not do this for humanitarian reasons; he simply wants to have more people escaping from the *ant-tanks* so that the demand for housing keeps increasing. On the other hand, Stanton Brose and the ruling class want to keep as many *tankers* underground as possible, so that they can preserve their privileges, including their vast rural demesnes. If, as Robinson seems to suggest, this novel is an example of the triumph of capitalism (this being the title of the chapter of his monograph which also deals with *The Penultimate Truth*), the political competition between different sectors of a capitalistic economy is not such an indefensible concept.

Brose's strategy to have Runcible indicted and then convicted includes the manipulation of the past by means of a time machine. There is a Precious Relics Ordinance (48) which compels the owners of the demesnes or any other portion of the Earth's surface to hand in any major archaeological find to the government; those who do not comply may be arrested and their possessions requisitioned. So Brose plans to send some forged skulls and weapons, some of them Terran, some of them non–Terran (92–3), six hundred years back to the past; these would be evidence that aliens landed on Earth centuries before Europeans settled in North America, fought against the natives and were forced to leave the planet. The artifacts include skulls that should belong to more evolved humanoids than Homo sapiens (93) and technologically advanced weapons. Having been sent to the past, the artifacts would not just look six hundred years old; they would "*be* six hundred years old" (95) when Runcible will find them in the land he has purchased to build new residential units, and would easily pass the carbon-14 test.

This plot has been overlooked by Robinson and Suvin, yet I think here Dick goes well beyond what we may find in Orwell. *Nineteen Eighty-Four* shows the scientifically managed production of fake evidence of historical events, the manipulation of traces. The equivalent of this process in Dick's novel are the two fake documentaries shot by Gottlieb Fischer (Chapter 10), the forerunner of the Yance-men: they deal with World War II, and present two reconstructions of how things really went during that war that support the propaganda of the Wes-Dem (USA and its Western Allies) and Pac-Peop (USSR and the Warsaw Pact). The two versions of the documentary are called

A and B respectively; the former rehabilitates Hitler (72) and "proves" that Franklin Delano Roosevelt was "a Communist agent. Under Party discipline" (75); the latter "proves" that "the Allies [held] back the Normandy landings for at least a year so that Germany [could] use all her armies on the Eastern Front to defeat Russia" (78). Both versions are aimed at discrediting the enemy of each bloc, and both are as bogus as the issues of *The Times* that Winston Smith rewrites in Orwell's novel.

But the time scoop in *The Penultimate Truth* does not produce fake evidence; it produces *authenticity*—something that seems to have escaped the attention of postmodern-oriented critics (e.g., many of those who contributed to the second special issue of *Science-Fiction Studies* on Dick in 1988).[16] It allows the *direct* manipulation of the past, which is the ultimate form of power and control. Joseph Adams immediately understands this, once Brose has explained his plan.

> We could shoot back scientific data, constructs of unfathomable value, to civilizations in the past — formulae for medicines ... we could be of infinite aid to former societies and peoples; just a few reference books translated into Latin and Greek or Old English ... we could head off wars, we could provide remedies that might halt the great plagues of the Middle Ages. We could communicate with Oppenheimer and Teller, persuade them not to develop the A-bomb and the H-bomb — a few film sequences of the war that we just lived through would do that. But no. It's to be for this, to concoct a fraud, one implement in a series of implements by which Stanton Brose gains more personal power [96].

Adams imagines a good use of the time scoop as opposed to Brose's ethically questionable machination, yet one might ask what the "humanitarian" manipulation of the past might bring to. Adam's dream of benevolent omnipotence may be as short-sighted as Brose's small-scale plot to frame Runcible; in any case, it resembles the apparently well-meaning tampering with the past of the USEA government in *The Simulacra*, or Palmer Eldritch's dubious encouraging Barney Mayerson to relive and possibly correct his own past. Unlike Molinari, who looks for a sustainable future among several more or less dangerous alternatives, here we have the dream to delete an unpleasant past and replace it with something more palatable to our sensibility — a power dream nonetheless.

And, in the oldest tradition of science-fiction, a well-meaning scientific discovery generates a monster: David Lantano. He is introduced in Chapter 7, after about ¼ of the story has been told. He is one of the Yance-men, like Joseph Adams, a PR professional in charge of writing the speeches of the android president, Talbot Yancy, which are broadcast via coaxial cable to the underground shelters, being the main propaganda tool of the invisible ruling elite.

Since his first apparition, Lantano is a puzzling character. He is described as a young man of Mexican descent (56), and this should explain his dark skin; but after a few pages Lantano's dark complexion is partly explained as a radiation burn (59), the effect of reclaiming land for his demesne which is still polluted by nuclear fallout. Also his age is uncertain: at times he may seem young, or young and sick, but he may also look definitely old: "Time curled and poked at him, tinkered insidiously at the metabolism of his body. But — never totally overtook him. Never really *won*" (148). Lantano is a contradictory being; old and young, but also sick and healthy: "It was as if he oscillated; he swung into degeneration, into submission to the radioactivity with which he had, twelve hours a day, to live ... and then, as it ate him, he pulled himself back from the edge; he was recharged" (148). There is an enigma about Lantano (150), greater than the enigma about Goltz, possibly as big as the enigma about Palmer Eldritch.

Lantano's strangeness has something to do with time. Joseph Adams muses: "*Time .... It's as if a force that grips us all in a one-way path of power, a total power on its part, none on ours, had for him divided: he is moved by it and yet simultaneously, or perhaps alternately, he seizes it and grips it and then he moves on to suit his own needs*" (150). Lantano is actually a "collateral victim" of the time scoop: a 15th-century Cherokee chief accidentally kidnapped from his time by Brose's scoop, and brought forward to 2025. There is no doubt that Dick was recycling his old idea of the time-traveling Native American chief Corith we found in *Dr. Futurity*, but here Lantano is not just a would-be (and failed) avenger of the oppressed, he is also an ambiguous manipulative figure like Goltz in *The Simulacra*. Lantano is revealed to have taken part in Gottlieb Fischer's making of the two fake documentaries on World War II: he played the part of general Dwight D. Eisenhower (175), and was then the model on which the face of Talbot Yancy, the artificial president, was molded. The connection between Eisenhower and Yancy is not surprising inasmuch as *The Penultimate Truth* is a remarkably composite novel, drawing from three different short stories, one of which, "The Mold of Yancy" (1955) proposed the idea of a bogus president and poked fun at the then current U.S. president whose election owed much to the efforts of advertising agencies, with the then innovative use of television ads (also used by his contender Adlai Stevenson); Dick himself acknowledged that Yancy was based on president Eisenhower (*CS4* 376).

The resemblance between Lantano and Yancy allows Dick to put another twist in his tale, because the time-traveling Cherokee plans to replace the android president, and start "visiting representative ant tanks" (182), like Winston Churchill did in World War II. The fake president would then be replaced by a *real* fake president, an actor replacing a machine. This is not a problem for Lantano, as he has already declared that "[a]s a component in his makeup ... every world leader has had *some* fictional aspect. Especially during the last century" (161–2). Thanks to the direct manipulation of history by means of time travel, the USA of 2025 will be ruled by a Dwight D. Eisenhower looka-like, who is also a Native American chief— a most paradoxical situation, and a splendid example of Dick's corrosive deadpan humor.

However, Lantano is not just the most striking figure of Dick's satirical portrait of his own country. The novel may well be, as Butler said, "Cold War paranoia at its height," hence connected to Dick's production of the 1950s, but Lantano's time-traveling ability ties this novel to the most psychedelic works of the 1960s, such as *Stigmata*; Lantano is a toned down version of Palmer Eldritch, another ubiquitous and scheming arch-villain whose plot stretches across different times — and ages (the characters in the novel unsur-prisingly keep asking themselves and Lantano who or what he is, just like Barney Mayerson and others do in *Stigmata*). But the time scoop allows Dick to play those games with narrative time that we have already found in other major novels, such as *Martian Time-Slip, Now Wait for Last Year*, or *Ubik*. In this novel Lantano may utter this odd sentence: "You know who I am, Foote. Or rather, who I have been in the past, in 1982. And who I will be" (175). The present, the past and the future are all encompassed by Lantano's ubiq-uitous *I*, and this foreshadows the famous sentence we find in *Ubik*: "I am Ubik. Before the universe was, I am ... I am. I shall always be" (190).

Lantano as a semi-divine being, then, like other Dickian characters — be they evil like Palmer Eldritch, or good like Molinari? Lantano as another demiurge, a manipulative second-rate god like the ones we shall meet in Chap-ter 7? Or Lantano as one of the many embodiments we find in Dick's fiction of the ruthless, almost animal survival instinct or will to survive, which is easily readable as a derivative of the Nietzschean will to power? I do not think any of these interpretive lines can be discarded, but what I find more interesting is reading Lantano as a character which produces the sort of ontological uncer-tainty about what has been, not just about what is, which we have already found in the two other novels we have analyzed in this chapter. The narrative consequences of this condition make for the twisted, multi-layered, multi-dimensional structure of the plot of these and other novels by Dick, and may well explain much of their literary value. The radicalization of traditional nar-rative devices of science-fiction allowed Dick to build destructured narratives not so far from the not-wholly-consistent stories of postmodernist fiction writers, from Vonnegut to Pynchon.

But there is another political aspect that we should consider, one that Robinson does not seem to have taken into account when he distinguished (33) between inessential time travel accomplished by means of machines (in

Penultimate and *Simulacra*), and artistically productive "private cosmos" time travel (as in Wait)—misunderstanding what are the real effects of JJ-180. Regardless of its being machine- or drug-produced, time travel may be a way to achieve a sort of immortality, and this is what the will to survive demands; and longevity may be a form of class struggle, as Fredric Jameson suggested in his essay on immortality in George Bernard Shaw and Robert A. Heinlein (Jameson 1996). It is in the latter, a writer towards whom Dick had ambivalent feelings, that we find the apotheosis of an immortal *and* time-traveling hero, Lazarus Long, who is only immortal in *Methuselah's Children* (1941), but then also travels backwards in time at the end of *Time Enough for Love* (1973), where Lazarus has sexual intercourse with his mother, so that he is—like Goltz in *Simulacra*—his own parent; he subsequently reappears in *The Number of the Beast* (1980), *The Cat Who Walks Through Walls* (1985), and *To Sail Beyond the Sunset* (1987). According to Jameson, Lazarus assumes a paternal function (Jameson 1996, 337); but, as an alter-ego and ideological mouthpiece of the author, he is also a patriarchal figure. Lazarus Long's omnipresence and invulnerability is a form of omnipotence, and it undoubtedly stems from the dream of transcendence rooted in Golden Age science-fiction. It is just one of the paradoxes or time-slips of this not-always-linear genre that Dick's corrosive criticism of time-travel as an instrument of manipulation and total control—as represented by the three novels we have read—came well before Heinlein added the ability of time-travel to Lazarus Long's immortality.

However Dick's final achievement along this line of development is not to be found in one of his novels, but in one of his best short stories. Most of Dick's short fiction, as we know, was hastily produced in the 1950s, and it includes scores of stories whose literary value is rather small; Dick himself was well aware of this. But when his output decreased, in the 1960s and 1970s, it is difficult to deny that quality replaced quantity. Among the eleven stories Dick wrote and published after 1970 we have one of the bleakest yet most fascinating time paradoxes ever written, "A Little Something for Us Tempunauts" (1974) where Addison Doug, the commander of the first U.S. crew of time-traveling explorers, deliberately causes a fatal accident on re-entry, thus locking "an absolutely unyielding loop" (350), a closed train of events which will endlessly and circularly repeat itself for ever and ever (the loop includes the participation of the three tempunauts in their own solemn funeral [341–2]). This nightmarish destiny, which resembles the dire real situation of the group of characters in *A Maze of Death* (Ch. 7), is actually sought for by Addison as a form of immortality; not individual, but collective.

> He saw, in his head, himself in other parades too, and in the deaths of many. But really it was one death and one parade. Slow cars moving along the street in Dallas and with Dr. King as well ... He saw himself return

again and again, in his closed cycle of life, to the national mourning that he could not and they could not forget. He would be there; they would always be there; it would always be, and every one of them would return together again and again forever. To the place, the moment, they wanted to be. The event which meant the most to all of them.

This was his gift to them, the people, his country. He had bestowed upon the world a wonderful burden. The dreadful and weary miracle of eternal life [351–2].

If we do not forget that there is a dream of eternity in every empire (let us not forget that Dick was familiar with Hitler's idea of a Thousand Year Reich), this is one of the most provocative images of the American Empire — not the actual reality of the USA in any given time, but the myth of the nation. An imperial myth of power and eternity, materialized thanks to an original use of the old device of time travel whose political implications Dick had already explored in his novels of the 1960s.

Yet the dismal miracle of eternal life does not completely hide the particular times that this story powerfully evokes: the funerals of John F. Kennedy on November 25, 1963, and Martin Luther King on April 7, 1968 (to those we could add Robert Kennedy's funeral on June 8 of the same year). After the death of president Kennedy, the assassinations and funerals of the other two American leaders must have triggered a sense of déjà vu in Dick, which he rendered perfectly in his short story. It is then a final paradox that these works which depict the manipulation of the past through time travel, materializing Benjamin's fears "that even the dead will not be safe," are deeply rooted in the historical moment in which they were conceived, written, and published.

Chapter 6

The Android Cogito: *We Can Build You* and *Do Androids Dream of Electric Sheep?*

"Golem stories are all hard telling"
Gustáv Meyrink

In his synoptic analysis of Dick's major novels of the 1960s, Fredric Jameson underscored the importance of Descartes' ontological investigation for a better understanding of a key area in Dick's fictional world, that of individual consciousness, which in his opinion includes such major Dickian motifs as androids and simulacra, empathy vs. the lack thereof, technology, enemies, and the future (Jameson 2005, 379). Jameson argues that the problem of individual consciousness cannot be reduced to pop psychology: it must be dealt with on a philosophical level. Dick's doubts about identity (some of which have been presented in Chapter 2, while others will be discussed here and in the following chapters) are not far from the Cartesian doubt, which posited a *malin genie* ("evil dæmon or genie") which may cheat the inquiring mind of the philosopher by presenting its senses with a complete illusion of an external world — including other people — and an illusion of his own body. It is a rather Dickian situation of ontological uncertainty, even if it appeared in print in 1641 as *Meditations in First Philosophy*. Descartes solved the problem by positing the human mind as something which doubts, that is, thinks: a "thinking thing," or *res cogitans* (Descartes wrote his philosophical essays in Latin). You can doubt an external reality with all the people in it, you can even doubt your own body; but how can you doubt, while doubting, that there is something that is doubting, that is, thinking? That became the basis of Cartesian ontology.

Dick, according to Jameson, went one step beyond. He did that by putting artificial intelligence into the picture: once mental processes can be technologically reproduced, or simulated, "what emerges at length is what I will call the 'android cogito': I think, therefore I am an android" (Jameson 2005, 374). Jameson then focuses on the scenes in *Blade Runner* (Ricley Scott's celebrated 1982 film based on Dick's novel *Do Androids Dream of Electric Sheep?*) in which people are tested to check whether they are androids,[1] and suggests that "the external issue of testing" is reversed "into a permanent rift within self-consciousness itself" (Jameson 2005, 374): it is thus not coincidental if the discussions about *Blade Runner* moved from the tested people or replicants to the tester him- or itself, to understand "whether Rick Deckard ... might not be an android himself" (Jameson 2005, 374).

Jameson's argument is quite cogent inasmuch as Dick sees solipsism as a suspicious condition, bordering on insanity. Descartes' foundation of the knowing (and doubting) subject on itself would not be satisfactory for the author of "I Hope I Shall Arrive Soon" (1980), a short story based on what we might call a recreational use of virtual reality. The protagonist of the story, Victor Kemmings, unexpectedly regains consciousness during a ten-year-long interstellar journey. He should have traveled in cryosleep, as there is no space (nor other vital resources) on board the ship; since the ship's artificial intelligence cannot repair the malfunction, Kemmings is doomed to remain conscious but paralyzed. To protect his sanity, the AI replays Kemmings' memories to him, but they are not at all pleasant, and he finds himself in the same situation of Barney Mayerson under Chew-Z in *Stigmata* (Ch. 7), re-living a lifetime of failures and mistakes. The ship AI then asks Kemmings what he wants most, and since his greatest wish is that the trip is over and he may reach his destination, the AI constructs such a scenario for Kemmings and repeatedly plays it to him for the next ten years. When the ship finally arrives at its destination, Kemming cannot tell reality from virtual reality, and thinks that his arrival is no more than another simulation: he is clinically insane.

Whenever characters are isolated in a solipsistic situation where the world around them is no more than a backcloth, possibly something they themselves have created, the result is terror and ultimately madness — not the "creative" madness that we find in *Clans*, but reaching that dreadful condition in which "nothing ever happens" (*Time-Slip* 143) to the psychotic again: the Tomb World which so scared Manfred and Jack Bohlen (which reappears in the eighteenth chapter of *Do Androids Dream of Electric Sheep?*, when John R. Isidore plunges into it due to the shock at the androids' cruel behavior). Thinking alone makes me a thinking machine; an android, not a human being.

The "android cogito" is part of the ontological uncertainty which dominates Dick's fiction. The characters of his novels and short stories may think that someone is a real human being while s/he actually is an android (this already happens in Dick's first published novel, *Solar Lottery*, where a remotely controlled android pretending to be a human being, Keith Pellig, is built to escape the bodyguards of the Quizmaster); but — which is a more genuinely Dickian situation — they may discover that *they* are androids, robots, replicants, electric ants, like Olham in "Imposter," or Garson Poole in "The Electric Ant."[2] This particular form of ontological uncertainty will guide us in a reading of two novels, one of which is among the most famous Dick ever wrote, *Do Androids Dream of Electric Sheep?*, as it was turned into the film which made the writer really famous outside the sf ghetto, *Blade Runner*[3]; the other is not as famous, though I believe that it should be ranked among Dick's best literary achievements, *We Can Build You*.

We will start from the less famous work, because it should be read as an important moment in the definition of the issue of the android cogito (no wonder it was discussed by Jameson, who also connected it to *Androids*), which will find its full development in the celebrated story of replicant-hunting cum philosophical inquiry. To do this we have to invert the chronological order of publication. While *Androids* was completed in 1966 and published in 1968, *Build* was sent to Dick's agent in October 1962 and was probably written immediately after *The Man in the High Castle*, though it only found a publisher as a magazine novelette in 1969–70 (on *Amazing*, as "A. Lincoln, Simulacrum") and as a paperback novel in 1972. This ten-year delay tells us that *Build* had a troubled story, and was not easily accepted by publishers. Dick himself explains why:

> [*We Can Build You*] essentially was not designed by me as science fiction. That was one of my hybrid books.... That was a book that would bridge science fiction and mainstream. And that was supposed to be one of them. Where there'd be science fiction elements but there'd also be elements of a mainstream novel.
>
> And that was the main one. It would be a continuum from *The World Jones Made* to *We Can Build You* to *Confessions of a Crap Artist*, would form a[n] ... unbroken continuum, where there's no sharp delineation between the three. And so I was trying to make a continuum out of my two parallel streams of writing, my science fiction and my mainstream [Rickman 1988, 175].

One might wonder why Dick saw such a heterogeneous trio of novels as a continuum, yet if we read his comments on *Jones* it will be easier to make sense of what he told Rickman. "[In *Jones*] I tried to transfer some elements from my quality or literary novels ... when you read it over you find a little more character development, it's a little more sophisticated in terms of character development" (Rickman 1988, 114). Besides, in the last months of 1954, when Dick wrote *Jones*, aimed at the science-fiction market, he was devoting most of his energy to the composition of those realistic novels that should have allowed him to become a professional writer for respectable and better-paying publishers; as far as we know, he was working on *Mary and the Giant* when he completed *Jones*. Dick's idea that *Jones*— albeit far from satisfactory in terms of overall quality — may have more technical sophistication than *Solar Lottery* (Rickman 1988, 114) is not so outlandish, and may well explain why Dick linked it to a definitely ambitious novel like *Build* and to the only unambiguously realistic novel that he managed to publish in his lifetime, that is, *Confessions* (whose history is just as troubled, having been published 16 years after its completion).

If, as Dick told Rickman, the two parallel streams of his writing (the two genres he practiced) were science-fiction and mainstream (i.e., realism), *We Can Build You* is sandwiched between two pure specimens of the two genres: *The World Jones Made* has space travel, psi-powers, aliens, colonization of another planet, genetic engineering, a world government; *Confessions of a Crap Artist* is an ordinary story of ordinary people in Northern California in the late 1950s, told by a rather odd narrator, Jack Isidore, whose utter naivety (possibly explained by his being mentally retarded) allows Dick to give a particular (and remarkably effective) twist to his narrative. If a continuum unites the three texts, it is evident that *We Can Build You* must be a hybrid, a text which mixes some sfnal elements with the characterization, the more careful plotting and the stylistic quality of the realistic works; its hybrid nature could then explain the problems it encountered in finding a publisher.

According to Robinson, such a duality or heterogeneity can also be found in the plot itself of the novel: the first half is pivoted upon "the abilities of the simulacra," that is the two androids reproducing Edwin M. Stanton and Abraham Lincoln respectively, climaxing in the "illuminating argument between Lincoln and the big businessman [i.e., Sam K. Barrows] concerning the differences between man and an intelligent machine" (Robinson 105). But this plot is abandoned, the narrative "jumps tracks" and tells the story of Louis Rosen's self-destructive pursuit of Pris Frauenzimmer (aka Pristine Womankind) which ultimately brings him to madness and internment in an asylum. Robinson regrets that "[w]e never return to the story of the simulacra and the business battle over them" (Robinson 106); this judgment follows Suvin's reading of the novel as split in two parts, the Dickian beginning with androids and the Jungian ending with Pris (Suvin 1975, 14).

Robinson sees the shifting of the narrative as a sign that the novel is "broken-backed" (Robinson 105), like other minor (and failed) novels Dick published in the late sixties (it is compared to *The Crack in Space* and *The Unteleported Man*). The critic implicitly suggests that Dick moved from one plot to another because he was unable to fully develop the initial plot (Robinson 84–7), so that these works bespeak Dick's creative crisis in those years. Robinson then attempts a half-hearted defense of the novel saying that "the division into two parts [could be] a deliberate formal device that reinforces the preemptive strength of the second story-line," because "[m]adness preempts any other business at hand, no matter how interesting" (Robinson 106).

But philology contradicts this interpretation. Already Warrick noticed that, though published at the very end of the 1960s, *Build* had been written well before, "during the same year as *Martian-Time Slip*" (Warrick 65), and was concerned with schizophrenia, like its more prestigious and accomplished companion. It is then impossible to assess its value on the basis of its belonging to a period of creative sterility. Warrick also deems *Build* to be a minor work, but for a different reason: it is weak because it is a mainstream work, while Dick was a powerful science-fiction writer: "in [*Build*] the characters talk and talk, driven to make certain they have told all about schizophrenia" (Warrick 66).

While Warrick's placement of *Build* in the first plateau period of the early 1960s is undisputable, her reading of the novel as mainstream is highly questionable; in it we have androids, space travel (Sam K. Barrows, the reckless interplanetary realtor, plans to use the androids as artificial neighbors for families who settle on other planets [114–6], so that the settlers do not feel lonely), electronic Penfield organs that may control the moods and emotions of their users, and a futuristic USA where citizens may be sent to Federal asylums by the omnipotent Federal Bureau of Mental Health — which seems to have replaced the good old FBI (172) — if they fail to pass psychiatric tests; the workings of this repressive apparatus are described in several pages of the novel, especially when Louis fails his tests and is sent to the Kasanin Clinic in Chapters 17 and 18. The science-fictional component is so strong that we cannot talk about bestseller realism here, and the difficulties to sell the novel to non-sf publishers prove this beyond any doubt; though Dick saw it as a hybrid (which is the best way to describe the text), it was ultimately published on a science-fiction magazine and then as a science-fiction paperback.

However Warrick does have a point when she highlights the connection between this novel and *Martian Time-Slip*. An intertextual reading may tell us much about *Build*, and it should not surprise us that Fredric Jameson dealt with it in his synoptic reading of a group of novels which also included major works like *Stigmata*, *Androids*, *Bloodmoney*, *Ubik*, and *High Castle*. Actually the issue of schizophrenia is not something that Dick conjures up when the plot about the simulacra and the struggle of the little men Louis and Maury Rock against the big businessman Barrows "fizzles out" — to put it in Suvin's terms — but an issue which is already introduced in the third chapter of the novel, when Louis meets Pris, who has been recently been dismissed from the

Kasanin Clinic in Kansas City, where she was interned because of "dynamism of difficulty" (26), a legal euphemism for her schizophrenic condition.

Besides, the issue of mental health is suggested in an indirect fashion earlier in the novel. Previous commentators of *Build* seem to have not wondered why the first simulacrum built by the MASA Associates, before the one reproducing Lincoln, is the Stanton. Edwin M. Stanton (1814–1869) is surely not as famous a historical character as the U.S. President who won the War Between the States, abolished slavery and was assassinated while still in office; but there is a feature of Stanton's personality, suggested by any synopsis of his life, that might have appealed to Dick's sensibility: it was characterized by a striking paranoid streak. In at least two key moments of Stanton's political career (his activity as Secretary of War under Lincoln and the investigations after Lincoln's assassination) he was bent on the persecution of people who conspired against the Union or the President: army officers suspected of having traitorous sympathies for the South or suspected accomplices of John Wilkes Booth — this fear of conspiracies was so strong that it led Stanton to hand-pick the members of martial courts and suborn witnesses.

Be it paranoia or schizophrenia, insanity is strictly connected to what is arguably the main issue of the novel, the attempt to define — at least in a tentative fashion — what is human; an attempt which was troubled at least, because Dick has also applied his strategy of ontological uncertainty to *Build*. Surely the strategy is more manifest in *Androids*, where one of the main issues is ascertaining who is human and who is not (so that the psychiatric tests used in *Build* to detect psychos are applied to the hunting of runaway androids in *Androids*); but in the earlier novel (in terms of composition) there is uncertainty as to who qualifies as a human being regardless of its/his having been built/born. The title of the magazine version of the novel was "A. Lincoln, Simulacrum," an oxymoron that couples a historical character whose reality is not to be doubted and an artificial entity (androids are called *simulacra* in the novel) which is no more than someone's representation; it suggests an ambiguity, putting together some*body* who is authentically human (albeit long time dead) and some*thing* which is not.

The title of the paperback edition sounds much less ambiguous, as it is something humans might tell simulacra: "we can build you, hence you are not authentic: you are artifacts, manufactured devices, products." Ontogeny, however, does not guarantee that all those born of man and woman are human(e), neither it ensures that the simulacra in the novel are no more than machines. There is a political side to the novel which Suvin only began to detect when he noticed that "the conjuring up of the past probity from the heroic age of the U.S. bourgeoisie against its present corruption cries out for more detailed treatment" (Suvin 1975, 14); but the purpose of resurrecting

Stanton and Lincoln is not just a way to insert a sort of moral touchstone in the novel, though surely the comparison between Lincoln and such a shallow and mean character like Barrows may also suggest thoughts similar to those of the critic. In fact we should not forget that the main issue of the War Between the States was slavery — its diffusion and then its abolition — and slavery is based on a distinction between those who are fully entitled to human rights — and a human identity — and those who, being not entitled to civil rights, are second-rate citizens, less-than-human individuals. Being completed in October 1962, the novel was written (like *The Simulacra*, which should be considered as another companion piece, as we shall see) during the 100th anniversary of the Civil War, which is also mentioned in the novel — set in 1982 — as "a flop" where "[a] few souls got out and refought a few battles" (15). While *Simulacra* ironically pays homage to the American Civil War by depicting a futuristic civil war (cf. Ch. 5), *Build* represents in a science-fictional context the basic question of that war, "the only and first national epic in which we Americans participated" (14), that is, "who (or what) is human?" — which is also known as the question of racism.

Racial discrimination, which was the core issue of the Civil War and was still a hot issue in the early 1960s (1961 was the year of the Freedom Rides), is an undertext which surfaces in many episodes. Both the protagonist/narrator of this 1st-person narrative, Louis Rosen, and his business partner Maury Rock are of Jewish descent; Louis' father Jerome still uses Yiddish words and phrases, Louis seems to be familiar with German; Maury changed his real "original old-country" (9) surname, Frauenzimmer, into Rock, possibly because he felt ashamed of his Jewish origins. Putting two Jewish families in the foreground necessarily hints at the issue of race and racism which was also central in the Civil War.

The Jewish roots of the narrator may also be connected with the legends about the Golem, an animated clay man purportedly created by Judah Loew ben Bezalel, aka the Maharal of Prague in the 16th century, and made famous by Gustav Meyrink's 1914 fantasy novel *The Golem*. The artificial man was created, according to the legend, to protect the Jewish community of Prague from threats of pogrom or expulsion by the Holy Roman Emperor Rudolph II; Jameson, on the other hand, sees the two simulacra as "adjuvants" or "helpers" after Propp's narratological theory (Jameson 2005, 376). But the Lincoln, and then the Stanton, help MASA Associates to defend itself from the machinations of Sam Barrows (cf. in particular the eleventh chapter), so that the two helpers are also protectors, just like the Golem.

The racial issue is however more insistently hinted at than the Golem legends. It is central, for example, in the argument between Lincoln and Barrows about the differences between man and an intelligent machine, which takes place more or less at the middle of the novel (Chapter 9, 111–3) and is pointed out by Robinson as the climactic moment of *Build*. Actually the argument begins when the Lincoln objects to Barrows' intention to purchase him and the Stanton (108); the simulacrum asks the businessman "how [he] could acquire [him] or anyone else, when Miss Frauenzimmer tells [him] that there is a stronger impartiality between the races now than ever before" (111). The Lincoln thus equates the purchase of simulacra to the purchase of human beings, that is, slave trade.

Barrows' answer is that the concept of human "doesn't include mechanical men" (111), that is the traditional justification of racial discrimination (and slavery): some humans can be treated in a different way (possibly be sold and bought) because they do not qualify as fully human, be they Africans or Jews. The Lincoln then counters Barrows' argument by asking the businessman to tell him what is a man (111). Barrows quotes Shakespeare's line where Falstaff calls man "a forked radish" (in *King Henry IV, Part II*), and then proposes a mock definition of man as "an animal that carries a pocket handkerchief" (112). The Lincoln then asks Barrows to define an animal, since he understands that the possession of a soul, the traditional distinction between man and animals, is meaningless to Barrows (he will later say that "[t]here is no soul [...]. That's pap" [113]), and the definition of the animal should apply to humans too, as opposed to simulacra. Barrows maintains that an animal "has a biological heritage and makeup which [simulacra] lack" (112), because simulacra are machines, like spinning jennies or steam engines. Asked to define a machine, Barrows tells the Lincoln that he is one of them, something that has been made by someone and belongs to him or them. It is a matter of being produced, then; but the Lincoln objects that also Barrows is a machine, for he has a Creator, God, like the people who have built it. In other words, if humans can tell simulacra "we can build you," the simulacra may object that "somebody built you too"—God, for those of religious persuasion, or natural evolution, for those who trust Darwin. If a man is nothing else than a more sophisticated animal, and animals, according to Spinoza (quoted by the Lincoln) are no more than "clever machines" (113), then, since Barrows thinks that there is no soul, "a machine is the same as an animal.... And an animal is the same as a man" (113), which means the distinction between humans and simulacra is at least problematic, and not as clear-cut as Barrows likes to think.

Barrows' reaction is quite annoyed, and bespeaks the inability to properly counter the thrust of the Lincoln; he only repeats the former argument that "an animal is made out of flesh and blood, and a machine is made out of wiring and tubes" (113), a terribly weak idea in Dick's world where artiforgs (artificial organs) abound and cyborgs are quite common. Stanton Brose in *Simulacra* and Palmer Eldritch in *Stigmata* are both also made "of wiring and tubes," and this is not enough to make them totally non-human (besides, this applies today to many people in our koinos kosmos of 2010). Barrows' final argument is "I know you're a machine; I don't care" (113), and it expresses the typical arrogance and shallowness of those who think they are always right just because they are rich and powerful.

But Barrows' annoyance, which is quite clearly expressed by his words, proves that the Lincoln is able to discuss a complex issue with him, thus giving the lie to Barrows' claim that what the simulacra say has just been recorded on a tape, and that they are just "the familiar mechanical man gimmick" (111). Barrows has scathingly compared the simulacra built by MASA to "Pedro the Vodor," one of the technological *mirabilia* on display at the 1939 San Francisco World Fair, which was no more than "a keyboard-operated talking machine invented by the Bell Telephone Laboratories" (Domzalski 114). All this shifts the argument between the Lincoln and Barrows from the realm of noble (or questionable) philosophical and political principles to the prosaic world of business transactions. Barrows' underestimation of the technological innovation achieved by MASA is a tactic aimed at lowering the price the businessman could eventually have to pay for the simulacra and their projects. Dick was well aware of such tactics, because he carefully depicts a business negotiation where they are used in his non-sf novel *Puttering About in a Small Land* (Ch. 8), where Roger Lindahl's business proposal is first unenthusiastically received and then nonchalantly stolen by a store owner. If this is what Barrows is really driving at, his move is thwarted by the simulacrum, who proves it is much more than a "Pedro the Vodor" device, even though Barrows does not want to admit it.

The argument also suggests that things are not as simple as they may seem. The borderline between human and artificial, between wo/men and machines is not so easy to trace. The simulacra may have a switch that allows humans to turn them on or off like a vacuum cleaner or a TV set, but shutting the Lincoln off is something that Maury hates to do, and Pris finds dreadful (125)—almost like killing a real human being. On the other hand, Louis' brother Chester is a "radiation-mutant" (19) whose face is upside down; he belongs to the group of those tactfully called "[s]*pecial birth* persons," and one wonders whether they are (considered) completely human if "there is so much discrimination and prejudice in so many fields that most professions of high status are closed to them" (19). We should then not forget that there was a time and a place (Nazi Germany, 1933–45) in which people like Chester and Jews were not considered persons, and this was surely something the author of *The Man in the High Castle* was well aware of. But the greatest problem can be said to be represented by the two newborn creatures, the Stanton and the Lincoln, and their creator, Pris Frauenzimmer.

The two simulacra may be endowed with on/off switches, but do not behave like machines at all. They are also endowed with free will, as Louis tells Barrows (111); the Stanton's decision to leave Boise and go to Seattle and remain there, without informing his creators (94–5) is proof of this. There is a moment that the Stanton seems to be ready to work for Barrows; only a shrewd move by the Lincoln (offering the other simulacrum the position of "Chairman of [the] Board of Directors" [141]) persuades him to remain with Louis and Maury. The two simulacra are able to make decisions and take the initiative, just like humans. This description of the Stanton talking to Louis' father, taken from the second chapters, tells us that the simulacra are also endowed with charisma: "... it was impressive, the two old gentlemen standing there facing each other, the Stanton with its split white beard, its old-style garments, my father looking not much newer. The meeting of patriarchs, I thought, like in the synagogue" (21).

The Lincoln is even more charismatic. When Louis first talks to it, he faints (83); just before that, he cannot help calling the simulacrum "Mr. President." Louis' reaction to this is worth quoting: "My going up to it and speaking to it this way put me into the fiction, the drama, as an actor like the machine itself; nobody had fed me an instruction tape — they didn't have to. I was acting out my part of the foolishness voluntarily. And yet I couldn't help myself" (83). Being part of the fiction means being artificial, playing a part; but Louis has to deal with the Lincoln as if it were another human being (the only one who stubbornly strives not to treat the Lincoln as a person is Barrows, who "did not offer to shake hands with it, nor did he say goodbye to it" [120], though he discussed with it and found it a tough opponent). Moreover, when Louis' own schizophrenia starts surfacing, it is the Lincoln that he empathizes with: "Lincoln was exactly like me. He might have been remote, but he was not dead emotionally: quite the contrary. So he was the opposite of Pris, of the cold schizoid type. Grief, emotional empathy, were written on his face" (188). The Lincoln itself (or should we say *him*self?) acknowledges this bond when he says that Louis and it (him?) have much in common (193).

Moreover, even though the narrator does not seem to be aware of this (but Louis is not, as we shall see, totally reliable), the Lincoln appears as the mastermind of the plot. Robinson thinks that the first plot, the struggle between Barrows and the MASA Associates about the use of the androids, is abandoned when Louis' unfortunate quest for Pris comes to the fore; yet a careful reading of the second part of the novel (which follows the climactic argument between the Lincoln and Barrows) might show that, though the narrator is distracted by his obsession with Pris, he nonetheless provides readers with information about the destiny of MASA. Once the firm is managed by the Stanton and the Lincoln, Barrows' plan is thwarted, and the moves the Lincoln suggests to Louis are effective — even when he apparently misdirects Louis, telling him that Pris might be at Colleen Nild's apartment (211); in fact Louis will find his father there, but this will allow his relatives to rescue him when his schizoid hallucination fully erupts (215–9). If the Lincoln's purpose was to stop Barrows' takeover, he manages to do that when Pris "kills" the Booth simulacrum and breaks with Barrows in the other climactic sequence of the novel, Chapter 16 (without Pris' talent, any simulacra Barrows could build would be as shallow and unimpressive as the Booth).

It might then be argued that the Lincoln and Barrows are the two competing masterminds of the plot, and that — as it happens in so many novels, e.g., in *The Great Gatsby*— the 1st-person narrator is a secondary character who does not know everything about what is really going on (Dick was knowledgeable about Fitzgerald's novel, even if he considered it a failure because "it fell completely apart in the ending" [*SL1* 56], as he wrote in a letter written in 1960). Besides, what is Barrows' move to ultimately defeat his would-be competitors? After having secured the two creators of the simulacra, Pris Frauenzimmer and Bob Bundy, he has a Booth simulacrum built (202); its purpose is to eliminate (or scare) the Lincoln, not Maury or Louis. This move tells us that, notwithstanding his scathing attitude towards the artificial men, Barrows is well aware that his most dangerous enemy is the Lincoln, not the humans who built it — directly or indirectly.

On the other hand, the material creators of the two simulacra, though legally human, have both mental problems; Pris is schizophrenic, while Bob is hebephrenic (and this is the reason why he was fired by the Federal Space Agency [11]). Bundy never appears in the story; people talk about him, but he never takes part in any scene. We have to rely on Louis' description to somewhat picture him: "His clothes are dirty, his hair uncombed, his chin unshaved, and he won't look you in the eyes. He grins inanely.... If someone asks him a question he can't figure out how to answer it; he has speech blockage" (11). Bundy's speech impediment should be compared to the brisk but effective use of language by the Stanton or the Lincoln's articulate eloquence. Barrows insists that the simulacra are not human, and nothing new, because they are no more than mindless "talking machines" (like Pedro the Vodor); but it is the legally human Bundy who is unable to speak properly, though he is "damn fine" (11) with his hands. Being mentally and linguistically impaired, Bundy can be said to belong to the group of less-than-human characters, like Louis' brother Chester.

What is more impressive, however, is how Louis sees the woman he catastrophically falls in love with. It is not just that Pris is or has been insane; it is that "[b]eside her the Stanton contraption is all warmth and friendliness"

(33). Though Louis is in love with Pris, he is well aware of her pathological coldness; she clearly tells Louis that he is in love with her *because* she is abnormally unemotional: "I'm sexually desirable when I'm cruel and schizoid, but if I become MAUDLIN, THEN I'm not even that" (127). When Pris defects from MASA to join Barrows, Louis is depressed (and this will trigger his insane trip to Seattle), but he muses: "What a woman, what a *thing* to fall in love with" (155). The thingness or inhumanity of Pris is repeatedly stated: Louis complains that he "was doomed to loving something beyond life itself, a cruel, cold and sterile thingthing — Pris Frauenzimmer" (184). Pris' coldness is such that she is "two times thing."

We might obviously doubt Louis' reliability when it comes to describing the woman, or better the entity, he loves. To him Pris is not a real woman; she is a deity, the Mediterranean Magna Mater, as explained by doctor Nisea: Ishtar, Cybele, Attis, "Athene" (or better Athena), more a goddess than a human being (227). Pris, as seen by Louis, is cosmic, so that he may tell Barrows that "[y]ou've lost Pris .... That's everything" (207). Louis is eventually diagnosed as a psychopath, suffering from "the dynamism of difficulty which we call the Magna Mater type of schizophrenia" (227)[4]; and Nisea explains that what Louis is loving, or better worshipping, is a projection of the part of himself (the anima posited by Jung) "onto the cosmos" (227). Nisea's psychoanalytical diagnosis should warn us readers that we are not presented with Pris as she "really" is, but as an increasingly deranged mind perceives her.

There is however a sort of double bind at work here. On the one hand, we may disbelieve what Louis tells us because he is insane; on the other hand his insanity is sanctioned by the same psychiatric apparatus, the FBMH, which diagnosed Pris as insane when she was a teenager, and interned her in the same mental hospital where Louis chooses to go. The FBMH tells us that Louis is not a reliable narrator, so that we could call in doubt his description of Pris as an emotionless "thingthing"; but then the same organization twice diagnoses Pris as a schizophrenic, because Louis meets Pris again in the Kasanin Clinic (244), and when he last meets her she reveals that she is much too sick to be released, so that she might remain in the clinic for a long time, possibly forever (252).

Louis is then a partly-reliable, partly-unreliable narrator: such a condition amounts to a form of ontological uncertainty that we already know. Our reading of *Martian Time-Slip* (*Build*'s companion piece, it should be underscored) showed how madness may foster ontological uncertainty; when the narrative focus is put on a mentally diseased character (be it Manfred, Jack Bohlen or Louis Rosen), we are not sure that what we are told corresponds to some hypothetical objective reality or at least to the fictional *koinos kosmos* we should be presented with. Here the narrator himself is not reliable, and

all we know about the fictional world of the novel must be filtered by his
instable mind. But ontological uncertainty in this novel is not only caused
by the unsettling comparison of simulacra's behavior with that of "humans,"[5]
or Louis' schizophrenia. At the Kasanin Clinic Louis undergoes a form of
psychiatric therapy, the *controlled fugue* (237), which consists in drug-produced hallucinations, that is, the creation of a series of Finite Subjective Realities where he can live a happy life with Pris, as we can see in the table below:

Table 6.1
Louis' Controlled Fugues

I	238–9	Louis and Pris are in Jack London Square in Oakland feeding pigeons; he asks her if she loves him, and she answers she does not.*
II	240–1	Louis and Pris are travelling by car; she once more refuses him.
III	241–2	Pris and Louis are walking in the train station of Cheyenne, Wyoming; they are married; Pris considers committing suicide.
IV	242–3	Pris and Louis are in the Jack London Park in Oakland; she says she feels "dead and empty," but then announces she is pregnant.
V	243–4	Pris and Louis are married and have a son, called Charles.
VI	245–6	Pris is older; they have been married for years; they are doing the washing-up and Louis tells his wife he has met her in the Kasanin Clinic.
VII	249–50	Louis is in a supermarket with Pris and their son. Louis wonders whether what they are experiencing is real; Pris tells him she cannot stand his "eternal philosophizing" (250). Louis tells her he will not accept other "derogatory opinions" and then slaps her.

*This scene is similar to the ending of another novel by Dick, *Mary and the Giant*. The character of Mary Rittersdorf belongs to the type of dark-haired girls which also includes Pris
Frauenzimmer, and, as we shall see, two androids in the other novel we will discuss in this
chapter, *Androids*: Pris Stratton and Rachael Rosen.

These seven controlled fugues, which can be seen as drug-induced FSRs
similar to those conjured up by Chew-Z in *Stigmata* (Ch. 7), show us moments
of an alternate life where Louis manages to marry Pris and live with her for
years. It might be seen as a form of wish-fulfillment, if we were not presented
with the unpleasant aspects of their ménage in all these FSRs; Pris may have
married Louis and borne him a son, but her intractable character does not
seem to have changed very much. These are, however, the experiences that
Dick shows us; Louis is told by doctor Shedd that he underwent many other
controlled fugues (up to 220 are counted [247]). Louis has forgotten many
of them, and realizes he has lost track of the days he has spent in the clinic;

it is a dismal awareness of an entropic time-slip, a loss of memory which signals a loss of time and a sort of narrative black hole, because we skip days and then weeks and months of Louis' stay at the Kasanin, summarized by this piece of inner monologue: "How much time had passed? How many times had we been together, now? A dozen? A hundred? I couldn't tell; time was gone for me, a thing that did not flow but moved in fitful jolts and starts, bogging down completely and then hesitantly resuming" (243).

The impression readers get is that the therapy is not working, and that Louis is coming dreadfully near to the "stopping of time" that Jack Bohlen (another schizophrenic) sees as the essence of psychosis in *Martian Time-Slip*: "once the person becomes psychotic, nothing ever happens to him again" (143). It is then interesting to see that if time-slips are part of the content of *Time-Slip*, but also one of its main structural features, they may also be found in the final chapter of *Build*, which, being set in an asylum which is also a sort of prison, a closed space of potentially endless repetition, embodies what Jack Bohlen called "[t]he end of experience, of anything new" (143).

However, it is in the place of madness and perverse time-slip, a place where Louis lives an illusory virtual life and loses the time of his real life, that an odd kind of salvation takes place. And here we have another paradox: if Louis could find empathy and humanity in the Lincoln, a simulacrum, he may find the way to escape the clinic and its dismal therapy thanks to Pris, a diagnosed and interned schizophrenic. Pris tells Louis what to do to stop the relentless sequence of controlled fugues: "Tell [Shedd] you're not sure you're getting anything out of it anymore. And then when you're in it, tell your fantasy sex-partner there, the Pris Frauenzimmer you've cooked up in that warped, hot little brain of yours, that you don't find her convincing any more" (248–9).

It is interesting that the key to escape the drug-induced FSRs is to express doubts as to their reality. Louis' problem was that he could no more tell hallucination from real life; if he starts doubting the reality of the controlled fugues, he might qualify as sane again. In other words, it is not certainty that may help you to escape madness, but uncertainty: asking yourself if an evil dæmon is not cheating you. This is a rather original version of Descartes' thought experiment.

Uncertainty however rules in the ending of *Build*. During the sixth controlled fugue Louis tells Pris that he saw her the day before in the hall of the Kasanin Clinic (246). Does not this amount to suspecting their ménage is not real? And it happens before Pris (in the Clinic) suggests him to tell Pris (during the controlled fugue) he does not find her convincing any more. One cannot help wondering whether Louis *really* met Pris in the clinic. Doctor Shedd says he cannot have met her, because he checked the records and did not find her name; to him their meeting is just "an involuntary lapse into psychosis" (246). Louis then finds out that Pris is at the Kasanin Clinic under her father's assumed name, Rock (247), but this is what is told us by a diagnosed psychotic who has already suffered from hallucination concerning Pris (the scene where Louis hallucinates sexual intercourse with Pris at the end of Chapter 16),[6] and has been undergoing a treatment with hallucinogenic drugs. Can we trust such an untrustworthy narrator?

Telling fictional reality from fictional hallucination, be it drug- or schizophrenia-induced, is not easy. If the two simulacra are declaredly "fiction," because they are the artificial reproduction of long-dead historical characters, then Louis (and the other characters) are "put into the fiction," because they eventually interact with the Stanton and the Lincoln as if they were real people; and we have seen that the Lincoln has enough intellect, volition and agency to be a match for a shrewd human like Barrows. Yet also Barrows' humanity appears dubious to Louis, well before his schizophrenic outbreak: the businessman seems to be controlled by "some servo-system or some feedback circuit of selenoids and relays, all of which was operated from a distance off" (34). This is actually a description of a character in the first novel Dick published, *Solar Lottery*, where the villain tries to liquidate the new Quizmaster using an android, Keith Pellig, which is remotely controlled by a pool of operators, so as to escape the surveillance of the telepaths which should protect the Quizmaster.

Besides, Barrows' inhumanity is also stressed by his being definitely on the side of deliberate and carefully planned simulation, aimed at cynically swindling others. He dismisses Maury's naïve idea of using the simulacra to re-enact the battles of the American Civil War (a grandiose theatrical display where spectators would in any case know that the soldiers fighting and dying before them are not human beings [24]); he proposes instead to "use a number of them designed to look exactly like the family next door. A friendly, helpful family that would make a good neighbour" (114). This should persuade Terrans to emigrate to the colonies on other planets, because they would not feel lonely and miserable in those "empty, barren wastes" (115). Barrows says that the actual settlers would know that their neighbors are simulacra, but Maury and Louis suspect that the businessman has other plans. Louis even suggests that the simulacra might be quietly pulled back out "as more and more people got hooked" (115), and Barrows concludes "I think it would work." This is, in Louis words, "[a]ppearance built up over the fake" (117)—something definitely unacceptable in Dick's fictional world. Barrows belongs to the series of Dick's evil entrepreneurs, like Palmer Eldritch or the Karps in *The Simulacra*.

Here we may find a full development of Barrows' idea of artificial neighbors. They are the *famnexdos*, clearly derived from what is only imagined in *Build*. Also in *Simulacra* those who emigrate to Mars feel terribly lonely; but they may buy a group of simulacra reproducing a typical American family, and that is the meaning of the term famnexdo: *fam*ily *next-do*or (the same words used by Barrows in *Build*).

> Four simulacra seated in silence, a group: one in adult male form, its female mate and two children. This was a major item of the firm's catalogue; this was a famnexdo....
> A man, when he emigrated, could buy neighbours, buy the simulated presence of life, the sound and motion of human activity – or at least its mechanical near-substitute – to bolster his morale in the new environment of unfamiliar stimuli and perhaps, god forbid, no stimuli at all [58–9].

Baudrillard's comment on this scene also applies to *Build*: "Models no longer constitute an imaginary domain with reference to the real, and thus leave no room for any kind of transcendentalism" (Baudrillard 310). The travel to Mars does not carry settlers Elsewhere, perhaps to meet some unthinkable Other; it takes them to a hyperreal neighborhood where their neighbors have surely been given "the colors of the real, the banal, the lived." They go to another planet just to get exactly what they had at home, nuisances included (58). Baudrillard again: "SF of this sort is no longer an elsewhere, it is an everywhere: in the circulation of the models here and now, in the very axiomatic nature of our simulated environment" (Baudrillard, 312). Dick's comment on the famnexdos chimes in with the analysis of the French sociologist: "Communication with them [i.e., the simulacra of the famnexdo] was in essence a circular dialogue with oneself; the famnexdo ... picked up the covert hopes and dreams of the settler and detailed them back in an articulated fashion" (59). What does such an artificial environment reproduce, or re-circulate? Probably California.

Barrows' real estate speculations on other planets are no more than the anamorphic replica of models derived from the urban history of California, where such speculations had started even before Dick moved there with his family. He depicted such ambiguous economic transactions in *The Man Whose Teeth Were All Exactly Alike* (where the realtor Leo Runcible is ready to do anything to protect the value of his investments), and in *Humpty Dumpty in Oakland*, where Harmon suggests Jim Fergesson to invest his money in a garage in a brand new suburb. Dick had a first-hand knowledge of California's suburbanization, and he simply projected it on other worlds; and Barrows, like many characters involved in such speculations, is a greedy and ruthless individual, surely not an example of humanity and empathy. Suffice it to say that, after having presented his plan to induce people to settle in the neighborhoods he is building on other worlds, he clearly tells Maury and Louis:

"It's an environment up there that once you've seen it ... well, let's put it this way. About ten minutes is enough for most people. I've been there. I'm not going again" (116). Barrows is then less a human being than a cold-blooded and unsympathetic predator.

Who are the humans in this novel, then? Chester is a freak; Louis is mentally impaired, and his love for Pris is more an inhuman obsession with an artificial, overpowering image than a human passion; Colleen Nild and Mr. Blunk, Barrows' assistants, are two life-size puppets; as for Pris, she is characterized by a sort of mechanical coldness, but maybe her real problem is that she is not living her own life, but a fiction of herself, having read Herman Wouk's novel *Marjorie Morningstar* (1955), which tells the story of a Jewish girl who replaces her real name Morgenstern with a more Anglo-Saxon surname in order to facilitate her career as an actress. This is somewhat similar to what Maury has done when he changed his surname from Frauenzimmer to Rock. Pris went several steps further, adopting an artificial identity as Pristine Womankind, and starting a career as a local celebrity thanks to Barrows' money and connections (156–62).

Quoting Ezra Pound I might say that there is no clear demarcation between human and artificial. Being made of flesh and blood or wiring and tubes is ultimately unimportant; it is what characters do, strive to do, or do not do which is really relevant. Dick expressed such a view much later in his life, in his 1976 essay "Man, Android, and Machine": "As one of us *acts* godlike (gives his cloak to a stranger), a machine *acts* human when it pauses in its programmed cycle to defer to it by reason of a decision" (212). The issue of the novel is then who is acting human and who is not, and this is something that cannot be decided once and for all, so that we are asked to judge scene by scene, act by act.

However, the borderline dividing the two simulacra (and those that will be built) from the biologically human individuals is ultimately not as important as the one which divides 75 percent of the U.S. population, made up by fully human — i.e., mentally sane — Americans, from the 25 percent of those that have been diagnosed insane based on the Benjamin Proverb Test and the Vigotsky-Luria Block Test (37), the same tests which certify the sanity of our unreliable narrator at the end of the novel (251). While the two simulacra act in a passably sane and humane way, one American out of four has been or is interned in a mental hospital, and Louis recalls a long list of people he knows that have been victims of certified madness (37–8), so long that one may suspect that just anybody could be declared mentally insane and interned in the near future devised by Dick. Are those who do not pass the mandatory tests fully human? If they are, why are they forced to go to a clinic (which disquietingly resembles a prison) and undergo dismal therapies like the controlled fugue applied to Louis? However, the insane 25 percent of the population does not enjoy full civil rights — just like the Afro-Americans in antebellum USA, or the segregated racial minority in Southern states before 1955, or the Jews under the Nazi and Fascist regimes of the 1930s. Or the two simulacra, if Sam K. Barrows self-serving distinctions were turned into laws.

The Lincoln and the Stanton are there to embody the main argument of the novel, which is the difficulty (or, for pessimist interpreters, the impossibility) to have a clear demarcation that may separate what is human from what is not. The ontological uncertainty which reigns in the novel, heightened in the final chapter by the controlled fugues, should induce readers to question their standard definitions of authentically human and inhuman, when even Abraham Lincoln, an illustrious representative of the category of the Great Man, can be a simulacrum, and be occasionally switched off. On the other hand, the authentic human who tells us the story, Louis Rosen, the character we should know and understand better, is eventually revealed as a madman ready to go to Seattle with a .38 pistol, who sees himself as "the stranger in town, armed, and with a mission" (166), a mission which might just be a killing spree. Here Louis reminds us of the fictional Travis Bickle, the protagonist of Martin Scorsese's 1976 movie *Taxi Driver*; or the historical Mark David Chapman, the murderer of John Lennon[7]; and this could be an excellent variation on Jameson's android cogito, where the certainty of the "I think" is promptly neutered by the conclusion that "therefore I am an android"; in a metaphoric rewording, Louis' motto might be "I tell, therefore I am a madman."

Dick could not publish *Build* for eight years, so it should not surprise us that he started recycling ideas and characters taken from it in other works. We have already noticed that the famnexdos in *The Simulacra* were at least imagined (by Barrows and Louis) in *Build*; *Simulacra* was completed less than a year after *We Can Build You*, and unsurprisingly features such an old acquaintance as Maury Frauenzimmer — back to his original German surname — as the manager of the Frauenzimmer Associates, which builds the famnexdos and is then awarded a contract to build the android president of the USEA, *der Alte*. In this novel the Man in the White House is not as charismatic as the Lincoln in *Build*, but it is even more artificial; being not endowed with an autonomous mind, he can only utter the speeches prepared by the White House staff, like Yancy in *The Penultimate Truth* (Ch. 5).

But other elements reappear in *Simulacra*: unlike Pris, who is seen by Louis as an overpowering Magna Mater, but appears skeptical about the Pris Frauenzimmer he has cooked up in his "warped, hot little brain," the First Lady Nicole Thibodeaux *deliberately* plays the part of the archetypal Great Mother: the young woman embodies an archetypal figure, "the image ... of

the Bad Mother. Overpowering and cosmic" (98). Psychoanalysis is not as important here as it was in *Build*, but there is a narrative thread about a psychother-
apist, Dr. Egon Superb (another of Dick's onomastic puns), and Dick hints at
a psychoanalytical interpretation of the "national neurosis" (98), the psychological weakness felt by males in the novel in relation to Nicole: "I'm terrified
of her and that's why I'm scared of Julie, I guess in fact of all women ... It's
because of weak-fibred men like me that Nicole can rule ... I'm the reason
why we've got matriarchal society" (98), confesses one of Dr. Superb's patients.

"Bad Mother" is here an equivalent of the Magna Mater, as we can see
when another character explains his feelings towards Nicole. "She's a Magna
Mater figure to him. As she is to all of us.... The great primordial mother"
(184). She is a dreadful figure, even though all male characters seem to be fascinated by her beauty: when Ian Duncan meets Nicole in the White House
he is evidently starstruck, but also scared by the First Lady, whose semi-divine
status is revealed by an involuntary pun by Ian, who after hearing Al Miller
say "We ate, Mrs. Thibodeaux" thinks "*We ate Mrs. Thibodeaux*," thus hinting
at Christian Eucharist, where believers eat god; but then he adds "Doesn't
she, sitting here in her blue-cotton pants and shirt, doesn't she devour *us*?
Strange thought..." (162). Not so strange if we think that there were human
sacrifices to pagan gods, so that those deities might as well be seen as devouring
gods. Nicole, as an embodiment of the Magna Mater, is a voracious, canni-
balistic figure. Nicole's archetypal role explains her place in the power structure
of the USEA and her ascendancy as depicted in the novel: something imported
from Nazi Germany, where the dominating figure was the Führer — undoubtedly a patriarchal authority figure — while in the USEA there is a totalitarian
matriarchy which requires "spiritual-moral emasculation ... a present day pre-
requisite for participation in the *Ge* class, in the ruling circles" (36).

But then Nicole is unmasked as a young actress who has replaced the
original First Lady, who died many years before, so that she is just one of the
many simulacra in this overcrowded novel; she may not be built, but her
agency is severely diminished by fact that she receives orders from a secret
Council ultimately masterminded by Goltz (cf. Ch. 4). In this bitter satirical
novel simulacra pass for humans and humans are actually puppets, and such
an idea is a development of the world of sane simulacra and insane humans
depicted in *Build*.

But there is another novel which is strongly connected to the one we
have analyzed in the first half of this chapter, one which Warrick saw as a
powerful reworking of the then still unpublished manuscript (Warrick 66):
Do Androids Dream of Electric Sheep? When Dick was interviewed by Rickman
he did not talk about the connection between *Build* and *Androids*, but it is
quite evident that he considered it one of his best novels, written in a moment

of economic and emotional stability (Rickman 1988, 171). His comment high-lights the psychological metaphor underlying the text:

> ... I was contrasting Nancy's warmth with the coldness of the people I'd known before. I was beginning to develop the idea of the human versus the android, the bipedal humanoid that is not essentially human. She had shown me for the first time what a real human being could be like, tender and loving and vulnerable. And I was beginning to contrast that to what I had been brought up with [Rickman 1988, 171].

Another version of this comment is found in one of his last letters (dated July 1, 1981), where Dick overtly connects *Build* to *Androids*, and he does it in such a way that we are authorized to apply what we have found in the former to the latter:

> I guess the essence of my artistic vision is to try to formulate what con-stitutes the authentic human being, as contrasted to what I call the "android" (a metaphor) or reflex machine; that is, the creature which resembled a human, is human biologically yet lacks, really, a soul. This is a preoccupation with me that first finds expression in my early novel WE CAN BUILD YOU (written in the early sixties) and attains a sort of peak in DO ANDROIDS DREAM OF ELECTRIC SHEEP? which is the novel BLADE RUNNER is based on [*SL6* 178].

Many interpretations of this novel have been written, and the temptation to read it in a biographical key is understandable: Dick felt he had to contrast Nancy (the authentic human being) with people like his parents, his distant father and his cold mother (metaphorically androids, or reflex machines). This obviously leads to those analyses which, like Robinson's short but effective discussion, show that in *Do Androids Dream of Electric Dreams?* beside the Humane Humans (such as John R. Isidore) there are the Cruel Androids (Roy Baty, his wife Irmgard, Pris Stratton), but also Cruel Humans, such as bounty-hunter Phil Resch (Robinson 92). It is something we have also found in *Build*. Humans in *Androids* are not necessarily cruel, but they are surely lacking in emotions, which should be among the main features of the real human being. In fact Rispoli noticed that "humans in the world of the novel are so unable to experience any kind of emotional response that they have to use the mood organ even to get negative moods" (Rispoli 100, translation mine), like Iran — the wife of the protagonist — uses to do.

What I find questionable, however, is Robinson's idea that there are Humane Androids, with Luba Luft, the opera singer, as the representative of this group. Dick's opinion is overtly expressed in a letter to his literary agent where he says that Rick's view has won out: "the androids are vicious machines which must be destroyed" (*SL1* 230) — without exception. Rick Deckard may find Luba humane and warm, but she is ultimately as cunning and potentially lethal as the other, more aggressive androids, Polokov and Baty; she does not hesitate to have Rick arrested by the police officer from the fake Hall of Justice on Mission Street (Ch. 9), even if that means his death (Rick is only accidentally rescued by Phil Resch, who apparently behaves like an android but is human); then, when Phil and Rick get back to the Opera House to retire her in Chapter 12, she tries to set Rick against Phil by declaring that the latter is an android (102). Rick's reaction to Luba's words once more confirms what is more or less overtly suggested by the novel: he is not the best bounty hunter in the Los Angeles area, being the substitute of Holden, the top bounty hunter in town (25), wounded by Polokov while he was testing it.

What is clear, if one reads this novel in connection to *Build*, is that the two narrative foci of *Androids* are not much more reliable than Louis was in the former novel. John Isidore is a chickenhead or special, that is, an individual who has been mentally impaired by radiations; he may be a warm person from the emotional point of view, and there is no doubt that he is one of the most humane characters in Dick's gallery, but has troubles when it comes to analyzing others' behavior with some detachment. On the other hand, Rick is not a very competent bounty hunter at the beginning of *Androids*; he is almost cheated (and killed) by Polokov, is shrewdly manipulated by Rachael Rosen (as we shall see), and at least confused by Luba's allegation that his colleague is an android — even though she had already accused him to be one just a few hours before (79).

Believing what Luba tells him during their second meeting (even if he should be well aware that the android singer is able to lie easily and effectively) Rick almost fights with Phil, and this might offer Luba the opportunity to escape, or to shoot both bounty-hunters (we have already seen in her first meeting with Rick that she is armed). Moreover, since Rick believes her when she accuses Resch of being an android (he will only test him, and discover to his dismay that the cruel bounty-hunter is indeed human, only after Luba has been retired [108]), he might kill him straightaway if he were as trigger-happy as Phil Resch — hence the android's lie might lead to the killing of a human being. Rick may not be a complete fool, yet he is a typical representative of those Dickian Little Men who are not impeccable professionals, but only passable workmen. Rick manages to retire all the Nexus-6 androids in 24 hours in the end, but he needs help to do that: Phil's help during the retirement of Luba, and Mercer's help when he attacks the last three remaining androids in Isidore's apartment. He may make serious mistakes, and he almost makes one in Luba's case; then he makes another when dealing with Rachael, as we shall see.

Though Luba's attempt to imitate the human (103) may allow her to be an artist (she does sing Mozart's *The Magic Flute* wonderfully [76–7]), it does not mean that she has also developed the empathic faculties that would turn her into a Humane Human in Robinson's scheme. While simulacra are better than humans in *Build*—with the possible exception of the disquieting Booth —androids are all worse than humans in *Androids*, even if they may have a fascinating artistic talent like Luba's, or be sexually attractive like Rachael Rosen.[8] And that is exactly Rick's problem, which is not accidentally explained by Resch, a more competent and expert bounty-hunter: Rick had problems with Luba "[b]ecause she—it—was physically attractive.... We were taught that it constitutes a prime problem in bounty hunting. Don't you know ... that in the colonies they have android mistresses?" (110). Deckard does not know (though he is aware of the attraction female androids may exert [75]), hence his problem with Luba, and the greater problem with Rachael.

Robinson's superficial interpretation of Luba's behavior might be explained with a confusion which takes sometimes place between *Androids* and its famous cinematic version, *Blade Runner*. While androids are selfish and merciless creatures in Dick's novel, some of them are endowed with a remarkable dignity in the film, where Roy Batty proves to be a humane android when he spares the life of a human bounty hunter (in the original version of the film, where Deckard is a man) or proves to be capable of solidarity (in the *Director's Cut*, where both he and Deckard are Nexus-6 androids, but the latter does not know yet). While Ridley Scott's ultimate version of the film shows that androids may be better than humans (with the possible exception of Gaff), something which pushes Deckard to revolt, Dick uses androids, cold and emotionless beings whose only purpose is selfish self-preservation at the expense of others, to present us with anamorphic images of those human beings who are as cold, selfish and cruel as them — the epitome of the Cruel Human being Phil Resch, whose cynical (and morbid) approach to a female android is "[g]et to bed with her first ... and then kill her" (111), which sounds like a line recited by one of the streetwise, cynical characters of noir movies.

Yet the comparison between the novel and the movie is not necessarily misleading, provided we pay attention to all the shifts that take place between Dick's text and the movie as it was re-released in 1992 (the *Director's Cut*). We should also remember that there is something that the two works have in common, their radical differences notwithstanding. That *Blade Runner* mixes a science fiction background with elements drawn from film noir is something which was almost immediately noticed and discussed by critics (cf. Doll & Faller, but also the essays collected in Judith B. Kernan's *Retrofitting Blade Runner*); yet the presence of crime fiction elements in *Androids* is not something which has often been discussed, even though Stanislaw Lem spotted this aspect in one of the first academic essays on Dick's science fiction, when he said that this novel "we see the sad picture of an author who squanders his talent by using brilliant ideas to keep up a game of cops and robbers" (Lem 1972, 89). Lem, who was all too eager to make a distinction between the "desperate case" (sf as pure entertainment product, belonging to the despicable "Lower Realm" [Lem 1972, 47]) and the exceptions (sf as respectable literature belonging to the "Upper Realm" or "Olympus" [Lem 1972, 48]), could evidently not accept the crime component in Dick's novel since it belonged to the Lower Realm.

Today we do not see the picture of Dick mixing androids and a police investigation as such a disreputable one, because we know that — notwithstanding the fact that a great part of crime fiction belongs to the lower realm — several crime fiction authors (among which two who were also based in California, Dashiell Hammett and Raymond Chandler) are now considered part of the upper realm; we also know that the iron curtain dividing the two realms (Lem 1972, 49) was more a rhetorical device than a historical reality. What is more interesting is that the crime element is probably what Dick added to turn the materials he had already elaborated[9] in *We Can Build You*— still an unpublished text and a failure in 1966 — into a novel that might be more palatable to sf publishers and readers. Besides, we shall see in the next chapter that he could take a narrative model from crime fiction in a moment of creative dearth and build a passable science-fiction novel on it, *A Maze of Death*.

The importance of noir themes, imagery and aesthetics in *Androids* has not been discussed, probably because Dick's essays, fiction and letters do not mention of Chandler, Hammett, or any other writer involved with noir film or hard-boiled fiction (he only mentions Mickey Spillane in a letter he wrote less than a month before his death [*SL6* 313–4]). I am not suggesting that Dick deliberately attempted to hybridize his sf with noir movies or hard-boiled fiction in particular: it is however undeniable that the relevant difference between *Build* and *Androids*, since the central issue of human vs. android (with all the metaphoric implications we have found in the former text) is the present in both novels, is the insertion of plot devices typical of crime fiction in *Androids*, such as the investigation, the hunt for criminals (here runaway androids), the interrogations (here turned into the Voigt-Kampff tests), so that an analysis of these elements is unavoidable.[10] One might for example consider how Dick took a rather secondary character in *Build*, the Booth simulacrum, which is by definition a murderer, and turned it into the threatening and cold Nexus-6 androids in *Androids*; he gave the androids all the features of the schizophrenic mind as depicted in the earlier novel, but above all turned them into criminals — like the historical John Wilkes Booth.

If we follow the names and surnames of characters, it is easy to see that Eldon Rosen, the powerful owner and chief of the Rosen Association, may well be a descendant of Louis Rosen in *Build* (Jameson 2005, 375), which is an ironic reversal, inasmuch as the small firm of losers turned into a powerful and successful corporation.[11] So it is not a surprise that one of the androids is called Pris, even if the surname is not Frauenzimmer: Pris Stratton physically resembles her schizophrenic namesake in *Build*, and her android nature leads her to be as abusive to John R. Isidore as the first Pris was to Louis Rosen.

But the character that most closely resembles Pris Frauenzimmer is Rachael Rosen, who appears in one of the most remarkable episodes of ontological uncertainty (which Ridley Scott and/or his screenwriters could not omit), when Rick Deckard is summoned to the premises of Rosen Association, shown their collection of precious animals and invited to submit Rachael to the Voigt-Kampff test (Chapter 5). Here we have uncertainty about her nature (is she human or an android?), which is obviously one of the main issues of this novel, an uncertainty which Dick dramatized by turning the artificial characters (who helped the protagonist/narrator in *Build*) into dangerous and hunted outlaws (who mostly attempt to kill one of the human protagonists, and almost enslave the other), and having one of the two narrative foci on a bounty hunter. And, though there is always deception at work in this novel whenever the androids appear (e.g., Luba desperately trying to imitate humans — which is also a mimetic ruse that should prevent her identification as an android —,[12] Polokov pretending to be a visiting Soviet policeman, Roy and Irmgard Baty hiding in a desolate suburb where only specials live, probably hoping to pass as radiation mutants), the most impressive episodes of ontological uncertainty are tied to Rachael (with the remarkable exception of the fake Hall of Justice, which is visited after Rick's failed attempt to retire Luba and masterminded by Garland, the bogus police officer, who is actually an android).

Rick initially identifies her as an android, but is immediately told by Eldon Rosen that Rachael is human, albeit emotionally defective because born and raised on board a space ship, in a sealed and artificial environment (43–4). This scene has heavy implications: if the Voigt-Kampff test can fail to identify as human someone suffering from mental disorder, it is unreliable, and this could discredit the activity of bounty-hunters. This revelation, the typical Dickian abrupt reversal, is followed by an attempt to blackmail and corrupt Rick, so that he certifies that Nexus-6 androids can be detected by the test, so that the Rosen corporation may continue their production and sale (47)—it is a matter of money (recalling the shady dealings which abound in hard-boiled fiction, especially in such novels as Hammett's *The Glass Key* and *Red Harvest*, where corruption is a main issue).

In a further reversal Rick manages to correctly identify Rachael as an android, and ward off Eldon's deception, by asking her one more question from the test and measuring her reaction time; what arouses his suspicion is a little verbal detail, the fact that Rachael keeps calling the precious specimen of owl owned by the corporation "it" (48), showing no affection to it. Rachael is actually too sincere; the owl is another fraud, an artificial animal like Rick's electric sheep and the toad he will find almost at the end of the novel (180). The presence of android animals adds another form of ontological uncertainty to the novel, which in the episode of Rachael's test further complicates the main human vs. android opposition.[13]

But the revelation that Rachael is an android, even if she is not aware of it (49), does not lead to her retirement (or liquidation); since she belongs to the Rosen corporation (which designs, tests and builds androids), her presence on Earth is not illegal. This paves the way for another important episode in the novel, that is, Rick and Rachael's night at the motel, when they have sex. Their second meeting is prepared by a video call from the android girl, who offers Rick to take part in the hunting of the remaining Nexus 6 androids. This amazes the bounty hunter, who wonders: "[w]hat kind of world is it ... when an android phones up a bounty hunter and offers him assistance?" (71). He takes this as an example of something humans give for granted, that androids cannot properly cooperate because they lack empathy. Rick believes in this, when he tells Garland that "You ... don't exactly cover for each other in times of stress," and it agrees because "it would seem we lack a specific talent you humans possess ... called empathy" (95).

Rachael's good will seems confirmed when she proposes a strange deal: "[g]*o to bed with me and I'll retire Stratton*" (147). This seems to be precious help, because Rick has just realized that Rachael and Pris do not just belong to the same Nexus 6 model, but also to the same batch of female androids with the same body and face. This had been already suggested by Pris, when she told John Isidore that her name was Rachael Rosen (55); it was arguably a mistake, and Pris immediately realizes this when John connects her to the powerful corporation: she immediately tells him that her name is Pris Stratton (which might well be made-up). When Rick realizes that Pris is a look-alike of Rachael he understands that if he goes to bed with the latter he will not be able to retire the former, because a powerful empathic (or sentimental) relation will be established. Hence Pris' apparently helpful offer to kill Pris.

I say "apparently" because Rachael belongs to a type of character whose ability to cheat is remarkable; we might say that their main role in the sort of narratives where they appear is to cheat or betray the male protagonist. I am obviously talking of the so-called *dark ladies* so often found both in noir movies and in hard-boiled fiction. I might add that one of the classical theorists of noir cinema, Damien Hirsch, defined these complex figures as "amoral destroyers of male strength" (Hirsch 20–1), and though subsequent critics of the genre have expressed different opinions on female characters in noir movies (cf. Cowie), that definition fits Rachael perfectly.[14] In fact, after their sexual intercourse, she tells Rick that "[y]ou're not going to be able to hunt androids any longer .... No bounty hunter has ever gone on ... [a]fter being with me" (149) — the only exception being Phil Resch, described as cynical and nutty (his lack of empathy being a possible symptom of borderline schizophrenia or some other light mental disorder). So Rachael is exploiting Rick's (and other bounty hunters') empathy to destroy their psychological strength, the ability to keep hunting and eliminating runaway androids. That she does this by exploiting her sexual appeal should not surprise noir connoisseurs: it is the typical situation of the male protagonist in those films, because Pris is, like other dark ladies, a "not innocent woman ... to whom [the protagonist] is sexually and fatally attracted" (Damico 54).

The attraction is fatal inasmuch as empathic (sentimental and/or erotic) involvement with a female simulacra may disable any bounty hunter save the psychopathic ones like Resch — who might be dangerously eager to kill the suspect, even if they are not sure he or she is an android (something that outrages Rick during the retirement of Luba Luft [103]). But this is just a part of Rachael's plot[15]: the fact that she and Pris are two specimens of the same android model will be also exploited by Pris when she will go towards Rick on the stairs of Isidore's conapt building (166), hiding a laser tube (167), and telling him "[for] what we've meant to each other" (166) — something which would be nonsensical, since Pris has never met Rick before, if we did not take into account the fact that Rick almost mistakes Pris for Rachael (this mistake is also caused by his belief that Rachael will reach him to keep her promise to retire Pris). Pris knows that Rachael exists and that they are almost undistinguishable; but she cannot know that Rick has gone to bed with Rachael and believes she will reach him to help him — *unless Rachael has told her*. It is one of those tricks that one can expect from the canonical dark ladies of noir movies, and it tells us how devious Rachael really is; no wonder that she is the only android to escape the 24-hour slaughter unscathed.[16]

Rick is only saved by the direct intervention of Mercer, the odd godhead of the religion practiced by most humans in the novel. This is a science-fiction novel, after all, and a Dickian novel, so technological *mirabilia* (like the androids, the artificial animals, space travel and laser tubes, flying cars and the empathy box) live together with supernatural events, like Mercer's apparition in Chapter 19, just before the final shootout (which resembles the apparition of the Intercessor in *A Maze of Death* that will be discussed in the next chapter). Mercer not only saves Rick's life, thus averting the machinations of the dark lady, but he also solves the moral quandary of the novel, even if the solution is terribly bitter.

Other interpreters have noticed Rick's moral dilemma (Fitting 1987, 135; Robinson 91; Warrick 127–8), which is formulated well before his night with Rachael at the hotel: if androids must be hunted when they reach Earth, because they have killed their owners to escape the colonies on other planets (29), and because, lacking empathy, each one of them is a dangerous "solitary predator" (28), the hunter — which must be human — will only be able to retire them if he has no empathic bond with them. A biological parallelism is suggested: the androids are like predators, which must not be endowed with empathy to survive (28), while men are "like herbivores" endowed with a "group instinct," being "omnivores who could depart form a meat diet" (28). This implies that all the humans in the novel are vegetarians, since eating meat would contradict the generalized veneration of animals required by Mercerism. Yet some men, the bounty hunters, must retire androids, that is, kill them; and while the simulacra in *Build* were electronic devices, the androids in this novel are the product of genetic engineering, even though Dick did not use this phrase. They look like humans, hence the necessity of the tests to identify them, and here rises a contradiction: how can a man go on killing androids once he establishes an empathic bond with some or all of them, due to their human (and sometimes attractive) appearance, and cannot simply see them (like Rick does at the beginning of the novel) as "the Killers" (28–9) and obey Mercer's commandment that "*You shall kill only the killers*" (28)?

The basic idea in the *Director's Cut* of *Blade Runner* is there to solve this problem: Rick is a replicant, expediently used by the police (and possibly controlled by Gaff) to retire runaway replicants. But this is not the case in the novel. Rationality will not solve this dilemma, also because the fact that androids are purely rational prevents them from understanding Mercerism and empathy: unrestrained rationality is on the side of inhumanity. If this is a mystery, in the religious meaning of the term (especially used by Eastern Christianity and Roman Catholics), here is how Mercer enunciates it: "You will be required to do wrong no matter where you go. It is the basic condition of life, to be required to violate your own identity.... It is the ultimate shadow, the defeat of creation; this is the curse at work, the curse that feeds on all life. Everywhere in the universe" (135). Jameson described this as a "*Bhagavadgita* moral" (Jameson 2005, 366), because also the sacred Hindu *Bhagavad Gita* contains a contradiction between the principle of *ahimsa* (avoidance of violence) and just war (one which is not tainted by selfish concerns). So Rick may have an empathic bond with his prospective victims and kill them all the same; he can paradoxically kill more efficiently because he may empathize with them and see the world from their point of view (whenever he fails to do this, as with Rachel or Luba, he is cheated). He is not cynical, like Resch (or the real protagonist of a classical noir), so he will suffer for what he must do — hence the deep emotional exhaustion which besets him after he has retired Pris, Roy and Irmgard Baty, in chapters 20 and 21 (also caused by the killing of the goat [170]). Rick cannot hide what he is doing behind an euphemism; he is well aware that he is not just "retiring" androids but slaughtering them, and the scene of the final killings (166–9) has a dry brutality of an intensity that one rarely finds in Dick, a man who intensely disliked physical violence and never indulged in graphic descriptions of carnage in his fiction.

All in all, this novel is also a theodicy, that is, a meditation on the presence of evil in the world, hence similar to *High Castle* (Ch. 3), and *Stigmata*, as we shall see in the next chapter; the philosophical implications of the existence of evil were evidently a long-term concern for Dick, also noticed by Link, who chose to devote a section of his overview of Dick's themes to the "Theodicy Problem" (Link 73–9). *Androids* is a science-fictional theodicy which — we cannot say whether accidentally or intentionally — has many elements in common with noir movies and hard-boiled fiction: the dark lady, as we have seen; the convoluted plot with a series of coups de théâtre (as it is usual in Dick but also in Hammett's novels, be they *Red Harvest* or *The Dain Curse*); but above all the character of Rick Deckard, which Jameson correctly describes as a "middle-class bounty hunter" (Jameson 2005, 367). This may have been inspired by Marc Vernet's contention that the hero of noir cinema, the private detective, "is a petty-bourgeois jealous of his independence, convinced of his moral worth and concerned with protecting what is, in his eyes, the exemplary value of American democracy" (Vernet 18).[17] There is little doubt that Rick (as depicted in the novel, with his wife, his electric sheep, his wish to buy a real animal frustrated by his scant salary, and his independent position as a bounty hunter) is a typical Dickian Little Man, closer to Vernet's petty-bourgeois class than to a really proletarian character like John R. Isidore (I tend to see the androids as a group outside the class system, similar to Marx's *Lumpenproletariat*; it is too difficult to see them as a "wronged lower class" as suggested by Suvin [14]). If Dick's Rick Dekard, as distinguished from Ridley Scott's character, has some traits in common with the heroes of noir movies (though lacking their street wisdom, vitriolic sense of humor, and baroque verbal skills),[18] it should be then added that the roots of his contradictory moral are not necessarily as exotic as Jameson suspects (though one should always take into account Dick's familiarity with Oriental philosophies and religions).

On the one hand the contradiction of the predator (Rick) endowed with empathy can be solved from an ethological point of view. Not all predators are lonely killers; lions and wolves (two animals that Dick did not mention in this animal-crowded novel) hunt in well-organized teams, and they have both social instincts and killing skills. On the other hand, Rick's plight —

that is, to empathize with his victims, kill them and suffer — may bear some relation with D.H. Lawrence's definition of the essential American soul, that he posited as "hard, isolate, stoic, and a killer" (Lawrence 68). Maybe Rick is not as hard as Phil Resch, and he is luckily not isolate (though he isolates himself in chapter 21, after the final slaughter), but there is no doubt that he kills most of the six androids and that the experience allowed by the empathy box, the fundamental ritual of Mercerism, has a remarkably stoic quality: climbing a desolate slope hit by stones thrown by invisible tormenters asks for those virtues of self-control and fortitude that stoics considered paramount.[19]

Is Rick Deckard a representative American, after all? It is not something that may be ruled out, given Dick's powerful democratic (and sometimes populist) frame of mind. It should be said, however, that he is the only professional killer in Dick's gallery of characters — if we exclude the sometimes psychotic and almost always android-like thugs, such as the Nazi commandos which try to eliminate general Tedeki, mister Tagomi and herr Wegener in *The Man in the High Castle*.

We should conclude our discussion of these two novels by pointing out that these are — as usual — multi-layered texts where ontological uncertainty asks readers to reconsider their notions of human, machine, and android. But other received notions are at stake in these texts. It is in fact interesting that Peter Fitting asks a very simple question, when he notices that "there are few reasons given why anyone would want to go to the expense and trouble of developing a robot which could pass for a human being — especially since this resemblance is the source of considerable anxieties" (Fitting 1987, 133). It is a sensible questions if one considers *Androids* (and *Blade Runner*), though one may wonder whether Rachael's sexual intercourse with Rick (and Rachel's love story with the replicant hunter in the movie) are not enough to explain what can be done with these beings which almost perfectly imitate humans though they are not legally recognized as humans.

All in all, however, Fitting's question finds an answer in *Build*, and one which reconnects the two novels that the tradition of science-fiction: there Pris perceives the quasi-religious aspects of building the Stanton and the Lincoln, first by connecting them to resurrection (69), then to the sacrament of the Eucharist (69), though not without doubts; but a clearer statement of the religious implication in what she and the MASA Associates are really doing is expressed later in the novel, when she tells Louis: "We're like gods ... in what we've done, this task of ours, this great labor. Stanton and Lincoln, the new race..." (91). By creating life, man becomes god; but this was already clear to Mary Wollstonecraft Shelley when she chose to use these three lines from Milton's *Paradise Lost* as the epigraph of *Frankenstein; or, the Modern*

Prometheus: "Did I request thee, Maker, from my clay/To mould me man? Did I solicit thee/From darkness to promote me?"

This religious aspect of the human-android relation is present in *Build*, but it is even blatant in *Blade Runner* (where the killing of Tyrrell by Roy may amount to a Luciferian rebellion or a resurrection of the monster's conflictual attitude towards his creator, Victor Frankenstein, cf. Desser). On the other hand, it does not seem to be active in *Androids*, where the issue of religion is represented by Mercerism and its stoic morality; yet it might be argued that if *Build* describes the past of *Androids*, and Eldon Rosen is a descendant of Louis Rosen in the earlier text, then the consequence of Pris' act of hubris — creating a new race and turning into gods — is the gloomy and decadent world of *Androids*. Here it is not clear anymore who is human and who is not: just anybody could be a runaway Frankenstein's monster without revealing electrodes and scars, ready to laser us to death, and decent men like Rick must turn into stoic killers to survive. Ontological uncertainty cuts both ways: it may create such a situation where the injustices of racism are denounced and a more equalitarian society may be glimpsed — one where the Lincoln could be an excellent president of a posthuman USA — but also lead us to a paranoid world of mistrust and suffering, where the Dickian little man feels he has became "a scourge, like famine or plague" (169). Once again Dick is questioning the ideology of transcendence through technology which underpins the narratives of Golden Age science-fiction. It is not then strange that, after stating the godlike status she has achieved, Pris Fraunezimmer adds "and yet by giving them life we empty ourselves. Don't you feel hollow, now?" (91).

I do not know whether there is an echo of T.S. Eliot's hollow men in these words; however it is plain to see that the religious undertones of *Androids* may tell us so much about it. So much may stem from the two different situations of ontological uncertainty at work in the two novels, which are both however pivoted upon the basic opposition of authentic vs. fake, or human vs. android. The absence of a clear demarcation in these narratives may lead to such a condition that "no man can find site for his dwelling," to quote Pound once again (is not that a condition of radical uncertainty?), but it surely allows for rich and hopefully fecund interpretive work. Dick believed he had exhausted the issue of androids vs. humans, as this "is his last significant extended statement in fiction on the android" (Barlow 1991, 77); given the complexity of *Androids*, he had good reasons to think so.

Last but not least, the bleaker tone in the second novel in order of completion, that is, *Androids*, prepares us for the reading of the darkest novels Dick wrote, which will be discussed in the next chapter; it also introduces the issue of Dick's creative crisis in the late sixties and early seventies, which will be dealt with there.

Chapter 7

Psychedelic Demiurges:
The Three Stigmata of Palmer Eldritch, Ubik, A Maze of Death and *Flow My Tears, The Policeman Said*

> "I could be bounded in a nut shell and count myself
> a king of infinite space, were it not that I
> have bad dreams."
> William Shakespeare

The three novels in the fourth chapter are united by the themes of madness and community, and seem to express a moderately optimistic stance (with at least a utopian possibility glimpsed at the end of *Time-Slip*, and utopian undertones in *Bloodmoney* and *Clans*—surely stronger in the latter than the former); the four novels I will discuss in this chapter—*The Three Stigmata of Palmer Eldritch* (1964), *Ubik* (1969), and *A Maze of Death* (1970), and *Flow My Tears, The Policeman Said* (1974)—present us with four different variations on the theme of finite subjective realities, and it is a remarkably bleaker quartet than the previous trio (with the partial exception of *Tears*).

I will not use the terms utopia and dystopia to differentiate these two groups of novels because there is no fully developed utopian component in *Martian Time-Slip*; even Fredric Jameson reads the ending of that novel, with Manfred's final visitation (discussed in chapter 4), admitting that it is a single episode "in the most depressing of all his novelistic 'realities,' the settlements on Mars of *Martian Time-Slip*" (Jameson 2005, 383). On the other hand, three of the four novels we are going to discuss do not qualify as dystopias, a term which can only be used for *Flow My Tears* (plus the two subsequent works, *A Scanner Darkly* [1977] and *Radio Free Albemuth* [posthumously published in 1985 but actually completed in 1976]); hence I disagree with Darko

173

Suvin's contention that "[u]p to *The Three Stigmata of Palmer Eldritch* the novels by Dick that are not primarily dystopian ... are better forgotten" (Suvin, 1975, 7). The problem with such a formulation is not that it dismisses a novel which should not be forgotten at all (*The Cosmic Puppets*), but that it is difficult to qualify the major works before *Stigmata* (published in 1964) and some of the following as *primarily* dystopian.

In his essay on science-fiction, utopia and dystopia, Tom Moylan defines the third genre, drawing from such previous theorists as Sargent and Suvin (Moylan 155), as a narrative text that offers a detailed description of a non-existent society which is worse or significantly less perfect than the society in which the contemporary readers lives; but this society must be presented and/or judged as such from the point of view of a representative of a discontented group or class. The lack of a detailed description in Dick's novels of the 1960s tells us they do not really qualify — with the possible exception of *The Man in the High Castle*. In all the other novels (with two remarkable exceptions), even if the world described is bleak, oppressive, even totalitarian (like the One Happy World in *Time Out of Joint*), the stress is more on individual adventures and misadventures than on the collective level. In Dick's novels we never find something like the essay-within-the-novel *The Theory and Practice of Oligarchical Collectivism* by Emmanuel Goldstein that Orwell grafted on his *Nineteen Eighty-Four* to describe in detail the workings of the totalitarian regimes in Oceania, Eurasia, and Eastasia. There is a text-within-the-text in *High Castle*, Abendsen's *The Grasshopper Lies Heavy*: it is however an alternate history novel, which does not analyze or explain the world Mr. Tagomi and the other characters live in, but conjures up another world altogether; it complicates the plot, as we have seen, rather than clarify it, as Goldstein's hyperfictional essay does in Orwell's novel.[1]

The future societies devised by Dick are mostly backgrounds, seen from the perspective of the ordinary people who live in those societies; a perspective which usually allows only sketchy descriptions of how those societies work. Moreover, the future societies in Dick's science-fiction are often anamorphic images of the United States as seen by Dick (this is true for the Martian settlements in *Time-Slip*, but also for the USEA in *The Simulacra*, cf. Chapter 6), or they may be derivative of stock despotic governments easily found in commercial science-fiction (which Dick knew quite well and also produced). Christopher Palmer is in fact right when he observes that "popular fiction ... commonly implies that the ruling structures of society are inadequate or corrupt and that average people are helpless or incriminated, so that a superhero or — what is much the same thing — a private investigator must come to the rescue" (Palmer 161).

I might object at Palmer's a bit too nonchalant superimposition of pulp science-fiction (whose pulpiest representatives are surely superhero comics)[2] and hard-boiled detective stories, but his remarks are quite fitting: unjust or oppressive governments are a staple in cheap science-fiction, and they are unfailingly found in those novels Dick wrote as apprentice works or to make ends meet: *Solar Lottery, The World Jones Made, Vulcan's Hammer, Our Friends from Frolix 8,* etc. In these works the overthrow of dystopian governments is correctly diagnosed by Robinson as "wish-fulfillment" (27). There is a certain difference between Dick's dismal worlds, which are often nightmarish (even in their "pulpier" versions, such as *The Game-Players of Titan,* which Kim Stanley Robinson finds disturbing even if he considers it a failure [Robinson 53]), and the programmatically evil world depicted by Orwell, Zamjatin, Huxley, Atwood. Characters in real dystopias are mere probes which allow writers to show their readers the awful workings of those hellish societies; they may also be ethical/political touchstones, as Moylan theorized following Suvin, as they embody the discontented group or class which rejects that society.[3] But in Dick's fiction characters are central, even if they are destructured, fragmented, split, mad, neurotic, amnesiac, or any combinations of these, because Dick is above all a pure-bred novelist. *Tears* might almost qualify as a dystopia if only the representatives of the discontented/repressed class in it presented that world or expressed an articulate judgment; their (often unhappy) feelings and experiences of love are however more important. Even in Dick's only full-fledged dystopias, *Scanner* and *Albemuth,*[4] characters and their lives are more important than the sfnal societies they live in.

However, though one has to reject Suvin's stress on the dystopian dimension, in the same essay there is an interesting remark which may tell us something about *The Three Stigmata of Palmer Eldritch* and the three other novels we are going to read in this chapter. The Croatian critic was evidently annoyed by *Stigmata*: in the first page of his essay he says it is "a flawed but powerful near-masterpiece" (Suvin 1975, 2). Then he explains that "the political theme and horizon begin here to give way to the ontological" (9); the problem is Palmer Eldritch, of course, the interplanetary entrepreneur and drug-dealer whose drug Chew-Z not only allows its consumers to live in imaginary worlds where their wishes may allegedly come true, but allows him to control those virtual worlds or FSRs to such an extent that Chew-Z users do not know whether they are in the real world or in one that only looks real, but is actually another FSR conjured up by Eldritch. The classical "what is real?" question, that some interpreters see as Dick's main obsession, is here more ostensibly central than in *High Castle* (though we should now see that Dick has simply heightened the ontological uncertainty which characterized *The Cosmic Puppets, Eye in the Sky* and *Time Out of Joint*). Suvin understands that "the ontological dilemmas have a clear genesis in the political ones" (9), but shifting the issue of power from human institutions to mysterious entities is something that a Marxist — albeit unorthodox — intellectual like him cannot accept.

Suvin probably sensed something that underlies the whole novel, written — as Dick told Rickman — "in connection with [his] becoming an adult convert to the Episcopal Church" (Rickman 1988, 149): in that church, the United States province of the Anglican Communion, there is the sacrament of the Eucharist, which is considered by some Anglo-Catholic Anglicans as a transubstantiation, a change of bread and wine into the body and blood of Christ. This mystical transformation evidently fascinated Dick, which devised "a diabolical Eucharist" (Rickman 1988, 149), having elaborated "a fairly profound idea" of the sacrament. The mysterious entities — Eldritch and the Chew-Z he markets — were unpalatable to Suvin because he realized that those entities were above all religious, or derived from theological concepts.[5]

Stigmata was completed in March 1964, developing an idea that Dick had already presented in his 1963 short story "The Days of Perky Pat." The months in which he wrote the novel are a time of marital crisis, but also a moment of psychological malaise. Sutin tells us that Dick saw a face in the sky in the second half of 1963, a metal face with "empty slots for eyes" (Sutin 127); it was cruel, and it was God. Dick said that he "didn't really see it, but the face was there" (127); Sutin suggests that Dick's abuse of amphetamines, that he took to sustain his hectic writing habits (Dick himself says he saw the ominous face when he was going to the shack where he wrote eight hours a day and more), may have caused the hallucination.

Dick's involvement in the Episcopal Church was an attempt to find spiritual comfort vis-à-vis that terrifying vision, which was explained by a priest at Dick's church as an apparition of Satan (that's in any case what the writer wrote in a text which might not be very reliable, an unpublished headnote for a story collection [Sutin 326]); but that vision had a strong resemblance to the sight of Dick's father Edgar wearing his Great War gasmask when he told little Phil about his horrifying combat experiences on the Western Front (Sutin 127). Dick himself acknowledged that the face in the sky was that "metal, blind, inhuman visage ... now transcendent and vast, and absolutely evil" (Sutin 127). Moreover, Dick wrote in an unpublished headnote to "The Days of Perky Pat," the short story he expanded to write *Eldritch*, that "my father appears as both Palmer Eldritch (the evil father, the diabolic mask-father) and as Leo Bulero, the tender, gruff, warm, human, loving man" (Sutin 132).

Sutin rightly warns that no single event can explain the creation of a literary text like *Stigmata*; the face in the sky may have pushed Dick towards the Episcopalian church, with its sacrament of the Eucharist; the Eucharist, which should offer salvation through ingestion, might seem somewhat similar to the relief from tiredness that amphetamines offered; the ominous face in the sky reminding Dick of his father[6] may well have been turned into the ghastly face of Palmer Eldrich, with artificial Luxvid eyes and steel teeth (implanted due to an accident)[7]; but there are other elements to be taken into account. According to Sutin, Dick was fascinated by the symbology of the Eucharist, which led him to read Carl Gustav Jung's 1941 essay on "Transformation Symbolism in the Mass," and that essay hinted at the Gnostic roots of the sacrament (Sutin 128). In Jung's opinion, Christ dies because he has created a flawed world: "the *auctor rerum* [world creator] was a lower archon who falsely imagined that he had created a perfect world, whereas in fact it was woefully imperfect" (Jung 1941, 334).

Here we may see how Dick's synthetic imagination worked (being not different, be it clear, from that of most writers): in fact archons were servants of the demiurge in Gnostic doctrines. The demiurge is the lord of the imperfect world we live in, who pretends to be the real God — who is hidden, and can only be reached through *gnosis*, or spiritual knowledge.[8] It is easy to see that Palmer Eldritch is an archon of sorts, inasmuch as he thinks (or says) he creates perfect worlds of wish-fulfillment, who are actually imperfect; the worlds or Finite Subjective Realities can be accessed by taking Chew-Z pills, in a blaspheme parody of the Eucharist; those FSRs may seem real, like the imperfect world created by the demiurge, but they are not; and though the worlds conjured up by Chew-Z seem to offer an opportunity to recover what one has lost (Barney could get back to the happy days of his marriage to Emily, before their divorce [Ch. 5]), thus having a positive value, they are actually "like being in hell," a hell that is "recurrent and unyielding" (158). The worlds created by Eldritch's drug carry his stigmata, "the evil, negative trinity of alienation, blurred reality and despair" (203). This is what lies under or behind Eldritch's prosthetic organs, that are clearly recognized by a Martian telepathic jackal, a creature living in the wilderness which seems to have a more direct perception of the nature of things; Barney, having used the Chew-Z, assumes now and then the aspect of Eldritch, sporting metallic eyes, teeth and arm; he is thus declared "Unclean" — hence uneatable — by the hungry jackal, as "there's something intolerably wrong" (197) with him.

Are we then allowed to read this novel as an allegoric narrative whose two main characters, Leo Bulero and Barney Mayerson, try to fight a sort of cosmic villain, Palmer Eldritch, who embodies in a science-fictional setting Evil itself? Is this novel a translation into science-fictional language of the ancient Gnostic theology? Before a general interpretation is attempted, we should pay attention to the architecture of the novel, especially to the parts of it which are set in drug-produced finite subjective realities, or virtual realities.

Table 7.1
Virtual Realities in *The Three Stigmata of Palmer Eldritch*

Kind of virtual reality	Agent	Pages	Content
Shared artificial world	Can-D	42–7	The colonists in the Chicken Pox Prospects translate into Perky Pat and Walt in California (as it was before the global heating)
Finite Subjective Reality	Chew-Z	69–99	Leo Bulero is trapped in several delusional worlds controlled by Palmer Eldritch, including one which seems so real that Leo is beguiled; it includes a contact with the men of the future with the visionof the monument to Leo Bulero (92–8); it is interrupted by a short sequence with Barney Mayerson (narrative focus)and Felix Blau (76–9)
Finite Subjective Reality	Chew-Z	150–157	Barney gets back to his life with Emily; then to the morning after his night with Roni Fugate; Eldritch intervenes by superimposing himself on Hnatt
Finite Subjective Reality	Chew-Z	168–85	Barney meets Leo in the future as a phantasm, then talks to his future self, and replaces Palmer Eldritch in his final trip from Venus, to be killed by Leo in Eldritch's place

All in all, slightly more than one fourth of the whole novel (59 pages out of 209) describe what happens to Bulero or Mayerson in the virtual realities produced by drugs. Most of the artificial worlds are produced by Eldritch's drug Chew-Z, and a single episode shows what is experienced by users of Can-D, the drug manufactured and sold by Bulero. It is quite clear that there is a fundamental difference between the two substances: Can-D allows its users to *share* a pleasant reality of Earth as it was before global heating forced people to emigrate to Mars; Chew-Z sends those who use it to different subjective worlds, as Leo understands while he is imprisoned in one of them (85). Of course, one might object that the happy-go-lucky virtual California, where Perky Pat and Walt Essex do not have to care about the impending environmental disaster, seems to be more an opiate for the masses than a real communitarian experience — but, compared to the nightmarish microworlds of solipsistic isolation conjured up by Chew-Z, the artificial koinos kosmos of Can-D appears rather harmless.

Moreover, the FSRs created by Chew-Z are *controlled* by Eldritch, who uses them as means to an end. If we consider the three larger sequences of virtual, drug-induced reality in the novel, we easily see that the first, which involves Leo Bulero, is aimed at forcing the businessman to accept Eldritch's conditions, and the terms of his capitulation are clearly stated by Eldritch (90) while Leo is still imprisoned in the FSR; the other two sequences, involving Barney Mayerson, can be said to be part of Eldritch's B plan. Once the cyborg entrepreneur understands that Bulero will never accept his commercial proposition, and this means that Bulero will eventually kill Eldritch (something that the latter knows thanks to the ghostly time-traveling capacity provided by Chew-Z), he tries to persuade Barney to replace him on board the doomed starship that will be destroyed by Bulero.

Once again a twisted theological subtext can be easily detected: Eldritch is an anti–Christ (Warrick 110–1), one who is not ready to die for humankind's sin, but asks a man to die in his stead. And, at the end of the eleventh chapter, Eldritch's B plan seems to succeed, when the "great translation" is accomplished, and Barney discovers that "[i]t will be [him] ... that Leo Bulero will kill. [Him] the monument will present a narration of" (179), because now he *is* Palmer Eldritch.

Here the term *translation*[9] hints at transformation (it refers to the very specific transformation taking place when people use Can-D and are embodied in the two characters/dolls in the layouts, Perky Pat and Walt), but the key concept — or metaphor — in this novel is rather a religious one, transubstantiation. It is the Roman Catholic and Anglican/Episcopalian belief that bread and wine change into the flesh and blood of Christ in the Eucharist, an ontological translation similar to those which take place in the novel. Thanks to Can-D (something which is ingested, like the Host), a layout with dolls is transmogrified into a temporarily inhabitable world (Perky Pat and Walt's sunny and carefree pre-disaster California); the comparison between this (pharmaceutical) experience and the Holy Communion is suggested by Anne Hawthorne, who is a believer and belongs to a relatively traditionalist church (114–6). But once Chew-Z enters the scene, transubstantiation is more frequent; smaller and greater transformations take place both in and outside the FSRs controlled by Eldritch. When Barney becomes Eldritch, Eldritch turns into Barney (183), so that we have a double transubstantiation. The use of the theological term is appropriate because, though the host and the wine retain their appearance, believers know that they are actually changed into Christ's flesh and blood; in *Stigmata* Barney finds himself in Eldritch's body on board a doomed starship, while the entrepreneur is safely hidden in Barney's body. In Aristotelian terms, the appearance of the two characters is a mere accident, while what counts is the substance within — their soul, to use an old-fashioned name.

But there is another transubstantiation which repeatedly occurs in the novel, and that is when someone (not just Barney, who has been in such close contact with Eldritch that "neither of [them] can ever become completely separated again" [187]) suddenly assumes Eldritch's appearance, showing Luxvid eyes, steel teeth and a prosthetic arm; this happens more than ten times in the novel,[10] and involves all the main characters, Leo Bulero, Barney Mayerson, and Anne Hawthorne. The phenomenon initially occurs in the FSRs created by Chew-Z, so that it may seem no more than a hallucination caused by the drug, but then it takes place even *after* characters have gone out of the virtual realities and are again in the koinos kosmos. This happens for example in chapter 11, when Barney sees Anne Hawthorne with Eldritch's stigmata, while she tries to prevent him from using Chew-Z again when it is too soon (168); we subsequently learn that also Barney appeared to Anne *sub specie* Palmer Eldritch (194) in that crucial moment. These apparitions could be explained as after-effects of the drug, but in the final pages they also extend to characters like Felix Blau, who have not used Chew-Z (201), so that they undoubtedly contribute to the condition of generalized ontological uncertainty that dominates in the novel.

Ontological uncertainty is generated in the drug-induced idioi kosmoi, when the characters are not sure if they are still the artificial world or have managed to get out of it (this repeatedly happens to Leo in his Chew-Z experience), and anybody (or anything) can turn into Palmer Eldritch. But it also impacts on them when they are out of the FSRs produced by the drug, and there is no certainty that they are really out of them, as Eldritch keeps appearing in the koinos kosmos (one of these apparitions, when Eldritch is superimposed to Leo's secretary [167] has been noticed by Jameson); in Leo's words "once you get into one of [the virtual realities] you can't quite scramble back out" (165). This might admittedly render my previous scheme pointless, though I believe that mapping Dick's novels can always help us grasp his textual strategies: the simple fact that most of the psychedelic fireworks triggered by Chew-Z arrive when 1/3 of the novel has elapsed tell us that the crescendo architecture we found in such a minor work as *The Game-Players of Titan* (Ch. 1) still applies to this major work.

Talking about ontological uncertainty in *Stigmata* is particularly appropriate, as ontology is overtly mentioned in the text; in fact Anne Hawthorne admonishes Barney not to "talk ontology," reminding him that if "the map is not the territory, *the pot is not the potter*" (193), even emphasizing it, so that he should not "say *is*"; but Eucharist is a fundamentally ontological sacrament, where bread *is* flesh and wine *is* blood (their appearances notwithstanding, but this is once again a matter of accident and substance). As we have seen, in this novel everybody can be Palmer Eldritch, and a suitcase can be a psychiatrist (7) called Dr. Smile. Displacements of identities and objects abound; uncertainty undermines any conclusion Barney and other characters may think they have reached (or wish they have) also because it cuts both ways. Chew-Z is a de-realizing, hallucinogenic drug, hence what you see while under its effects should be false, bogus, artificial; yet Leo, during his Chew-Z trip, reaches a moment in the future — well after Eldritch has been defeated and killed by him — thanks to the "time-overtones" of the drug (97), and contemplates a monument celebrating his victory over his rival.[11] Chew-Z is Eldritch's instrument, but it may offer a vision of a world where Eldritch has been defeated; it is hallucinogenic, but it may offer a revelation.

Besides Eldritch himself is a most ambiguous figure. He might be the embodiment of absolute evil, a ruthless alien invader who entered the body of the businessman while he was traveling from Proxima Centauri to Earth, and uses his product to dominate humankind (92, 164, 188–9). Yet he (or it) is also a superior form of life, with a "vast, reliable wisdom" (188) that helps Barney to make a fundamental choice about his own future. Barney had formerly described him as "an evil visitor oozing over us from the Prox system" (136), imagining him (or it) as the pulpish alien menace from outer space; but then Eldritch is much more than that, as Barney suspects that when people turn into Palmer Eldritch what is taking place is not just a superimposition, but a revelation of "absolute reality. The essence beyond the mere appearance" (194). Though Anne rejects Barney's suggestion that Eldritch is God, because "it's a creature fashioned by something higher than itself" (192), Barney maintains that if Eldritch manifests himself even to those who have not used Chew-Z, it may mean that he is more than he seems to be; he somewhat underlies the surface of reality. Barney insists on the stigmata (the artificial eyes, the steel teeth, the prosthetic arm) as "symbols of ... inhabitation" (194), and then goes on to describe the helplessness of humankind vis-à-vis this disquieting presence, as "we have no sacraments through which to protect ourselves; we can't compel it, by our careful, time-honored, clever, painstaking rituals, to confine itself to specific elements such as bread and water or bread and wine" (195). This takes us to the Eucharist again, where we have what the theologians have called the "real presence" of Christ. Eldritch is both alien invader out of pulp sf and a divine entity; but if he is God, he is neither a kind, loving, and caring heavenly father, nor a self-sacrificing redeemer.

Eldritch's genesis connects him to Dick's real father Edgar; Eldritch is a patriarchal god, because he, unlike Christ, is not a Son ready to die for his Father (and us), but "*the* superior power asking us to perish for *it*" (195). Such an inversion of the core of Christian theology smells of sulphur. Dick himself told Rickman that this "is essentially a diabolical novel," and that he accepted its definition as a "Satanic bible," with a "diabolical Eucharist" (Rickman

1988, 149). Do we have Palmer Eldritch as the Devil, then? In Rickman's interview Dick says that he aimed at "explaining just what [he] felt was the absolute evil in the world" (Rickman 1988, 149), something he had tried to grasp in *The Man in the High Castle*.

If we are satisfied with the idea that this is another science-fictional theodicy, another exploration of the problem of evil, then it is Barney who eventually offers an explanation, because if Eldritch is the embodiment of absolute evil, his fundamental drive seems to be "nothing more or less than the desire of ... an out-of-dust created organism to perpetuate itself" (195). It is the instinct of self-preservation that pushes Eldritch to ask Barney to perish for him, as he eventually admits when he says that his ultimate aim was to "perpetuate [him]self" (198). This idea returns in other important works by Dick, such as *Do Androids Dream of Electric Sheep?* (Ch. 6), but was already present in one of his earliest short stories, "The Preserving Machine" (1953), where a stereotyped sfnal inventor builds a device that may turn the great masterpieces of music (by Schubert or Wagner) into animals, so that they may survive the passing of time and "the reshuffling of societies" (*CS1* 149). But once the machine translates the music animals back into musical scores, the wonderful harmonies and melodies of great composers are turned into something "distorted, diabolical, without sense or meaning" (*CS1* 155), because the struggle for survival, the self-preserving instinct has corrupted them. In this early story we already have transubstantiation, the transformation of something into something else that should somewhat remain what it originally was under a different appearance; and the overpowering force of the principle of self-preservation.

We should not forget that Dick has also smuggled the Gnostic idea of the Demiurge in his novel, and Eldritch, being a semi-divine creator of false realities can be seen as a sfnal Demiurge. If we take the Gnostic subtext into account, we have to add another layer to our interpretation of *Stigmata* as a quite unconventional theodicy: evil is a de-realizing principle, just like Ahriman in *The Cosmic Puppets*, and there is no doubt that Eldritch is a master illusionist, "a damned magician" (100) in Leo Bulero's own words.

All this might well induce us to get to a little lower layer of meaning, to paraphrase Melville's Ahab, and ask ourselves whether Eldritch is not a sort of anamorphic self-portrait of the author as a novelistic demiurge. It is the conception of the author-as-god which Carravetta proposes as the representative figure of an important current in postmodernist fiction (Carravetta 505–8). Dick, the ultimate creator of the worlds in *Stigmata*, operates and intervenes through an archon who is no more than a servant of the real demiurge, namely the novelist. We should not forget that, unlike *Castle* and *Time-Slip*, *Stigmata* was written for the pulp paperback market; it was completed after the "publishing disaster" of 1963 that we have already discussed in the previous chapters, and its prose and structure bespeaks a much hastier writing process. This is not said in order to underestimate this novel, but to explain its rollercoaster, hectic rhythm, and the evident fact that Dick unashamedly plays the Game of the Rat once again, the same game he had played in his *The Game-Players of Titan* (completed nine months before *Stigmata*). While the Rat is invisible in the earlier novel and just occasionally hinted at (Ch. 1), here the game-player appears with his scary face and prosthetic arm: he is the arch-conjuror Palmer Eldritch, who can manipulate the fabric itself of reality, who creates a condition of radical ontological uncertainty—just like the hack sf writer Philip K. Dick, always ready to pull whatever sort of science-fictional rabbit out of his apparently inexhaustible hat.

Dick's identification with Eldritch may not be something that was clear to Dick himself, though the connection of Eldritch's face with his father's may well hint at that. Identification with one's father is always a viable psychological option, even for those who have a troubled relation with their male parent, like Dick did. The relation between Dick and Eldritch may also entail a generous dose of ambiguity (like everything else connected to Eldritch); the cosmic drug dealer may stand for a negative version of creativity, one that cheats humans (and readers), to be opposed by the real creative force belonging to artists (here represented by Emily Hnatt, the potter). But if Eldritch is a flawed artist, only able to concoct unsatisfactory worlds (universes falling apart, to paraphrase the title of one of Dick's most celebrated essays) which ultimately inexorably turn into recurrent and unyielding hells, he might be dangerously close to Dick, creator of unsatisfactory novels rejected by respectable publishing houses and sentenced to the repetitive toil of the hack writer.

Eldritch fails in the end, defeated by the little men Barney and Leo; we cannot obviously deny that Dick always sympathized for the little man who bravely struggle against absolute evil, like Mr. Tagomi, or Joe Chip in *Ubik*, but here the canny creator of FSRs is Eldritch, a failed conjuror of idioi kosmoi like Dick himself. This may allow us to reinterpret Barney's final remarks, when he wonders whether some responsibility for Eldritch's misdeeds does not lie on God after all—*if* Eldritch cannot be identified with God—because "it was a portion of God's Creation" (200). Eldritch is in fact a character in a novel created by Dick; if he *is not* Dick, because we cannot talk ontology, he is a portion of Dick's creation, so part of the responsibility lies in any case on the author of *Stigmata*. Then one of Dick's most famous sayings, which ends the plot pivoted upon Barney Mayerson, "there was such a thing as salvation. But—Not for everyone" (200), may be a bitter remark on Dick's fate as both writer and man.

That Eldritch is directly (as Dick's fictional alter-ego, because they are both demiurges) or indirectly (as the archon of Dick, the demiurge of the bogus world depicted in *Stigmata*) should then not surprise us, because the ending scene of the novel, with Leo Bulero turning into Eldritch to such an extent that he even forgets who he is, and asks Felix Blau "'Leo'? How come you keep calling me 'Leo'?" (204), is not just a way to provide a sardonic punch-line to the novel, but aims at reminding us that if Eldritch is evil, there is Eldritch in all of us, even in the man who will slain the arch-villain in fair combat (97).[12] Hence there had to be some Eldritch also in Philip Kindred Dick.

This metafictional interpretation does not exclude other approaches. I have for example proposed a reading of Palmer Eldritch as the embodiment of technology in all its manipulative capabilities (Rossi 1994), in a paper which drew strongly from Heidegger's meditation on *Technik*. To counter a certain interpretation of Dick as a herald of the postmodern condition — a condition where the uncertainty about reality is heightened by the mass media apparatus made up by several technologies — which was burgeoning in the 1980s and which was flattening the complexities of Dick's oeuvre, I identified Eldritch with mass media technologies and the FSRs they produced, and showed Dick's negative presentation of those artificial worlds. Such a reading is not incompatible with the analysis that I have proposed in this chapter, inasmuch as cheap pulp paperbacks aimed at a mass market were definitely not outside the mass media apparatus of the 1960s (nor they are today). Dick managed (once more) to use the tools of conventional science-fiction (Mars, space travel, alien invasion, psi-powers) and deconstruct them; he remained in the ghetto of a then still discredited popular genre, but managed to dismantle its mechanisms: the whole story of the colonization of Mars is a demolition of the expansionist myth underlying most of the Golden Age sf. While apparently catering to the unsophisticated appetites of purportedly lowbrow sf fans, Dick presents his readers with a display of alienation (the colonists in their hovels), blurred reality (the dominating ontological uncertainty, which cannot be simply read as a fake reality, but as something indistinct, hence beguiling, like Eldritch's virtual realities) and despair (Barney's final situation, when he is purposelessly stranded in the middle of the wasteland called Mars). This is, after all, an attack to a central principle of Golden Age sf, the programmatic optimism about the wonders that science and technology will offer us. Sf historians tell us that the 1950s, after the bombing of Hiroshima and Nagasaki, started to depict scientific progress as a mixed blessing, and Dick is among those representatives of sociological sf which replaced the gung-ho attitude of Campbell and his disciples with a more cautious exploration of the futures that might stem from nuclear weapons, the mass media, computers, space travel. But in *Stigmata* the dreams of omnipotence and transcendence-through-science of Golden Age sf are somewhat recapitulated in Eldritch's offer of eternal life as an easily-available commodity; and immortality is one of the myths of scientific transcendence repeatedly proposed by Robert A. Heinlein in his Lazarus Long stories and novels, from *Methuselah's Children* (1941) to *To Sail Beyond the Sunset* (1987) (Ch. 5).

Like Golden Age sf, Eldritch says he can deliver eternal life, which means transcending the mortality of man through science and technology; but immortality in *Stigmata* is only achieved in Chew-Z-produced Finite Subjective Realities, that is in a virtual, imaginary condition. Death is actually not overcome, because it is already inscribed in the plot of the novel: Eldritch's death *has already taken place* when we arrive to the ending, i.e., to Barney's last conversation with the drug dealer and entrepreneur, which takes place in linear time *before* Leo Bulero destroys Eldritch's space ship (here the opposition between *fabula* and *sujet* posited by Russian Formalists and structuralism finds a most original application); Eldritch is well aware that he cannot escape death (199). Hence I cannot agree with Robinson when he maintains that "the novel ends before the deed is actually accomplished" (62), where the "deed" is Eldritch's defeat, because the scene immediately preceding Eldritch's death is shown in Chapter 12 (183–5); the deed is thus accomplished in a prolepsis, which should not surprise us in a novel which begins with another, less evident prolepsis, Bulero's "interoffice audio-memo" (5) which, according to Dick, was "the *real* ending of the novel" as it "indicates that Leo has been successful in freeing his mind from delusion, that he has indeed remembered who and what he is" (*SL5* 135). This is no mean time-slip: the memo appearing as an epigraph at the beginning of the novel was "dictated by Leo Bulero immediately on his return from Mars" (5), which is told in Chapter 12. Besides, we know of Eldritch's final defeat thanks to the story the guards tell Bulero and the monument he sees during his Chew-Z experience in Chapter 6. The novel may end (*if* the ending is chapter 13) before the deed is actually accomplished, but what comes after the ending has been already told, *pace* Robinson, in a totally non-linear fashion — maybe less blatant than the labyrinthine temporal displacements in Joseph Heller's *Catch-22*, but almost as effective.

However, even in the Chew-Z-generated FSRs, neither Leo nor Barney achieve eternal life. Leo is described as a phantasm (95) by one of the guards watching the future monument; Barney is told by a future Leo he is a phantasm too (170). A phantasm may be an illusion, but it is also a ghost, a disembodied soul, what is left of a dead person; hence Chew-Z, by turning its users into phantasms, ultimately brings them to a sort of displaced death. It is not much better than the deadly Substance D in *A Scanner Darkly*.

There is a strong connection between *Stigmata* and the three other novels

I am going to discuss in this chapter, and it becomes evident if we compare
them to the three novels we have analyzed in Chapter 4: while *Bloodmoney*,
Time-Slip and *Clans* are multi-plot and multi-foci novels (the first two being
the best specimens of this technique with *The Man in the High Castle*), *Stigmata*, *Ubik*, *Maze*, and *Tears*, though presenting their readers with a group
of characters, do not offer a full-blown multi-foci narrative, but either a
"stripped down" (Robinson, 93) version of it, where the points of view of one
or two characters prevail (Leo and Barney in *Stigmata*; Joe Chip in *Ubik*; Taverner and Buckman in *Tears*), or a meager multiplicity of points of view, as
in *Maze* (with a prevalent focus on Seth Morley). Besides, compared to the
gallery of well-distinct personalities that we meet in *Castle*, *Time-Slip* or *Bloodmoney*, the group of colonists on Delmak-O in *Maze* is only weakly differentiated; the same may be said for the inertials around Joe Chip in *Ubik*. In
Stigmata, the clash among the three main characters (Leo, Barney and Palmer
Eldritch) does not offer others many opportunities to shine (with the possible
exception of Anne Hawthorne, who plays a more important role in the plot
than has been acknowledged by critics so far). Compared to these novels *Tears*
could seem out of place, as the characters met by Taverner in the novel are
strongly characterized, and some of them (Kathy Nelson, Ruth Rae, Mary
Ann Dominic, Alys Buckman) are definitely remarkable, some of them foreshadowing the powerful portraits of drug-addicts and dropouts in *A Scanner
Darkly*.

Besides, Dick himself saw a connection among the novels discussed in
this chapter. In a fragment of the *Exegesis* he wrote: "JOINT, EYE, STIGMATA,
UBIK, MAZE & TEARS are progressive parts of one unfolding true narrative"
depicting "the spurious world for what it is" (*Pursuit* 165). This statement,
written in 1977, is connected to Dick's frantic attempts to explain his 2-3-74
experiences: he saw those novels — all connected by the issue of bogus worlds,
or FSRs — as hinting at the religious revelation that he was striving to grasp,
according to which the writer was only apparently living in California in the
1970s, while he was actually one of the first Christians in A.D. 70. You may
believe his theories about the 1974 experiences or not (but if you do do you
will have to choose which one you should believe, because Dick spun so many
of them — sometimes in his essays, more often in his letters — not always consistent with each other), but I find this statement more interesting from the
point of view of literary criticism.

Dick then added a list of titles, each with a brief description of the precious information it conveys. Here is what he thought about the four novels
discussed in this chapter: "3) STIGMATA plural hallucinated worlds concocted
by an evil magician-like deity 4) UBIK messages of assistance penetrating the
simulated world(s) 'from the other side' by/from a salvific *true* deity 5) MAZE

simulated world fabricated by us, to escape an intolerable actuality 6) TEARS the nature specifically of that actuality (an intolerable one — the BIP *Acts*)"[13] (*Pursuit* 166). The idea of a bogus world hiding a reality that may be intolerable, but which is quite different from the one we know, is then present in all these novels.

Another fragment (written in 1978) reworks this idea thus: "EYE, JOINT, 3 STIGMATA, UBIK & MAZE are the same novel written over and over again. The characters are all out cold & lying around together on the floor, mass hallucinating a world" (*Pursuit* 177). The situation described by Dick is what we have found in *Eye in the Sky*, with the seven victims of the Bevatron accident unconscious and visiting a series of FSRs; yet it is clear that there is indeed a common element in these novels, namely the FSRs. Created by an imaginary physical phenomenon, as in *Eye*; by the combination of a vast conspiracy and a retreat syndrome, as in *Time Out of Joint*; by hallucinogenic or reality-altering drugs, as in *Stigmata* and *Tears*; or by two different sorts of Virtual Reality, as in *Ubik* and *A Maze of Death*, it does not really matter. What is at stake is the reality or unreality of a world, be it finite or infinite. Here ontological uncertainty does not just involve, as in Dick's android/simulacra stories, single individuals, who might or might not be human; here worlds may be faked. In all these novels we have characters or groups of characters trapped in FSRs they did not choose to live in (with the possible exception of *Maze*, but also the deliberately selected artificial shared world of Delmak-O may be seen as a prison, and it is ultimately threatening and dismal, as we shall see); moreover, in all these novels the FSRs have been created by someone or something whose intentions are questionable or absolutely bad.

The FSRs we are mapping in this chapter could be easily considered as private or partially shared hells. These realities are not subjective because they are pure idioi kosmoi, solipsistic microworlds with a population of one; these are rather ontologically uncertain infernos devised by a single, possibly deranged mind, but inhabited by a small bunch of damned souls (or, in *Tears*, a single damned who is aware that the world around him has changed, plus all the others who are unaware). It is the destiny of those souls which compels us to differentiate between the first two novels in the first list and the remaining four. While in *Eye* and *Time* an escape is not impossible,[14] in the four novels written in the 1960s escape is impossible or (as in *Tears*) quite difficult.[15]

Let us then read *Ubik*, considered by most critics as one of Dick's masterpieces, on a par with *Castle* and *Time-Slip*. We should start by saying that when Dick linked this novel to *Eye in the Sky* and *A Maze of Death* he was quite accurate, as in these three works you do have a group of characters "all out cold & lying around together on the floor, mass hallucinating a world"; on the other hand the characters of *Time Out of Joint* may be mass-hallucinating a world but are not unconscious; in *Stigmata*, as we have seen, there is group-hallucination when Can-D is used, but Leo's and Barney's FSRs are definitely individual and solipsistic; in *Tears* there is a peculiar sort of FSR, whose only difference from the koinos kosmos is the non-existence of a single man — the only individual who is aware of this. This should remind us that Dick's own comments on his works should always be read *cum grano salis*, allowing for the slips of a rather disordered memory (let us not forget that the Rickman interviews took place in the early 1980s, more than ten years after Dick had written *Ubik*, more than twenty years after the publication of *Time Out of Joint*).

Dick did not consider *Ubik* one of his best works: he told Rickman that it was "a rather desperate effort to infuse something original" into a conventional plot; moreover, he thought that in this novel readers could perceive "the beginning of an ossification in my writing where I *am* beginning to repeat myself" (Rickman 1988, 172). This novel that was wholeheartedly praised by Stanislaw Lem, Kim Stanley Robinson, Peter Fitting and others, including Suvin, who saw the second half of the 1960s as a downbeat period in Dick's oeuvre, but considered this "richest and most provocative novel" as an exception [Suvin 1975, 2]; its narrative architecture may seem simpler than the polyphony we find in *Castle* or *Time-Slip*, though interpreters like Robinson have shown that its stripped-down structure has its bewildering complexities. Yet *Ubik* bore — in the opinion of its author — the marks of ossification, decay, maybe even death.

Surely the time when the novel was written was not one of the worst in Dick's life: in 1966 his marriage with his fourth wife, Nancy Hackett, was quite serene. But there is a dark and haunting atmosphere in *Ubik*, which is above all a novel about death: what else could be said about the story of a group of characters who gradually discover that they are dead, and that what they are experiencing is not life but half-life, a form of virtual reality conjured up by residual electric activity in the brains of corpses preserved in cryogenic suspension? There is a double reversal, in this plot, which is ultimately rather depressing; while in the first half of the novel Joe Chip and the other survivors of the explosion on the Moon think their employer Glen Runciter was the only victim of the bombing, a series of strange events can only be rationally explained by Runciter's jeering message "LEAN OVER THE BOWL AND THEN TAKE A DIVE. ALL OF YOU ARE DEAD. I AM ALIVE" (111); here is what Dick meant by "messages of assistance" (*Pursuit* 166). In the last seven chapters of the book (10–16) we discover that only Runciter survived the attack, while Joe and the other members of the team died and were put in cryogenic suspension, with their boss trying to keep in touch with and help them. But then there is a reversal of the reversal when, in the brief last chapter, Runciter notices that on the fifty-cent pieces he is giving his secretary there is the profile of Joe Chip; since the appearance in the virtual reality of coins with Glen Runciter's profile was one of the signs that there was something wrong in Joe's world,[16] readers may well conclude that also Runciter died in the bombing and that he is in half-life too. Quoting Orwell, the characters of *Ubik* could declare "we are the dead," and such a bleak situation may well justify Dick's uneasiness with this novel.[17] If we don't forget that the bleakest period of Dick's life started in 1969, the year *Ubik* was published, we are authorized to read it also as a harbinger of a major psychological crisis in the life of its author.[18]

Not all the commentators consider the situation at the end of *Ubik* hopeless. Proietti suggests a political reading of the novel, where the final apparition of the 50 cents coins with Joe Chip, by revealing that all the characters are "on the same ontological plan" (Proietti 2006, 215), leads to a rejection of the previously suggested hierarchical relation, which saw Runciter as privileged because alive; Proietti then reads Ella Runciter's statement that "[t]his battle goes on wherever you have half-lifers" (183) as hinting to a stubborn opposition to an evil trinity of "evil, the capital, and entropy" (Proietti 2006, 215). Also for Kim Stanley Robinson the ending is not necessarily pessimistic, but must be read as a sort of sabotage of certain traditional narrative devices of sf. The ending heavily impinges on the interpretation of the novel, inasmuch as it creates a major logical inconsistency: in fact, if all the characters had died in the attack, "there would have been no one to get them to the Moratorium" (Robinson 94), that is, the place where dead people are kept in cryogenic suspension and can communicate with their relatives and friends. This leads Robinson to interpret the inconsistency as the result of a deliberate narrative strategy by Dick, as he "made certain that no explanation will cover all of the facts" (Robinson 95): it is not a matter of sloppy writing, but a move to purposefully thwart any rational explanation of the events told.[19] When Robinson wrote his monograph he could not quote another piece of evidence which demonstrated that the logical inconsistencies of this novel could not be explained away with hasty or careless writing: his PhD dissertation was published in 1984, while the text of the screenplay based on *Ubik* (written by Dick in 1974 for French filmmaker Jean-Pierre Gorin, whose project to film the novel failed for lack of funding) was only published in 1985 (as *Ubik: The Screenplay*). So Dick had an opportunity to change the plotline as much as he wished eight years after its original composition; if he chose *not* to change those crucial elements (the Runciter and Chip coins), it should mean that whatever inconsistencies are in the text are deliberate, not accidental.

In his monograph Robinson follows Stanislaw Lem's suggestion that inconsistency in literature is not always the result of incompetence, but may indicate the repudiation of certain values (such as logical consistency) for the sake of others (Lem 1972, 60–1); in other words, the oddities of, say, Surrealist art are not the result of Salvador Dali's or René Magritte's poor craftsmanship. But what are the "other values"? Robinson does not clearly tell us, though his quoting Fitting at the end of his essay may well mean that he accepts the basic thesis of Fitting's "Ubik and the Deconstruction of Bourgeois SF": Dick aims at the denunciation of "the anthropomorphic presuppositions of science and of SF" (Fitting 1975, 45). Fitting's essay is a typical representative of the earliest season of Dick scholarship, where the Marxist approach was paramount, and Dick's fiction was read as a form of socio-political criticism; though not all the conclusions drawn by those readings are fully persuasive today, the idea that *Ubik* is an attack to certain presuppositions of science-fiction is still worth considering.

Half-life, with the ontological uncertainty it generates, can well be a way to short-circuit and somewhat sabotage the idea of objectivity and rationality which Golden Age Sf propounded. But there is more to it than that: we have seen that Palmer Eldritch — who can mass-produce and deliver eternal life — is an embodiment of the dream of transcendence-through-science[20] which was typical of Golden Age Sf. He boasts that Chew-Z enables men and women to live whatever life they like, to attain immortality, even to change what is by definition unchangeable, that is, the past; it is then a way to achieve a sort of omnipotence, or total control. Half-life is not so different, inasmuch as it should deliver a sort of eternal life, or at least a prolongation of life beyond death — it also enables the living (like Runciter) to exploit the dead, to use them as consultants (this is what the entrepreneur does with his wife Ella right from the start), and this is what Proietti seems to suggest in his essay.

But Jory's domination on the half-lifers gives the lie to the hopes for a prolonged life, and unmasks the artificial afterlife as a nightmarish hell. Moreover, the final discovery disrupts any dream of rational control. Until we believe that only Runciter is dead and the others are alive, or Joe Chip and the inertials are dead and only Runciter is alive, we think we have at least one narrative focus outside the virtual reality of half-life, which should provide us with a grasp on the much needed objectivity of koinos kosmos. But the last chapter tells us that there is no external and reliable point of view. This does not really mean, *pace* Robinson, that there is no consistent explanation: one might imagine that after the bombing police forces intervened and put all the victims in a Moratorium; Jory's malignant intervention may then explain the separation of Runciter and his employees which leads he and them to believe they have survived the explosion. The final coup de théâtre, abolishing any external point of view at the end of the novel, determines the lack of a *certain* logically consistent explanation — we are well into ontological uncertainty once more, admittedly in a more radical fashion than in *Stigmata*.

Yet something important ties the two novels: in both *Stigmata* and *Ubik* it is the villain who maintains and controls the virtual reality. Jory clearly says that every fixture in the pseudo-world where most of the novel takes place "is a product of [his] mind" (174). Jory explains that the energy he absorbs from the brains of people in cryogenic suspension is used to maintain a small world (175), just enough virtual space to host the minds of those he is deluding. This is rather strange, and the strangeness of this behavior also strikes Joe Chip, who asks "What's the point of keeping this hotel and the street outside going for me now? ... Now that I know [that it is all bogus]?" (175). Jory's answer is scoffing: "But I always do it this way"; it does not really explain, and this may be part of the strategy of sabotaging any rational explanation that we have already discussed. But it might also be explained in a different way, if we connect this to something Ella Runciter tells Joe in a subsequent episode, that is, that "there are Jorys in every moratorium" (183).

Ella, being part of the virtual reality, might be untrustworthy, but her role in the plot is antithetical to Jory's. While the cruel and voracious boy embodies the destructive principle, propelled by sheer and avid self-preservation (174), and only interested in "eating" other minds to survive (just like Palmer Eldritch, though in a coarser fashion), Ella helps Joe survive by means of the reviving Ubik spray can. We have bitheism again, a dualistic world view where a principle of death and decay (originally represented by Ahriman in *Puppets*) is countered by a principle of life and growth (Ormazd and Armaiti in the same novel); no wonder then that Ella is represented as a young and beautiful woman. This resurfacing of an old symbolic opposition in Dick's fictional world should not however put us off the fact that wherever there is a moratorium — i.e., a space of virtual reality, however short-lived and flickering it may be — there is a Jory, that is, someone or something who maintains and manages the virtual reality, to a certain extent (the fact that Joe can protect himself from decay and death with the Ubik spray means that Jory's control of the artificial reality is not as total as he would like).

Who controls the virtual reality, then? In other words, who controls the fiction? The metafictional answer is that Dick himself, the game-player, the Rat, controls the game. And there is no doubt that also *Ubik* is another Game of the Rat, where readers' and characters' expectations and hypotheses are perversely belied by the repeated twists in the tale. Like Palmer Eldritch before him, Jory may be another anamorphic portrait of the author as a mischievous and twisted boy. This should not surprise us, because the childlike or adolescent character of SF (as it was, or as it was perceived from outside the ghetto) was already an issue Dick had explored in *Time Out of Joint* and then in his short story "Small Town" (see Ch. 1 and 2).[21] The fact that the author could portray himself as such a ghastly and despicable character as Jory chimes in with his not wholly positive opinion on the novel, and the gloomy atmosphere haunting it (though countered in several episodes by Dick's indestructible deadpan humor). A writer who had failed to escape the Sf ghetto (like one of his former colleagues, Kurt Vonnegut Jr., who was moving to recognition outside the genre in the very years Dick was stuck in the cheap paperback market), whose most ambitious works had been rejected by serious publishers, whose private life seemed to repeat a pattern of marital failure (which consisted in the inability to assume an adult role as a husband and a father) could well paint his self-portrait as a cruel boy who can only manipulate those who are trapped in his virtual reality — that is, a writer who picks on his characters.

The presence of the positive, protective figure of Ella Runciter is then another sign of a duality in Philip K. Dick's mind. I will not go so far as to talk about split or multiple personality, but the importance of Dick's dead twin Jane as a symbolic figure is something that scholars cannot ignore today. If half-life is an anamorphic image of Dick's science fiction, including his interest in time and its derangement (hence the strange regressive force at work in the novel, a time-slip in its own right, which transforms modern airplanes into old biplanes, television sets into thermoionic tube radios, etc.), it is to be expected that *Ubik* is the place of a "battle [which] goes on whenever you have half-lifers" (183), the battle between the two drives which struggled in Philip K. Dick's mind as depicted in his fiction (and possibly in his real emotional life). Of course those two drives are here represented by Jory and Ella Runciter.

Dick's feeling of ossification, his perception of a waning of his creative powers as a writer, is then depicted in the novel as the typical "universe falling apart"; the virtual reality that Jory maintains is precarious, decaying, and there are several moments (like the harrowing scene in the hotel in Chapter 15 or the gloomy episode in the drugstore in chapter 16) in which the lights are almost off and the annihilation of Joe's consciousness is almost accomplished. The virtual reality in *Ubik* is not as solid and resistant as the alternate universe in *Castle*; it is always on the verge of ultimate dissolution. If Jory is a demiurge to the half-life, his powers are remarkably weaker than those of Palmer Eldritch; he can be exhausted by sustained efforts of world-projection (175), as during Joe's flight from New York to Des Moines at the beginning of Chapter 11 (though we are only told this in Chapter 15). Joe's experience in the virtual world conjured up by Jory is often one of utter tiredness and sickness. In fact Dick told Rickman that the composition of Ubik had been quite an effort; an almost failed novel, saved *in extremis*, that the author "had to pull ... out of the fire," so that "there is an element of desperation that began to show up in the writing" (Rickman 1988, 172).

The third novel in this group, *A Maze of Death*, was described by Dick as "a desperate attempt to come up with something new," a failed attempt because "in no way it is new. It repeats familiar things with a multi-foci basis and the epistemological theme, the reality versus irreality. That's the last gasp of those things that had become my stock in trade" (Rickman 1988, 172). The novel was probably written in autumn 1968, and this was surely a much less peaceful time in Dick's life; his literary mentor and friend Anthony Boucher had died in April; Dick and his family had moved to a new and larger house in Santa Venetia the year before, a decision that put some financial strain on his budget (the house had to be registered in the name of his mother and her new husband due to Dick's poor credit rating [Sutin 158]); Dick had problems with the IRS from 1967 to 1969; to all this we should add his increasing addiction to amphetamines, which he took in increasingly larger doses. Writer's block, in such a precarious financial situation, could mean disaster.

No wonder, then, that Dick recycled older materials to write *Maze*. Much older, as the basic device of the novel dates back to 1939: in fact, the idea of fourteen people stranded on a faraway planet called Delmak-O, and killed one by one by an unknown murderer — possibly one of them — is too similar to the story of ten people lured to Soldier Island, on the coast of Dorset, and then inexorably killed by someone who might be part of the group, to consider it a mere coincidence; but this is the plot of Agatha Christie's *And Then There Were None*, aka *Ten Little Niggers*.[22] There is no direct evidence that Dick had read the novel, but in a dialogue two characters who meditate on their dire situation seems to suggest how Dick would rework the plot of Christie's novel:

> 'It's like some awful dream. I keep feeling that things like this can't happen.' ...
> 'I know. Presently a tap will come on the door, and early morning tea will be brought in.' ...
> 'Oh, how I wish that could happen!' ...
> 'Yes, but it won't! We're all in the dream! ...' [Christie, 180].

The series of murders in *And Then There Were None* is not a dream, and all the events are logically and exhaustively explained in the final statement written by Justice Wargrave, who is the murderer and mastermind of the plot. But Dick literalized the metaphoric sentence "We're all in the dream," because this is what we discover in the fifteenth and penultimate chapter of *A Maze of Death*: the characters only dreamt their frightening experiences on Delmak-O. The fourteen colonists are actually the crew of a spaceship, the *Persus 9*, forever orbiting a dead star due to an accident that also killed its captain and irreparably damaged its transmitter. The crewmembers know all too well that they will never be able to repair the ship or the transmitter, so that they are forever imprisoned in their orbital jailhouse; the only way to stave off

creeping psychosis, generated by seclusion in such a small space, is "the polyencephalic mind.... Originally an escape toy to amuse us during our twenty-
year voyage" (183). The device is connected to the ship's computer, TENCH
889B, and its working anticipates the cyberspace that would be introduced
more than ten years later by another science-fiction author, William Gibson,
in his 1982 short story "Burning Chrome." The main difference is that Gibson's cyberspace is a virtual reality which is patently artificial, "an abstract
representation of the relationships between data systems ... the consensus-
hallucination that facilitates the handling and exchanging of massive quantities
of data" (Gibson 196–7), so that the console cowboys in "Burning Chrome"
and *Neuromancer* are well aware that they are operating in a virtual space. On
the other hand, the virtual reality created by the polyencephalic mind is realistic enough to cheat the minds of those who are connected to it; besides,
their memories of life on board the *Persus 9* have been replaced by "manufactured recall datum," fake memories "implanted in [their] mind during the
fusion, to add the semblance of authenticity in the polyencephalic venture"
(182). This is why Dick saw the gist of the novel as the depiction of a "simulated world fabricated by us, to escape an intolerable actuality" (*Pursuit*
166).

Here Dick is recycling one of his classical devices, the amnesiac character,
that he had already used in *Time Out of Joint* and in the short story "We Can
Remember It For You Wholesale" published two years before the completion
of *Maze*; it should be added that the amnesiac hero was something Dick had
developed from A.E. Van Vogt's *The World of Null-A*, one of the classics of
the Golden Age of Science-Fiction. But other elements of the plot derive from
Dick's earlier works. Before the final denouement, there is a false revelation
in Chapter 14, when — after discovering that they are on Earth, not on Delmak-O (156–8) — the survivors assume that they are former inmates of a giant
asylum, the Aviary, where all the humans who could not stand the trauma of
interstellar travel have been committed; the fourteen characters could have
managed to escape, or have been set free in an experiment that should test
their ability to resume a normal life. If this were true, they would be a small
replica of the community of madmen and -women in *Clans of the Alphane
Moon*, and this hypothesis is strengthened by the fact that some of them have
mental problems or deviant behaviors: Tony Dunkelwelt has mystical hallucinations, Ben Tallchef is an alcoholic, Ned Russell is obsessed by cleanliness,
Betty Jo Berm is addicted to psychotropic drugs, Maggie Walsh has a mild
religious mania, Mary Morley is a control freak with a remarkable aggressive
component, Milton Bubble is hypochondriac, Ignatz Thugg is a zoophile and
has a strong homicidal drive (*nomen, omen*). But, unlike the clans of the
Alphane moon, the small community of deranged individuals on Delmak-O

is completely dysfunctional, because we eventually discover that the characters have killed each other (167–9).

Even when the events told in chapters 1–14 are revealed to be a synthetic experience generated by the polyencephalic mind, madness is still present; the violence in the virtual reality of Delmak-O bespeaks the derangement seeping into the minds of the crew members. "How long, really, can we keep on?" muses Seth Morley, brooding over the dismal virtual experience. "Not much longer. Thugg's wits are scrambled; so are Frazer's and Babble's. And me, too.... Maybe I'm gradually breaking down, too. Wade Frazer is right; the murders on Delmak-O show how much derangement and hostility exists in all of us" (187). Seth's disconsolate conclusion is that each artificial world produced by the polyencephalic mind "will be more feral." This view of madness is in marked contrast to the optimistic approach in *Clans of the Alphane Moon*.

We should also notice that *Maze* returns — or strives to return — to Dick's narrative strategy of the early 1960s, the multi-foci and multi-plot diegetic structure. But it is a half-hearted effort. If we check who are the narrative foci of the novel in each chapter, we find out that Dick did not achieve a full-fledged polyphony, as in *Bloodmoney* or *Time-Slip*.

Table 7.2

Chapter	Narrative focus/foci	Pages	Chapter	Narrative focus/foci	Pages
1	Ben Tallchef	9–15		Betty Jo Berm	115–6
2	Seth Morley	15–27		Maggie Walsh	117–20
3	Ben Tallchef	27–36		Tony Dunkelwelt	120–4
4	Seth Morley	36–44	10	Seth Morley	124–31
	Milton Babble	44–51		Glen Belsnor	131–6
5	Seth Morley	51–6		Roberta Rockingham	136–8
	Ben Tallchef	56–60	11	Glen Belsnor	138–41
	Seth Morley	60–1		Maggie Walsh	141–4
6	Seth Morley	61–73		Seth Morley	144–5
	Susie Smart	73–7	12	Seth Morley	145–51
7	Seth Morley	78–91	13	Seth Morley	151–62
	Susie Smart	91–6	14	Seth Morley	163–78
8	Glen Belsnor	96–105	15	Glen Belsnor	178–81
	Seth Morley	105–9		Seth Morley	181–6
9	Seth Morley	109–10	16	Seth Morley	186–9
	Maggie Walsh	110–1		Mary Morley	189–91
	Wade Frazer	111–2			
	Mary Morley	112–3			
	Ignatz Thugg	113–4			
	Ned Russell	114–5			

As we can see the pages of the novel are not equally distributed among the characters. Seth Morley acts as a narrative focus in about 90 pages, more than half of the novel. The rest must be divided among some of the others, among which Glen Belsnor, Ben Tallchef, Maggie Walsh and Susie Smart have larger shares. All in all, the narrative focus and protagonist of the novel is Seth Morley, and the events are occasionally told from the point of view of other characters, without a wholehearted effort to achieve a complete narrative polyphony (something Dick himself admitted in the Author's Foreword [5]). Only in Chapter 9 we have a frantic change of point of view, which strongly contributes to the effectiveness of this part of the novel, where each character sees what he or she wishes to see in a mysterious building discovered on the barren surface of Delmak-O (so that Ignatz Thugg sees it as a HIPPERY HOPPERY, that is a place where you can have sex with animals [113], while Seth Morley, who loves good wines and cheeses, visualizes it as a WINERY [110], and so on). The shifting of narrative foci continues at a lower speed in the two following chapters, then Dick relies on Seth's point of view for three chapters in a row.

Also the characters in the plot are more sketched than carved or etched. Usually Dick strives to portray at least a few rounded characters, and his impressive achievements in terms of characterization have been acknowledged by several critics, among which Ursula K. Le Guin with her essay "The Modest One" (Le Guin 1979); but here only Seth Morley can be said to have been painted in detail, and he is the umpteenth Little Man à la Frank Frink, Joe Chip, or Barney Mayerson, only remarkable because he is not a repairman or a professional, but the cook of the *Persus 9*.

There is no doubt that Dick built this novel with wreckage of his previous works, even though he managed to build a compact, suspenseful work which is excellent entertainment, and is endowed with an atmosphere of doom and menace with a remarkable impact. *Maze* is in any case an important document for Dick scholars, bearing witness to Dick's creative exhaustion. For example, there is a remarkable difference between *Maze* and the two other novels that we have already read in this chapter: in *Stigmata* and *Ubik* the idioi kosmoi (in the former), or fake koinos kosmos (in the latter) are conjured up by human figures, by individuals which — identified as Gnostic demiurges or archons — can well be interpreted as avatars of the author; but here there is no central manipulative game-player, no Rat directing the play behind the scenes. The artificial koinos kosmos of Delmak-O is the consensual product of several minds coordinated by a machine, TENCH 889B, a computer. On the one hand we might read this a sign of Dick's tiredness with the Game of the Rat: he felt that, as a hack writer producing pulp fiction, he was no more an artist, not even a respectable artisan, but a machine which kept churning out book after book monotonously repeating itself. A machine which cannot sustain the koinos kosmos it has projected on the characters' (and readers') minds for long, however; when asked "WHAT IS PERSUS 9?" (173) by the surviving colonists, the tench, the avatar of the ship's computer in the virtual reality (disguised as a mysterious alien creature, a "cube of gelatinous mass" [125] that is able to answer to written questions with enigmatic, sibylline answers [126–9]), explodes in a cataclysmic paroxysm (174–8) and the characters are abruptly ejected from the virtual reality and wake up on board the doomed starship. Another universe falling apart, like the FSRs of *Stigmata* and the half-life in *Ubik*. But this may be a universe that Dick himself is tearing apart, as Robinson suggested that "[j]ust as in the Christie's novel, Dick kills off the characters one by one. *A Maze of Death* is a rampage by Dick through his character system, a desperate attempt to kill off a cast that has obsessed him for over twenty years, in over twenty books" (Robinson 104). The systematic slaughter already took place in *Ubik*, but there Joe Chip could resist thanks to Ella Runciter's heaven-sent spray can; here no one gets out alive.

On the other hand the novel turns out to be even bleaker once we realize that behind this disintegrating reality we do not have, this time, an evil mind that masterminds the misadventures of the characters; the destructive drives that turn Delmak-O into a nightmare *are already in the minds of the dreamers*, and this bespeaks a much more pessimistic stance of the author/demiurge. Besides, the koinos kosmos that the characters get back to at the end of the novel is not less desperate and asphyxiating than Delmak-O; if we read it as an anamorphic image of our world, where we orbit a dying star on a planet which technology and globalized economy have made smaller and smaller, while virtual realities projected by the mass media distract us from the inescapable end of our life, i.e., death, it is a terribly bleak image, maybe the bleakest Dick ever presented his readers with (Warrick 150). *Maze* suggests an abysmal pointlessness of life, the world and also history; space travel, which was a glorious adventure towards an amazing future history in Heinlein and other Golden Age authors, only leads to a dreadful dead end in this novel — it is once again the frightening mental place imagined by Jack Bohlen in *Martian Time-Slip*, where nothing ever happens anymore.

Yet someone manages to escape the event horizon of this novel (the *Persus 9* orbits a dead star, not a black hole, but the situation is remarkably similar as there is no escape in both cases). When Seth Morley is ready to open the vents of the space ship, so that the atmosphere may get out and the crew can reach its "only comfort," death (188), someone appears to stop him. This apparition marks an ontological twist in the tale resembling the apparition of the Joe Chip coins in the last chapter of *Ubik*, because Seth is approached by a bearded young man, "with flowing, pale robes, ... erect, with a pure, shining face" (188); not a member of the crew, hence somebody who should not be there. He is the Intercessor, one of the divine entities of the fictional religion which was part of the virtual reality created by the polyencephalic mind, a syncretic mix of "all the data they had in their possession concerning advanced religions ... Judaism, Christianity, Mohammedanism, Zoroastrianism, Tibetan Buddhism" (182–3).

The Intercessor should belong to the virtual reality of the polyencephalic fusion; yet he invades the "real" universe of the doomed starship. If we applied the same reading strategy we have used with *Ubik*, this should mean that either Dick is once again playing the Game of the Rat, preventing us from rationally interpreting this novel, and plunging also the clarifying ending into ontological uncertainty again; or he is telling his readers that the "real" reality depicted in the last two chapters of *Maze* is in any case science-fiction — possibly cheap science fiction! — an imaginary universe conjured up by a writer who also is beginning to show serious signs of overwork. One should however be careful not to explain away this episode as a further sign of Dick's creative exhaustion or impending writer's block: this scene is after all a replica of the apparition of Mercer in *Androids* (Ch. 6), when the sfnal messiah, just declared a fraud by Buster Friendly (something Mercer himself does not deny), appears in the "real" world to offer Isidore and Deckard comfort and advice; and *Androids* was not written in a moment of creative dearth.

The apparition of the Intercessor offers Seth a possibility to escape the space ship, so that he does not try to kill himself and the others, by fulfilling Seth's wish to become "a desert plant ... that would see the sun all day" (188). This is read by Robinson as a sign that "at this ultimately low point in Dick's work, a miracle is the only hope. If a miracle cannot be summoned up, the alternative is endless horror" (Robinson 105). Becoming a cactus is a quite weird form of salvation, but then much in Dick's novels is weird; one may then wonder whether Seth's wish should not be taken ironically, as an elaborate, maybe pataphysical joke.[23] Yet we cannot downplay a simple fact that Robinson does not mention: while in *Stigmata* the religious subtext was tied to Palmer Eldritch, so that the figure with religious connotations is an evil god or an imposter (demiurge or archon), here the bogus religion concocted by the polyencephalic mind manages to somewhat save the protagonist, because Seth does leave the *Persus 9* (Dick takes care to shift the point of view on his wife who looks for him in vain, so that we cannot think that the meeting with the Intercessor was a hallucination or a dream), and his companions get back to another polyencephalic fusion, on Delmak-O again (a repetition which strengthens the claustrophobic atmosphere of the novel, like the dreadfully repetitive circular orbit of the *Persus 9*).

Unless we accept Mackey's straight interpretation of the scene as a real miracle (Mackey 101), and read *Maze* as a religious novel in its own right — something that is not critically untenable per se — the apparition of the Intercessor should be read as suggesting that there is a further ontological level. Delmak-O is a virtual reality; *Persus 9* seems to be the real koinos kosmos, but the intervention of the Intercessor means that it is no more than another FSR, a bogus world that can be accessed from an unimaginable Outside — by God (if one prefers Mackey's reading) or the author (metafictional reading) who, pace Robinson, may be tired of exterminating his characters and possibly melts with pity. His saving Seth, the most humane character in the novel, and letting him get out of the doomed ship is then an act of metafictional mercy.

However, such a reading does not contradict the ontological uncertainty which dominates this text. Several (though not numberless) alternative, conflicting explanations are possible; all of them, however, will have to take into account the interplay among the three alternate realities (or textual levels) in the novel.

Alternate realities are also the key element of a novel that could seem to belong to another phase of Dick's literary activity, *Flow My Tears, The Policeman Said*. Published in 1974, it might seem nearer such works as *A Scanner Darkly* (1977) and *Radio Free Albemuth* (completed in 1976 and posthumously published); but documental evidence tells us that the novel was actually written in 1970. It was published only four years later because Dick's private life in 1971 and 1972 was in such a turmoil that he could not work on it; suffice it to say that the manuscript of the first draft of *Tears* was finished in the bleakest moment of Dick's life, when his fourth wife Nancy had left him with his second daughter Isa, amphetamine addiction had reached a dangerous climax (he didn't take pills, but handfuls of pills [Sutin 169]), and his house was a meeting-place of drug addicts, dropouts and other weirdoes; it had been practically turned into a sort of commune (Sutin 177).[24] If we add his increasing problems with the IRS, it is easy to understand Dick's psychological instability in 1971, which prevented him even to work on an almost completed manuscript like that of *Tears*. It was real writer's block at last, which made his financial problems devastating.

The psychological impact was overwhelming: in August 1971 Dick asked to be hospitalized in Marin General Psychiatric Hospital and Ross Psychiatric Clinic, due to bouts of depression. He was visited by his attorney William Wolfson in Ross, and gave him the manuscript of *Tears* for safekeeping. This was a wise decision indeed, because on November 17, 1971 Dick's house in Santa Venetia was burglarized and his fireproof file cabinet forced open with explosives (Sutin 181–3). If the manuscript had been there, it could have been destroyed or stolen like other documents that were in the cabinet.

The 1971 break-in is a definitely Dickian event, marked by a deep uncertainty: Sutin lists eight possible explanations of the burglary, whose culprits have never been identified (one of the hypotheses being that Dick simulated it), but what is relevant to us is the fact that the manuscript of *Tears* remained in Wolfson's custody until late 1972, when Dick's situation had greatly improved and he had moved to Southern California. When he resumed the composition of *Tears* he worked especially on the ending scene, which he claimed to have rewritten ten times (*SL2* 139). The long pause in the writing of this novel and the repeated rewriting of at least a part of it[25] allowed Dick to have more control on the text, and it shows: *Tears* is more carefully built and woven than the novels of the late 1960s which immediately precede it, such as *Maze* or *Our Friends from Frolix 8* (1970); its prose is even more accurately crafted than what we find in such major works as *Stigmata* or *Ubik*.

Tears is undoubtedly the link between two phases of Dick's life and literary production; it has much in common with his novels of the 1960s (Robinson 106), but it also foreshadows Dick's concerns in the 1970s and early 1980s. One of the key elements of the novel, for example, is a sfnal drug called KR-3, used by one of the main characters, Alys Buckman; it is a deadly substance, which enables its user to manipulate the ontological frame of reality, and to access alternate worlds. It then resembles JJ-180 in *Wait*; but its world-creating power also bears relation with Chew-Z in *Stigmata*. However, in the uncannily realistic setting of *Flow*, whose futuristic elements are fewer than those one could find in the two earlier novels, KR-3 is less a sfnal device than something threateningly similar to amphetamines or heroin, paving the way for the devastating Substance D in *A Scanner Darkly*, an illicit drug whose direct effects are never described by Dick, so that it may be seen as a sort of archetypal ur-drug representing all the illicit substances used by whatever drug-addict one may imagine. In *Scanner* the drug does not directly produce ontological uncertainty, but its effects on its users are so unsettling that they live in an ontologically uncertain world: the main character, S.A. Fred, an undercover nark, is led to believe that Bob Arctor, his fake identity on the drug scene, is actually another person. KR-3 in *Tears* is more straightforward: it does change reality, it does bring the characters in the novel from one world to another and then to a third one; but its deadly effects are not just told, they are shown in the ghastly scene in Chapter 21, when Jason Taverner finds what is left of Alys, reduced to a skeleton (148).

Commentators have pointed out the strong autobiographical elements in *Tears* (Robinson 107): Dick's troubles with amphetamines, plus his stay in a Canadian rehabilitation centre, X-Kalay, have also been connected to Alys Buckman and her addiction to KR-3, though they have generally been tied to *Scanner*. Love and bereavement, the main argument of the novel according to Warrick (Warrick 158–9) and Dick himself (Rickman 1988, 177–8), are connected with an event in the writer's life, the painful break-up with his fourth wife Nancy. On the other hand the strong dystopian frame of the novel bears relation with Dick's growing anxieties about his being targeted by the police, the FBI or some other repressive apparatus, as a political dissident, due to his signing a petition against the Vietnam War in February 1968 (Sutin 160)—but also, and this is a more Dickian sort of fear, that he had "somehow, by accident, ... depicted a classified secret in his SF" (Sutin 161), in other words that he actually was like Ragle Gumm, not in a merely metaphorical sense. The 1971 break-in reinforced Dick's fears, and the revelations about COINTELPRO and the Watergate scandal (which started with another, more famous burglary) led him to believe, as he wrote in a 1974 letter to Richard M. Nixon, that he was "one of those whom [Nixon's] Administration sought to destroy" (*SL3* 64). Besides, Dick had already written in a previous letter that "the fascists almost took over, almost seized absolute power in the U.S., in a vast secret coup" (*SL2* 237). The world police state depicted in *Tears*, ruled by police marshals, with concentration camps and hi-tech surveillance devices (like those planted on Jason and neutralized by Alys [128–30]), stems from Dick's protracted fears which eventually brought him to write, from 1973 to 1975, the notorious letters to the FBI (cf. Philmus) where he strives to prove he is a law-abiding citizen eager to inform the authorities about a Communist conspiracy targeting him. A whole book could (and probably should) be written about these episodes in Dick's life, also because they may shed light on the split personality of Fred/Bob in *Scanner*, a character who is at the same time part of the repressive apparatus and one of its victims; suffice it to say that those letters show that Dick's fears about conspiracies and undercover surveillance were definitely not a pose.

However, *Tears* is a novel we must discuss because it features one more situation of ontological uncertainty which bears relation to the three earlier works we have already analyzed. We have already mentioned the reality-altering drug KR-3, whose effects are only explained in Chapter 27; the explanation is delayed because Dick wanted to exploit the suspense generated by the effects of the drug, which creates an absurd and disorienting situation of uncertainty. In the first chapter we are presented with the main character, Jason Taverner, a popular TV emcee and singer, whose *Jason Taverner Show* is watched by thirty million people (11); but after Jason is attacked by Marilyn Mason—a wannabe singer who had an affair with the TV celebrity to be subsequently dumped by him—and hospitalized, he wakes up in a "cheap wino hotel" (22) in Watts and finds out that nobody knows him anymore. The TV star is and has always been a nonentity; no one even remembers Jason was famous and successful, neither his agent Al Bliss, nor his attorney Bill Wolfer, nor his lover Heather Hart.

The situation is similar to what we have found in *The Cosmic Puppets*: there Ted Barton finds himself in a town where he does not exist, because he died when he was nine. But Jason's plight is even stranger: in the world where the novel is set after the first chapter he was never born — just like George Bailey in Pottersville (Ch. 1). It is also interesting that Taverner owes much of his success to the fact that he is a six, a genetically-engineered superman (117–9), so that here we have a mutant with enhanced intellectual powers like those in Van Vogt's novels, only he is not amnesiac at all: he remembers all too well who he is (or was), it is the world around him that apparently suffers from amnesia. Jason then becomes the victim of the repressive apparatus because he is the descendant of those Variable Men found in Dick's sociological sf of the 1950s (Ch. 2): the only man without proper IDs and records in a world where everybody is under surveillance.

Actually Taverner "passed over to a universe in which he didn't exist" (186), a parallel universe without a Jason Taverner; his passage, or translation, was brought about by Alys Buckman under KR-3,[26] but "when the drug wore off he passed back again" (186). We would then have a threefold scheme like this:

Table 7.3

Primary text	*Secondary text*	*Primary text*
Chapter 1	Chapter 2–21	Chapter 22-Epilog
Jason exists and is famous	Jason does not exist	Jason exists and is famous

This threefold structure resembles the one we had in *Puppets*, with the final restoration of the same reality which was challenged by the secondary text. We could then read the secondary text where Jason does not exist as an evil unreal world of occlusion, being the product of a KR3-addicted demiurge like Alys — who also uses other drugs, like the mescaline she gives Jason (134) or the "hexophenophrine hydrosuphate" she is on when we first meet her (80), and practices forms of sexual perversion by means of neurosurgery, which impact on her lucidity (82). If the secondary text is the product of such an unstable and obfuscated mind, where uncertainty reigns (as "she doesn't play by the rules" [95]), it must be an "occlusion, hiding the real world," as Zina Pallas will explain Emmanuel in *The Divine Invasion* (Ch. 9). This chapter focuses on novels featuring FSRs created by evil demiurges or archons, and we may see that Dick carries the idea to extremes in *Tears*: unlike the pocket universes in *Stigmata* or *Ubik*, or the deserted virtual planet Delmak-O in *Maze*, the alternate universe to whom Jason is dragged by Alys is populated by billions of individuals who ignore him; it may be a subjective reality, as it is somewhat masterminded by Alys, but it is not finite. Moreover, here the archon or demiurge is somewhat debased if compared to Eldritch, Jory or the polyencephalic fusion in Maze: the world Jason is trapped in has been conjured up by a decadent, perverted, mischievous, dying junkie.

It may be easily argued that this is another, even more pessimistic, anamorphic self-portrait of Dick: let us not forget that Alys is the twin brother of Felix Buckman, so that she may be another sfnal avatar of Dick's twin sister Jane, who was at the same time the author's missing half and the person he often identified with. Surely Alys is a world-creator like Dick; in Chapter 19 we are told that she is — like her brother — a collector of stamps (one of Dick's hobbies), antique snuff boxes (Dick loved snuff) and music records (another of Dick's passions)[27]; moreover she is a drug-addict like Dick was when he wrote the first draft of the novel.

But the relationship between textual levels and alternate realities is actually more complex than the one I have suggested. There are textual inconsistencies that call in doubt the identification of the reality accessed by Jason and the other characters in chapter 22 with the one depicted in Chapter 1; such inconsistencies were noticed by Robinson, who maintained that *Tears* "is another of the novel in which inconsistency is part of the structural fabric, only in this case it is unclear what purpose the inconsistency has, if any" (Robinson 107).[28] Once again, the pioneers of Dick scholarship were penalized by the limited availability of important documental sources, such as the writer's speeches.[29] It is there that an important inconsistency is explained as a deliberate textual move; in fact at least a commentator has noticed that while in Chapter 3 the hotel clerk mentions the law that forbids Afro-American couples to have more than one child (29), evidently devised to perform a "soft" genocide (in fact Blacks are few in the novel, and *Watts* is a depopulated neighborhood), the black man met by Felix in the final scene of the novel tells him that he has three children (197), and Rispoli interprets this as proof that Buckman spends some time (like Mr. Tagomi in *High Castle*) in our world (Rispoli 2006, 224).

If Robinson had been able to read (like Rispoli probably did) the text of "If You Find This World Bad, You Should See Some of the Others" (the speech Dick delivered in Metz, France in 1977) he would have understood that in Dick's interpretation of his own novel, the inconsistent detail was aimed at telling readers that "[s]omehow, just as Mr. Togomi (*sic!*) slipped over briefly into our alternate present, General Buckman in *Flow My Tears* did the same thing" (*Shifting Realities* 247). Hence the scheme should be changed thus:

Table 7.4

Primary text	Secondary text	Primary text	Zero Text
Chapter 1	Chapter 2–21	Chapter 22–27 (until page 194)	Ending of Chapter 27
Jason exists and is famous	Jason does not exist	Jason exists and is famous	Felix visits our world and meets Montgomery L. Hopkins

For the sake of clarity I did not add a fifth column to this table, which should contain the Epilogue, as it is certainly not set in our world but in the one depicted by the primary text. However, the brief episode purportedly set in our world should be read — according to Dick — as having an important psychological (and ethical) meaning. It is preceded by a dream (194) where a procession of medieval knights led by an old, white-haired king, reaches a house where Jason Taverner has sealed himself up; the posse enters the windowless house and kills Taverner, something which strikes Felix with "absolute and utter desolate grief." Due to the dream, Felix does not just feel devastatingly sorry for his sister Alys, but also for Taverner, the man he has just ordered to be arrested and arraigned for Alys' death (which Felix considers a murder).

Dick maintained that this dream "was a graphic depiction in General Buckman's mind of the transformation taking place objectively; it was a kind of inner analog to what was happening outside him to his entire world" (*Shifting Realities* 248) because Felix "underwent an inner change appropriate to the qualities of the better world, the more just, the warmer world in which the tyranny of the police apparatus was already beginning to fade away as would a dream upon the awakening of the dreamer" (*Shifting Realities* 249). Dick then adds that also this scene (and the dream) has an autobiographical meaning:

> In March 1974, when I regained my buried memories (a process called in Greek anamnesis, which literally means remembering) — upon those memories reentering consciousness I, like General Buckman, underwent a personality change. Like his, it was fundamental but at the same time subtle. It was me but yet it was not me [*Shifting Realities* 249].

The "buried" memories are those of Dick's alleged alternative life as an ancient Christian in A.D. 70 which will be discussed in more detail in the next Chapter. However, there are inconsistencies also in Dick's explanation of the inconsistency in *Tears*, and they are quite subtle. The writer tells us that the world where Felix meets Montgomery is the Zero Text, our world. Why do both Felix and Montgomery reach the gas station on quibbles (195), then? If Montgomery were a black man from *our* reality, free to have more than one child, he should travel on a car, not a quibble. Dick does not bother to describe quibbles in detail, though it is clear that they are definitely not our cars: they can fly, like the vehicles in *Blade Runner*. Montgomery should drive a Ford or a Chevrolet (or, like Dick for a short time in the 1970s, a FIAT); and the landing of Felix's quibble should amaze him.

But there is another inconsistency, and this is an internal one: first Dick tells us that Felix "slipped into our alternate present" (*Shifting Realities* 247), then he states that it is a "better world," one "in which the tyranny of the police apparatus was already beginning to fade away" (*Shifting Realities* 249); but we did not have the tyranny of the police apparatus in our world, at least not the variety depicted in the novel. Someone might complain that the 2001 USA PATRIOT Act is equivalent to such a tyranny, but the ubiquitous police force imagined by Dick, which in the novel has replaced all the local police authorities of the USA (and extends also to other countries, being "planetwide" [203]) is something that not even president G.W. Bush ever proposed. The gradual dismantling of the police apparatus, "too cumbersome to threaten anyone" is accomplished in 2136, when "the rank of police marshal was abandoned" (203), and this means that it is not something that may happen in "our alternate present." If Montgomery's three children mean that the world where Felix meets him is a better alternate reality than the one he comes from, the dismantling of the world police may belong to that world, but the presence of quibbles means it is not the world in which you are reading this monograph on Dick. Though a quibble is an evasion of the point of an argument by raising irrelevant distinctions or objections, the presence of quibbles as vehicles in the scene raises a relevant objection to Dick's own interpretation, and asks for a different scheme of how textual levels are structured in *Tears*:

Table 7.5

Primary text	*Secondary text*	*Tertiary text*
Chapter 1	Chapter 2–21	Chapter 22-Epilog
Jason exists and is famous; Afro-Americans are threatened by genocide due to the one-children law	Jason does not exist; Afro-American are threatened by genocide due to the one-children law	Jason exists and is famous; Afro-Americans are not threatened by genocide; the planetwide police will be dismantled

The passage from the first to the second world, and then to the third, makes for the atmosphere of ontological uncertainty, which is heightened and highlighted by the moral uncertainty of a dystopian world where anyone can be an informer of the police, ready to betray anyone else to reap real or imaginary benefits (imaginary like those expected by Kathy Nelson, who became an informer to save her husband Jack's life, unaware that he had actually been dead for a long time): here too things — and people — are seldom what they seem. Police general Buckman, one of the heads of the repressive apparatus, is actually a humane individual who shut down several concentration camps thanks to a legal catch (139) and prevented the final shootout between the police and students barricaded in the besieged university campuses or "kibbutzim" (140); he even "saw to it ... that in the kibbutzim the students were bathed, fed, their medical supplies looked after, cots provided" (140). But the "good cop" is also the man who decides that Jason Taverner must be arrested for the murder of his sister, claims he wants to kill the TV celebrity (188–9) and then cynically justifies the unmotivated prosecution of Taverner because "[t]he real, ultimate truth is that despite your fame and your great public following you are expendable.... And I am not" (192). Besides, Felix Buckman is quite good at cheating, as when he first meets Taverner and tells him that he is not impressed by his being a six, because the general is a seven (117); it is a lie, because sevens do not exist, but it helps Buckman to deal with the genetically-engineered supermen and -women. Once again, skim milk masquerades as cream.

On the other hand, it is the deranged, perverted, and wanton Alys Buckman who offers Buckman an opportunity to escape the nightmare world of non-existence: she is the first and only person in the secondary text who remembers Jason, his songs, and his TV show (132); she is then the equivalent of Will Christopher in *Puppets* (Ch. 1). But one might suspect that she does much more than confirm Jason's memories: since Taverner reaches a world where he is again famous only after having met Alys, his liberation must be tied to the woman; it is explained with Alys' death, because the death of the drug-addict demiurge must wipe away the false world (186) and let Taverner — and others, like Felix, officer McNulty, the policeman who investigates on Jason, and Phil Westerburg,[30] the chief coroner — return to the real world. But if the world at the end of the text (Tertiary Text) is neither the same we were presented with in Chapter 1 (Primary Text) nor the one where Jason is a nobody and where most of the novel takes place (Secondary Text), Alys' death is not sufficient to explain everything. If the death of the demiurge should terminate the effects of KR-3, Jason and the other character should return to a world where (a) Taverner is famous and (b) Afro-Americans are only allowed to have one child. Someone might object that the one-child genocidal law only exists in the Secondary Text, but this is not the case; when the hotel clerk mentions the law (29), Jason is not surprised by it, and shows he knows the workings of the law (such as the "birth coupon" that Afro-American women have to surrender when their first and only child is born); this means that the law also exists in the Primary Text. Hence the world where the novel ends is not the one where it started from; and how could Jason, and the other characters — including above all Felix, who will meet Montgomery — reach another alternate reality?

Maybe this is another of those inconsistencies noticed by Robinson; but we have already seen that one of them was actually something Dick had deliberately planted in his text. Could not this be another? If Jason ends up in an alternate world which may be acceptable to him, because he is a celebrity again, but is not the one he started from, his situation is quite similar to that of Hamilton at the end of *Eye in the Sky* (Ch. 2). We have an open ending, also because we cannot help asking what has really happened in Chapter 21; if Alys' death alone was enough to bring everybody back to the Primary text, it was not sufficient to take them to a third alternate reality, so what did move everybody to that world? There are two possibilities: either Alys is not dead, but is still alive, and is keeping Jason, her brother and the others in the third, better world by means of KR-3; or somebody else has taken KR-3, and that could be Jason, who has been given a pill by Alys (134) which might not be mescaline, after all, but KR-3 — this would be consistent with the fact that Jason desperately wishes to get back to his old life of fame and privilege.

There is another unclear element, though, because Jason "conjectures that his whole career as a TV star had been a drug-induced hallucination" (Mackey 104), and this conjecture, though discarded in the ending of the novel, indirectly casts light on a detail of the beginning: when Chapter 1 ends, Jason has been struck by the deadly Callisto cuddle sponge (20), an alien parasite which may enter a human body by means of its feeding tubes; Jason manages to kill the sponge, but the feeding tubes have penetrated in his chest (21), and it is not sure that the surgeons may do something to save his life.

This episode is not mentioned any more in the novel: when Jason wakes up in the dingy hotel at the beginning of Chapter 2 he is healed and shows no trace of a surgical intervention (22). How was he saved by the effects of the attack? We are not told. One explanation might be that Jason could not be operated and died, killed by the feeding tubes; and that the world he wakes up in is his afterlife (of half-life), where his status as a nobody is a sort of retaliation for his arrogance and insensibility. Hence this novel could be much closer to *Ubik* than previous interpreters have surmised, and it might be set in a highly allegorical FSR where a soul (Taverner's) may reach a better realm (the Tertiary Text) after having expiated his sins of pride and lack of empathy in a dismal world of dystopian oppression and obscurity.

Once again, ontological uncertainty makes for several effects of signification. It also allows us to interpret this novel as an anamorphic image of Dick's own situation in 1972–3, when he completed it; Warrick and Robinson already pointed out how sentimental bereavement was explored in *Tears*, due to the failure of Dick's fourth marriage; but this novel also unfolds the author's fear and uncertainty vis-à-vis the break-in and its meaning, and his paranoid anxiety for the situation of the country he was living in, the paranoid scare that the Nixon administration and the conservative backlash which had brought it to the White House could usher in a totalitarian regime — among whose victims there might have been Dick himself. He depicted such a scenario in *Radio Free Albemuth*, where a fictional Phil Dick ends up in a concentration camp for political prisoners. *Albemuth* must have been written between February 1973 and August 1976, and shares some elements with *Tears*; the dystopian setting is rather similar, though it is less sfnal (something which is to be expected in a story set in the contemporary USA, while *Tears* takes place in the then near future of 1988); the autobiographical component is even stronger, because it features Dick among his characters (anticipating what the writer will do in *VALIS*, cf. Ch. 8), and the co-protagonist Nick Brady has a lot in common with the author (he could be considered as an alternative Philip Dick who did not become a pro writer but found a job in the music industry).

Tears does not only stage Dick's fears and sorrows. It also offers some displaced self-portraits. Alys Buckman can be read as an anamorphic image of Dick; the applies to her twin brother, if the Jane-Phil/Alys-Felix analogy is tenable, as both twins are Dick's portrait of the artist as a split subject (something we also have in *Albemuth*, *VALIS* [Ch. 8], and *The Divine Invasion* [Ch. 9]). But another character stands for the author: Mary Anne Dominic, the potter, whose surname is nothing more than "Dick" with a few additional phonemes. Once again the creative artist is a woman, like Pris Frauenzimmer in *Build* (Ch. 6), Emily Hnatt in *Stigmata*, Sadassa Silvia, the folksinger in *Albemuth*, or Linda Fox, the singer in *The Divine Invasion* (Ch. 9). It is Mary Anne's blue vase which survives all the characters of *Tears* (204), and her work deserves to be mentioned at the end of this long chapter on fictional demiurges: to all the dismal universes falling apart conjured up by evil or insane archons, we may oppose this small and beautiful (and fragile) creation, which nonetheless abides and is "openly and genuinely cherished." It should obviously remind us of another precious artifact, Frank Frink's pin, the piece of jewelry which somewhat allows Tagomi to visit the Zero Text in *The Man in the High Castle*. In that novel, after refusing Paul Kasoura's offensive proposal to market the jewel as a cheap good-luck charm in Third World countries, Robert Childan muses: "Life is short.... Art, or something not life, is long, stretching out endless, like concrete worm. Flat, white, unsmoothed by any passage over or across it" (179). Like Frink's pin, Mary Anne Dominic's blue vase is unsmoothed by any passage over or across other worlds — and it may well be an anamorphic image of those other works of art which could open those labyrinthine passages: Dick's own novels, of course.

Chapter 8

Amateur Questers: *VALIS* and Its Quandaries

> "O you Doppelgänger! you pale comrade!
> Why do you ape the pain of my love
> Which tormented me upon this spot
> So many a night, so long ago?"
> Heinrich Heine

The last three chapters of this monograph are not incidentally devoted to the three parts of the VALIS Trilogy, which is Dick's final literary achievement. Obviously one has to be aware that only the "brute fact" of Dick's death granted these novels (i.e., *VALIS*, *The Divine Invasion*, and *The Transmigration of Timothy Archer*) such a conclusive value. The biographer tells us that Dick wanted to write another novel right after *Archer*, whose title should have been *The Owl in Daylight* (Sutin 281): the fact that Dick was planning another novel should warn us that reading the VALIS Trilogy as a sort of literary testament containing Dick's own final "message" is a rather risky critical move (cf. Fitting's doubts about those interpreters who look for "something akin to religious truth" in Dick's writings [Fitting 1989, 243]).

However, there are reasons which lead us to consider the trilogy as another climax of Dick's literary career, though this opinion is not shared by all critics. In fact the strong presence of religious symbols, motifs and subtexts has been a problem for several commentators: Fredric Jameson chose to steer his analysis away from Dick's religious thematics (Jameson 2005, 363) thus avoiding his last novels; Carl Freedman was more drastic, as he liquidated *VALIS* and *The Divine Invasion* as "pretentiously tedious" (Freedman 2000, 165)[1]; Rabkin went so far as to declare the whole trilogy the product of an insane mind (Rabkin 186). A more positive appreciation can be found in Christopher Palmer's monograph on Dick (Palmer, 221–37), while other critics deem these novels to be among Dick's most important literary achievements, one of them being Darko Suvin. He considers these three novels (plus the posthumously published *Radio Free Albemuth*, which was anyway written before *VALIS*) as parts of a second artistic plateau (Suvin 2002), rivaling that of the "canonic" novels of the 1960s — usually considered Dick's best achievements (from *High Castle* to *Ubik*). Highly positive appreciations were also expressed by Gabriele Frasca and Kim Stanley Robinson (Frasca 2006; Robinson 111–27); a balanced and open-minded judgment on the religious themes in Dick has been formulated by Antonio Caronia, who reads it as an attempt to somewhat tackle ethical (and ultimately political) quandaries (Caronia & Gallo, 211–6). Here I can only say that the three parts of the VALIS trilogy are excellent examples of that principle of ontological uncertainty which is so important in Dick's oeuvre, and that they are among the most intriguing to a critic among those the Californian writer ever wrote. But if a defense of these works is needed, it will carried out in the analyses of the single novels, in this chapter and in those which follow it.

What should be briefly discussed here, before starting a detailed reading of *VALIS*, is why Dick's last three novels are to be considered a trilogy, notwithstanding the indisputable fact that the characters of the three works are not the same and the settings are different, as *VALIS* takes place in Southern California, *The Divine Invasion* on the extrasolar planet CY30-CY30B and then on the East Coast (only the ending is set in California), while the scene of *The Transmigration of Timothy Archer* is the San Francisco Bay area (with a single episode set in Santa Barbara). As for plot continuity, there is a link between *VALIS* and *Invasion*, because in the latter two characters — Elias/Elijah and Emmanuel — talk in Chapter 6 about "a very old movie" whose title is *Valis*, "made by a rock singer in the latter part of the twentieth century" (69): the title and description of the film clearly say that it is the same movie which gives *VALIS* its title, and is described in detail in Chapter 9 of that novel, when the protagonists watch and then discuss it; such an overt reference to the first part of the trilogy tells us that *VALIS* is set in the past of *Invasion*.[2] But there is no connection like this between any of these two novels and the third part of the trilogy, *Archer*. Moreover, the three parts belong to quite different genres; but it is exactly this difference which may help us understand what sort of unity can be hidden behind such a heterogeneous trio of narratives.

Invasion is undoubtedly a sf novel, we might also say an exasperated sf novel: extrasolar planets with aliens, space travel, a totalitarian world government, cryogenic suspension, flying cars — Dick put almost all the traditional ingredients of pulp sf in this book, thus leading Kim Stanley Robinson to suggest that *Invasion* could have been written by Horselover Fat, the deranged and visionary half of Dick's fictional self-portrait in *VALIS* (Robinson 112).

The overt presence of God in this novel is also sfnal, as he (if such a sexist pronoun is allowed) is a character that we can meet in several classics of sf, from C.S. Lewis' quite orthodox Space Trilogy (1938–46)—quoted in *VALIS* as Lewis is David's favorite writer — to Michael Moorcock's provocative novel *Behold the Man* (1969).[3] But Dick's most original move is to stage an invasion of Earth, this most sfnal event (since H.G. Wells' original *War of the Worlds*), where Earth is invaded not by the usual Martians (or other bug-eyed-monsters), but by the Old Testament God (embodied in a little child), supported by a Holy Family of sorts (the literary avatars of Joseph and Mary being not even married) plus prophet Elijah.

On the other hand *The Transmigration of Timothy Archer* is fundamentally a realistic novel (and as such it was sold to Simon and Schuster [Sutin 278]) where there is no more than the ghost of a fantastic element,[4] that is, the imaginary ancient sect of the Zadokites who might have used a hallucinogen substance called *anokhi*, thus creating the basic ideas of Christianity two hundred years before Christ. This is just a provocative hypothesis whose truthfulness is uncertain, held by bishop Timothy Archer — and it is ultimately less important than the sometimes merciless cross-section of the countercultural generation that Dick presents us with. Through a brilliant use of the technique of flashback Dick shows us what happened to the dreams and the delusions of a quite representative bunch of Californian protagonists of the "years of discord," and he does this starting from the fateful year 1980, when John Lennon was killed and Ronald Reagan elected. The novel is thus tightly pegged to the historical reality of the 1960s and 1970s in the USA.

VALIS is possibly more complex than the two following parts of the trilogy, as we will see in the detailed analysis that will be carried out in the rest of this chapter. Suffice it to say that the novel oscillates between religious sf and realism, and that such oscillation is not resolved, not even in the ending: it so exemplifies the principle of ontological uncertainty that has guided us in our survey of Dick's fiction like no other text we have read so far.

Hence what we have is a sf novel, a realistic novel, and a novel which is neither sfnal nor realistic, or both sfnal and realistic, or something that lives in a weird middle space between the two genres[5]— a situation that reminds us of a novelette by another American writer, Henry James' *The Turn of the Screw*. In other words, in this final trilogy we have the two literary genres which Dick practiced in his life: sf, which gave him an undeniable popularity in the sf ghetto and a cult writer status outside it; and realism, which is the genre of all the posthumously published novels (with the single exception of *Albemuth*) plus two novels Dick managed to publish in his lifetime, *Confessions of a Crap Artist* and *Archer* (remarkably, the preternatural elements present in this last novel belong to the fantasy genre he started from [Ch. 1]). Hence the

Trilogy is a representative sample of what Dick could do as a writer, and it is a trilogy also because it presents the whole gamut of narrative strategies that Dick mastered. It explores the possible games (of the Rat, of course) that a novelist can play when hybridizing two only apparently incompatible genres; it may have been Dick's own way to show the world (respectable publishers included, those who had so often — albeit not always — snubbed him) what he could do.

However, one should take into account what Dick himself said about the trilogy, because he suggested that there is a unifying element for these three novels. In fact, a June 1981 interview — possibly his last — the writer said:

> I would call *VALIS* a picaresque novel, experimental science fiction. *The Divine Invasion* has a very conventional structure for science fiction, almost science fantasy; no experimental devices of any kind. *Timothy Archer* is in no way science fiction; it starts out the day John Lennon is shot and then goes into flashbacks. And yet the three do form a trilogy constellating around a basic theme [Boonstra 1982].

Dick however does not say that the "basic theme" is. We have a clearer suggestion in the published selection of the *Exegesis*, where Dick says that the trilogy is about his mystical experiences called 2-3-74 (meaning February-March 1974, the period when he purportedly had visions and received enigmatic messages quite similar to those received by Horselover Fat in *VALIS*), and his contact with "not Elijah; the *spirit* of Elijah" (*Pursuit*, 239).[6] Usually such statements have been politely ignored by critics or taken as proof that Dick was insane when he wrote his final works. Since I am not a psychiatrist and believe in a critic's duty not to sweep under the carpet what does not fit an interpretation, I think it is from here that we should start.

In his July 9, 1981 letter to his daughter Laura and her husband Joe, Dick wrote:

> The topic of the trilogy is Christ; it is a study of the essence of Christ, what the term means, and how Christ is encountered and — in a certain real sense — brought into being.... In looking over the three novels of the trilogy I can see how Christ becomes progressively more and more real, but only is truly there in the third and final novel. And even in that novel Christ only 'occurs' at the end [*SL6* 178–9].

We should not underestimate the fact that the protagonist of the third part of the Trilogy is called Angel, inasmuch as that name derives from the Greek word ἄγγελος (*angelos*) which originally meant "messenger." A messenger announces something; a messenger can also reveal something previously unknown. In fact these three novels are about *revelation*. It does not really matter whether Dick's mystical experiences were real or not, that is, if he really was contacted by God. I dare say this is a matter of religious beliefs which each reader should sort out by him or herself.[7] What is important for literary critics is what is in the novels and what Dick did with that, and the concept of revelation is surely the theme that the writer has developed through sophisticated variations in the three movements of his fictional concerto. The fact that in 1981 Dick thought that the two parts of the trilogy he had already written (in this fragment he does not mention *Archer*) had as their "final ulti- mate purpose ... to predict ... the imminent coming — i.e., return — of the Savior" (*Pursuit*, 238) should not lead us to hasty judgments based on our religious beliefs, whatever they may be, or lack thereof, but to question what the coming of the Savior may *mean* from a literary point of view and what is its *meaning* in these three novels.[8] It is interesting to notice, by the way, that Dick's statements about his mystical experiences are rather contradictory, as in the same collection of excerpts from the *Exegesis* we have a self-examination (written in 1979, when the writer had already completed *VALIS*) where the author himself explains his visions of February-March 1974 as psychosis (*Pur- suit* 241–6).

Revelation has then to be taken here as a literary theme or motif. The three novels are pivoted on revelations of some sorts, and characters' reactions to those revelations are different in the three parts of the Trilogy: in *VALIS* Fat's experience, the revelation of a God that communicates via pink beams carrying impressive amounts of information (God as a broadband data down- load, we might say today), is met by his friends (and himself) with an alter- nation of belief and skepticism; in *The Divine Invasion* there is no doubt about the presence of God, which is revealed through indisputable facts (and an authoritative messenger, prophet Elijah), though there is a series of further revelations after the initial manifestation of Yah (concerning the character of Zina, as we shall see); in *Archer* there is a bewildering revelation about the origins of Christianity, and then the announcement of bishop Tim Archer's reincarnation, which are met by the 1st-person narrator, Angel Archer, with incredulity and a much stronger — and effective — skepticism than that dis- played by Phil and Kevin in *VALIS* (there is another, much more effective revelation when Angel meets Edgar Barefoot [Ch. 10]).

Surely revelation is a category which originates in religion, and the three novels are unsurprisingly crowded with religious terms, symbols, narratives: at least one of them, *Invasion*, is a religious sf novel, though one should wonder why the novel which stages the manifestation of God in the most straight- forward and indubitable manner is the only "pure" science-fiction novel of the trio (science-fiction being, as we all should know, a non-realistic genre). However, the strong and overt religious subtexts are a unifying element of all the trilogy, and this may even suggest an underlying symbolism. Since Christian symbols and concepts are paramount here (especially those from the Protestant traditions, as Dick considered himself an Episcopalian), the Holy Trinity may be a very important key to understand this trio of literary texts. Since the Trinity is composed of Father, Son, and Holy Ghost, it is difficult not to see that the quest for God is the main theme in the first novel, and that an incarnation (the embodiment of God in the Son) is only attempted there through the birth of Sophia, but fails. On the other hand the incarnation is successful in the second part of the Trilogy, whose protagonist is Emmanuel, a strange boy which is also God Incarnate, a new Christ who should not repeat the mistakes of the first. As for the third part, the presence of the Holy Ghost may have something to do with the ghost of Timothy Archer, which manifests itself in the last chapters of the novel; with the spiritualist teachings of one of the main characters, New Age guru Edgar Barefoot; and with the fact that the novel is powerfully influenced by Paul's epistles and the Acts of the Apostles, which were written (and take place) after the Ascension of Jesus, when the apostles are left with the Holy Ghost in their effort to covert the heathens.[9]

These and other religious elements will be discussed when each of the three parts of the trilogy will be analyzed. But before our reading of *VALIS* may begin, a last unifying structure of this weird triptych should be highlighted, as it is strongly connected to the leading issue of ontological uncertainty. The three movements of the trilogy can be said to be related to the present, the future and the past. It is the everyday present of late 1970s-early 1980s that Dick depicts in *VALIS*, and the two alternative readings of Fat's experience (divine revelation, or epiphany, vs. psychotic delusion) stand for two different visions of that present, two alternative or laminated present moments ("laminated" being, as we shall see in the rest of this chapter, a key Dickian word first used in *VALIS*): one of messianic hope and the other of despair and dissolution. The opposition of a living vs. dying present is quite important if we want to fully understand this novel.

It is quite obvious that the future is the favorite (albeit not the only) time of science-fiction, and that is the genre that *The Divine Invasion* undoubtedly belongs to. Here we are presented with two alternative futures, one of dystopian oppression and despair (a future Earth dominated by a two-headed world dictatorship), the other a more sustainable time where oppression can at least be fought. The two futures are embodied — in sfnal fashion — in two parallel universes, which the novel explores in turn: both however should be read as alternative futures stemming from Dick's present in 1981.

As for the last part of the triptych, *The Transmigration of Timothy Archer*, it is not just the massive presence of analepses that tells us this novel is dominated by a very peculiar sense of the past: *Archer*, as we have already said and will see in more detail in the last chapter of this essay, is fundamentally a reckoning of Dick's past life, told against the background of the rising and ebbing countercultural tide. No wonder then that the only undisputed fantastic element in this realistic novel (haunted, as many American realistic novels, by allegorical echoes and hints) is the past — or better ancient — story of the Zadokite sect and its scrolls. What is at stake in the novel is definitely not an alternative present or future, but an alternative, counterfactual past.

We can then end this preliminary discussion by saying that the unity of the VALIS trilogy should be understood as the way in which Dick applied his strategy of ontological uncertainty to the present, the future, and the past, indissolubly linking these three novels not by means of narrative continuity or recurring characters, but through a series of variations of his favorite theme. This should not surprise us, since we are dealing with a writer who was deeply in love with music (and *Invasion* can also be read as a celebration of the redemptive power of that art).

Once again, our reading of *VALIS* will be based on the detection of genre shunts, a technique already applied to *The Game-Players of Titan* (Ch. 2). This narrative starts like a realistic novel describing the nervous breakdown of a middle aged man, Horselover Fat: the setting is California in the 1970s, the years of the ebbing of the countercultural tide of the 1960s, and the story begins with the suicide of Fat's friend Gloria, which triggers his breakdown. There is nothing supernatural or science-fictional in Chapter 1, and the book adopts a rather traditional realistic narrative mode, only complicated by fast-forward narrative leaps which quickly move the story from a year to another: "This was 1971. In 1972 he would be up north.... In 1976 ... Horselover Fat would slit his wrist..." (10). The realistic atmosphere is strengthened by the fact that Fat is no more than an alter-ego of the author, who tells us "I am Horselover Fat" (11), and justifies this disguise as a narrative device which, through the distancing third-person narration, should help him "to gain much-needed objectivity." Is there anything more realistic than an autobiographical narrative in the first person?[10]

This narrative move is however ambiguous, because it could either be read as a deliberate literary creation (which was also carried out with the help of Dick's agent, Russell Galen [Rickman 1988, 196–7]) or a psychotic projection, as Dick explained in his July 12, 1980 letter to Galen: "[i]t is not the case that Fat is psychotic; Fat is the *narrator's* psychosis, objectively given" (*SL6* 18). But — be it artistic creation or psychotic delusion — the split is what generates the narrative itself. Which is a remarkably ambiguous narrative, as the rest of this chapter should prove.

In fact we move from autobiographic fiction to something quite different with the first genre shunt, placed at the beginning of Chapter 2, when Phil (the narrating I, who should coincide with the author) tells us how Fat managed to overcome his suicidal impulses: "The first thing that came along to save him took the form of an eighteen-year-old highschool girl ... and the second was God" (18). This cryptic hint might make us think that Fat simply (and realistically) found consolation in religion (plus womanly beauty). But what befalls him two pages later is absolutely not a conventional moment of religious inspiration:

> God, he told us, had fired a beam of pink light directly at him, at his head, his eyes; Fat had been temporarily blinded and his head had ached for days. It was easy, he said, to describe the beam of pink light; it's exactly what you get as a phosphene after-image when a flashbulb has gone off in your face. Fat was spiritually haunted by that color. Sometimes it showed up on a TV screen. He lived for that light, that one particular color [20].

Fat's experience or vision is not directly *shown* to us as readers: we (and Fat's friends) are *told* about an experience which occurred in an undefined moment in the recent past. One should compare this passage with one of the letters where Dick described his 2-3-74 experiences, like the one he wrote on June 28, 1974 to Peter Fitting (the earliest one about his experiences that I have managed to find), where he describes "colored graphics which resembled the non-objective paintings of Kandisky and Klee, thousands of them one after the other, so fast as to resemble 'flash cut' use [*sic!*] in movie work" (SL3 142–3). This is followed by more detailed descriptions, which are however not explained as a religious experience, but as a bewildering phenomenon maybe triggered by an overdose of vitamins (*SL3* 141), where information from the future was transferred by means of tachyons. Unlike Fat, Dick tried to explain his experiences with scientific theories[11] in this letter, and maintained that "[w]ithout the tachyon theory I would lack any kind of scientific foundation and would have to declare that 'God has shown me the sacred tablets in which the future is written' and so forth, as did our forefathers" (*SL3* 143).

What Dick's personal experience — as depicted in the initial letter — and Fat's vision have in common is their sfnal character. In fact, God does not communicate in the traditional ways, by means of a miracle, an acousmatic voice, or an inner feeling or illumination; he hits Fat with a beam of pink light, resembling the laser weapons of cheap science-fiction, acting like a mysterious alien entity. Thence the reader is presented with two alternatives: (a) Fat is the victim of a hallucination (which is not surprising given his difficult psychological situation)[12] and *VALIS* is a realistic novel telling the story of a madman (with a hefty dose of irony and black humor), or (b) Fat has really been contacted by some alien entity by means of a technology so advanced that it seems miraculous (or science-fictional) to us, and *VALIS* is a sf novel about contacts with aliens (or God).

Phil, the sensible narrator of Fat's antics (or the sane part in a split mind whose deranged half is Fat), does not subscribe to his friend's (or alternate personality's) mystical point of view, but chronicles his subsequent search for God: in fact Fat embarks on a frantic quest for the ultimate truth behind his vision, whatever it, he, or she may be. He starts writing a journal (called *Tractates: Cryptica Scriptura*) which should keep track of his meditations and discoveries, which are frequently quoted in the novel (starting from p. 23); this text really exists outside *VALIS* the novel, as the quotations come from Dick's own *Exegesis*. But the attitude of Phil the character in the novel is not very respectful: he calls Fat's (and P.K. Dick's) journal "the furtive act of a deranged person" (22).

Besides, Fat's quest is a rather wild enterprise: not the scholarly research of a trained scholar, but the rambling pursuit of a self-taught thinker. Christopher Palmer has objected to these frantic quotations from the most different sources, from Plato to the Tibetan Book of the Dead:

> Each of these colorfully different texts, torn out of historical context, bathed in the warm solvents of esotericism, says the same thing, although, admittedly, what that same thing is changes from speculation to speculation. And this blurring of differentiation should be connected to an underlying literalism of interpretation... [Palmer 232].

There is a name for this "adventurous syncretism" (Palmer 232), nonchalantly mixing so many sources from Plato to the Rusicrucians: textuality. Textuality is a condition where "text speaks to text" (Palmer 230–1), where quotation answers quotation and a new, esoteric name replaces the previous name (which stands for a previous interpretation/explanation of the phenomena); textuality is also a condition, typical of postmodernist literature (Palmer describes the atmosphere in the novel as "rhapsodic postmodernist restlessness" [Palmer 232]), where characters (and their adventures) are a textual artifact only, a self-referential construct. Hence, according to the Australian critic, "Dick's attempts to restore 'thingness,' phenomenological substance, to humble objects, are not successful here as they were in earlier novels" (Palmer 232); he quotes as an example an episode in the twelfth chapter of *VALIS*, where the narrator secretly baptizes his son using hot chocolate and a hotdog bun (207–9), which the Australian critic finds unconvincing (Palmer 233).

Palmer does not seem to have noticed that this scene can also be found in the eighteenth chapter of *Radio Free Albemuth* (169), and that — according to Sutin — it mirrors instructions Dick received by means of the information-rich pink beam which hit the writer during his 2-3-74 experiences (Sutin 218).[13] Yet this is one of the many elements in the text which could bolster

Palmer's thesis that *VALIS* suggests — even to those who do not know that many episodes of the novel "are recounted and analyzed as events in Dick's life, in his Exegesis and in interviews" (Palmer 235) — that the author believed in VALIS. But this "literary effect ... denies textuality" (Palmer 235): this may look like a postmodernist novel which playfully quotes a heterogeneous constellation of texts and does not pretend to have substantiality; it may resemble the quotationist works of Borges, Barth, or Pynchon — but it is actually a text which, by staging the author's belief in what has been revealed in his February-March 1974 experiences (the author is then unsurprisingly present in the novel as the narrating I "Phil Dick"), is reduced "to a screen through which we look at Dick's belief in the existence of VALIS" (Palmer 235).

Though Palmer's discussion of *VALIS* might in some points read like a denunciation of Dick as a charlatan,[14] what the Australian critic really aims at is rejecting Scott Durham's postmodern reading of the novel as a text where the author as a subject is abolished (Palmer 234), something which is declared in the title itself of Durham's article, quoting Roland Barthes' "death of the subject" (Durham 188–9). How can the subject be abolished, or die, seems to be Palmer's objection, if it is somewhat reasserted, if "the novel defeats our attempt to defend ourselves by saying that it is only a novel," as it "denies its fictionality" (Palmer 236)? What Palmer finds in *VALIS* is a "collision between ethical seriousness and a postmodern sense of the textuality of meaning" (Palmer 237): on the one hand we have the actual suffering of characters (committing suicide, suffering from cancer or depression) and Dick's direct implication in the novel as a believer in the reality of VALIS; on the other hand the quotationist extravaganza which seems to annihilate the substantiality of meaning in a "threat to differentiation" (Palmer 237) where all texts mean the same thing. This collision brings to a "painful blockage" (Palmer 237), not a dissolution of the subject in textuality.

Actually Durham's article seems to have been presented in an oversimplified fashion by Palmer, inasmuch as its complete title is "From the Death of the Subject to a Theology of Late Capitalism": Durham quotes, as an example of the death — or better disassembling — of the subject, a scene in the fourteenth chapter of *The Simulacra* (a novel published and written well before *VALIS*) where telekinetic (and schizophrenic) pianist Richard Kongrosian literally turns himself inside out (Durham 189), a moment when the sfnal device of telekinesis turns the metaphor of madness as "delirious dissolution of subjectivity" (Durham 189) into a literal dismemberment. On the other hand, Dick's last novels hint at a possible resurrection of the subject, no more individual but collective, as the critic sees the theological component in *VALIS* as helping to conceive "a collective subject capable of grasping such contradictions," i.e., the contradiction between "the subject of countercultural experience and the subject of hegemonic social memory" (Durham 197), respectively embodied in the two halves of *Scanner's* split protagonist, Bob Arctor the junkie and Special Agent Fred the undercover nark. According to Durham, in *VALIS* there is a momentary reunion of "the subject of memory to the delirious subject of experience" (Durham 197), and this may have a political meaning because the "theological madness ... proves to be the method by which a counter-culture attempts to think a counter-memory" (Durham 198).

Palmer's and Durham's analyses of *VALIS*, both stemming from the postmodern season of Dick scholarship (well represented by the 1988 special issue of *Science-Fiction Studies*, which included Durham's article), are interesting because — their divergence of views notwithstanding — they are both pivoted on a contradiction which is undeniably present in the novel, and this chimes in with my reading. There is a split, a chasm, a conflict in *VALIS*. No wonder that the protagonist/narrator is split, then; no wonder that the text mixes scores of erudite quotations and episodes from Dick's own life; no wonder that it is difficult to trace the borderline between fiction and autobiography; no wonder, eventually, that there are two different works of art in a single book, struggling against each other, belonging to two different literary genres: autobiographical novel and religious science-fiction. The split, the chasm, the conflict is evidently the constitutive element of *VALIS*, and this means that any discussion of the novel which aims at finding a unified interpretation, a monological reading, will always fall short of the fascinating duplicity of this book. Palmer's collision is there, and it is that collision which gives *VALIS* most of whatever literary value it may have.

What we are going to do in the remainder of this chapter is to map the collision, by showing where and when the contradiction between the two literary genres that *VALIS* might belong to are textually embodied; the shunts (Ch. 1) which shift the plot from realistic quasi-autobiography to religious sf and back. There is an oscillation between these two genres, so that Palmer's collision is actually a constellation of small collisions, which fosters a condition of ontological uncertainty.

It is in fact quite interesting that Fat, after his pink beam experience, does not achieve certainty. He does not have a truth to preach to the heathens; he is no Christ, no rabbi[15] teaching his apostles a transcendental verity. Fat — unlike real prophets and messengers of any God worth considering —[16]does not come equipped with the Way, the Truth and the Life. Above all Fat does not have positive knowledge: the pink beam experience is mostly an enigma to him. Let us read an important passage of the novel where Phil describes what happens when Fat's mystical experience is discussed:

> David continually quoted C.S. Lewis; Kevin contradicted himself logically in his zeal to defame God; Fat made obscure references to information

fired into his head by a beam of pink light; Sherri, who had suffered dreadfully, wheezed out pious mummeries; I switched my position according to
who I was talking to at the time [29].

If, according to Palmer, this novel wants to make us believe in Fat's (and
Dick's) 2-3-74 experience, such scenes are far from effective: here the experience is presented as the manifestation of something unclear, obscure, enigmatic. Palmer rightly suggests that "[t]he possibility that is allowed to grow,
to vary and to permute ... is best defined ... as the possibility that Philip K.
Dick believes in VALIS" (Palmer 235–6); but believing that something happened to Fat (and his author Philip K. Dick) is one thing, saying *what it is
or was* that is something completely different. VALIS is the name of an enigma,
not a revealed truth. In fact, most of what happens in the 23 pages between
the first mention of the pink beam and the second twist in the plot is not the
announcement of some revelation, but the unquiet questioning of a puzzling
event — or its exegesis[17]; hence the series of hypotheses, or speculations, that
explain the event in different fashions. The quotation of Heraclitus in Chapter
3, "The nature of things is in the habit of concealing themselves" (39) is probably less tied to ontology than to hermeneutics: concealed truths, the "latent
structure," must be laboriously deciphered, and may well remain hidden. The
pink beam actually *opens* a quest, a search for meaning and truth.

However, Fat's religious but cryptic experience has not really saved him
from his psychical turmoil, as he attempts to commit a spectacular (and redun-
dant) suicide "with the pills, the razor sharp blade and the car engine" (43).
If the so far undetermined message delivered through the pink beam should
save him from his initial nervous breakdown, we have to admit that what was
told him was disappointingly ineffective. "Encountering the living God had
not helped to equip him for the tasks of ordinary endurance, which ordinary
men, not so favored, handle" (46): Phil's comment indirectly tells us that Fat's
experience was not illumination but madness, that "his brains are fried" (47).
The supernatural element is discredited, and here we have a shunt which takes
the narrative back to realistic fiction.

This return to realism leads to one of the worst moments in Fat's life,
when he is detained at the Orange County mental hospital (43),[18] which is
practically a prison. Should we then be surprised by the curious political-his-
torical bent Fat's visions assume in this part of the novel, when he starts to
see the California of 1974 mysteriously superimposed to the Imperial Rome
of A.D. 70? If the mental hospital is a prison, where Fat can be kept for an
indefinite time (50), it is not that strange that Fat "discerned within the superimposition [of contemporary California and ancient Rome] a Gestalt shared
by both space-time continua, their common element: a Black Iron Prison"
(48). The reference to Gestalt psychology should make us aware that the Black

Iron Prison is a form which may organize and define the single parts of which it is composed; a form that may holistically define the political situation of Imperial Rome, or modern California,[19] or the very personal predicament of Horselover Fat, a wrecked individual prisoner of a mental hospital — and madness. The religious and esoteric symbols can be thus read as referring to a very concrete and mundane reality of suffering and despair (acknowledged by Palmer [233]); an individual reality, one should add. Let us not forget that the novel begins with Fat's nervous breakdown, *not* with the pink beam.

We should also notice that this ghostly apparition of another time and place, superimposed to late 20th-century California, reminds us of the ghost-like apparitions of Ubik (in its several embodiments) in the homonymous novel, and is another manifestation of ontological uncertainty. The never ending Imperial Rome is in fact also a parallel universe, an alternative history or layer of reality which might be hidden by our only apparently real *koinos kosmos* of A.D. 1974. Once again, the fictional reality conjured up by the Game-Player and so far accepted by readers thanks to the usual willing suspension of disbelief (helped by the realistic Californian setting) might in any moment dissolve to reveal a far weirder and unfamiliar world.

However, the novel moves — after the suicide attempt and Fat's hospitalization — towards a new shunt, that is, the intervention of doctor Stone. This unorthodox therapist cures Fat by means of a language that he may understand and accept, that of his religious obsession (in what Stilling defines a "metapsychanalitical" sequence [96]). He first solves a contradiction between the two superimposed moments (the 1970s and A.D. 70) in Fat's vision, by pointing out that — according to Fat himself— time ceased in A.D. 70: actually they are still in Roman times. Modern day California is no more than a dream: humankind is still under the domination of Rome, as a symbol of absolute political power.[20] From Phil's point of view, Stone's intervention is in any case worse than the illness it should cure: "Now Fat would never depart from faith in his encounter with God. Dr. Stone had nailed it down" (63). Stone's subsequent therapeutic move is even more successful, though it once again ratifies his patient's faith in the supernatural character of his experience: when asked an opinion on the Nag Hammadi manuscripts,[21] one of the fundamental elements in Fat's (and Dick's) home-made theological system, Dr. Stone replies: "You would know.... You're the authority" (65). With this reinstatement of Fat's faith in himself, the psychological collapse triggered by the departure of his wife and, before that, Fat's failure to save Gloria's life, seems healed. The quester may not know who or what exactly fired the beam at him, but he knows that there is an explanation which transcends ordinary reality — so the novel is once again a search for something preternatural, or better — since we are in a science-fictional atmosphere — for something alien.

It is not a harmless quest, though: Fat, once discharged from the asylum, goes to live with Sherri Solveig, his friend who suffers from cancer, animated by a morbid self-destructive drive, as she "did not merely plan to get sick again; she like Gloria planned to take as many people with her as possible" (73). It is quite clear now that behind the first and most evident oppositions which structure the plot of the novel — Realism vs. Science-fiction, Sanity vs. Madness, Ordinary reality vs. Supernatural entities — there is also an arguably more fundamental semic opposition: Freud's classical dichotomy of Eros vs. Thanatos (Stilling 94). Fat is basically threatened by death, embodied in the suicidal impulse which gets hold of him after Gloria's suicide: the self-destructive drive is like a contagious disease which may easily spread to individuals with no or not enough spiritual antibodies — people weakened by physical suffering like Sherri, or by a crazy mixed-up life, like Fat. While the novel oscillates between realism and fantasy/science-fiction, Fat more or less successfully strives to keep far from death and reach life. It is through therapy[22] that Dr. Stone has helped Fat to stave off death and grasp life again — and that is Eros; while Sherri involves him in her own destruction, and that is surely Thanatos. One might even say that Fat's predicament is like Joe Chip's in *Ubik*, with the divine spraycan replaced by VALIS/Zebra.

However, Fat's decision to live with Sherri marks another genre shunt, because the question arises about how a man who has been enlightened by God (via pink beam) can make such a blatant mistake as "to bind himself to the Antichrist" (74), i.e., to Sherri, who "planned to take as many people with her as possible" (73). Phil's understated question is: if God is on the side of life and healing (Eros), how can one who has really been touched by God deliberately chose Thanatos?[23]

Yet the critical, ironic distance between Phil and Fat seems to decrease after the beginning of chapter 7. Palmer noticed this loss of distance: "Philip begins to participate in the obsessions and textual riffs that the split seemed to have assigned to Fat rather than to the often impressively wise and blunt Philip" (Palmer 235). Suvin, following Palmer, sees Phil as a device aimed at persuading readers, a "disbelieving patsy" whose incredulity was "set up so that [it] can be confounded, wiping out the reader's disbelief too" (Suvin 2002, 383). But we should remember once again what the sensible Phil tells us almost at the beginning of the novel: "I am Horselover Fat and I am writing this in the third person to gain much-needed objectivity" (11). The apparent distance between Phil the sceptic and Fat the visionary is exactly that: apparent. It is a fictional device which is craftily exploited by Dick to curb Fat's interpretive obsession, but his interest in esoteric literature and ancient religious texts cannot be completely neutered because Fat and Phil are the same man, after all — or maybe two conflicting drives in the same mind.

However, even if Phil is confounded, and this means that Fat is right (an oversimplified interpretation, as we shall see), once again Fat does not have a truth to teach; he has several conflicting hypotheses about truth, like Dick, and the many interpretations he suggested in scores of letters in Volumes 3–6 of the *Selected Letters* prove this. On April 6, 1977 he sent a letter to his literary agent where he declared that he believed that the Zebra Principle, the entity behind his 1974 mystical experiences, was "not just a fictional device for the purpose of novel writing" (*SL5* 67), but something he really believed in (*SL5* 68), though it is explained in a quasi-materialistic fashion by an essay written by psychologist Julian Jaynes that Dick had just read.[24] But in two letters written four months later the writer explains his experiences with the intervention of the Holy Ghost, with no mention of Jaynes' theories (*SL5* 90–3). Other theories are formulated in the scores of letters to Claudia Bush and Patricia Warrick. Dick even hypothesized that the "Biblical apocalyptic terms" (*SL6* 51) he was using in the early eighties to explain his mystical experiences had been suggested by the macro-brain (another embodiment of the mysterious intelligence Dick used to call VALIS) to camouflage itself: by using those terms Dick discredited himself, so nobody would believe his description of the enigmatic entity.[25] All in all, even when Fat and Phil (and their friends Kevin and David) agree, they do not agree on some ultimate truth; they agree on carrying on a quest for truth, and Suvin seems to have missed this, as well as the many tell-tale references to Parsifal's search for the Holy Grail scattered throughout the novel, which may induce us to read *VALIS* as Dick's own, very personal version of *The Waste Land*.

Doubts lurk everywhere: not many pages after Phil begins to discuss the same esoteric texts that Fat loves so much (as the hymn by Ikhnaton quoted at the beginning of ch. 7 [101–2]), there is a moment of radical uncertainty: it is Phil who, "without getting Fat's permission" (117), quotes Heraclitus and then one of his interpreters, Edward Hussey: "the infinitely old divinity is a child playing a board game as he moves the cosmic pieces in combat according to rule" (117). The image of a god who treats humans like "pieces on a board" (118) must have chimed in with Dick's paranoid streak: but the idea of characters like pawns manipulated by a superhuman game-player hints at *The Game-Players of Titan* (Ch. 1), and Dick's own Game of the Rat, where the manipulation of genre conventions (and readers' expectations) plays a fundamental role. One might then suspect that Dick is playing with us once again.

In fact the pink beam broadcast something, but that message, however important, is not easy to decode: hence the moves of the child god may be totally obscure to his pawns. Also because God may be very different from mortal creatures, as different as some alien form of life from another planet: what we call God may not be what we have always meant by that term (118).

Both Fat and Phil are prey to a radical and unstoppable form of doubt, more puzzling than Descartes' ontological doubt.

It may even be, as Phil suspects, that the being which fired the pink beam at Fat is not God, but Fat himself, or better Fat as he will be in a future moment. The identity of Zebra (the code name that Fat has assigned to the entity that has contacted him [102]) could thus be something that is not transcendental at all: "Zebra is all the selves along the linear time-axis, laminated into one super–or trans-temporal self which cannot die, and which has come to save Fat" (132). This hypothesis creates another textual shunt, because if we take this laminated self as someone or something that can retroactively act on his old self by moving backwards in the time flux, we have to accept the idea of time-travel, albeit limited to information: this is a typical science-fictional idea based on the tachyon theory quoted in the letter to Fitting (*SL3* 141–8) we have already quoted (a theory featured e.g., in Gregory Benford's 1980 solid sf novel *Timescape*), so *VALIS* moves from theological science-fiction to hard science-fiction.

But Zebra, considered as the sum of all the selves along the time-axis laminated into one trans-temporal self might simply be Philip Kindred Dick writing his own story in 1978, staging his own 2-3-74 experience with considerable hindsight (in any moment our self is made up of all our past selves), and communicating with his own fictional alter-ego Horselover Fat (the idea that the laminated self cannot die may also be read as a new version of the old topos of the immortality of literature and its authors). Here we have postmodernist metafiction, not religious preaching, as the image of the child playing a board game already suggested; then also *VALIS* could be part of the Game of the Rat. VALIS might simply be the author himself.

In any case, the novel does not end here, and the oscillation takes us back again to theology and supernatural entities when Kevin, Phil's and Fat's ultra-skeptic friend (a purported portrait of Dick's real friend K.W. Jeter, another science-fiction writer),[26] invites them and David to see "a science-fiction film" (138), *Valis*, whose screenplay has been written by Eric Lampton, the leader of rock group Mother Goose. The film is described in detail by Dick (139–44); suffice it to say that much of its plot is a rehashing of the storyline of *Radio Free Albemuth* (which has been considered an earlier version of *VALIS*, though the differences between the two novels are so extensive that they can be read as independent works). What is important, however, is that the film contains a welter of allusions to what Fat has seen in his mystical visions: pink light beams, three-eyed aliens, the meaningful little clay pot, the Christian fish sign. Some of these images are in the background, so that only the initiates may recognize them; some are explained in an unexpected way, such as the source of the information-rich beam, which is fired by an alien satellite called VALIS, i.e., Vast Active Living Intelligence System; or the fish sign, identified with Crick and Watson's double helix model of DNA (146). The vision of the film radically changes Fat's friends' attitude to his "lurid schizophrenic episode": "Kevin had gone to the movie and now he was not so sure; the Mother Goose flick had shaken him up" (153).

The film persuades Fat & C., now dubbed "Rhipidon Society" (a name that Dick derives from the early Christian *Ichthys* or fish symbol, as *rhipidon* means "fin" in Greek [171]), after more wild hypotheses and interpretations of *Valis*, to contact Eric Lampton and his wife Linda, plus their friend Brent Mini,[27] an experimental musician who composed the soundtrack of the movie. Already the phone call before the actual meeting marks an important change in the novel: when Phil says that it was not he who was "told things" (168), that is, received information from VALIS, because "[t]he information was fired at my friend Horselover Fat," Lampton immediately deconstructs his fictional alter-ego: "But that's you. 'Philip' means 'Horselover' in Greek ... 'Fat' is the German translation of 'Dick.' So you've translated your name." One might object that *dick* is the German translation of "fat," but Lampton has in any case decoded Dick's interlinguistic pun, and reminded us, after more than 150 pages, that Dick and Fat are one. This might mean that Lampton, who is not cheated by Dick's fictional device, is endowed with the truth, or, gnostically speaking, with Sophia, the divine wisdom.

In fact when Rhipidon Society meet the Lamptons in Sonoma they discover that their guests are indeed endowed with Sophia, because that is the name of their 2-year-old daughter (189), who is introduced by Eric Lampton as the reincarnation of the Messiah (which is Christ but also Buddha [169]): "This time ... for the first time, the Savior takes female form" (189). But before this revelation another shunt operates in Chapter 11: after talking with the Lamptons, Phil tells David that "they're crazy" (181), because what they have said may also chime in with the findings of Fat's esoteric research, but when they claim to belong to Ikhnaton's race, three-eyed aliens with claw-like hands (175–6), they push their act too far, mixing the story of pharaoh Akhenaten, or Ikhnaton — who strove to push Egypt towards monotheism — with aliens out of conspiracy theories on Area 51.

Fat's quest for truth may seem as crazy as other (more or less symbolic) pursuits of ultimate truths, be they Parsifal's quest for the Holy Grail or Ahab's hunt for Moby-Dick, but here the questers will not settle for some second-hand nonsense. And when they finally meet Sophia (190), in the climactic twelfth chapter of the novel, they discover that the little girl who should be the embodiment divine wisdom has a remarkably no-nonsense approach to life: "Your suicide attempt was a violent cruelty against yourself," she tells Phil, and when he tries to parry by saying "It was Horselover Fat," she replies

"Phil, Kevin and David. Three of you. There are no more." Horselover Fat is exposed as a projection of Phil's sick mind, at the same time a product of his madness and the representation of that madness. Sophia can heal the split personalities, and make Phil whole again; if this, as we have seen, is the sign of her belonging to the side of Eros, not Thanatos (while the Lamptons, as we shall see, will ultimately ally themselves to the forces of destruction), we should also understand that her message is not at all deranged or nonsensical.

Another critic acknowledged this, namely Kim Stanley Robinson, who suggests that what Sophia says "is very simple, very humanistic" (Robinson 116–7), and quotes two highly relevant passages of the novel (198, 213) which express an idea of God as something which is inside man, as a salvific force in the human mind. "[H]uman beings should now give up the worship of all deities except mankind itself" (213): here is a summation of Sophia's message to Phil and his friends, something that strikes me as surprisingly closer to the ideas of such a canonized poet as William Blake than to the ravings of a madman. We should also add that here (190) the genre shunt turns the theological science-fiction novel to a straight religious novel, because readers might now easily take Sophia as a metaphorical or symbolic figure of a wisdom (this is the meaning of her name in Greek) which may be directly and preternaturally inspired by God, but also reached thanks to a process of inner growth.

However, since Dick was definitely not a preacher, but remained a novelist till the end, this truth does not come as something ultimate and incontrovertible. The novel enters the territory of theological science-fiction once again when Phil is struck by a pink beam which also causes a time slip (204); this mysterious episode helps him to escape the deranged Lamptons, so that the Rhipidon Society will not be involved in Sophia's accidental death. That tragic event evidently marks another shunt in the novel, as it compels readers to doubt the divine nature of the little girl. There are already doubts about Sophia when the Rhipidon Society is in the Lamptons' house in Sonoma (195–6), but Kevin, the stubborn skeptic, says that one thing is sure: Sophia healed Phil: "[y]ou stopped believing you were two people. You stopped believing in Horselover Fat as a separate person" (196–7).[28]

However, a much stronger threat to the persuasion that Sophia is the Savior comes when — after the return home of Phil, Kevin and David — Linda Lampton phones the writer and announces that Sophia died in a failed experiment in which Brent Mini tried to gather information from the child through laser beams (215). "[I]f Sophia was the Savior, how could she die?" asks Linda, expressing the radical doubt that also the other characters (and we readers) must share: how could the thanatoid forces of psychopathy (Mini's crackpot experiment) prevail if Sophia was the embodiment of Eros/God? Doubt strikes back, and this obliges me to disagree with Suvin's reading of the novel as divided into two parts, one of skeptical and frantic search before the viewing of the film, the other of wholehearted belief after the viewing of *Valis* and the meeting with Sophia (Suvin, 383).

We might instead quite easily read the novel as a realistic narrative depicting a sometimes comic case of madness (the split between Phil and Horselover Fat) plus the tragedy of a small sect of self-deluded individuals (the Lamptons and Brent Mini). Dick was well aware of the dangers of fanatical religious faith: its effects are represented by the tragedy of the Lamptons, and they are also evoked by the brief hint at the 1978 mass-suicide in Jonestown (220), organized by religious leader Jim Jones. Is this the ultimate meaning of the novel? Or does the comeback of Horselover Fat (216), at the beginning of the fourteenth and last chapter, ultimately shunt it towards the area of theological science-fiction, since Fat starts spinning his theories again and manifests his intention to continue his quest (217)? Phil tells him to go away (220), and this might amount to a refusal to continue the quest, foreshadowing Angel's rejection of the quest in *Archer* (Ch. 10), but this time Fat does not disappear: he becomes a wanderer who looks for an explanation of his experience in the farthest corners of Earth, and gets now and then in touch with Phil (usually via mailgrams [221] or phone calls [227]).

Does one of the two possible interpretations ultimately prevail? I think that we may try to answer this question only if we carefully read the ending paragraph of the novel. We are told that Fat has left, and is searching for truth all around the world, but Phil has not followed him: he has stayed at home, and this choice seems to be quite important, if the novel ends by restating it: "My search kept me at home; I sat before the TV set in my living room. I sat; I waited; I watched; I kept myself awake. As we had been told, originally, long ago, to do; I kept my commission" (228). This ending paragraph is a modern-day rewriting of a key passage in another text which Dick knew quite well, the Gospel of Mark; when Phil says "I waited; I watched," he clearly refers to the ending of the "Little Apocalypse" (Mark 13:35–7), where Christ exhorts to watch "for ye know not when the master of the house cometh"— this is probably what "we had been told, originally, long ago."

The Little Apocalypse is a very important part of the gospel, and there is a Biblical scholar, Etienne Trocmé, who hypothesized that Mark (which, according to the majority of New Testament scholars, was the source or one of the sources of both Matthew and Luke) originally ended here, when Christ says "And what I say unto you I say unto all, watch" (Kermode 71–2), and what follows Mark 13 is an appendix subsequently added by an anonymous editor. This is not the right place for an exegetical discussion, but we should not overlook the fact that at the end of his novel Dick chooses to quote a part of Mark's Gospel which might or might not be the real ending[29]; because the ending of the fourteenth chapter of *VALIS* might not be the real ending of the novel.

In fact the paragraph I have quoted is followed by an Appendix which collects all the excerpts of Fat's (and Dick's) *Exegesis* scattered in the novel, something which might seem gratuitous, or worse, might be read as upholding Fat's crackpot esoteric revelations (being placed at the end of *VALIS*, these fragments might amount to the moral of the story) — were it not that the final fragment says: "From Ikhnaton this knowledge passed to Moses, and from Moses to Elijah, the Immortal Man, who became Christ. But underneath all the names there is only one Immortal man; *and we are that man*" (241).

Palmer contends that "[e]ach of these colorfully different texts, torn out of historical context, ... says the same thing" (Palmer 232); Dick was well aware of this, if he ends up the book *VALIS* with the revelation that we (he, his characters, his readers, everybody) is Christ, that is the Messiah, the Savior, the principle of Eros and healing, the divine wisdom, or Sophia. It takes some wisdom to understand this truth; to understand that Ikhnaton the monotheist pharaoh, Moses and Elijah the prophets, Christ the Messiah and all the other figures from esoteric and religious texts which have been mentioned, quoted and discussed in *VALIS*, once inside the space of fiction, all become fiction,[30] all become characters in a complicated story which maybe is not so complicate because after all we are talking about a man and his mortal terrors, his hopes, his feelings: *and we are that man*. Once again, as Horace already knew, *mutato nomine de te fabula narratur*.

The ending excerpts from the *Exegesis* might persuade readers to accept Palmer's basic idea that *VALIS* denies its fictionality (Palmer 236), not because it is autobiographic, but because it is a disguised religious pamphlet: the Appendix may read dangerously like a final revelation (with or without capital R). Yet, by placing at the end of the Appendix (which follows Dick's own Little Apocalypse, the ending of Chapter 14) a fragment which identifies prophets and messiahs with us readers, Dick ultimately brings everything to the only place where we all meet, believers and unbelievers, visionaries and skeptics: real life, our shared reality with all its laminations, the *koinos kosmos* where all the private worlds intersect in the most complicated ways.

Dick leaves to the readers the freedom to decide if we should bring Ikhnaton and those other characters down to our mundane level, or spiritually rise to the transcendental heights of religious truth. Both a materialist and a spiritualist reading are possible: the oscillation is not closed, not even in the second ending. And this ultimate form of tolerance and open-mindedness might well be another of the strong points of this most complex novel — possibly its strongest point.

It is Dick himself to explain this in one of his last letters, one he sent to his agent Russell Galen, on November 12, 1981. He starts by pointing out that the inner contradiction of the novel is a new version of Epimenides' paradox, that is, the Cretan who declares that all Cretans are liars (*SL6* 286): Horselover Fat says he saw Christ (aka VALIS), but he is a madman, hence not reliable; but the author of the book is Fat, writing in the third person about himself, and readers should wonder whether a narrative by a madman can be reliable. A blow-by-blow analysis of the consequence of this original logical paradox brings to this conclusion:

> What, then, if anything is asserted? It is impossible to tell. VALIS is a novel/VALIS is not a novel. I am Horselover Fat/I am not Horselover Fat. Horselover Fat is insane/Horselover Fat is not insane. I saw Christ/I did not see Christ. I assert I saw Christ but I am insane/I assert I saw Christ but I am not insane. I assert I saw Christ/I do not assert I saw Christ [*SL6* 287].

This barrage of alternatives somewhat mirrors the following scheme, summarizing the shunts in *VALIS*, which should help us understand that this novel does not lack of focus, as Suvin maintains (Suvin 2002, 383), but simply has two alternative foci — something Dick was well aware of.

Table 8.1

Page #	Description	From	To
20	Fat is struck by the pink beam	Realistic fiction	Theological science-fiction
43	Attempted suicide: Fat's desperation denies divine intervention	Theological science-fiction	Realistic fiction (a case of madness)
63	Dr. Stone confirms Fat's faith in himself ("you're the authority")	Realistic fiction	Theological science-fiction
73	Fat goes to live with Sherri: if God is in contact with him, why didn't he warn Fat?	Theological science-fiction	Realistic fiction
101	Phil begins to participate in Fat's obsessions	Realistic fiction	Theological science-fiction
132	Phil suspects that Zebra is Fat's supra- or trans-temporal self	Theological science-fiction	Science-fiction (time-travel) or postmodernist metafiction
138	Fat and friends watch the movie *Valis* which confirms Fat's visions	Science-fiction (time-travel) or postmodernist metafiction	Theological science-fiction

(cont. next page)

Table 8.1 (continued)

181	Fat thinks that the Lamptons are insane	Thological science-fiction	Realistic fiction
190	When Phil and friends meet Sophia, Fat disappears	Realistic fiction	Religious novel
204	Phil is struck by the pink beam, and manages to escape the deranged Lamptons and Mini	Religious novel	Theological science-fiction
215	Sophia dies in Brent Mini's experiment	Theological science-fiction	Realistic fiction
216	Fat reappears, but Phil sends him away (220)	Realistic fiction	Open ending

Dick's final conclusion, as expressed in the letter to Galen, is that

> However, *something is asserted.* Assertions are made. The astute reader, then recognizes that assertions are made ... and then contradicted.... Dropping formal logic for a moment, it occurs to the readers that *probably*— only probably —*some*— but only some — of the assertions in VALIS are true. *Parts*— but only parts — of VALIS are true. VALIS, then, is a new kind of thing never seen before; it is neither novel nor autobiography, neither true nor false [SL6 287].

Dick is right when he says that his novel is neither a "pure" novel (provided novels were ever pure: the earliest specimens of the genre were Daniel Defoe's fake autobiographies) nor an autobiography, but is wrong when he says that VALIS was a new kind of thing. There was an illustrious predecessor, published in 1969 and written by another sf writer who had managed to escape the ghetto and become an acclaimed writer, one of those quoted in the chapter of the prestigious *Columbia History of the American Novel*[31] devoted to Postmodern Fiction (Hite 699): Kurt Vonnegut, whose *Slaughterhouse-Five* also unashamedly mixes autobiography and science fiction. Like Dick, Vonnegut appears in his de-structured novel as a character (a secondary one, unlike Phil Dick in *VALIS*, but in his capacity as writer,[32] like Phil Dick in *VALIS*), and describes his horrifying wartime experiences in Dresden by conjuring up a fictional alter ego, Billy Pilgrim, who finds himself in the 1945 Dresden bombing and fire storm like the real Vonnegut.

Dick's *VALIS* is well inside one of the currents of postmodernist fiction, that of autofiction, covering "autobiographical fiction, or fictional narrative in the first-person mode" (Smith and Watson 186). Such texts are astraddle the borderline between autobiography and fiction, and use "textual markers that signal a deliberate, often ironic, interplay between the two modes" (Smith and Watson 186) — and I cannot imagine a more blatant marker than having two protagonists, one of which (the narrating I) is the author himself. There are other examples of this hybrid form; Smith and Watson mention *Roland Barthes by Roland Barthes* (1975), but there is another interesting specimen (also written by a former sf author), J.G. Ballard's *The Kindness of Women* (1991), which — like *VALIS*— has been read as part of a "life trilogy" also including the semi-autobiographical novel *Empire of the Sun* (1984) and the compact autobiography *Miracles of Life* (2008), whose three parts have different takes on the narrative materials of Ballard's own life (Rossi 2008).

Palmer may be right when he suggests that *VALIS* is a screen through which we look at Dick's belief in the existence of VALIS; but the character of Horselover Fat may be another screen through which Dick himself looked at his own belief in VALIS. Fictions like *VALIS* do work like screens, screening embarrassing and problematic memories to protect the mind of the writer, but at the same time screening those very experiences which cause embarrassment and disorientation; they resemble Freud's screen memories about childhood which retain insignificant facts, but are associated with important facts that have been suppressed because they are unacceptable to the ego. Mixing memories and fiction may be a way to tackle unsettling or painful experiences: let us not forget that the novel begins with one of these painful events, the suicide of Fat's friend Gloria Knudson, and an even more painful event which is only briefly mentioned, the fact that "Fat had lost his wife, the year before, to mental illness" (11).

Thus Dick was definitely not off the mark when he claimed that *VALIS* was "experimental science fiction" (Boonstra 1982), as it closely resembles other postmodernist authors' experiments in genre hybridization which short-circuit "reliable" autobiographic writing and fictional invention. Such experiences are conterminous with other experiments in hybridization, like Norman Mailer's New Journalism (as represented by *The Armies of the Night* [1968] and *Of a Fire on the Moon* [1971]), or Hunter S. Thompson's Gonzo journalism (*Hell's Angels* [1966] and *Fear and Loathing in Las Vegas* [1972]), possibly even Tom Wolfe's "nonfiction novel" *The Electric Kool-Aid Acid Test* (1968). Dick often mentioned Vonnegut in his letters (though not very respectfully), and he said that *VALIS* contained "certain modern elements associated with Hunter S. Thompson" (*SL6* 127).

It is also interesting that these texts all deal with events which have strongly characterized the 1960s and their countercultural wave, from the Apollo missions to the use of illicit drugs, from the October 1967 march on the Pentagon to the lysergic odyssey of Ken Kesey's Merry Pranksters across America. It is not difficult to understand that Fat's and Phil's quest for VALIS belongs to those years, even if it was published in 1981, when the Reaganite backlash was already wiping the countercultural wave away. Phil clearly says:

"This time in America — 1960 to 1970 — and this place, the Bay Area of Northern California, was totally fucked. I'm sorry to tell you this, but that's the truth" (11); and as an example of this totally fucked time, he quotes one of the climactic events of those years, but not one related with LSD, mysticism, or some form of more or less deranged creativity: "The day they moved Angela Davis, the Black Marxist, out of the Marin County jail, the authorities dismantled the whole civic center. This was to baffle radicals who might intend trouble" (12). This refers to Angela Davis' trial, held in 1972 for the August 7, 1970, shootout at the Marin County courthouse. Interestingly the events as witnessed by Fat are strange, almost sfnal:

> The elevators got unwired; doors got relabeled with spurious information; the district attorney hid. Fat saw all this. He had gone to the civic center that day to return a library book. At the electronic hoop at the civic center entrance, two cops had ripped open the book and papers that Fat carried. He was perplexed. The whole day perplexed him. In the cafeteria, an armed cop watched everyone eat. Fat returned home by cab, afraid of his own car and wondering if he was nuts. He was, but so was everyone else [12].

Strange days ask for strange chronicles and stranger chroniclers. Durham may then have got a point, and not a secondary one, when he claims that VALIS — considered as a postmodernist autofiction — may be the textual form "by which a counter-culture attempts to think a counter-memory" (Durham 198). Freedman persuasively argued that Dick is "a writer of the 1960s" (Freedman 1988, 147–51), not so much because he wrote his best works in that decade (Freedman's assessment of Dick's oeuvre is oversimplified [147]), but because Dick is perfectly attuned to the intellectual climate of those years, and can be considered one of their greatest singers.

Many of the historical events of the 1960s and early 1970s defy traditional concepts of reasonableness and verisimilitude; then the quandaries of the late-modern or postmodern histories must necessarily be explored by means of such partly-reliable, partly-unreliable narratives, that are at the same time both autobiography and science-fiction, both a skeptical debunking of religion and quests for a mutant form of religiosity — and, last but not least both comedy and tragedy.[33] Such texts tell us that ontological uncertainty, far from being a mere device to keep readers interested, may be the only viable method to map an ontologically uncertain age like ours.

All in all, Phil, Kevin, and David's quest is an open-ended one; it is quite different from the modernist version of the medieval chivalric quest as depicted in T.S. Eliot's *The Waste Land*, where the Chapel perilous is reached, but found empty ("There is the empty chapel, only the wind's home"), meaning that in the modern age there is no salvific Grail, no ultimate truth that can redeem our fallen world. In fact one could believe that Fat's departure towards faraway lands and Phil's resigned wait in front of a TV set at the end of the novel mean that the quest is endless, and that such and endlessness implies its pointlessness, as there is no salvation, no redemption, no hope; this also means no healing, as the novel, in Dick's opinion, could also be read as "the narrator's odyssey to exorcise his psychotic self," where Fat's return is triggered when Sophia's death "revives in him the original trauma" and "the narrator is again split into two people" (*SL6* 18). But we should never forget that *VALIS* is only the first part of a trilogy, and the quest actually continues in its second and above all its third part — because it is in *Archer* that an answer will be found to the quandaries *VALIS* leaves open.[34]

Chapter 9

The God from Outer Space: Reconsidering *The Divine Invasion*

> "And what rough beast, its hour come round at last,
> Slouches towards Bethlehem to be born?"
> W.B. Yeats

The second part of the trilogy is apparently less ambiguous and problematic than *VALIS*; no wonder that Dick himself said that it "has a very conventional structure for science fiction, almost science fantasy; no experimental devices of any kind" (Boonstra 1982). Here God — called Yah — undoubtedly exists, intervenes, operates, and is one of the characters of the story. We are even presented with his thoughts in several moments of the complicated plot. As we have already said, this is a science-fiction novel and the reader may expect weird events in it, even God's carefully planned invasion of planet Earth to defeat his Adversary, Belial, the personification of Evil. This might seem to wipe out any form of ontological uncertainty and its intriguing textual consequences, but a careful reading of the novel[1] may reveal us complexities which have been already perceived by another critic, Darko Suvin:

> This second novel in the trilogy ... is ideationally and narratively more coherent, though the following account streamlines Dick's gradual revelations but also his sometimes competing explanations, confusingly overloaded details and layers, and simple inconsistencies [Suvin 386].

There are indeed competing realities in this novel; two alternative worlds whose existence may justify and clarify the "competing explanations" and "simple inconsistencies" Suvin talks about. This is an important source of ontological uncertainty, but there are others. Contrary to what Christian theology has always taught us, i.e., that Christ's incarnation saved humankind — notwithstanding the evident fact that this is definitely not the best possible world (Palmer 39) — this novel tells us that the official (we might even say

Authorized) version of the first Coming is not true: things went wrong in A.D. 33 (and after). Hence we have a hidden truth behind the "official" history (or story) told by the four Gospels.

Moreover, in this novel we have once again the typical Dickian character whose memory is not totally reliable, and that is God himself, who suffers from amnesia due to a primary trauma. Since God must recover his lost memories, we also have a quest here, and the quest necessarily entails interrogations, inquiries, doubts, revelations which may seem ultimate but are sometimes given the lie by subsequent discoveries; all in all, that atmosphere of uncertainty which should be familiar to Dick's readers. Another game of the Rat.

However, any reading of *The Divine Invasion* must start from its *Entstehungsgeschichte*, that is, the history of how this novel was written, which begins with a short story published in 1980, "Chains of Air, Web of Aether." Its plot is set on the same star system CY30-CY30B where the novel begins; its protagonists, Leo McVane and Rybus Rommey — two of the Earth colonists living a boring and almost purposeless life under the airtight domes on the alien planet — are quite similar to Herb Asher and Rybys Rommey, two of the main characters of the novel (the name of the woman is almost the same); in both story and novel Leo/Herbert is a fan of interstellar pop star Linda Fox, who sings electronic arrangements of John Dowland's 16th-century lute songs; Rybus/Rybys is sick with multiple sclerosis in both texts, and undergoes a devastating chemotherapy; both Leo and Herbert grudgingly look after their ill neighbor, though they dislike her; both Rybus and Rybys detest Fox's music, and vocally express their negative opinion without considering Leo/Herb's feelings.

Dick recycled his short story to write the first five chapters of his novel, something that was not unusual for him, as we have already seen when we discussed, e.g., *The Penultimate Truth* (Ch. 5) and *The Three Stigmata of Palmer Eldritch* (Ch. 7). The differences between the story and the novel may tell us something about *The Divine Invasion* and its overall architecture. While in the novel Rybys, Herb and Emmanuel form a Holy Family of sorts,[2] in the short story there is no hint at the Christian image of the Holy Family; there is not even an affair between the two protagonists. Rybus is not pregnant and she does not return to Earth with Leo. The short story is focused on the destructive drives in Rybus, described as a dying person who wants to take somebody with her (431).[3] Notwithstanding his intense dislike of Rybus' destructive personality, Leo feels ethically compelled to assist her, but this entails paying a high price, because Rybus' jeering criticism of Linda Fox and her music spoils forever the pleasure he draws from her songs. What happens is synthesized in this sentence: "a human life won and a synthetic media image wrecked" (441). It is not a totally positive ending, as Leo is well aware that he "got [Rybus] through her ordeal and she paid [him] back by deriding into rubbish that which [he] cherished the most" (441). Moreover, Rybus' physical survival is somewhat neutralized by her psychological degradation: when Leo visits her dome after her multiple sclerosis has been healed, he finds her compulsively watching TV soaps (and it is quite clear that if Fox is just pop trash those TV programs are not much better) and almost unable to interact with another human being. "She's completely crazy. She is dead. Her body has been healed, but it killed her mind" (443) is Leo's almost final comment.

I say that this comment is *almost* final because it is followed by a moment of recollection, when Leo, watching Rybus who still wears her black glasses, thinks of a John Dowland song that the Fox uses to sing "on Christmas Day, for all the planets" (444). This might mean that Leo's love for Fox's versions of Dowland has not been completely destroyed by Rybus' insensitive derision. But we should be careful about the meaning of the lines quoted by Dick:

> When the poor cripple by the pool did lie
> Full many years in misery and pain,
> No sooner he on Christ had set his eye,
> But he was well, and comfort came again.

Is the "poor cripple" Rybus, who has not been healed by Christ's apparition but chemotherapy? Or is it Leo, turned into a spiritual cripple by the contact with Rybus' "thanatous" personality (according to the AI system consulted by Leo, which recommends "total avoidance on [his] part" [435])? And is the final "comfort" an effect of art's power to heal psychological wounds, or is it just an ironic thrust? The ending is rather ambiguous.

The story is however focused on the relationship between Leo and Rybus, and its main argument seems to be the value of art and beauty in an age when works of art (here music) are industrially produced like any other commodity. It is not just a matter of technological reproducibility or mechanical reproduction, as in Walter Benjamin's famous (and rather optimistic) 1935 essay; we are talking of a "synthetic media image" (441), something which is radically false, mass-produced trash animated, in Rybus' words, by "recycled sentimentality, which is the worst kind of sentimentality" (429). The story is pivoted on the clash between Rybus matter-of-fact mentality, focused on survival, indifferent to feelings and beauty, and Leo's sentimental approach to life, whose artistic sensibility is marred by amateurism (his attitude to the Fox is undeniably fannish [431]). It is not a resolved contrast, as we may disapprove of Leo's teenagerish selfishness, which brings him to refuse contact with another human being to cultivate his platonic love for a virtual woman, but it is difficult to subscribe to Rybus monomaniac harshness. Though she manages to defeat her illness, she turns into a sort of soulless robot, having sacrificed all those emotions that give life much of its meaning.

When Dick turned "Chains of Air..." into the first part of *Invasion*, he also turned the two conflicting characters of Leo and Rybus into a couple of sfnal Joseph and Mary, and added a child, Emmanuel, so that the Holy Family is complete — though Emmanuel is not Herb's son, as we shall see (but that is also true for Joseph and Jesus in the Gospels). The image of the Holy Family, be it overt or covert, virtual or actual, was present in Dick's fiction well before he started writing *Invasion* in 1980. Earlier embodiments of this image can be found in *Time Out of Joint* and above all in *The World Jones Made* (well before its evocation in *VALIS*), and it is this neglected novel that may shed light on the role the Holy Family will play in the second part of the VALIS Trilogy.

The World Jones Made (1956) is pivoted on the political takeover of Floyd Jones, a psi-empowered religious leader who succeeds in establishing a world dictatorship based on intolerance, and grandiose plans of space colonization by exploiting the xenophobic fears spreading all over the world because of the arrival of enigmatic alien creatures called "drifters." Jones' theocracy replaces the former tolerant, enlightened, and peaceful Fedgov administration, whose values are upheld by the protagonist of the novel, Cussick, a Fedgov serviceman; at the end of the story his family must flee Earth and settle on Venus in order to escape the revenge of Jones' followers (Cussick has accidentally killed Jones, thus turning him into a martyr).

In the last pages of the novel the protagonist, his partner Nina, and their son Jacky are shown as the only depositors of the old values of open-mindedness and tolerance, and have to insulate themselves — first by leaving Earth, then by sealing themselves into an airtight transparent bubble protecting them from Venus's atmosphere (like the domes on CY30-CY30B). Religious symbols abound in the novel: Jones is a Jesus-like figure (notice the similarity of their names) who manages to prevail thanks to his death (foretold by his precognitive faculty and possibly premeditated by the religious leader). In this context it is quite easy to see Cussick's triadic family under its bubble on an alien planet as Dick's sfnal version of the Holy Family's flight into Egypt. The fact that the sfnal flight to Egypt occurs *after* Jones' death is not inconsistent with the reverend's purported messianic features: it is quite clear, at the end of the novel, that Jones is a false messiah, actually an Antichrist of sorts, and that his followers are even worse than him.

Cussick, Nina and Jacky preserve the ethical and political values of tolerance, a political issue that ties the novel to the historical context of the 1950s. Jones' intolerance may well relate to the activities of Joseph McCarthy's

Subcommittee on Investigations, the House Committee on Un-American Activities (one of its members being Dick's political nemesis, Richard Nixon),[4] or the Senate Internal Security Subcommittee, plus the beginning of the struggle for the civil rights. However, if Cussick's triadic family is the embodiment of a repressed political truth, it is also a symbol coming from the Christian tradition. The religious subtext is quite evident in *The World Jones Made*, thanks to the presence of the negative messiah Jones.[5] However, these religious materials are endowed with a strong political charge, which fuels a radical and ironic criticism of Eisenhower's *America Felix*. Religious subtexts are not here part of some escapist fantasy, but provide a symbolic frame which orients the overall ethical meaning of the novel.

When the ethically charged family in *The World Jones Made* must leave Earth because it is under the domination of and evil authoritarian regimes (re-enacting the Flight to Egypt, but with the ancient North-African country replaced by Venus), its flight sanctions at the same time its "subversive" value, and the domination of Earth by the powers of evil. On the other hand, it is quite clear that the return of the Holy Family might amount to a challenge to the authoritarian domination that has enslaved Earth. It is a quite simple political symbolism, once we understand how Dick superimposed religious symbols to sfnal topoi. This will turn the rather static plot of "Chains of Air...," which is confined to the claustrophobic domes of the two colonists on CY30-CY30B, into an eventful novel with a hectic rhythm,[6] where the return of the Holy Family to Earth is staged.

Much of the complexity of the plot derives from its non-linear architecture, shaped by a massive use of analepses. The story begins *in medias res*, when a lot has already happened, both in the near and far past, and all these previous events are told or shown through flashbacks. For example we are told that it all started with Yahweh's retreat from Earth, with a revelation which is both political and theological: God was exiled, leaving our planet to the Adversary (Belial),[7] in a definite moment in time and space, A.D. 73 (or C.E., as Rybys says), when the Roman Tenth Legion "Fretensis" crushed the last remnants of the Jewish rebellion at Masada. It is then that the Incarnation failed.

This historical event, overtly mentioned in the novel (54–5), is evidently an episode of imperialist/colonialist repression of the freedom and independence (mostly political, but also religious) of a small people. We know that Dick repeatedly used the idea of the Empire as a visionary symbol of (a) oppressive power in general, (b) the United States of America as a hegemonic superpower,[8] and/or (c) evil itself. In Dick's own home-made variety of Gnosis—as it is expounded e.g., in *VALIS*[9]—the fact that we live in a bogus world, the Black Iron Prison, concocted by a bogus god (the Demiurge), is also connected to the idea that the Empire never ended, that we are still living in the age of the Roman empire (*VALIS*, 48–63).[10]

Crackpot historiography? Delusional mysticism? If we read Dick's fiction as a history book such accusations might stick, but this is fiction and it should be read as such[11]: from a symbolic point of view the superimposition of Imperial Rome and the imperialist USA is a legitimate move, which appears even clearer today after Negri and Hardt's *Empire*.[12] However, the synchronic superimposition of different moments in time is an important feature of *VALIS*, but not of *The Divine Invasion*: the departure of God from Earth after the fall of Masada is placed in a far past and it remains an antecedent, though it has consequences on the present depicted in the novel (actually a sfnal future). After God's defeat there have been different forms of oppression on the Earth, all of them related to Belial: different empires have ruled according to the principle of technological and political power, the last of which may look odd in 2009, but was definitely not in 1981.

Earth is dominated by two competing institutions which actually buttress each other (in a way that foreshadows the construct called Empire by Negri and Hardt, created by the interplay of different global entities): the twin institutions are the Christian-Islamic Church, whose supreme leader is the Chief Prelate, Cardinal Fulton Statler Harms, and the Scientific Legate, headed by the Procurator Maximus, Nicholas Bulkowsky (the two characters and their plots are first introduced in Chapter 7). Suvin reads them as Church and Party, and interprets their "behind-the-scenes struggle" as modeled on the "medieval Papacy vs. Empire" (Suvin 386); Butler says that this "sub-plot about the leaders of the Communist/Catholic Alliance ... never quite fits in" (Butler 110–1). Schmid sees it as an "amusing invention" (Schmid 3), then seems to get lost in the complex architecture of this novel when he says that "[t]he pseudo-reality as represented by Cardinal Harms and Procurator Bulkowsky is as far as it is concerned nothing but a hologram" (Schmid 3) and supports this interpretation quoting a conversation between Elias and Emmanuel where the former says "[a]n artificial satellite that projects a hologram that they take to be reality," to whom Emmanuel replies "[t]hen it's a reality generator" (69)—actually the two characters are talking, as we shall see, of an old film called *Valis*.

Actually the sub-plot with the machinations of Cardinal Harms and Procurator Bulkowsky, occupying a small part of the novel, is fundamentally an exasperation of what Dick knew all too well as a U.S. citizen in the late 1970s-early 1980s: the global competition between the two superpowers, USA and USSR, the former trusting in God (and supporting the Muslim Mujahideens in Afghanistan),[13] the latter purportedly believing in Marxist scientific thought and technocratic materialism. The Christian-Islamic Church and the Scientific Legate are two sfnal inventions which remind us of H.G. Wells' Morlocks and Elois: while the two humanoid species in *The Time Machine* are the result of Darwinian evolution applied to the British working class and bourgeoisie respectively, the two competing institutions which rule Earth in *The Divine Invasion* are the result of an imaginary historical evolution, which turned two competing super-nations into a double-headed totalitarian global government. Both leaders are instrumental in Belial's domination of the world; both are the result of a typical sfnal projection of present realities on a reasonably far future.

Dick took pains to make it clear that the world in *Invasion* is *our* future; he did that by having Elijah and Emmanuel talk about "a very old movie" (69) whose title is *Valis*, "made by a rock singer in the latter part of the twentieth century" (69): this is an overt reference to the first part of the trilogy, where rock star Eric Lampton directs *Valis* the movie (Ch. 8), and clearly tells that *VALIS* is the past of *DI*. This is also a way to connect the two novels, and stress the continuity between Dick's present (California in the 1970s) and the dystopian future (surely not near, judging by its technological advancement) depicted in *Invasion*. But there is more than this in the conversation on the film *Valis*, as we shall see.

However, God's defeat can be reversed, as "God can be defeated, but only temporarily" (56): the Holy Family must get back to Earth, in a well-organized raid that may place the Messiah well inside "the zone of Belial" (96). The mastermind of the operation is Elias (who is actually the prophet Elijah), who explains that Rybys is not just sick with multiple sclerosis but also three months pregnant thanks to Yah's intervention (55); the disease is no more than a trick to get Rybys (and the Messiah, her son) past Earth's Immigration, and Herb is part of the ploy, as he will play the role of the father. So Rybys' pregnancy, which is in itself a supernatural event (a woman conceiving without sexual intercourse), we might even say a sfnal event, contributes to the composition of the image of the Holy Family, but it is also a propulsive element of the plot, as Rybys' womb will be the vehicle of the divine invasion: her son Emmanuel will be the new Messiah.

Between Masada and the raid of the Holy Family from outer space Elijah kept the resistance against Belial active. He proudly lists a series of historical moments when he intervened, times of important political upheavals: "I was with Graf Egmont in the Dutch wars of independence, the Thirty Years War; I was present the day he was executed. I knew Beethoven.... We engineered the American Revolution.... We were the Friends of God at one time and the Brothers of the Rosy Cross in 1615... I was Jakob Boehme" (97). Some references in this list might be obscure and must be explained: Lamoral, Count of Egmont is a Dutch aristocrat and commander who protested against the harsh Spanish rule in the Netherlands and was executed in 1568 (Dick surely knew the Dutch statesman through Beethoven's 1810 overture and music composed for Goethe's 1788 play *Egmont*); his death triggered the rebellion of the Dutch against the Spanish domination, but this was called the Eighty Years War (1568–1648), though the Thirty Years War (1618–1648) was connected to it (suffice it to say that the Dutch funded all the countries which fought against the Catholic Habsburg empires in the Thirty Years War). Beethoven is mentioned due to his connection to Egmont via Goethe's play, but also for his attachment to the egalitarian and libertarian ideals of Enlightenment. The German mystical group of the Friends of God (*Gottesfreunde*) was founded in the 14th century in Switzerland, and spread to cities which are now part of Germany and France; Dick may have it mentioned by Elijah because the name of the sect was taken by John 15:15, a passage of the Gospel with a potentially egalitarian and democratic meaning: "No longer do I call you servants, for the servant does not know what his master is doing; but I have called you friends, for all that I have heard from my Father I have made known to you." The symbol of the Rosy Cross has been used in several contexts, but the date mentioned by Elijah probably refers to the publication of the two anonymous Rosicrucian manifestos, which occurred in Germany around 1615: the two texts declared the existence of a secret confraternity of alchemists and sages ready to revolutionize European arts, sciences, religion, and political and intellectual landscape. As for Jakob Boehme, or Böhme (1575–1624), a German mystic and theologian, he does not seem to have a particular political relevance, though his idea that the Fall is a necessary phase in the evolution of the universe may have a strong relation to the overall frame of reference of *The Divine Invasion*.

In fact we should not forget that this novel had as its working title *Valis Regained* (Sutin, 261) as a pun on Milton's *Paradise Regained* where the Fall was also seen as a necessary precondition of redemption — it is St. Augustine's theological concept of *felix culpa*, mentioned by Rybis in the novel (56). Yet Dick knew the Bible too well to ignore that that title was ultimately misleading, as VALIS is the name he came to assign not to Eden but to God (as in *VALIS*) or something that resembles God or connects man to God (as in *Radio Free Albemuth*, where VALIS is an alien communication satellite), so he switched to *The Divine Invasion*, but both titles are important to fully grasp what Dick was aiming at. On the one hand, this novel should tell us the story of how the disaster of the Fall was really remedied, since what Milton thought was the remedy (Christ's coming, or, in Elijah's terms, "mission") actually was an aborted attempt (56); the lost Paradise will be really regained only by means of God second incarnation through Rybys. On the other hand, the scriptural frame of reference is inextricably interwoven with materials and topoi from the sf tradition, and that is underscored by the ultimate title of the novel: God, in order to defeat Belial, must *invade* Earth, and this invasion is seen by the Earthmen — whose mind is benumbed by evil — as a threatening alien attack, something out of Wells' *War of the Worlds* or the unconscious fears behind it and most pulp sf. So Rybys' son Emmanuel is a new version of "the monster from outer space" (65), as she realizes in a most dramatic scene (63–6) when she accepts her dire destiny.[14] In fact Elijah's (and Yah's) invasion plan is not completely successful. After the Holy Family has reached Earth an air accident (arranged by Belial) occurs, where Rybys dies, though she manages to give birth to Emmanuel, who is immediately tutored by Elijah, also because Herb suffers severe brain damage in the accident and has to be put in cryonic suspension. These events too are told through a series of analepses (and re-lived by Herb while he is in cryonic suspension [9–10]).

Most of *The Divine Invasion* is actually a sort of chess game between Emmanuel and Zina, a girl that the child messiah meets on his first school day, at the beginning of the novel (9). Zina cannot be just an ordinary little girl: like Emmanuel, she talks and behaves like an adult, and is abnormally knowledgeable about religious texts from different traditions. We (like Herb and Elijah/Elias) know that Emmanuel is Yah(weh) in disguise, who managed to infiltrate Belial's fortress: but we are not told who Zina actually is, and some of her words may also lead readers to believe that she is not friendly (Elias mistrusts her and suspects that she may be Belial or one of his agents).

The turning point in the relation between the two *enfants prodiges* is when the girl dares Emmanuel to visit her realm (141). This comes just after the moment when the boy has clearly said that there will be war between him and Belial and it will be nothing less than Armageddon (140). Hence Zina's invitation to visit "the Secret Commonwealth" (142), a place whose name is enough to scare Elijah (surely not a faint-hearted man); readers are induced to suspect that something in that place may endanger Emmanuel or hinder his plans. The trip to the Secret Commonwealth might also be, however, something that Emmanuel himself has planned: though he is God, and is obviously omniscient, he suffered a "brain damage" (143) that made him forget something — actually there was a split which "caused part of the Godhead to fall" so that it *"lost touch with a part of itself"* (145). Obviously an omniscient God would be the end of any narrative; the amnesiac God allows Dick to have the Christian godhead in the picture and save the suspense of a plot whose developments are unknown to both readers and characters. This highly unorthodox idea of a schizophrenic God, suffering from a cosmic trauma which caused amnesia (Warrick 191–2), and struggling to recover some of his memories (that he might also have deliberately hidden to foster his own plans) is one of Dick's typical moves to generate ontological uncertainty, but it has a theological basis being an adaptation of Isaac Luria's Kabbalistic theory of *tzimtzum*, the contraction or constriction of God to leave space to his creation, and that of the "Breaking of the Vessels" (which was made famous in literary studies by Harold Bloom's 1982 essay), according to which sparks of God (*nitzotzot*) were disseminated in all worldly matter (the part of the Godhead that fell, according to Emmauel). Once again these religious concepts, this time taken from the Jewish Kabbalah, are superimposed to sfnal topoi: we know how often Dick has already used amnesia and anamnesis as narrative devices, from *Joint* (Ch. 2) to *Game-Players* (Ch. 1) and beyond.

The Secret Commonwealth is not a very remarkable place at first, as Emmanuel discovers when he enters it through the disappointingly ordinary door of a savings and loan building (which is anyway shaped as a Golden Rectangle, like the doorway Emmanuel has already seen in his self-induced experience of accelerated time [59–63])[15]: is not very different from the world Emmanuel and Zina have just left, but the differences are important: in fact the little girl turns into a young woman, Miss Zina Pallas. The relation between them is now such that Zina can lecture Emmanuel about all the things he does not know: for example, she tells him that his world lacks beauty and fertility. "You were always partial to arid land.... You have gone from the wastelands to a frozen landscape — methane crystals, with little domes here and there, and stupid natives.... You skulk in the badlands and promise your people a refuge they never found" (150). Zina's world is a place of spring, unlike the Sinai and other Middle Eastern deserts where God usually appears in the Bible, and the desolate planet CY30-CY30B where Yah took refuge after his defeat. Zina's declared aim (152) is to show Emmanuel/Yah the beauty of her world, and to persuade him not to destroy it: to "postpone [his] great and terrible day," because she says that "[t]he power of Belial is mere occlusion, hiding the real world, and if you attack the real world, as you have come to Earth to do, then you will destroy beauty and kindness and charm" (152-3).

Then the question obviously arises if the world we have been shown so far is the *real* world. Surely for us readers it is not the real world of 2011, nor it was the real world of 1981 when the novel was first published. One should however wonder whether the Earth dominated by the two-headed authoritarian regime of the Christian-Islamic Church and the Scientific Legate (and secretly ruled by Belial) is the real world *in* the novel, the world we readers should recognize as real thanks to the customary willing suspension of disbelief that fiction in general — and science-fiction in particular — ask for. The answer, as we understand once we venture into Zina's Secret Commonwealth, is that it may seem real, but it might be "mere occlusion," a dismal appearance hiding a better reality, hence similar to Ahriman's decaying Millgate in *Puppets*

(Ch. 1) or the Black Iron Prison world with the repressive police state in *Tears* (Ch. 7). However, there is no doubt that the world where we and Emmanuel are taken in chapters 12–20 is not the same where the first 11 chapters are set, something Dick overtly acknowledged (Rickman 1988, 189). The Secret Commonwealth is a place where Zina is a young woman, as we have already said; Rybys is still alive and married to Herb, though their marriage is evidently unsuccessful; they have never been to CY30-CY30B and have no children; when they meet Zina and Emmanuel (who are now brother and sister) they do not recognize the boy; Elias is a colleague of Herb, who works in the latter's small hi-fi business. But the differences are greater than these. In fact Zina tells Emmanuel:

> The Communist Party has not the world power that you are accustomed to. The term "scientific legate" is not known. Nor is Fulton Statler Harms the chief prelate of the C.I.C. inasmuch as no Christian-Islamic Church exists. He is a cardinal of the Roman Catholic Church; he does not control the lives of millions [164].

So the two autocrats who ruled Earth in the first part of the novel are here demoted to cadres of organizations that do not have (yet?) the pervasive power they wielded before Chapter 12 (195–8). This also suggests us that Zina's world is somewhat better, less bleak and oppressive than the world where the story started. Emmanuel is not eager to accept this idea: he protests that Zina's world is just an illusion. But Zina's answer refuses to accept the idea of a simple dualistic real vs. fake dichotomy: "The world you see here, my world, is an alternative world to your own, and equally real" (164).

Zina's world is an alternate reality which does not coincide with the sfnal world where the first part of the novel takes place. We have — once again — a Primary and Secondary text in Dick's novel, projecting two different ontological levels; Zina and Emmanuel are well aware of this. But the novel hints at a third alternate reality, or better an alternate past. In fact when Elijah and Emmanuel discuss *Valis* the movie the prophet describes it as set in "an alternative U.S.A. where a man named Ferris F. Fremount is president," featuring Valis, "[a]n artificial satellite that project a hologram that they take to be reality" (69). In fact this very short descriptions fits the movie Fat, Phil, and David watch in the ninth chapter of *VALIS*, at the prompting of Kevin (*VALIS* 139–44)— and that film is a sort of surrealistic hallucination of the plot of another novel by Dick, the posthumously published *Radio Free Albemuth* (1985), actually written by Dick before *VALIS* and *Invasion*.

The plot of *Valis* the movie in *VALIS* the novel is a disjointed, dreamlike tale, actually aimed at transferring subliminal messages (*VALIS* 144); besides, it is directed by an amateur, rock star Eric Lampton, a character whose sanity is dubious at best (Ch. 8). Yet it evokes the dystopian history —

sfnal, but not at all oneiric — of the totalitarian USA ruled by evil president Ferris F. Fremont (whose initials may be numerically read as 666, hence hinting at his connection with the Lord of Flies, aka Belial) in whose fictional reality Valis is a satellite, not a movie. Hence the movie deals with an alternate reality, by showing in *speculum, per aenigmata*, the dystopian near future depicted in *Albemuth*. In 1980, when Dick was working on *Invasion*, that novel was no more than a forsaken manuscript, a discarded earlier version of *VALIS*: it amounted to a lost memory of a dismal alternate reality. By recalling it in *DI*, Dick seems to be telling us that there may be more than two realities in the fictional world conjured up by *Invasion*— with different degrees of reality.

This is what Zina and Emmanuel discuss when they evaluate the pros and cons of the real world vis-à-vis Zina's Secret Commonwealth (163–6), a discussion that brings Emmanuel to acknowledge that Zina's Earth is not so bad, and it "should not be scourged by fire" (166). During the discussion Emmanuel objects to Zina's alternate world being an illusion (166); there are many worlds, protests Zina, but Emmanuel/Yah explains that they are "potentialities that do not become actualized" (165)— this may also hint at the suspended status of *Albemuth*, then a manuscript which had not turned yet into a published novel. Emmanuel eventually decides that he will make Linda Fox real, because, being God, conferring being is his job; and this leads to a bet between Emmanuel and Zina, where what is at stake is the relation of Herb Asher with his idol Linda (who, in the world of the two-headed dictatorship, does not really exist, but is just a media-created image meant to soothe the oppressed — in other words, an opiate of the people). Emmanuel thinks that Zina's dreams of happiness are nothing, that "the quality of realness is more important than any other quality" (163), so he will make Linda Fox real to make it up to Herb; Zina, on the other hand, thinks that Linda Fox is worthless both as a media myth and as a real woman, so that Emmanuel will not achieve anything by making her real.

This bet might remind us of the Book of Job in the Bible, where it is God and Satan who bet; but, as we discover in Chapter 16, Zina is not the Adversary, nor an agent of his, but the lost part of God, which is called Malkuth in the novel, after the name of the tenth sefiroth, or emanation of God, in the Jewish Kabbala. By discovering the real identity of the girl he met at the beginning of the novel, Emmanuel completes the process of anamnesis and the split between him and his lost part is healed. This symbolic reunion of the male and female part of God might be read as a happy ending, which mirrors the successful meeting of Herb and Linda, which will soon turn into love.

The ending of the novel is a complex, multilayered allegory, which

Robinson seems to have only partially understood; he maintains that "the mock reality ... at the end of the book ... corresponds very closely to a fantasy that Herb entertained about Linda Fox, long before he began his adventures on CY30-CY30B" (Robinson 120). If this were true, we would have no more than a happy ending whose substance is mere wish-fulfillment. The ending is more than that, but it is also a display of those coups de théâtre that Dick could pull out of his hat with the consummate craftsmanship of the pulp writer he also was, and it takes more than one reading to fully understand it. One should however not forget that Emmanuel's decision to make Zina's world real means that Herb will be able to meet Linda Fox, but Linda will be a real woman with her period who may occasionally burp (189)— otherwise she would be a "nonentity" (185), as Zina says. Dick took pains to make clear that Linda as she is presented her in the final chapters is not a fantasy (part of Zina's realm) but has been "imparted substance" (185), entering Emmanuel/ Yah's realm.

The ending is more complicated than Robinson's "illusory world" (120), because just after the anamnesis, and Emmanuel/Yah's reconciliation with Zina/Malkuth, there is in fact another, unexpected fall: Zina unwittingly sets free an apparently harmless goat which is actually Belial himself (207). Dick is aware that no tale only made of words can remedy the ills and evils of the world by itself. The reunion of the two parts of God could admittedly please him (being also an anamorphic image of the reconciliation of two sides of his mind, or a symbolic resurrection of his dead twin sister Jane, the archetype of all the dark-haired girls in his fiction) and satisfy his reader's love of symmetry; the final solving marriage (the final union or macrocosmic syzygy [239] should mean that this is Dick's own *Divina commedia*, as classical comedies must end with a marriage) could be an original happy ending; but Dick knew that the symbolic apotheosis he stages in his novel cannot really redeem the world around him. Dick wrote *Invasion* in May-June 1980; too soon for the Republican National Convention, held in July, but not too soon for the news that George H. W. Bush, Reagan's remaining opponent in the quest for the Republican nomination conceded defeat (May 26). Reagan's victory only took place in the October elections, but Dick surely disliked the Republican candidate, the man who had ordered the National Guard to occupy Berkeley in May 1969. Reagan was not the U.S. President yet when Dick was writing *Invasion*, but the possibility of his victory loomed large, and it was not something welcome for Dick.

No wonder then that Belial strikes back in the ending; he does that by having Herb Asher arrested by a policeman while flying to California and Linda Fox; what is even worse, Herb hears again the all-string version of *South Pacific* (210)— the same sort of mawkish muzak he had to listen to while in cryogenic suspension (10–5). He then suspects — in a classical Dickian fashion — that he is still in cryonic suspension (210–1), and that all the events following his release are no more than one of those delusions experienced when "he was in that part of his cycle when he was under the impression that he was still alive" (9). The final chapters suggest that if Zina is on the side of creative imagination, and Emmanuel/Yah's business is solid being, Belial is the master of de-realization and fakery — of such a ghastly delusional condition as the half-life in *Ubik*, more or less the same condition Herb was in at the beginning of the novel.

Herb in any case manages to escape the policeman who has arrested him, in one of Dick's funniest scenes, with a display of musical expertise (including listing all the instrumentation that Gustav Mahler's *Second Symphony* is scored for, which is a form of Sophia in its own right; besides, Mahler's symphony is also called "Resurrection" — an escape from half-life, no doubt). Herb is set free also because the policeman is — unlike his boss — a decent person, in which Herb sees "some response ... some amount of human warmth" (22). Persuading the policeman to release him is a small, almost irrelevant victory, in Yah and Belial's cosmic battle — but it is a victory against Belial nonetheless.

Herb subsequently tells Elijah abut the soupy string music he is hearing, and the prophet/repairman suggests him to "patch into that FM station whose sound [he] hears" (222), to turn it into an instrument of enlightenment and liberation. Elijah thinks the radio station should only broadcast his fiery speeches, but Herb suggests also playing "something interesting, something that stimulates the mind" (224) — also Linda Fox's music. What Herb and Elijah have in mind is a free radio, much like Dick's Radio Free Albemuth in his then unpublished novel. And radio is usually the liberating medium in Dick's fiction (Rossi 2010).

Good music may counter Belial's threat; human relations (call them empathy, call them solidarity, love, agape) may stave off his evil lack of reality and his dismal simulations. Elijah's words may unmask his lies. But — and this should teach something to those commentators who, like Robinson,[16] have complained about Dick's purported inability to create positive female characters or his conservative stance vis-à-vis the issue of abortion[17] — it takes a woman to defeat Belial when he takes control of Herb's body, appearing as an only apparently harmless little kid[18] (227–34). In fact it is Linda Fox who immediately recognizes the Adversary, cheats him and then singlehandedly slays him (234).

Linda's toughness behind her appearance as an ordinary girl who looks "a little like a pizza waitress" (187) can only surprise those who are not familiar with the rest of Dick's oeuvre. In Dick's fiction there are destructive female characters, but there are also warrior women, usually dark-haired girls like Zina; Juliana Frink in *High Castle* (Ch. 3), a martial arts instructress who kills the Nazi hatchet man Joe Cinnadella; Pris Frauenzimmer in *Build* (Ch. 6), who disables the John Wilkes Booth simulacrum built to liquidate the Lincoln; Donna, the undercover agent in *A Scanner Darkly*. Zina belongs to this typology of characters, as her surname is Pallas, an attribute of Pallas Athena, the Greek goddess of wisdom, but armed with the typical weapons of the Greek *hoplites* (armored infantry) because she also was the goddess of rationally planner warfare, superseding the old, primitive male god Ares. Zina may say "I am not Pallas Athena" (154), meaning that she is not *just* that, but Yah correctly identifies her as Malkuth, and her identity also includes — in Dick's syncretistic mythology — her being "Pallas Athena, the spirit of righteous war" (195).

It is Linda, not Zina, who defeats Belial, but Linda is — behind her harmless and ordinary appearance — another tough woman; we might say that she is more than a human being, as she is Herb's *yetzer ha-tov*, his Advocate, a sort of spiritual protector (once again Dick is stealing ideas and words from the Jewish tradition, where the *yetzer ha-tov* is actually man's tendency to do good, as opposed to *yetzer ha-ra*, his inclination to do evil), sent by God to defend those who are accused by Belial (235). Linda Fox is revealed at the beginning of Chapter 20 as the ultimate embodiment of the type of the tough, streetwise, determined, dark-haired girl who often manages to do what Dick's little men cannot. If Linda is Herb's Advocate, it means she is his lawyer — surely a job for tough people. She paves the way for Dick's most impressive female character, Angel Archer in his last novel (Ch. 10), the ultimate embodiment of these strong, no-nonsense figures who play important roles in some of Dick's most celebrated novels.

The complexity of the final scenes is heightened by the fact that Linda is a singer, that is, an artist, and her relation to Herb is also aesthetic: Dick is also suggesting that there is a redemptive power in music, and this may explain the otherwise incongruous fact that Linda and Emmanuel/Yah (240) speak — of all languages — German when they meet after the defeat of Belial. One might expect Hebrew (because of the Torah) or Greek (the Gospels), but German is the language of music for Dick, used by some of his favorite composers of vocal music, such as Wagner, Schubert, Beethoven, and Bach. It is then in German that Emmanuel/Yah tells Linda to sing forever for all people, throughout eternity (240); to sing her *Zauberton* (a compound word which should mean "magic note or sound"), her *Musik*. There is such a redemptive power also in the other arts, of course including that branch of literature called science-fiction, and this is tied to the fact that Emmanuel and Zina — or Yah and Malkuth — can be also interpreted as two aspects of the writer's mind, and that their relationship may be a complex and original allegory of literary creation.[19]

Compared to the bleak ending of *Radio Free Albemuth* and *A Scanner Darkly*, this novel seems to offer quite a different perspective on the political situation of the USA in the last years of Dick's life. The writer seems to be suggesting that the reality of any given historical moment is something complex, a laminated world where the potential horrors of a crushing totalitarian regime are superimposed on interstices of quasi-utopian opportunities. The readers' world, in other words, is one where Belial rules, through repressive surveillance apparatuses like those depicted in *A Scanner Darkly*; yet it is also one where a little man like Herb Asher can survive Belial's aggression, possibly helped by a spiritual Advocate. The redemptive power of art (Fox's music) can help the victim of brutalization to heal. Surely the defeat of Belial is a small, temporary event, not the ultimate triumph that Yah/Emmanuel aims at; however it is real, inasmuch as it takes place in the world that Yah has made real.

What we have at the end is not the passage from a dismal dystopian world to an utopian reality, but the passage from a dystopian reality (another embodiment of Dick's Black Iron Prison, like the police state in *Tears*) to a sustainable reality (Zina's world), which is however threatened by Belial, who stands for evil (in a metaphysical, even religious sense) but also repression (in a quite concrete political sense). In the last chapters we actually have an oscillation between the sustainable world where Herb may have a truly satisfactory life with Linda (neither imprisoned in the prison domes of CY30-CY30B, nor damned in the cold hell of cryogenic suspension), and Belial's dystopian world, which can always get back (its return immediately triggering Herb's solipsistic paranoia of being in cryogenic suspension). Yah's Armageddon has been postponed sine die; yet this does not bring to an unconditional surrender to the forces of evil. We have rather guerrilla warfare, with small victories achieved by little men like Herb, with the precious help of tough women who know how to deal with the Prince of Darkness.

The oscillation between the two alternate realities can be read in many ways — just like the interplay between alternate histories in *The Man in the High Castle* (cf. Chapter 3) — but it is difficult to deny that the ontological uncertainty inherent in this laminated reality is another of Dick's variations on his favorite theme. However we should ask ourselves if what is at stake here is just the passage from a bleak future to one which looks much less bleak (though Herb is stopped and almost arrested by the Police there), or the oscillation between those two worlds; we should also ask us if the alternative realities here are just two or more, because we also have the heavenly Palm Garden, repeatedly mentioned in the novel (and briefly glimpsed at p. 147). Could this be read as a psychologization of our cognitive relationship to the world, so that the kosmos we live in is ultimately determined by our state of mind? Such an interpretation obviously puts *The Divine Invasion* in the context of Dick's life: we might associate the oppressive world under the two-headed world regime in the first part of the novel with Dick's bleakest years (late sixties-early seventies), and the very dark mood which pervades *Flow My Tears* and *A Scanner Darkly* (both dystopian drugs novels); getting out of that world and entering the Secret Commonwealth might be psychologically equivalent to Dick entering the relatively more serene last years of his life.

Is it just a private matter? Since the years 1968–1974 are possibly Dick's most troubled time, but also the years of a strong conservative backlash and the presidency of Dick's political bugbear, Richard Nixon, also a historicist reading is possible. The Secret Commonwealth is not a perfect world (it is still threatened by Belial, after all), but it is decidedly more inhabitable than the stifling dystopia where the first part of the novel takes place. We should not forget that the domes on CY30-CY30B are prisons, after all, that the very travel to Earth is an act of rebellion (promptly repressed by the political authorities), while Herb and the other characters enjoy a greater freedom of movement in the second part (Herb and Rybys in the Secret Commonwealth have *never* been secluded on the dismal planet where the story begins). Probably Dick — personal problems apart — saw the late seventies of President Carter as a relatively more tolerable world than the U.S. under Nixon. As for Belial striking back, it might hint at Reagan, as we have already said, and it is then interesting to quote one of Dick's letters, written in February 1981, after Reagan's victory, commenting on his administration:

> The President we have now is worse than any we have had before. He is worse than Nixon. The plans of the new regime are worse than the plans Nixon had. The FIA (Freedom of Information Act) is to be cancelled (really). It will soon be legal for an FBI undercover operative to commit murder in order to maintain his cover (really). Two billion dollars will immediately go into a nerve-gas program. The MX missile will be approved. Likewise the neutron bomb. Likewise the B-One bomber. Likewise a central data bank to gather information on domestic sedition, or suspected sedition, which includes "terrorism," probably defined as any group of two or more blacks with a .22 pistol and a couple of lids of grass. The Director of the CIA now holds cabinet rank for the first time. Fanatical madmen are at the helm and the suppose themselves to be in possession of a mandate [*SL6* 123].

One may subscribe to Dick's outline of Reagan's politics or not, but this letter proves that, though he was writing about angels and demons, godheads and archons, he did not forget what was happening in the koinos kosmos of the early 1980s surrounding him. Surely here we have a tangle of individual and collective history, a node where Dick's *idios kosmos* is tuned to the *koinos kosmos* of those years. We cannot help feeling that the cripple in John Dowland's song, quoted once again in the last page of *The Divine Invasion* (243), the wretch who "after many years in misery and pain" is finally well and receives comfort, may well be Philip K. Dick himself. Like *VALIS* before it, and *The Transmigration of Timothy Archer* after it, this novel may also be, among other things, a very original exercise in anamorphic autobiography.

Chapter 10

A Counterfactual Counterculture: *The Transmigration of Timothy Archer*

"One generation passeth away, and another generation cometh"
Ecclesiastes

Before we start discussing *Archer* we should deal with Warrick's contention that it does not really belong to the VALIS Trilogy. This should be done because Patricia Warrick is an authoritative interpreter inasmuch as she is one of the few scholars who was in contact with Dick for quite a long time, with a regular exchange of letters beginning in November 1979. According to her,

> *The Owl in Daylight*, the novel in progress when he died, was to be the final work in the trilogy. The writing of *Timothy Archer* gave him a chance to catch his intellectual breath, to retrace his creative leap in moving from the depression of *Valis* to the transcendence of *The Divine Invasion*. We recall that he saw those novels as analogous to *Paradise Lost* and *Paradise Regained* [Warrick 185].

Warrick's monograph was published in 1987, so she had to base her reconstruction of Dick's plans only on the long letters he had sent to her before his death (mostly contained in the sixth volume of the *Selected Letters*). But she could not access the letters Dick had sent others; the publication of Dick's letters only began in 1991, and the sixth volume with the letters that are relevant to an understanding of the *Entstehungsgeschichte* of *Archer*, covering the period 1980–1982, was only published in 2010.[1] Warrick could not then read all those letters written by Dick to different addressees where he maintains that *Archer* is the third part of the Trilogy.[2]

252

The fact that he indicates *Archer* as the third part of the Trilogy in letters to different people is quite important, inasmuch as even a cursory reading of Dick's letters shows that he always tried to please the person he was writing to, and this occasionally brought him to write different and contradictory things in letters sent to different addressees; a good example of this is the letter he sent to Ursula K. Le Guin on May 13, 1981, on the very day he sent the manuscript of *Archer* to his agent, where he tells the sf writer and critic — who had criticized Dick's female characters in *VALIS*[3] and did not approve of Dick's theological concerns in his last novels (cf. *SL6* 137) — that the most important element of the new novel was Angel Archer, a woman who is "quite anti–Christian and very against the sort of mushy mysticism that I've involved myself in" (*SL6* 151); one might then read this as Dick's rejection of the religious concerns which had animated his fiction after 1974 (though, as we have seen, they were already present in earlier novels). But less than two months later, in a letter to Laura and Joe Coelho, Dick states that Christ "becomes progressively more and more real" in the three novels, "but only is truly there in the third and final novel" (*SL6* 179), that is, *The Transmigration of Timothy Archer*.[4]

As a general rule I have not trusted what Dick wrote in a single letter to a single person, but only what he repeatedly said to different people — with some unavoidable exceptions, like the so far unidentified and unconfirmed Japanese novels which he repeatedly pointed out as the models of the multi-foci and multi-plot architecture used in *Castle*, *Time-Slip* and *Bloodmoney* (Ch. 4). I have accepted what Dick said in a single letter if it was not contradicted in other letters and was consistent with what we find in his fiction or can be found in other sources. Hence the five letters that include *Archer* in the Trilogy seem to me enough to call in doubt Warrick's contention that *Owl* should have been its third part.

Besides, *The Owl in Daylight* does not really exist; saying that it would have fit the first two novels in the Trilogy better than *Archer* may be a rather risky interpretive move. Though Dick wrote letters with outlines of the plot, such as the one he sent to David Hartwell[5] on July 14, 1981 (*SL6* 180–1), Butler lists other sources of information about the content of the projected novel, and notices that Dick's descriptions are not consistent, as he probably kept changing his mind about the plot and the ideas to be expressed in *Owl*, sensibly concluding that "[g]iven the way *Valisystem A* [i.e., *VALIS*' working title] shifted between first draft and VALIS, [*Owl*] could have borne no resemblance to any of the notes" (Butler 2007, 114). All we can say is that theology would have been once again an important component of the novel; that Dante's *Divine Comedy* would have been a major inspiration (after having also played an important role, as we shall see, in *Archer*); that Dick wanted to reconcile the three concepts of *Umwelt*, *Mitwelt* and *Eigenwelt* derived from existential psychoanalysis (Ch. 2) with the three realms visited by Dante in his other-worldly voyage (*SL6* 156, 174); and that he wanted to use again the Buddhist concept of *bodhisattva* (*SL6* 156) that plays a crucial role, as we shall see, in the ending of *Archer*. Something Dick wrote in a letter, that *Archer* was "the third and *presumably* final novel of the VALIS trilogy" (*SL6* 178, italics mine), might on the other hand induce to suspect that the Trilogy could have become a tetralogy if and when *Owl* had been completed.[6]

Warrick's contention may be easily explained if we take into account what she wrote about *Build* (Ch. 6): she considers that novel proof of Dick's "weaknesses as a mainstream writer" (Warrick 66). This judgment arguably stems from Warrick's interest in "Dick's technique to make the metaphorical literal" (Warrick 29), which she saw well represented in one of Dick's earliest short story, "The Eyes Have It" (1953), where a naïve or deranged reader interprets literally all the metaphors (some of them actually idiomatic expressions like "his eyes slowly roved about the room" or "he took her arm") and mis-construes a piece of mainstream fiction as the description of an alien invasion of Earth. If Dick's literary value lies mainly in his extraordinary ability to materialize metaphors (a good specimen might be *The Penultimate Truth*, where the tankers in their underground shelters believing that World War III is ravaging the surface of Earth is a materialization of Plato's Metaphor of the Cave), it is his science-fiction that is worth discussing: in fact Warrick declares that in his sf Dick "paints metaphors that show the reader his meaning" while in *Build* (and in his realistic novels) "characters talk and talk, driven to make certain they have told all about schizophrenia" (Warrick 66).[7]

Warrick's misjudgment may be excused with the undisputable fact that most of Dick's non-sf novels were unpublished or out of print when she wrote her monograph. However, if she deemed Dick's realistic fiction inferior to his sf, it is to be suspected that she would not see *Archer* as part of the trilogy because it, unlike *VALIS* and *Invasion*, is basically a realistic novel — something Warrick does not clearly say in her reading of Dick's last work, but may be the basis of her hypothesis about the composition of the Trilogy. However, Warrick devoted some pages of her monograph to Dick's last novel, pointing out that the structure of the novel "echoes that of *Valis*," though "in *Valis*, the character of Phil Dick is much less hostile to Horselover Fat and his mania than is Angel Archer to Tim Archer and the Dyonisian madness that drives him to his death" (Warrick 188–9).

Also Robinson connected *Archer* to *VALIS*, identifying bishop Tim Archer as "the visionary [which] fills the same role in the narrative that Horselover Fat does in *VALIS*" (Robinson 120), though he considers it as the novel that Phil Dick, the lucid and skeptical narrating I in *VALIS*, could have written (as opposed to *Invasion*, which might have been written by Horselover Fat). If this parallelism works, and I think it does to a certain extent, Angel Archer offers Dick a distancing screen that may help him to objectivise Tim Archer's frantic and impulsive religious quests, be they aimed at interpreting the Zadokite scrolls (transparently inspired by the Qumran and Nag Hammadi findings), at discovering the mysterious and miraculous *anokhi* mentioned in those ancient documents, at contacting his dead son Jefferson through mediums, at finding the anokhi, once it has been identified as a hallucinogenic mushroom, in the Dead Sea Desert — a final quest which will bring Tim to his death.

Though Tim is a fictional portrait of one of Dick's best friends, bishop James Pike, who actually died in the Israeli desert in September 1969, he does have much in common with Horselover Fat, who in turn is, as we have seen, a fictional depiction of Dick himself, or at least of what he felt was a part of himself. The remarkable difference between *VALIS* and *Archer* is that in the former novel the distancing screen is Phil Dick, a literary avatar of the author himself, which unavoidably leads to an interpretation of the novel in terms of split personality or a fractured subject; while in the latter text Dick uses as a screen a character that is as different from him as possible: a woman, younger than Dick, more educated, skeptical, pragmatic, an atheist, an avid reader (not a writer), who works for a law office and then a record shop. Yet Angel and her creator have something important in common: love of music and Berkeley (where Angel still lives at the beginning of the novel on December 8, 1980, when a giant analepsis summons up all the events pertaining to the death of her husband Jeff, her father-in-law Tim and her friend Kirsten Lundborg).[8] These are not lesser elements: Berkeley becomes the symbol of a certain lifestyle in the novel, and stands for a place where Angel lives and her psychological condition; music is — as we have seen in our reading of *Invasion* — not just Dick's hobby, but a powerful force in his fictional world.

Two more characters are important in the novel. The first is the son of Tim Archer, Jefferson, Angel's husband, who kills himself in Chapter 5 — though, given the rather loose and spoken modality of telling used by Dick, the event is mentioned before that chapter because after all we are "listening" to Archer, who is not always recollecting events from her past in an orderly fashion. Tim is indeed one of the protagonists, but *in absentia*: he is already dead in chapter 1 (before the analepsis begins), and the events recollected after Chapter 5 (9 chapters out of 16) all take place after his death. Notwithstanding this, his suicide is tied to all the main events in the novel: Jeff's self-destructive act is caused by the love affair between his father and Kirsten Lundborg, one of Angel's friends, which triggers Jeff's "emotional involvement" with Kirsten and morbid jealousy for his father (43, 56–7, 60–1); and it is quite evident that the train of events recollected in the 12-chapter analepsis starts with the meal that the four characters have at the Bad Luck Restaurant (a glaring case of *nomen, omen*), when Tim first meets Kirsten (20). Thus Jeff appears in the novel mostly like a ghost[9]; literally for Tim and Kirsten, in the period when they believe in messages from the afterlife (delivered via mediums like Dr. Garrett in Chapters 9 and 10); metaphorically for Angel, who does not believe in the supernatural events that Tim and Kirsten have experienced (the content of Tim's book-in-the-book *Here, Tyrant Death*).

The "quartet" of main characters in the novel is completed by Kirsten, who will commit suicide when she will be told she has an incurable lung cancer (171). While Jeff's personality is not very well outlined, which is not surprising for someone whose apparitions are prevalently spectral, Kirsten clearly stems from the lineage of Dick's negative female characters, the castrating bitches, though her personality is much more complex than the stereotyped domineering wives like Kathy Sweetscent in *Wait* or Mary Rittersdorf in *Clans*. Though often cynical and power-hungry, Kirsten is endowed with a corrosive sense of humor and has a deep relation with Tim; Angel appreciates her qualities, though well aware of her sometimes intractable character.

To these four main characters we should add Bill Lundborg, Kirsten's son, who suffers from schizophrenia and is not a constant presence in the novel, being often interned. Nonetheless, he plays an important role inasmuch as he counters Tim's intellectual and abstract turn of mind with his matter-of-fact, practical approach to life: he is not educated, but, being a mechanic, his link to the material world is stronger and steadier. In a memorable scene of the novel in Chapter 8, Bill is the only one who dares challenge Tim's belief in supernatural events and messages from the hereafter, and he does this by debunking the bishop's faulty inductive reasoning with his practical knowledge of cars and their working. Bill becomes more important in the ending chapters (Ch. 14–16) when he reappears at Edgar Barefoot's seminar and is "adopted" by Angel at Barefoot's suggestion, and subsequently claims to be the reincarnation of Timothy Archer—whose mind has supernaturally transmigrated into his brain, though it has not completely replaced Bill's one (Chapter 15), hence the title of the novel.

The presence of such a set of round characters with strong and in some case well-detailed personalities (especially Tim and Archer) is to be expected in a novel which was conceived as a "quality" narrative, as a literary book, as Dick repeatedly says in several letters included in *SL6*, especially the one to Rickman in which he complains that he could have written a cheap novelization of *Blade Runner* for $400,000 and chose instead to write a "quality" novel for $7,500 (*SL6* 167–70). Dick was disappointed by his agent's reaction (he "couldn't read" it [*SL6* 167]) and afraid that the publishing house might not like it (*SL6* 169), since his previous attempts at writing a mainstream novel (that is, a non-sf book) had not been successful, as we know, and he feared another failure. "Quality" meant, for Dick, stronger characterization; whatever we may think of the role played by flat characters in many post–World War II American novels considered masterpieces of postmodernist fiction (one might think of Heller's *Catch-22*, Pynchon's *Gravity's Rainbow*, or Vonnegut's *Slaughterhouse-Five*), Dick evidently associated flat characters with cheap sf, the very genre he wanted to escape (though he often wrote in his letters that he was at heart a sf writer and should stick to that). Moreover, some of the characters in this novel are based on real people, bishop James Pike and his lover Maren Bergrud (whose stepdaughter Nancy Hackett was Dick's fourth wife); we do not need to get into a detailed description of what is fact and what fiction in *Archer*, because Dick did it in a clear and detailed letter (*SL6* 224–5) to show that there was no risk of a libel action from the living relatives of Pike or Bergrud.

But if characters and their complex relations are paramount in this novel, one may be tempted to read *Archer* in a quite traditional fashion, as if it were a 19th-century realistic narrative; or, stressing the connection with *VALIS*, concentrate on the autobiographical component and analyze it as an autofiction (Smith & Watson 186), that is, one of those 1st-person narratives which conflate real and fictional elements (among whose most interesting specimens there is a novel like *The Kindness of Woman*, written by another sf author often compared to Dick, J.G. Ballard), and are often found in the territories of postmodernist fiction.[10] Though undoubtedly interesting, such a reading would remain outside of the issue of ontological uncertainty; and it is that line of inquiry that we must follow. In fact ontological uncertainty lurks in the pages of Archer, though it is much less exhibited than it is in *VALIS*, and of a different kind than the one at work in *Invasion*.

Robinson noticed that *Archer* only features a "single break away from strict realism" (Robinson 122), and this happens when Bill tells Angel "I am Tim Archer ... I have come back from the other side. To those I love" (226). This simple message hides a reference to the title of James Pike's essay *The Other Side* (1968), whose fictional avatar is Tim Archer's *Here, Tyrant Death*; in the real essay, Pike described the paranormal phenomena he had allegedly experienced after his son Jim's death by drug overdose in 1966. Jim's (and Bill's) "other side" is then afterlife; from our point of view, the "other side" is the genre of fantasy which would include *Archer* if we accepted what Angel Archer refuses to accept, that is, Tim's return from the hereafter and the communication of living people with the dead.

Since the narrating voice of the novel rejects Bill's revelation readers may be encouraged to take it as a symptom of mental disorder, and read *Archer* as a novel realistically depicting several forms of madness: Jeff's suicidal drive, strengthened by depression, a difficult relation to his father and (possibly) drug abuse (68); Kirsten's pathologic jealousy (166), and her deep rooted sense of guilt for Jeff's death, which brings her to an irrational faith in the paranormal; Tim's obsession with the paranormal first (though it is rejected after Kirsten's suicide [180–3]), and then with the *anokhi*, the mysterious entity or substance mentioned in the Zadokite scrolls; and, of course, Bill's madness that has been certified well before his final revelation. We might also include Angel among the mentally impaired people, due to her inability to leave Berkeley even when Tim implores her to go with him to Israel in the thirteenth chapter; Angel's exasperate attachment to the Berkeley area (and community) reminds us of Dick's agoraphobia, which often struck him, and made him difficult, though not impossible, to undertake long travels (and also shorter ones).

But how does Angel justify her disbelief? Here is what she tells us readers: "That the bishop had returned from the next world and now inhabited Bill Lundborg's mind or brain — that couldn't be, for obvious reasons. One knows this instinctively; one does not debate this; one perceives this as absolute fact: it cannot happen" (234). While Bill disputes the bishop's faith in the paranormal with a rational argument, calling in doubt the causal connection between the strange phenomena the bishop has experienced and his dead son (126–8),[11] Angel makes her rejection something instinctive — a matter of faith, though a faith that is opposite to the bishop's or, in this case, Bill's.

This bears relation to what Dick wrote about the difference between sf and fantasy (Ch. 1), when he said that it is "in essence a judgment-call, since what is possible and what is not possible is not objectively known but is, rather, a subjective belief on the part of the author and the reader" (*SL6* 153). This also applies to the borderline between realism and fantasy. A reader may not believe in reincarnation outside the fictional world conjured up by Dick, but he could believe that it takes place in the novel, regardless of what Angel's opinion may be, even if she warns readers that "I could quiz Bill forever, trying to establish the presence in him of facts known only to me and to Tim, but this would lead nowhere ... all data become suspect because there are multiple ways that data can arise within the human mind" (234).

Angel's mention of facts known only to her and Tim anticipates a crucial scene which takes place ten pages later, when Bill quotes the Gospels showing Angel a mushroom he has picked up, and declares "This is my body ... and this is my blood" (245). This is a famous passage that can be found, with slight differences, in Mark (14.22, 24), Matthew (26.26–7) and Luke (22.19–20); but the less famous passage he subsequently quotes "I am the true vine, and my father is the vinedresser. Every branch in me that bears no fruit he cuts away, and every — " is only found in John (15.1–2) — and in a previous chapter of the novel.

In fact Tim quotes this passage from John's Gospel while discussing the then still mysterious *anokhi* with Angel: "I am the true vine, and my father is the vinedresser. Every branch in me that bears no fruit he cuts away, and every branch that does bear fruit he prunes to make it bear even more" (82). When Tim quotes this passage, to explain that the Holy Writ cannot be read literally but must be interpreted symbolically, he and Angel are alone, in front of a small grocery store in San Francisco. It is a remarkable coincidence that Bill quotes precisely that (not very famous) passage of the Gospel in his conversation with Angel — *if* this is a coincidence. If it is, we are reading a realistic novel; if it is not, it is proof that Tim really transmigrated, and that he is speaking through Bill.

But this is not the only fact that could support a reading of *Archer* as a novel of the preternatural — a fantasy novel, then, belonging to the very genre Dick had practiced before moving to sf for commercial reasons (Ch. 1). When Tim and Kirsten consult Dr. Garrett, a medium living in Southern California (the only moment described in the novel that Angel leaves Berkeley), she tells them that Jeff said "The man at the restaurant was a Soviet ... police agent" (151). The man at the restaurant is actually Fred Hill, the owner of the Bad Luck restaurant, and many in Berkeley (including Archer and Jeff) do believe that he is a KGB agent (20–1). This is what Angel calls "a creepy residuum" that she cannot explain: "How could Dr. Garrett know about the Bad Luck Restaurant? And even if she knew that Kirsten and Tim had met originally at that place, how could she have known about Fred Hill or what we supposed was the case with Fred Hill?" (154). In fact neither Jeff nor Angel talk about the urban legend concerning Fred Hill when Tim and Kirsten are present, so Dr. Garrett could not have been told this by them or Mason, the medium they have consulted in England (106). Does this mean that the medium really contacted Jefferson Archer? Another judgment-call, of course.

Another element taken from fantasy fiction is fate: this is a novel where predictions are effective — no wonder then that bishop Archer discusses the ancient Greek term for fate, *ananke* (75). On the day of her first meeting with Tim Archer, Kirsten jokingly says that her body "is trying to die" (27); this is undoubtedly explained with the symptoms of an undiagnosed peritonitis which does not allow her to eat, but Kirsten's body is really trying to die because of a lung cancer which will only be discovered in Chapter 10. Her offhand remark sounds like a premonition, but there is not only that: a full-fledged prophecy is uttered by Dr. Garrett, the medium in Santa Barbara, who unambiguously tells Kirsten "You are going to die very soon" and then adds "His father will die soon after Kirsten" (156–7). Tim's reaction after

Kirsten's death is one of disbelief, and he solemnly states "Kirsten is dead ... because we believed in nonsense. Both of us.... Garrett and Mason could see that Kirsten was sick. They took advantage of a sick, disturbed woman and now she's dead" (180–1). With these words he is repudiating his previous faith in the preternatural, yet he will soon die in Israel and Dr. Garrett's prophecy will thus come true. It may be a scam, like Angel always thought and Tim comes to think only after the first half of the prophecy has been fulfilled; one might even think that Tim fulfils the prophecy by trying to resist, because he will travel to the place of his accidental death in order to find the *anokhi* (204–5) which could possibly save him from the tyranny of fate (and death). And this resembles a very old story told by Sophocles in his most famous tragedy, *Oedipus the King*, who fulfils a prophecy by trying to avert it — one of those ancient Greek tragedies which Dick knew and liked (Aeschylus' *Agamemnon* is quoted in the Bibliography of *Archer* [251]), though he does not explicitly mention Sophocles' masterpiece in this novel; one of those stories which confirm the overwhelming power of fate by showing humans' helpless attempts to escape its tyranny. Once again, if fate and prophecies really work, this is a fantasy novel (with remarkable gothic undertones); if fate and soothsayers are nothing more than a hoax, and those who believe them are fools, then this is a realistic novel.

Ontological uncertainty, as we can see, is also present in this third part of the trilogy. It depends on what readers believe — or what their willing suspension of disbelief allows them to believe while reading the novel. Besides, there is another matter of ontological uncertainty which looms large over *Archer*, but it is of such nature that it does not necessarily have the same impact and force for all readers: the Zadokite scrolls.

These have been based on the findings in Qumran, where a collection of Essene scrolls was found between 1946 and the mid–1960s, and those in Nag Hammadi, where an important set of Gnostic texts was found in 1946. What Dick drew from the real story of these portentous archaeological findings has been discussed in detail by Gabriele Frasca (in the last chapter of his monograph *L'oscuro scrutare di Philip K. Dick*, "Restare nel buio"); suffice it to say that the fictional Zadokite scrolls are nothing less than Q, or "Q source," or "Q document," the source of the three synoptic Gospels (60), a text whose existence has been only hypothesized by Biblical scholarship since the 19th century but which Dick conjures up in his novel. He was not faithful to scholarly hypotheses on Q, because these only posit it as a source for Matthew and Luke, on a par with Mark (this is called the Two-Source Hypothesis, according to which those parts of the two later gospels which are not in Mark derive from a lost written Q source); but *Angel* is fiction, after all, or better a complex mix of facts and fiction, where some facts may also be slightly twisted. However, the problem with the Zadokite scrolls is that if they are the Q document, since they "date from two hundred years before Christ" (60), they call in doubt all traditional beliefs about Jesus and his historical reality.

Either Christ was not the original source of those teachings and revelations that are found in the Gospels, but he simply reported much older religious truths stemming from forgotten sects; or he never existed, and those words which have been attributed to him come from others, possibly some anonymous master whose identity might remain forever unknown. This is not a very important issue for an atheist like Angel, but it is a devastating discovery for bishop Timothy Archer. Once again, it is a matter of belief or disbelief; but the consequences for an important member of the Episcopalian clergy like Tim are overwhelming. He feels he is morally obliged to "step down as Bishop of the Episcopal Diocese of California" (136)—a particularly outrageous act, because Tim Archer (like his historical counterpart James Pike) is a celebrity, who marched with Martin Luther King at Selma and was a friend of President Kennedy. But Tim's integrity compels him to resign, because, as he tells Kirsten and Angel, "I have no faith in the reality of Christ.... None whatsoever. I cannot in good conscience go on preaching the *kerygma* of the New Testament. Every time I get up in front of my congregation, I feel that I am deceiving them" (136).

As we can see, the matter of belief plays a fundamental role in this novel. For those who believe in reincarnation, this may be a realistic novel. For Angel, the transmigration of Timothy Archer did not take place, and there may be other explanations for the "creepy residua." For an atheist like Angel, or a Muslim, or a practicing Jew, the discovery of the Zadokite scrolls is not an epoch-making event as it is for bishop Archer (and his congregation, including an unorthodox Christian like Philip K. Dick). However, the discovery that Christ was no more than a disciple of a nameless and faceless "Zadokite Expositor" (78) is more than a matter of ontological uncertainty (we are not sure any more of what the past really was, of what *res gestae* may lie behind an untrustworthy *historia rerum gestarum*): it is a matter of radical metaphysical uncertainty for practicing Christians (like Tim, and also Philip K. Dick).

But the final discovery of Tim's quest (and the fact that he is another tireless quester once again ties this novel to *VALIS*), the ultimate—or better penultimate, as we shall see—truth, is another destabilizing move by Dick. The mysterious *anokhi* which gave the Zadokite sect eternal life is actually is a hallucinogenic mushroom (88); the Zadokites "were simply getting off on a psychedelic trip, like the kids in the Haight-Ashbury ... The Twelve, the disciples, were ... smuggling the anokhi into Jerusalem and they got caught" (88–9).

A first comment might be that, whatever Dick said in many of his letters, his deadpan humor never abandoned him; the idea that the Apostles were a bunch of stoned freaks pushing illegal drugs in Jerusalem is one of his funniest jokes. On the other hand, we have a further moment of ontological uncertainty, both for believers and agnostics: practicing Christians would be obviously shocked to discover that the revelations of the Gospels ultimately derive from the hallucinations of a small sect of drug-addicts; while atheists might be surprised by discovering that the idea of religion as the opiate of the masses could not be just a metaphor, after all, and that something (chemically) real lies behind the Holy Writ. This reconnects to with Jameson's argument about Dick's favorite forms of hallucination (cf. Introduction), those — such as drug-induced altered states — that generate ontological uncertainty.

But there is more to be said about the discovery of the real nature of the *anokhi*. This disconcerting revelation resembles the scene in *Do Androids of Electric Sheep?* when Buster Friendly discloses on TV that "Mercerism is a swindle" (158): his was a ham actor and an alcoholic, the scene of Mercer's agony on the stony slope was shot in a studio, the religion practiced by all humans in the novel (Ch. 6) is a gigantic media hoax. Yet Mercer appears to Rick Deckard and helps him to overcome the three remaining androids, even Pris Stratton, the one which appeared impossible to the not-very-competent bounty hunter. This revelation has a devastating effect on John R. Isidore, who goes into hysterics, starts breaking everything (160) and then retreats in a dismal hallucination, falling in the tomb world. Yet Mercer appears and saves him from his psychotic retreat, though the old man admits: "I am a fraud" (162). It is a paradoxical statement, and the fact that the self-proclaimed fraud manages to heal John and his spider, to somewhat comfort Rick (paradoxically again, because when they first meet Mercer tells him that "*There is no salvation*" [135], surely not a comforting truth) and then to save him from Rachael's and Pris' trap adds to the paradoxicalness of the situation.

The paradox remains such in *Androids*, though something Mercer tells John hints at an explanation. After having admitted that what Buster Friendly and his pals (actually a group of androids that have managed to escape the surveillance of the police and the bounty hunters) have announced is true, he adds that "[t]hey will have trouble understanding why nothing has changed. Because you're still here and I'm still here" (162). Buster friendly has revealed that Mercer was actually a bit player called Al Jarry; yet the fraud is there to save John, the spider, and Rick Deckard. Though the religious figure — half prophet, half persecuted messiah — that represents the main virtue of Mercerism is bogus, empathy still works. And it may save people, at least from a psychological point of view.

Maybe the point is symbolism itself. Something that symbolizes something else is not the symbolized entity—it is just a sign, an indicator. What is signified, what is indicated is important. Even if symbols are cheap, even if the moon in the background is painted and the rocks thrown at Mercer are made of soft plastic (156), and Mercer himself is a bit player (157). We could also say: even if the novel telling us the story of Mercer, Rick Deckard, John R. Isidore and the other characters in *Androids* is cheap pulp sf, it may hint at something serious, it may have something important to tell its readers.

In *Archer* the issue of a bogus religion (something started well before Christ by a group of drug-addicts eating hallucinogenic mushrooms) returns, and Dick seems to be better able to articulate what was only an enigmatic paradox in *Androids*. He does this by putting in the foreground Tim, who may be said to play the same role of Buster Friendly in *Androids*: like the android TV celebrity aimed at debunking Mercerism in the earlier novel, Tim wants to debunk Christianity in Dick's last novel. Not a mean feat; in fact the issue of discovering what lies behind the traditional truths of Christianity (we might also say "that which general opinion regards as true") is a much more important thread than Buster Friendly's disclosure was in *Androids*. Yet Dick did not think that Tim's disclosure could annihilate the "good news" of the Gospels.[12] Here is what he wrote in a letter sent to his daughter Laura a few weeks after completing *Archer*:

> In looking over the three novels of the trilogy I can see how Christ becomes progressively more and more real, but only is truly there in the third and final novel, and even in that novel Christ only 'occurs' at the end. It is as if the disparate pieces that make Him up come together: a part of Angel, a part of Tim Archer, a part of the boy Bill Lundborg, a part taken from the Sufi teacher, Edgar Barefoot; no single alone is Christ but when they join together they do form Christ, as if by an alchemical miracle [*SL6* 179].

This explanation may sound like one of the mysteries of Christianity, truths that we cannot really understand: a matter of faith, not reason. Yet, having been uttered by a writer who is trying to explain his last work to someone he loved, it should be taken seriously and understood in its literary implications. We may do it if we take into account the disclosure which takes place in *Androids* but does not change anything; because Mercer is there to help.

Edgar Barefoot is the character who may explain what is left once "that which general opinion regards as true" has been revealed as a fraud, once we know that the truth behind the truth, the ultimate truth Tim Archer strives to find, revelation after revelation, the ultimate experience that the *anokhi* should bestow upon him, is an undignified death in the Dead Sea desert. The story begins when Angel goes to one of his seminars, and ironically says that "it costs a hundred dollars to find out why we are on this Earth. You also get a sandwich, but I wasn't hungry that day" (7). Frasca noticed that this sentence is one of Dick's frequent "hidden prolepses" (Frasca 209), because Barefoot's lecture is not as important as the sandwich he offers his audience, and this is something we will only be told at the end of the giant analepsis which retrieves the sad story of bishop Archer, Kirsten, Jeff, and Angel, that is, at the end of the novel. It is then that Barefoot tells Angel that she is sleeping (in fact she has not really listened to his lecture, but recalled her sad story); then he tells her something even more important, which Dick felt had to be italicized: *you are starved* (215).

Barefoot explains this with clear words: "Spiritual things will not help. You don't need them. There are too many spiritual things in the world, far too many" (215). And the sandwich that Archer sarcastically mentioned in the very first page of the novel comes back with a vengeance: "When people come here to listen to me speak, I offer them a sandwich. The foolish ones listen to my words; the wise ones eat the sandwich" (216). This baffling revelation is much less cryptic if we take into account that feeding someone is a way to take care of him/her. It is then clear that the world of words, where revelation follows revelation, the world where Tim Archer lived, is an uninhabitable place if the sandwich is not eaten, if people starve there, feeding themselves only with words, and possibly tranquilizers, like Kirsten (128), LSD, like Jeff, or amphetamines, like Tim (52, 198) (cf, Frasca 213).

If the bread of the sandwich has a positive value, and symbolizes the ability to be anchored in the real world, keeping in touch with others, actions like eating or feeding are semantically charged in the novel, and it is no coincidence if during Angel's first meeting with Bill Lundborg the boy manages to feed Angel's cat, Magnificat, and she notices "[t]he care he took in spooning out the food... systematically, his attention deeply fixed, as if it were very important, what he had become involved in" (91). No wonder then that Magnificat, "a rough-and-tumble old tomcat who normally did not allow strangers to get near him" (90) lets Bill, the nourisher, pet him.

On the other hand, though Archer often meets her word-obsessed friends (Jeff and above all Tim) for lunch or dinner, something is always missing from their meals. When the four friends meet at the Bad Luck Restaurant, Dick (rather unusually) makes them tell us what they are going to have: minestrone, sweetbreads, veal Oscar (22); when Kirsten arrives, Jeff suggests her to order "toast and a soft-boiled egg" (27), but she refuses, saying that her body is "trying to die," and contents herself with white wine and cigarettes (26). In a novel where prophecies are a main theme (Kirsten's and Tim's untimely deaths are predicted by Dr. Garrett in Chapter 10) it is not a coincidence if a lung cancer kills Kirsten, given what she says in this scene. But the refusal of the toast is also meaningful as a toast is made with bread, and this is the food that the four guests will not have. One should also notice that Tim forgets to pay the check (27), thus bespeaking his lack of interest in nourishment and bodily life.

Another meal is hastily organized after Jeff's funeral: Kirsten proposes to have a takeaway dinner with pizza (73), but then changes her mind because "[t]here is no way [she is] going to be able to keep down pizza" (75), and asks Angel to buy boned chicken, rice or noodles, ginger ale and the unavoidable cigarettes (76). If we do not forget that pizza is basically a flat disc-shaped kind of bread, topped with a variety of food, we can see that also in this dinner bread is missing, or better refused. What is also remarkable is that Tim and Archer stop outside the grocery store (81–3) talking about Tim's religious quest, that is, forgetting nourishment to exchange words. They enter the shop at the end of chapter 5, but we are not shown the three eating.

There is a third meal, which unsurprisingly takes place after Kirsten's suicide (carried out by ingesting barbiturates): this time Tim and Angel meet in a Chinese restaurant: "This was Mandarin-style Chinese food, not Cantonese; it would be spiced and hot, not sweet, with lots of nuts. Ginger root..." (200-1). Once again, no bread. And Tim does not seem to be aware of what he is eating, because when Angel tells him it has been a wonderful dinner, he replies "Was it? I didn't notice" (208). His trip to Israel is much more important of what he is doing; Tim always lives in an immaterial future, not in the material present.

The series of scenes where food plays a role also include indirect references. When Angel suggests a literal interpretation of the passage in John's Gospel where Christ says he is a vine, ("Well, it's a vine, then [...] look for a vine" [82]), Tim rejects this suggestion as it is "absurd and carnal"—and carnal may mean something related to flesh. Some time later, Kirsten must be hospitalized for a peritonitis, which explains her lack of appetite (85), and this is a disease of the digestive apparatus. When they first meet, Bill tells Angel about his experiences in the asylum, where also drug-addicts were interned (consumers of drugs like Tim and Kirsten),[13] and says that being messed up from drugs "is due to malnutrition; people on drugs forget to eat and, when they do eat, they eat junk food;" and those addicted to amphetamines (like Tim and Dick before 1971) "don't eat at all" (98). When Kirsten gets back from England, she looks younger; she asks Angel if she thinks she lost weight (105), and one may wonder how a loss of weight agrees with Kirsten's claim that she quit smoking—however, one loses weight by eating less or not eating, so that once again lack of nourishment seems to characterize the three main characters. Actually Tim and Kirsten are not eating the right food, but thriving on words (Tim's, but also those of the mediums they are consulting).

Bishop Archer talks about food when he wants to show Bill that there is another world, on the other side of death, and starts by asking the boy "Do you create your own food? Do you out of yourself, out of your own body, generate the food that you need in order to live?" (125). But talking about food is not eating, and this is something Barefoot teaches Angel: "When your dog or cat is hungry, do you talk to him? No; you give him food" (216). Tim's (and Angel's) problem is that when they should have eaten the sandwich, to put it in Barefoot's terms (and this is what never happens in all the meals described in the novel, as bread is always absent), they have talked — or eaten something else, not even noticing what they were eating.

The crucial moment of Angel's life, the moment which defines her life, "the time of her birth into the real world" (146) is the sleepless night when she suffers from an abscessed tooth (145), and spends the whole night drinking cheap bourbon and reading Dante's *Divina commedia*. If the real world is that of books and words, there is really nothing to object; yet this is a night when toothache prevents Angel from eating (she obviously goes to the dentist "with no breakfast, not even coffee" [145], and coffee is all she has — with the inevitable pill — once she gets back home from the dentist [146]). No wonder that Angel is enthralled by Dante's supreme vision of the universe made up by scattered pages which are bound by divine love in a cosmic book — being a book-addict she reads it quite literally, not heading Dante's warning that "Quanto è corto il dire e come fioco/al mio concetto!" (Dante, *Paradiso*, XXXIII, ll. 121–2), which, roughly translated, means that the words he is using (*il dire*) fall short (*corto*) of the infinite entity (God) he is trying to describe, and that those words are too feeble (*fioco*) to render his concept (*concetto*) of what he has seen, a mental image which is in turn only a pale shadow of God himself (cf. also ll. 133–41). Dante was well aware of the limits of the language he could use like nobody else; while Angel, a professional student — but neither a professional scholar nor a professional writer — seems to be too confident of the power of words (and literature) *left alone*.

At the end of the novel Angel does not take the sandwich, and even a patient teacher (and therapist) like Barefoot seems to think hers is a desperate case: "Someday perhaps you'll come for the sandwich. But I doubt that. I think you will always need the pretext of words" (249). Angel does not answer, though she thinks "Don't be that pessimistic ... I must surprise you." This adds a further uncertainty which remains such: one wonders whether Angel will be able to escape her mental prison of words and no nourishment, her condition of professional student, too much in love with words to be able to live a full life, her psychological jailhouse called Berkeley, more a state of mind than a physical place.

The issue of not being able to leave Berkeley is particularly important inasmuch as Angel thinks of herself as the traitor of her friends (including her husband Jeff). "Traitor" is the secret name she confesses to have when asked by Barefoot (214), and there are at least three betrayals that beset her recollection of the past: having neglected the estrangement from her husband Jeff (61, 67), having seconded Tim's and Kirsten's madness about the preternatural for fear of losing them (112–3), and — last but not least — having rejected Tim's proposal to become her secretary (which she misinterprets as an advance Tim is making to her [201]) for his trip to Israel. Not eating the sandwich Barefoot has offered her should mean Angel has not completed yet the process that should heal her; she has acknowledged the grief for her friends' deaths and her responsibility for what has happened, she has started to abreact, but she has not gone all the way to a full recovery from her machine-like condition of spiritual death (210).

Yet there is hope: she has accepted to take care of Bill Lundborg, something Barefoot warmly encourages her to do (247). She does this because he is the only survivor of her lost affective world, being Kirsten's son and having once been Jeff's friend; it may be a form of nostalgia, but taking care of Bill is a lot better than living alone or wasting time with such unsatisfactory and nonsensical affairs like the one with Hampton (196), who behaves like a child, insensitively pokes fun at people who committed suicide (196–7), and eventually show "traces — rather more than traces — of paranoia and hypomania" (236). By taking care of Bill Angel may take care of herself— or better, Bill may take care of her, because dealing with people is something that may turn words into actions, possibly into acts of love. This may also involve preparing sandwiches and — who knows? — eating them.

If the issue of nourishment is a metaphor for human relations (we would better call them "humane relations," given the importance Dick assigns to caring, nurturing, sheltering, feeding, sharing food, etc. in the novel), it is opposed to Tim Archer's frantic quest, and these two opposite attitudes both relate to ontological uncertainty: Tim wants to solve all the mysteries, to debunk or sort out the episodes of ontological uncertainty that play a pivotal role in the novel (communication with the hereafter vs. delusion, prophecy vs. hoax, fate vs. accident, and ultimately fantasy vs. realism); Barefoot seems to be suspicious of such searches for an ultimate truth. When Angel tells him he is "another fisherman" (213), a spiritual man like Tim (of course the metaphor of the fisherman refers to Christ, as Dick was well aware of the Christian symbolism of the fish, already explored in *VALIS*), Barefoot answers "I fish for fish. Not for souls. I do not know of 'soul'; I only know of fish" (213). Another biographic element, because Dick is actually quoting his son Christopher who, at four, while the writer and his wife Tessa were talking about Jesus in the synoptic Gospels, declared "I am a fisherman. I fish for fish" (*Shifting Realities* 279). In Dick's 1978 essay which includes this anecdote ("How to Build a Universe That Doesn't Fall Apart Two Days Later") Christopher's words hint at a hidden, mystical reality; but in the novel they pave the way for Barefoot's concrete offer of the sandwich. Fish is food, after all, and refusing a metaphorical or symbolic interpretation of fish aims at stressing the importance of material life, of living beings — be they fish, or people. Striving to understand once and for all whether Bill is Tim Archer reincarnate, to grasp the ultimate truth behind the *anokhi* (or thanks to it), to fully understand what the impact of the Thirty Years War was on our koinos kosmos (Jeff's final obsessive self-imposed task, another endless quest), is fishing for souls — but that is not as important as fishing for fish, that is, deciding how to deal with the one who is still alive, Bill, how to practically help him, how to take care of him.[14] One thing is to discourse on the etymology of the word "love," as Tim does in his confrontation with Archer in chapter 4, and say that it is equivalent of the Latin word *caritas*, from which the word "caring" comes from; another thing is actually caring for or loving someone. In other words: you have to *live* in a condition of ontological uncertainty; you cannot sort out the riddles of shifting realities first, and *then* bother to live.

All this mirrored Dick's state of mind in the second half of 1981. In his September 5, 1981, letter to Le Guin, he writes: "I know that I do not know" and adds "I am beginning to lose vitality in this effort" (*SL6* 242); "effort" obviously refers to the relentless, home-made research and theory production that left us the ponderous *Exegesis*. In his last interview with Rickman, Dick declared, talking about his main obsession, the 2–3–74 experiences: "I saw something, and I can remember it very well, but I don't know what it was, what it signified.... I'll never know what it was" (Rickman 1985, 51). I do not believe that the truth (or truths) of a literary work are completely revealed by taking this or that event or statement in the author's life and positing it as the ultimate meaning of that work; but I think that a critic is authorized to read literary text intertextually, placing them in a network of texts, and Dick's huge production of letters, some of which not deprived of literary values, some rich in a twisted, proletarian, vernacular beauty and pathos, offers us other texts that we can connect to Dick's novels and short stories and essays. What these letters tell us is that six months before his death Dick was sick and tired of his endless exegesis, of his interpretive effort to understand the ultimate meaning of his weird personal experience. If Bishop Archer embodies his questing drive, Angel is the fictional embodiment of a state of mind that Dick recorded in his September 11, 1981 (talk about coincidences!) letter to Russell Galen:

> I have wound down my exegesis, at last, realizing that in seven and a half years that I have worked on it I have learned relatively little; ... My study of

Plato, Pythagoras and Philo (among others indicated that what I saw in March 1974 that I call VALIS is real, but what it is I simply do not know, nor do I expect ever to know [*SL6* 250].

That just three days later Dick was enthusiastically reading an essay by the Protestant theologian Paul Tillich, whose interpretation of Luther's idea of an omnipresence of Christ's body seemed to chime in with his 2–3–74 experiences, tells us that the oscillation between the obsessive quest and the pragmatic awareness that life had to be lived in the here-and-now was not resolved once and for all. Ontological uncertainty was not just a narrative strategy; it was Philip K. Dick's lifestyle.

The psychological dimension of the novel — Archer's sense of guilt, her and her friends' "madness," Barefoot's warning that words alone cannot save anybody — should not however hide another important aspect of *Archer*, that is, its being a tapestry of the life and times of the countercultural generation. In fact the counterculture of the 1960s is well represented by Angel Archer, the professional student of Berkeley, but also by her feminist friend Kirsten, her Berkeleyite husband Jeff and above all her father-in-law Tim, who quotes Romans 7.6, "But now we are rid of the law ... free to serve in the new spiritual way and not in the old way of a written law" (47), to show Angel that her fears about his affair with Kirsten are misplaced. Freedom was what the counterculture of the 1960s aimed at, and freedom from old rules and sometimes old written laws was part of the program, as well as the intellectual freedom to question all the old dogmas, everything that was held true because general opinion regarded it as true, or right, or licit. Surely the counterculture is more famous for his approach to the civil rights, free speech, the Vietnam War, women's liberation, environmentalism, lifestyle (including sexual liberation, use of drugs, alternative models of family), art (especially music and cinema); yet it cannot be denied that the countercultural period was one of widespread interest in the preternatural, *per se* or as something connected with the enlargement of consciousness to be hopefully achieved by means of psychedelic drugs. If science mistrusted paranormal phenomena, many people who adopted a countercultural stance mistrusted science, and experimented ESP and other forms of the preternatural — including séances with or without mediums. The historical James Pike did that, and published the results of his dealings with the hereafter under the title *The Other Side*.

Most of those countercultural issues I have listed above are present in the novel (especially sexual liberation, use of drugs and the civil rights movement, the latter being repeatedly stressed by Dick)[15]; the countercultural attitude was to be on the other side of whatever established truth was held true simply because the mainstream mechanically accepted it — and I am well aware that this sentence mixes keywords in Dick's vocabulary, but this should not surprise us, because, though older than most baby boomers (that is, the generation usually associated with counterculture), he partook in that cultural emotion (Frasca 217) since the beginnings of his career, when he lived in Berkeley (possibly the cradle of the countercultural movement) and already expressed his unorthodox opinions in his earliest short stories.

Angel Archer may have a skeptical approach to the preternatural, yet she is a typical representative of the countercultural mentality, for her use or abuse of marijuana (a bit too nonchalant when she shares a joint with Bill [237–40]), her political opinions, even her love of music, which ultimately brings her to work in a record shop. But also the historical thread of the novel has a strong countercultural undertone. Surely Dick inserted the reference to Wallenstein and the Thirty Year War to substantiate Jeff's scholarly turn of mind — even if he is just another professional student, not a real scholar — and mirror Tim's superstition, so that when he says that "What Schiller saw in Wallenstein was a man who colluded with fate to being on his own demise" (75) he is actually — a good example of tragic irony — talking about himself. But Jeff's search for the historical truth behind World War Two and Nazism, which brings him back to Wallenstein and the Thirty Years War, is not so different from Tim's attempt to find out what is the historical truth behind Christ, and then behind the Zadokites, and behind the *anokhi*— a countercultural effort to discover an alternative truth (which is also an alternate history — and reality). These quests resemble another counter-historical project, stemming from the cultural emotion[16] of the 1960s, and produces one of the masterpieces of postmodernist fiction, Thomas Pynchon's *Gravity's Rainbow*.

One of Dick's readers once asked him if he had read anything by Pynchon. He answered: "I have read no Pynchon — paranoia makes me dreadfully suspicious; viz: I suspect paranoia, which is a paranoid reaction!— but I understand he is very good" (*SL6* 147). Was this just his usual way to please those he was writing to? As far as I know, Dick only mentions Pynchon in another letter, written on January 6, 1973, to recommend the manuscript of a then unpublished novel, *Dr. Adder*, written by his friend K.W. Jeter: "It's somewhat like Thomas Pynchon's stuff" (*SL2* 128). He may not have read Pynchon, but he knew what Pynchon was writing, as he knew that Pynchon was a paranoid writer like him. Moreover, if Dick was aware of Thomas Pynchon in early 1973, before the publication of *Gravity's Rainbow* (which only reached bookshops on February 23), and the controversy about the 1974 Pulitzer Prize (which was not awarded to *Gravity* though the Pulitzer jury on fiction unanimously supported it — probably because it was too countercultural), he was presumably not informed about Pynchon's innovative fiction by newspapers or magazines, but by some of his acquaintances who had read either *V.* or *The Crying of Lot 49*. But, leaving aside the issue of a direct or indirect influence, it is remarkable how close *Archer* and *Gravity* are, notwithstanding the massive stylistic and structural differences: both aim at rewriting history, Pynchon with the partly factual, partly counterfactual conspiracy pivoted upon the Rocket and Dominus Blicero, Dick with the Zadokite scrolls. Both craftily mix fact and fiction: behind the Rocket there is the historical German V-2/A-4 ballistic missile; behind Blicero there is Wernher Von Braun, a former Waffen-SS officer, the father of the Nazi hi-tech weapons and the Apollo project; while behind the Zadokite scrolls there is the history of John Allegro's challenge to the orthodox history of Christianity. Both draw from personal experiences of their authors: Pynchon worked for Boeing in Seattle and took part in the BOMARC project, regarding an advanced anti-aircraft nuclear missile, in the early 1960s; Dick was a friend of James Pike and Maren Bergrud, and an avid reader of the Gospels and Paul's letters (whose influence on *Archer* has been thoroughly discussed by Frasca). Both deal with the countercultural wave of the 1960s: Pynchon in an indirect fashion, by putting characters which uncannily resemble the Californian hippies in war-torn post–1945 Germany; Dick in a metonymic fashion, by focusing on a small group of characters which well represent that decade and its aftermath.

All in all, these two novels stem from the countercultural wave, and would be unthinkable without the counterculture of the 1960s. And both writers are engaged in a highly countercultural and characteristically irreverent act: Pynchon populates the shattered cities of post–World War II Germany with stoned freaks or marijuana pushers like Bummer Säure; Dick imagines the real founders of Christianity as a bunch of hippies high on magic mushrooms. Both gestures are born from the same cultural emotion, the same refusal to accept that which general opinion regards as true.

But here is a remarkable difference between *Gravity* and *Archer*, one that may tell us something important about both novels: while the former, published in the early 1970s but written during the 1960s anamorphically mirrors the decade in which the counterculture blossomed and ripened, and still suggests that there is hope, because Pynchon counters the conspiracy around the Rocket with the Counterforce (appearing in the fourth part of his counter-historical novel), *Archer* witnesses the dissolution of the counterculture, symbolized by the murder of John Lennon,[17] which only leaves behind traumatized survivors like Angel, veterans of a lost war waged by a generation who wanted to give up war and dehumanization. Dick's final novel is then closer — and could be an inspiration — to Pynchon's 1990 novel, *Vineland*, focused on a group of survivors of the Summer of Love in the reactionary winter of Reaganite America. That Pynchon went out of his 14-year narrative silence after he had had time to ponder Dick's literary testament may be no more than a coincidence, as it may not — as far as we know today, it is a judgment-call.

Notes

Introduction

1. The history of Dick scholarship was quite short in the Appendix to Kim Stanley Robinson's *The Novels of Philip K. Dick* (Robinson 131–3), but it would not be so compact today. I have tried to take into account all the book-length contributions (be they monographs or collections of essays) that are available, with the exception of Samuel J. Umland's *Philip K. Dick: Contemporary Critical Interpretations* (1995), which today is a collector's item (unfortunately not available in Italian libraries); and to select those articles published on academic journals which might best help me in my exploration of ontological uncertainty in Dick's fiction. Dick scholarship was a pioneer settlement when Robinson first attempted to map it — much like Dick's depiction of Mars in *The Three Stigmata of Palmer Eldritch* — but it is a populated mid-size city today, rapidly growing to become a metropolis.

2. To these names we shall perhaps have to add that of Laurence A. Rickels, whose ponderous monograph on Dick, *I Think I Am: Philip K. Dick* (2010) reached me too late to be used and discussed as it could have deserved — its density and unorthodox approach to psychoanalysis and German culture in Dick's oeuvre made it impossible to include it in my discussion in a systematic and exhaustive fashion.

3. Here I refer to Avantpop as theorized and illustrated by Larry McCaffery in *After Yesterday's Crash: The Avant-Pop Anthology*.

4. A more balanced position is expressed by Christopher Palmer, who maintains that these novels "have not received much discussion, and it is not hard to see why" (Palmer 67), yet devotes a chapter of his essay (the fourth, "Mired in the Sex War") to two of them, *Confessions of a Crap Artist* and *The Man Whose Teeth Were All Exactly Alike*, with a reading focused on gender issues.

5. The main problem is Dick's style, though Gopnik acknowledges the raw power of Dick's fiction (and has partially grasped the main critical question in *VALIS*): "The trouble is that, much as one would like to place Dick above or alongside Pynchon and Vonnegut — or, for that matter, Chesterton or Tolkien — as a poet of the fantastic parable he was a pretty bad writer" (Gopnik).

6. Dick enjoyed a moderate prosperity only in the last years of his life, also due to the filming rights of *Do Androids Dream of Electric Sheep* as *Blade Runner* (1982).

7. Here Jameson is reintroducing a fundamental dichotomy which was already expressed by György Lukács in his fundamental 1920 essay *Theory of the Novel*, where the original equilibrium and harmony of subjective and objective in the classical Greek culture was split by Christianity, thus originating (among other philosophical consequences) the two different approaches to narration, centered on the self or the objective reality.

8. Jameson's model is more persuasive than Stanisław Lem's reading of Dick's fiction in his 1972 essay "Science-Fiction: A Hopeless Case — With Exceptions," where the peculiarity of Dick's fiction is explained thus: "[h]e is accustomed to let action issue from a clearly and precisely built situation, and only later in the course of a novel does decay, perplexing the reader, begin to undermine initial order so that the end of the novel becomes a single knot of fantasies. Dreaming and waking are mixed, reality becomes undistinguishable from hallucination, and the intangible center of Dick's fiction dissolves into a series of quivering, mocking monstrosities" (Lem 1972, 73–4). What is actually proposed

here is a model of Dick's fiction as literary entropy, where chaos gradually replaces order, but this is a rather simplified description of what really happens in those novels. Besides, Lem admits it is based on the reading of only seven novels (which do not include, say, *Time Out of Joint*, *Eye in the Sky*, *Dr. Bloodmoney*) and a few short stories (Lem 1972, 81). Moreover, Lem underestimates the importance of *Do Androids Dream of Electric Sheep?* (Ch. 6), so that his appreciation of Dick seems to be mostly based on *Ubik* (the only novel he quotes repeatedly) and — to a lesser extent —*Stigmata*. Often enthusiastically quoted in the 1970s, when the secondary bibliography on Dick was discouragingly thin, Lem's essay is definitely outdated today.

9. Jameson reads the characters of the novel as suggesting a provisional, unstable solution to material problems, that is, the shift from "the older ... world of empirical activity, capitalist everyday work and scientific knowledge" to "that newer one of communication and of messages of all kinds which we are only too familiar in this consumer and service era" (Jameson 1975, 360); in other words, the passage from a modern to a late-modern or postmodern condition. On the other hand Dick is interested in the "actual energy elements" in signals and messages (*SL4* 130), because he was desperately trying to understand his February-March 1974 experience: the transmission of high energy signals that he received as psychedelic visions presented itself as a viable explanation of those phenomena, at least in that moment.

10. Ontological uncertainty in Dick may bear relation to R.D. Laing's *The Divided Self* (1960), where the British psychiatrist contrasted the experience of the "ontologically secure" person with that of an individual who "cannot take the realness, aliveness, autonomy and identity of himself and others for granted" and consequently strives to avoid "losing his self" (Laing 41–3). Laing explains how we all exist in the world as beings, defined how others see us and how we see them; then our feelings and motivations derive from this condition of "being in the world" in the sense of existing for others, who exist for us. Without this we suffer "ontological insecurity," a condition often expressed in terms of "being dead" by people who are clearly still physically alive. Dick was an avid reader of psychiatric and psychoanalytic literature, especially in the late 1950s and early 1960s, the period in which Laing became famous; it is not impossible that he was influenced by *The Divided Self*, and its idea of ontological insecurity.

11. Though philosophers may be interested in narratives, cf. Ricoeur's *Time and Narrative*.

12. A particularly virulent critique was written by Stanislaw Lem (Lem 1974).

13. Dick discusses these two complementary concepts in his 1965 essay "Schizophrenia & *The Book of Change*" (175); they are derived from Heraclitus' fragment B89.

14. The relevance of Descartes to any reading of paranoia in Dick has been suggested by Jameson with his idea of an "android cogito" (Jameson 373–4): a foundation of ontological certainty on the self-evidence of the doubting mind (synthesized in the famous motto "I think, therefore I am") is questioned by Dick because the then purely sfnal device of AI technology enables a technical reproduction of the thinking (and doubting) mind. Jameson therefore ironically rephrases Descartes motto as "I think, therefore I am an android," thus highlighting the threat of de-humanization lurking in the solipsistic foundation of a transcendental (and ontologically certain) subject.

15. Whose implications have been thoroughly discussed in Pagetti's Introduction to the Italian edition, "Un sinantropo di nome Bill Smith" (Pagetti 2002) and my Afterword to the novel (Rossi Postfazione).

16. But there are other aspects of this complex, and unfortunately neglected novel, which Butler's brilliant article "LSD, Lying Ink and *Lies, Inc.*" has only begun to fathom (Butler 2005).

17. The most exhaustive discussion of *Scanner* is undoubtedly the third chapter of Frasca's *L'oscuro scrutare di Philip K. Dick* (Frasca 147–98), whose depth owes much to the fact that Frasca wrote an excellent translation of the novel into Italian in 1993.

18. One of the greatest practitioners of the sequential art, Art Spiegelman, was one of Dick's friends before his graphic novel *Maus* made him famous. Dick liked Spiegelman's comics, and he even wrote a short story in 1975, "The Eye of the Sybil," which Spiegelman should have illustrated "in a vivid and compelling way" (*SL4* 144), but did not.

Chapter 1

1. Suvin does not consider *Puppets* worth discussing, and he sentences it (and the next novel we will deal with) to a sort of *damnatio memoriae* (Suvin 1975, 7).

2. Moreover Warrick overtly declared that her "choice is to devote [her] attention to the great

novels and to ignore the others" (xiv), so that we may understand that in her opinion *Puppets* does not belong to the group of the major works.

3. But the novel could have been completed even before that date; in a letter written on September 16, 1954, Dick complains that there is a "fantasy novel" written two years before that his agent "won't handle ... because there's no market" (*SL3* 33). This could well be the manuscript of *Puppets*: its description as a story "whose beginning is natural, factual, normal" which then "progresses into greater and deeper levels of fantasy" does fit the plot of *Puppets*. This should mean that the novel had been written in 1952, at the beginning of Dick's career as a professional writer.

4. The letter was published in 1981 on a sf magazine, *Just: SF*, under the title "My Definition of Science Fiction," and then reprinted in the volume of collected essays (*Shifting Realities*, 99–100). Being something written for publication, its purpose should not be to gratify the addressee — like other statements found in single letters.

5. The same might be said of a later work, *Do Androids Dream of Electric Sheep?*, which would still be sf even if the protagonist were an android — like the Rick Deckard of *Blade Runner: The Director's Cut* (Ch. 6).

6. Here Dick is writing thirty years after the original publication of Hubbard's quasi-noir tale, and this confirms that it had left a lasting impression on his mind.

7. Maybe it is not just a coincidence if one of the secondary characters of *Time Out of Joint* is called Mr. Lowery.

8. I must simplify Hubbard's novelette here for the sake of clarity, because its ending, where the last words ("*Who ever heard of demons, my sister?*" "*No one at all, my brother*" [Hubbard 190]) are perhaps said by the demons (who speak in italics throughout the text). In fact *Fear* does lend itself to a double interpretation, which might superimpose a supernatural layer to its basic crime plot; though those final words may also be read as a monitory ending which warns readers about the demons which live in the minds of people even if they do not believe in a supernatural reality anymore, demons which are nonetheless strong enough to do mischief. No wonder that Dick was fascinated by such an ambiguous narrative.

9. The fact that Capra's movie is not mentioned in the first volume of the *Selected Letters*, which covers the years from 1938 to 1971 does not necessarily mean that Dick did not know *It's A Wonderful Life*; due to the 1971 break-in, many of the documents Dick kept in his archive were destroyed, including the carbon copies of the letters he wrote before 1971. Just a few of them have been retrieved by the editors of the *Selected Letters*, compared to the abundance in the following five volumes.

10. There is obviously a strong political subtext in the opposition Bedford Falls vs. Pottersville which has been noticed by Frasca (cf. Ch. 2 "La notte delle superfici"); suffice it to say that Bedford Falls embodies the ideals of Roosevelt's Keynesian economy, while Pottersville materializes the negative consequences of laissez-faire capitalism (what is today known as Neoliberalism).

11. Lorenzo DiTommaso has highlighted the syncretistic nature of the religious subtext in *Puppets*, showing that it also draws from Christian, Platonic, and Gnostic traditions (DiTommaso 2001, 53–5). Besides, the original title of the novel — *A Glass of Darkness* — is an unmistakable quotation of Paul's 1 Corinthians 13:12 (DiTommaso 2001, 53).

12. Also Will Christopher is cured, because in the last chapter he is no more a bum but a successful, enterprising TV technician, owner of "the most attractive shop along Central Street" (140).

13. Dick's use of concepts coming from existentialist psychoanalysis was first discussed by Tony Wolk in his 1995 essay "The Swiss Connection."

14. In the essay "The World of a Compulsive" by V.E. von Gebsattel (May, 170–90), which quotes Heraclitus' Fragment B89 thus: "When men dream, each has his own world (idios kosmos), when they are awake, they have a common world (koinos kosmos)" (May, 182).

15. Also the grave-world or tomb-world concept can be found in one of the most important essays in *Existence*, "The Existential Analysis School of Thought" by Ludwig Binswanger (May, 191–213), possibly the most important representative of existential psychoanalysis.

16. In 1967 Dick suggested Roger Zelazny to write a novel based on a board game where characters should move on the board, or better inside it, because each square is an alternate world; the game was to be controlled by "Cosmic Game-Players"; he quoted his "ACE book" *Puppets* as the model (*SL1* 226).

17. We might mention such short stories like "The Leech," "The Mountain Without a Name," and the highly representative "The Academy," plus his 1960 novel *The Status Civilization* which may be considered as a *summa* of his "sociological" period. Sociological sf also includes a good part of the

sf short fiction written by Richard Matheson in the 1950s, and some works by Ray Bradbury, *Fahrenheit 451* first and foremost.

18. One might then wonder whether purportedly "Dickian" films such as Andy and Larry Wachowski's *The Matrix* (1999), *The Matrix Reloaded* (2003), and *The Matrix Revolutions* (2003) actually are more VanVogtian than Dickian.

19. There could be some relation between Dick's shunts and what van Vogt *might* have told him at the sf Worldcon in 1954. The modal verb is necessary since we do not have sources that tell us what van Vogt actually told Dick; we just know what the *fictional character* of van Vogt tells the fan (who might be a fictional avatar of Philip K. Dick) in Dick's short story "Waterspider": "I start out with a plot and then the plot sort of folds up. So then I have to have another plot to finish the rest of the story" (*CS4* 224). So we have van Vogt's method in Dick's own words; however, what is interesting is the idea of a *discontinuity*, of an interrupted plot that must be superseded by another in order to complete a story. Unfortunately we have no external evidence telling us whether Dick faithfully — albeit not literally — reported van Vogt's words, or put in the character's mouth a statement that reflected his own modus operandi.

20. Especially in its Avant-Pop variety, well represented in the nineties by such novels as Patricia Anthony's *Happy Policeman* (1994), Jonathan Lethem's *Girl in Landscape* (1998), Steve Erickson's *Arc d'X* (1993) and Lewis Shiner's *Glimpses* (1993); cf. Rossi "From Daick to Lethem."

21. Besides, the name of the protagonist (Peter Garden) resembles the name of a property on the Monopoly Board, i.e. Marvin Gardens (Sutin 301).

22. There are at least three other novels where Dick traveled in a Sfnal territory which bordered on crime fiction: *Do Androids Dream of Electric Sheep?* (1968), *A Maze of Death* (1970), and *Flow My Tears, The Policeman Said* (1974). But some critics (Italian sf novelist and expert Valerio Evangelisti among them) noticed that also *Ubik* is indebted to Agatha Christie's *And Then There Were None* (cf. Ch. 6 and 7).

23. This name/surname seems to be one of Dick's favorites, since we also have Anne Hawthorne in *The Three Stigmata of Palmer Eldritch* (Ch. 7), and Hawthorne Abendsen, the writer in *The Man in the High Castle* (Ch 3). Valerio Massimo De Angelis argued that Abendsen's character might hint at Nathaniel Hawthorne (De Angelis 2006).

24. He completed *Stigmata* less than a year later; *Game-Players* was received by Dick's agent on 4 June 1963, *Stigmata* on 18 March 1964.

25. A good example of time travel outside sf is Washington Irving's 1819 short story "Rip Van Winkle."

26. Dick does not say in his June 3, 1957, letter to Anthony Boucher what were the other novels he had to drastically shorten (as for *The Man Who Japed* he says that 75 typescript pages were edited out): yet, given the date of the letter, they should be *The World Jones Made* and *Solar Lottery*. *Eye in the Sky* also underwent major changes, but those will be discussed in Chapter 2. However, Don Wollheim, the publisher, said that he never changed the plots of those Dick's novels he published (Sutin 90).

Chapter 2

1. Kim Stanley Robinson says that "the action of these narratives is in every case the successful toppling of the dystopian state" and concludes that "all of these novels are wish fulfillments" (Robinson 14); this is obviously not incompatible with their status of hastily written sf novels, whose primary aim is entertaining readers.

2. Dick's appreciation of the little man may have populist aspects, which will be discussed in the reading of *Do Androids Dream of Electric Sheep?* (Ch. 6). It is however interesting that Fallada's absolutely realistic depiction of a little man, an ordinary German young man struggling to maintain his little family, could be transmogrified into the Dickian Little Men struggling against futuristic world dictatorships and alien threats. It is one of Dick's many "deliberate anachronisms," his appropriation of characters, ideas, stories from other times (some of them definitely remote) to be "brutally" inserted in his futuristic or contemporary settings — we might mention his thefts from Gnostic theology, German romanticism, 17th-century poetry. A whole book might be written on this, and it would not be a work of pedantic erudition.

3. What Dick was not allowed to do in the 1950s he managed to do in the early 1980s, when he wrote a novel, *The Divine Invasion*, where one of the protagonists is Yah, the God of the Bible, cf. Chapter 10.

4. Also Robinson analysed this novel on the basis of Heraclitus' dichotomy (Robinson 15–7); but I prefer to introduce the concept of Finite Subjective Reality because in Lethem the private world is one that other people may access (albeit involuntarily), which is the same situation we have in *Eye* and in *The Three Stigmata of Palmer Eldritch*. Obviously a private world that may be somewhat accessed and shared turns into a small *koinos* kosmos or common world, but one where individuals are subjected to the will of the creator or dreamer of the FSR; this microworld is evidently a metaphor of literature (and other arts which may create a sustained virtual reality, such as cinema, theatre, etc.).

5. This choice is also motivated by the criticism of the not-well-meditated use of the *koinos/idios* kosmos concepts that has been expressed by Lorenzo DiTommaso (DiTommaso 2001, 57). We should in fact not forget that Dick's pocket universes or FSRs are quite different from what *idios* kosmos originally was in Heraclitus and its translation in psychoanalytical terms operated by existential psychiatrists.

6. According to Robinson this is Dick's way to suggest his readers to drop out of society, rejecting the American Fifties' *koinos* kosmos of conformism, intolerance and militarism (Robinson 16–7). One might object that starting a business is a rather weak way to drop out, but we should not underestimate the difference between a firm working on missile technologies and one producing harmless hi-fi equipment: the former serving the machinery of Cold War, the latter at the service of music, that is, one of Dick's favourite forms of artistic creativity.

7. Yet Dick thought that the ending, where Hamilton enters into a partnership with Laws, was "very daring and progressive" for 1956, the year when he wrote the novel (Rickman 1988, 125), when segregation was still mandated by Jim Crow laws in several states.

8. Moreover, there is at least a commentator which proposed a religious subtext for this novel, because Hamilton can be said to have had an experience of "awakening conscience" which allows him to fully understand the immorality of the bigoted political intolerance which has targeted his wife; this awakening is associated with a renewed "faith in oneself" (DiTommaso 2001, 60).

9. Hofstadter does not however apply his category of "paranoid style" to contemporary American politics, but also to earlier phases of US history; he traces the sources of political paranoia back to the spreading of Illuminist ideas in late-18th-century America.

10. An idea which would be later recycled by an older and more successful sf writer, Robert A. Heinlein, in his 1964 novel *The Moon is a Harsh Mistress*. In Heinlein's the opposition between the Lunar rebels and the Earth is seen as a science-fictional re-telling of the American Revolution, something which is not as evident in Dick's novel.

11. According to Sutin, *Confessions* was written in 1959 though it was published in 1975 (Sutin 298).

12. I have taken this phrase from Umberto Eco's discussion of Greimas' semantics (Eco 1979, 94); there *effect de sense* is something that is created by much smaller texts than a novel, but it may be said that a particular reading of a text much longer than a lexeme like the one analysed by Eco may also produce an effect of signification, and that several effects of signification may be produced by a single literary text.

13. It could be also argued that the character leaves the Peyton Place-like world of mainstream literature (but we would better use the term "best-seller realism" here) and is free to reach the world of science-fiction travelling on the archetypal icon of SF according to Thomas M. Disch: the starship.

14. In my 1996 article "Just a Bunch of Words" I suggested that Dick was aware that behind the Greek word *logos* used by St. John at the beginning of his Gospel, there was the Jewish term *dabar*, meaning both "thing" and "word." This hypothesis was subsequently contested by Lorenzo DiTommaso in his 1998 article "A *logos* or Two Concerning the *logoz* of Umberto Rossi and Philip K. Dick's *Time Out of Joint*," though one of the fragments of the Exegesis that have been published mentions the Jewish term (spelled as *dabhar*) (*Pursuit* 126) in connection with Philo of Alexandria's theory of Logos. Anyhow, the fragment was written in 1981, so it does not prove that Dick already knew about *dabar* and its peculiar double meaning when he wrote the park scene in *Time*.

15. Something similar can be found in the Introduction Dick wrote to his short story collection *The Golden Man* (*Shifting Realities* 93).

Chapter 3

1. Though the atrocities shown by newsreels left deep marks on Dick's mind (Platt 153–4).

2. The Fifth Marine Regiment was involved in heavy fighting in summer 1918, especially in the fierce battle of Belleau Wood (1–26 June); some episodes of those clashes were soon part of the Marines

mythology. The Fifth also played an important role during the final Allied offensive of Autumn 1918 which brought W.W.I to an end, fighting in the battles of Saint-Mihiel and the Meuse-Argonne Offensive (which is not casually mentioned in *High Castle* [66]). The Fifth was a prestigious unit which distinguished itself; no wonder then that Edgar Dick described himself as "a corporal like Napoleon and Hitler" (Sutin 14).

3. This story will be subsequently used as the plot frame of *The Penultimate Truth* (Ch. 6).

4. Here we follow Peter Jones' distinction of *combat novel* vs. *war novel*; the former focusing on the experience of soldiers (a good example could be *The Short-Timers*, written by one of Dick's acquaintances, Gustav Hasford, a Vietnam veteran), the latter also dealing with the civilian world, and showing the consequences of war, or contrasting the plight of combatants with that of civilians, etc. (two examples being Tolstoy's *War and Peace* and Pynchon's *Gravity's Rainbow*). Jones introduced the distinction in his 1976 monograph *War and the Novelist*, focusing on US war narratives; I extended it to other literatures in my essay *Il secolo di fuoco*, which also discusses *High Castle*.

5. Working with a respectable publishing house did not only mean more prestige for the author, but also an opportunity to work with a competent editor, like Peter Israel, who worked with Dick on *High Castle*: Israel's contribution was wholeheartedly acknowledged by Dick (Rickman 1988, 139–40).

6. Dick could have read the novel, as he had been deeply struck by Sinclair Lewis' *Babbitt* (1922), where he "found [his] character" (Rickman 1989, 211).

7. Already published as a standalone article on *Extrapolation* in 1991.

8. This is particularly evident in the treatment of Byron, who turns into "an uncompromising conservative" (Hawthorne 290) in the House of the Lords in his old age, or Bonaparte, who has been moved "from St. Helena to England" (Hawthorne 294). Though most of the story is about literature, it also possesses an important historical-political aspect.

9. It is quite clear that the knowledge of history may vary, and that we may imagine a reader so ignorant about 20th-century history that s/he might totally miss the point of the novel; but even if this hypothetical reader did not know anything of W.W.II and its outcome, he would be faced with two different versions of history *in* the novel, which would obviously lead him/her to wonder what really happened in 1939–45. We might say that *The Man in the High Castle* intrinsically forces the reader to question his/her referential code, even if he lacks information about the Second World War.

10. This should also bring to a revision of Barthes' idea of a Referential Code, which I have attempted in my doctoral thesis, *La prova del fuoco*.

11. It also accounts for an important episode of the novel, Mr. Tagomi's visit (in Chapter 14) to an alternate San Francisco where the Japanese are not respected and feared, but treated with racist contempt—another level of reality which should correspond to our one. Hence the novel also displays the Zero Text, and this is something Dick overtly said in one of his speeches (*Shifting Realities* 247).

12. I have collected all the *I Ching* hexagrams mentioned in the text in this table which might be useful for future interpreters:

Table 3.2 Note

Number and name	Description	Character who obtains the hexagram	Page
15, Ch'ien	Modesty	FRANK FRINK	18
44, Kou	Coming To Meet	F. FRINK	20
20, Ta Kuo	The Preponderance of the Great	TAGOMI	23
46, Sheng	Ascending	TAGOMI	25
11, T'ai	Peace	F. FRINK	53
26, Dà Chù	The Taming Power of the Great	F. FRINK	56
47, K'un	Oppression (Exhaustion)	F. FRINK	102
51, Ch'en	God Appears in the Sign of Arousing	TAGOMI	161
42, Yi	Increase	JULIANA FRINK	209
43, Kuai	Break-through (Resoluteness)	J. FRINK	209
61, Chung Fu	Inner Truth	TAGOMI	231
Idem	Idem	J. FRINK	267

Tagomi actually obtains Hexagram 61 at p. 194, so that it comes before 42 and 43, but Dick does not tell us in that page what hexagram is the result of Tagomi's query.

13. Even his family name is bogus: "Cinnadella" may sound Italian, but it is not a real, documented Italian surname.

14. I have discussed the character system in High Castle from a racial/ethnic point of view in my 2000 article "All Around the High Castle: Narrative Voices and Fictional Visions in Philip K. Dick's *The Man in the High Castle*," where I show how ethnic identity affects each character's point of view, and how the *I Ching* can be considered as a quasi-character.

15. According to Palmer the devices Dick used to do this are "fantasy, ... a textualist dissolution of the objective 'real,' ... a non-linear conception of temporality, and ... a theologizing of history" (Palmer 131); these are indeed components which play a role in the novel, and Palmer managed to outline their respective roles. One should add that these components fit Palmer's conception of post-modernism as an ideology of gnoseologic nihilism, and that is the reason why he chose to focus on them, overlooking the issue of paranoia.

16. In the former we have Leon Cartwright's elaborate plot to overthrow the despotic rule of Quizmaster Reese Verrick, and Verrick's less hidden counterplot to defend his own power; in the latter, a world dominated by computers endowed with artificial intelligence is torn by the struggle between two AIs, Vulcan 3 and Vulcan 2, based on deception and the manipulation of information.

17. Palmer is sceptical about DiTommaso's description of Juliana's "adventure" as a path to redemption, and says "it is hard to see why Dick has Abendsen praise her as something magical, a 'chthonic spirit'" (Palmer 129). Actually Abendsen's words do not sound like praise at all, as Juliana is also called a daemon; Caroline, Abendsen's wife says she is "terribly, terribly disruptive" (248); and a chthonic spirit belongs to the underworld (in ancient Greek religion), to the world of the dead. In Dick's oeuvre Juliana is another embodiment of that formidable female figure which is also described as Magna Mater, whose avatars are other dark-haired, streetwise, cold-blooded women, like Pris Frauenzimmer in *We Can Build You* or Donna in *A Scanner Darkly*; these dark-haired girls are often warlike and ready to fight (Juliana is a martial arts instructress), and they may also relate to a peculiar Olympian (not Chthonian) goddess, Pallas Athena, who was the Greek goddess of war and wisdom (one of the identities of another dark-haired girl, Zina Pallas in *The Divine Invasion*, cf. Ch. 9). Palmer may find her figure puzzling, but her meaning is not so difficult to interpret once she is read against the background of Dick's oeuvre, where characters are often recurring; in that intertextual system, it is the dark-haired, tough, warlike girl who must eliminate the Nazi thug.

18. A remarkable case of historical uncertainty, because more than forty years after they execution there is not absolute certainty yet about their being innocents unjustly killed or real Soviet spies; contradictory revelations about the couple were published as late as 2008.

19. While the numberless hints at the reality of the 1950s and 1960s scattered throughout the novel could be read as a series of more or less hidden prolepses.

20. Though he had to research his novel and study the details of W.W.II, something that has already been noticed by Palmer (Palmer 119). Dick was quite proud of his research work, cf. the Acknowledgements page (8). Suffice it to say that even major Ricardo Pardi, the commander of Joe Cinnadella's "crack artillery battery" (82) during the war in North-Africa, mentioned only twice in just one scene of the novel, really existed. In fact the commander of the first group of the Italian 2° Reggimento d'Artiglieria Celere in January 1942 (which was part of the Marcks group of the German Afrikakorps) was a major Pardi (whose Christian name was actually spelt Riccardo); he played an important role in the battle at Halfaya Pass, near Sallum, in June 1941 (mentioned in Paul Carell's *The Foxes of the Desert*, one of the historical essays Dick listed in the Acknowledgements [Carell 37–8]).

21. West was acknowledged by Dick as an influence on his *Confessions of a Crap Artist* (Rickman 1988, 133); though the writer added that "there's no evidence of a Nathaniel [sic!] West influence on the book when you read it," *Confessions* does read as a journey in the ordinary madness of ordinary people in California, just like West's *The Day of the Locust*: Jack Isidore may be just an updated (and less threatening) version of the fool in West's novel, Homer Simpson.

Chapter 4

1. Suvin ends his article wondering whether Dick will continue writing science-fiction, as the science-fictional elements of his most recent novel at that time, *Flow My Tears, The Policeman Said*, are "perfunctory" (Suvin 1975, 14).

2. On January 18 and July 31 respectively: the latter is quoted by Sutin in *Divine Invasions* (114).

3. Dick reiterated his claim also in one of the last letters he wrote, that of August 10, 1981 (*SL6* 206–7).

4. While writing *High Castle* Dick used the *Anthology of Japanese Literature* (1955) edited by Donald Keene, one of the major Japanologists in the United States (who suggested me to read Noma's *Zone of Emptiness*). That anthology, mentioned in the Acknowledgements of Dick's novel (7), does not cover the 20th century, though it mentions two other works by Keene, his 1956 anthology *Modern Japanese Literature* and his 1953 compact history *Japanese Literature: An Introduction for Western Readers*, none of which mentions the students of French literature at Tokyo University that Dick allegedly imitated.

5. *High Castle* was completed by November 29, 1961; Dick completed *Time-Slip* less than a year later, in October 1962.

6. They are Arnie Kott, Jack Bohlen and his wife Silvia, Leo Bohlen, Norbert Steiner and his son Manfred, Otto Zitte, Dr. Glaub. Suvin did not insert the psychiatrist in his scheme (Suvin 1975, 5) but David Bohlen, Jack and Silvia's son, though he cannot be said to have a point of view of his own.

7. Warrick posits four different networks or webs which connect the four settings of the novel (Warrick 68) and the episodes of the plot (Warrick 68–9); one of them is "the invisible network of human relationships" (Warrick 68).

8. We know Dick had the concepts of existentialist psychoanalysis in mind while he was writing *Time-Slip*, as he recommends Rollo May's collection of essays to Tony Boucher in his April 25, 1962 letter (written just six months before the completion of the novel), where he also mentions the *Umwelt* (misspelt as "Unwelt," *SL1* 65).

9. *Counter-Clock* was completed in late 1965, so it comes after the group of novels where Dick creates ontological uncertainty by means of time travel (Ch. 5) and *Stigmata*, where the hallucinogenic drug Chew-Z also allows a ghostly form of time travel; we might then say that the first half of the 1960s is a time in which time is a central concern for Dick, who experiments with both *Erzahlzeit* (the time of narrating) and *erzahlte Zeit* (the narrated time) as distinguished by Gunter Muller (Muller 1968).

10. Also Warrick noticed this passage, highlighting the blackout of consciousness that strikes Jack when the confrontation with Arnie occurs (Warrick 74); actually Dick does not really need to describe what happens once again, as readers already know it thanks to the repeated prolepses. This is not very different from what we will find in *Stigmata*, where the moment of Eldritch's death is not told because it has been already shown through Barney (Ch. 7).

11. Pagetti reads Manfred's *gubble* (which is Dick's rendering of both his destructured utterances and the way he perceives what other characters tell him) as "the annihilation of any verbal communication" (Pagetti 2002, 14), a sort of degree zero of language (and writing), but sees also Manfred as a sort of arch-Dickian character, whose deviant mind turns the private drama of alienation into a public issue — we might say that Manfred's private world powerfully impacts on the shared world (Pagetti 2002, 14–5).

12. Vallorani's 2006 essay "Con gli occhi di un bambino" reads Manfred's condition based on Bruno Bettelheim's essay on autism, but unfortunately ignores the existentialist psychoanalysis which inspired Dick's novel; however, Vallorani's reading effectively focuses on the paradoxical role of connector played by the autistic boy in the climactic scene on Dirty Knobby (chapters 15 and 16).

13. Interestingly one of the androids, which have been built to resemble historical characters, is a replica of Immanuel Kant (152); a possible hint at the *Ding-an-sich* issue, the radical split between an unknowable objective reality and the human mind which strives to grasp and order it through its categories.

14. This reading and other precious insights on this novel can also be found in Pagetti's 2002 Introduction to the Italian translation (written by Pagetti himself), "I procioni di Marte."

15. This seems to be the assumption that underlies Lejla Kucukalic's reading of *Martian Time-Slip* in the third chapter of her *Philip K. Dick: Canonical Writer of the Digital Age*, but the lack of a solid reconstruction of the historical background of the novel (something that earliest critics could afford to omit, given the small historical distance from the year of publication of the novel) renders her reading too unfocused and abstract. Kucukalic quotes Foucault as an example of the "corresponding intellectual climate" (62–6), where "contemporary" would have been a more fitting adjective than "corresponding," but does not mention Anti-psychiatry or its most important representatives, such as R. D. Laing, Thomas Szasz or Franco Basaglia; nor she connects the novel to other countercultural

texts or works of art which tried to promote a different image of and approach to mental disease in the 1960s.

16. And their plight, as Warrick points out that "[t]he Martian world may be imaginary, but Jack's struggle to escape the Tomb World is real" (Warrick 78).

17. If Mars is California, a synecdoche of the United States, could not Arnie Kott, the corrupt, power-hungry yet charismatic trade union leader, be an anamorphic image of Jimmy Hoffa, the Teamsters leader who had been pursued by Robert F. Kennedy since 1957? A whole book could be written only to pinpoint all the reference to US current affairs scattered in Dick's novels.

18. And, as Palmer suggests, Jack manages to escape both Arnie and Manfred (Palmer 147), because the boy is dangerous to him: "Manfred ... can infect others with his vision of reality" (Palmer 158). It is a vision invaded by the entropic *gubbish*, an inner wasteland of ruins and decay mirroring the desolation of the Martian landscape. Maybe a better description of the interaction between Jack and Manfred is that the former must escape the dismal tomb world in which the latter is trapped; the time-slip is somewhat contagious (in fact also Arnie is sucked down by it in chapter 15 and 16).

19. We do not know if Dick had read Kesey's novel; the name of the author of *One Flew Over...* is mentioned only once in Dick's letters (*SL4* 10), but in the January 10, 1975 letter it is misspelt as "Keasy," and there is no mention of his novel (in that letter Dick complained that he was unable to provide the publisher of *A Scanner Darkly* with a list of prestigious writers which could read and possibly endorse his new novel).

20. They are Bruno Bluthgeld, Hoppy Harrington, Stuart McConchie, Bonny Keller and her children Edie and Billy, Dr. Stockstill, Walt Dangerfield, Andrew Gill; to these we should add other minor characters, such as Eldon Blaine (175–9), who may occasionally act as narrative foci.

21. Actually the two novels are quite different, though it is true that the initial scene of *Voices* has striking similarities with the first pages of *Bloodmoney*; in the earlier novel there is a Modern TV Sales and Service shop, owned by Jim Fergessen (Hoppy's and Stuart's employer in *Bloodmoney*); there is an Afro-American sweeping the pavement, though he does not work in the TV shop; the name of the protagonist is Stuart Hadley (though he is white).

22. The details of the failure can be found in Rickman 1989 (304). Suffice it to say that, for example, *Mary and the Giant* was rejected by 25 publishers. Commentators have suggested reasons why the important New York publishers did not buy Dick's novels: according to Butler, it is a matter of the scandalous issues (incest, interracial couples, marital problems, etc.) Dick often dealt with (Butler 2007, 36, 40, 42, 45–6, 49, 52); Rickman believes mainstream publishers found the hidden message in Dick's novels unpalatable, as it revealed "that so many Americans were lying to themselves, about their jobs, about their lives" (Rickman 1989, 314).

23. Lawrence Sutin rejects Dick's narrative of the *Time-Slip* disaster, as he maintains that the novel which was submitted to several mainstream publishers was *We Can Build You*, completed in October 1962 but published only ten years later (Sutin 118). Here I suspect Sutin is missing the point; Dick was not deflated by the fact that *Time-Slip* did not find a publisher, because it did, in 1964, well before *Build*; he was depressed because after two novels published as hardcovers, he "was back selling to the goddamn paperbacks again, selling to Ace again" (Rickman 1988, 147). To this humiliation, we should add that *Time-Slip* was turned down even by Wollheim at Ace.

24. I have discussed the figure of Walt Dangerfield by putting it in the wider context of the media in Dick's oeuvre in my article "Radio PKD" and in the even wider context of US radio vis-à-vis Sixties counterculture in "Acousmatic Presences" (Rossi 2009, 88–9).

25. The graphic description of war and other forms of mass violence was not, however, Dick's forte. The two chapters which display the day the bombs fell are characterized by a distinctly oneiric atmosphere, though it might be argued that such a feeling is stronger or weaker according to the point of view adopted. If this is a choral novel, also the depiction of the catastrophe is choral, and differentiated. Compare, for example, the nightmarish, vaguely surrealistic paragraph where we see the nuclear holocaust as perceived by Bruno Bluthgeld (58–61) with Stuart McConchie's more concrete and frantic experience (61–3).

26. The title of the novel as it is now was concocted by the publisher (those proposed by Dick were *In Earth's Diurnal Course* and *A Terran Odyssey*), possibly to take advantage of the popularity of Stanley Kubrick's 1964 black comedy *Dr. Strangelove, or How I Learned to Stop Worrying and Love the Bomb*, also dealing with the nuclear holocaust.

27. In this novel Nixon is the Director of the FBI, but this is not a clue to the falseness of the world Dick presents us with; it is part of the construction of a near-future world, as we are told right

from the start that the year is 1981 (2). Nixon, who had just been defeated in the 1962 California gu-
bernatorial election when Dick was working on the novel, seemed at that time to have no political
future, hence his recycling in the intelligence field.

28. So Warrick disagrees with Jameson; interestingly she also disagrees with the widespread belief
that *Dr. Bloodmoney* is a utopian novel (Warrick 88).

29. Also Edie Keller believes in Bluthgeld's powers (236), but she is a little girl after all.

30. In my essay *Il secolo di fuoco* I discuss the issue of the radical difficulty of narrating and experiencing war as one of the key theoretical issues in the field of war literature criticism (Rossi 2008,
45–62); it is difficult to deny that *Dr. Bloodmoney* belongs to that very peculiar area of war literature
which deals with World War III, a war which never took place but looms large on the mindscape of
the late 20th century.

31. Here domestic disharmony is present in the crumbling marriage of Bonny Keller; and it is interesting to see how Dick could touch the theme of marital strife from the point of view of a woman,
regardless of critical commonplaces. For a more detailed treatment of marriage in Dick's oeuvre (especially in the realistic novels), see the fourth chapter of Palmer's monograph, "Mired in the Sex War"
(Palmer 67–84).

32. Interestingly, in a novel based on interpersonal relations, the asylum takes its name from an
American psychiatrist whose research on interpersonal relationships led to the foundation of interpersonal psychoanalysis. Dick had read Sullivan's 1956 essay, *Clinical Studies in Psychiatry*, which he
recommended to Tony Boucher in a letter written in 1962 (*SL1* 64).

33. Warrick only passingly mentions *Clans*, but files no complaint about its alleged sexism.

Chapter 5

1. Maybe some critics consider *Penultimate* a somewhat minor literary achievement by Philip
Dick because its binary structure is less complex, intriguing and ambiguous than the mazes we find
in the major works of the 1960s, such as *The Three Stigmata of Palmer Eldritch, Martian Time-Slip*,
or *Dr. Bloodmoney*. Moreover, *Penultimate* seems closer to the concerns of Dick's fiction of the 1950s
(the nuclear threat, Cold War propaganda, social status, the Grey Flannel Suit nightmare etc.), thus
it may have been read as a step back.

2. A model that has been subsequently imitated in many other countries, including Italy; no
wonder then that it took Europe about twenty years to articulate a discussion of mass-media politics,
which finds its most radical expression in Jean Baudrillard's works of the 1980s.

3. It should then be noted that the relation between Mussolini and Hitler was more complex than
the former falling under the spell of the latter; Hitler only managed to become Germany's prime minister in 1933, when Mussolini's Fascist regime had been in power for eleven years. Historians generally
say that it was Hitler who fell under Mussolini's spell, and imitated the older dictator (the Duce was
born in 1883, six years before the Fuhrer).

4. The issue of nostalgia and nostalgic objects in Dick has been thoroughly discussed by Jameson,
which subsumes Wash-35 and other artefacts which reproduce lieux de memoire under the category
of the *layout* (a term Dick used in *Stigmata*, cf. Ch. 7) in his "History and Salvation in Philip K.
Dick."

5. The effects of the law had already been shown in his 1958 short story with the eloquent title
"Try and Change the Past," which also belongs to the Change War cycle.

6. Dick was surely aware of Leiber's treatment of time travel when he wrote *Penultimate* because
on the December 1963 issue of *Galaxy* where "No Great Magic" was published there was also Dick's
short story "If There Were No Benny Cemoli"; but Leiber's Change War cycle was so famous in the
sf community (*The Big Time* won the Hugo Award in 1958) it is highly unlikely that Dick totally ignored it before that date.

7. Though there is no agreement on where exactly Drake landed, one of the prevalent hypotheses
identifies Nova Albion with Drakes Bay, situated on the coast of Marin County, California, not far
from Point Reyes, where Dick lived with his third wife Anne; hence Dick's interest in the Drake expedition.

8. The idea of a man who is "his own parent" obviously bypasses any female figure representing
motherhood, thus achieving a disquieting absolute fatherhood (cf. Jameson's discussion of Heinlein's
Lazarus Long novels quoted at the end of this chapter).

9. This is the position of Kim Stanley Robinson, who criticizes Dick for having put too many twists in the plot so that it "just doesn't work" (Robinson 72). Surely if we analyze the plot looking for the "rational explanation" Robinson demands we will find holes and even pratfalls, but one cannot help wondering what is the consistency of berating Dick for the lack of a tightly woven rational plot in *Simulacra* and then praising Dick's decision to make certain that "no explanation will cover all of the facts" (Robinson 95) in *Ubik*. *The Simulacra* is structured along an entropic process: order is gradually replaced by chaos, then mayhem — this structure works because it is charged with a political meaning, and can be even said to be prophetic, if one thinks of what happened in the USA from 1960 to the moment that Nixon had to resign, including the assassination of a President and a possible candidate to presidency, plus two prestigious Black leaders, urban riots, etc. Warrick's assessment of the novel as pessimistic political satire is more perceptive (Warrick 89–93).

10. We know that *Wait* was completed on December 4, 1963. Less than a month later Dick sent another manuscript to his literary agent, *Clans of the Alphane Moon*: though we know that Dick wrote fast, it is difficult to believe that he was not already working on *Clans* when he was still completing *Wait*. *Stigmata* was completed by March 17, 1964; the day before he had sent another manuscript, *The Crack in Space*, and this should mean he worked on both novels in winter 1963–64. Dick repeatedly said that it took him a short time to write a novel, but that he kept meditating on its plot and scenes for a long time before he started typing the first draft, only jotting down short notes now and then (Rickman 1988, 55). The strong connections between *Wait* and *Stigmata* may then be explained by the simple fact that while materially working on the former Dick was already composing the latter in his head.

11. This echoes another historical event, the so-called Doctors' Plot, an anti–Semitic campaign hatched by Stalin in the last months of his life (1952–53); Stalin thought that Jewish doctors had caused the death of several Soviet leaders, and that they might try to assassinate him too.

12. There is an evident political subtext in this novel that deals with racism, an issue that was particularly hot in 1963, when Dick wrote *Wait*. Anthropocentrism leads Molinari to ally himself with the Lilistarians, thus making a fatal mistake; a racist group kills Molinari for his tolerance to aliens. Racial issues were also present in *Dr. Futurity*, and they play a very important role in *The Crack in Space*, a novel Dick completed only three months after *Wait*: it tells the story of the first Afro-American president of the United States, Jim Briskin, who has to solve the problem of all the unemployed citizens (the so-called *sleepers*, most of whom are Black) who are kept in cryogenic suspension. I have already discussed this issue in the Afterword to the Italian translation of *Crack* (Rossi Postfazione).

13. This marginal figure is a perfect example of helper, a role often played by alien creatures which are mostly benevolent in Dick's fiction, whose function is what Jameson has defined "counsel" (Jameson 2005, 376–7, 379); his name then is reminiscent of Kafka's characters (another writer often mentioned in relation to Dick, and one whose name Dick himself sometimes dropped in his interviews).

14. A revelation which is anticipated by Bert Hazeltine, the manager of the firm which manufactures the drug, who suspects that "the time period entered by the subject under its influence is phony" (140).

15. It is interesting that Dick does not use the usual US political terminology to define the offices of the future government: Stanton Brose is not a Secretary, but a Minister; Dick is using a term which is not usual in Anglo-Saxon political systems, but is typical of Continental European governments. Germany has Ministers, and the term was also used in the Third Reich. Dick may have derived the term from his research on Nazi Germany, and used it to suggest the totalitarian character of the world government depicted in the novel.

16. On the other hand, it is something that Dick still remembered almost twenty years later, when Rickman asked him to comment on this novel (Rickman 1988, 154); Rickman told Dick that "[a]ny other novelist would have built a whole novel around that idea, and you just toss it off as a plot device," without realizing that often Dick's "small" plot devices, taken together, create the bewildering and overpowering effect of radical uncertainty which characterizes his fiction.

Chapter 6

1. The objection that *Blade Runner* is not a novel by Dick but a film based on *Do Androids Dream of Electric Sheep?* is not relevant, inasmuch as the idea that Rick Deckard might be an android is also suggested in the novel, as we shall see, even if it turns out to be false.

2. For a survey of Dick's sf about androids, robots, and simulacra, cf. Barlow's "Philip K. Dick's Androids."

3. It also started the current PKD craze in Hollywood, with several films based on Dick's novels or stories and more films being made. I am not interested in the movie versions of Dick's fictions (be they adaptations that strive to be faithful to the text, like Linklater's *A Scanner Darkly* or action movies where the name of Dick is just a pretext, like Tamahori's *Next*), but this is an aspect of his impact on our culture that has been repeatedly discussed, cf. Fitting 2006, La Polla 2006, Kerman 1991.

4. Dick must have taken the figure of the Magna Mater from Jung, who considers it one of the archetypes (cf. Jung's essay "The Psychological Aspects of the Kore"). The so-called Magna Mater schizophrenia is thus a fictional mental disease assembled by Dick himself (and possibly rooted in his difficult relation to his own mother).

5. I wish to repeat it to make it as clear as possible: when simulacra/androids/replicants are clearly recognized as such they are not the direct cause of ontological uncertainty. Things are different when it is not clear whether one or more characters (including the protagonist) are or are not artificial — like in "Imposter" or, on a vaster scale, in *Androids*.

6. In a novel fraught with ambiguity and ontologically uncertain situations, especially in the last three chapters, something said by Barrows may well call in doubt our understanding of that scene: the businessman remarks "That girl in there is underdeveloped. Everything slides back out. What's she doing there in the bedroom anyhow? Has she got that skinny body—" (219). Does Barrows really say this, or is Louis also hallucinating these comments? And if Barrows really says this, does this mean that Pris is in the room, notwithstanding what we have been told a few pages before (214), that Louis found his cigar-smoking father in the bedroom? Many pitfalls are scattered in this most beguiling novel.

7. Another event that struck Dick, since he decided to open his last novel, *The Transmigration of Timothy Archer*, on the day that Lennon was shot (Ch. 10).

8. Once again a comparison with *Build* is enlightening: in that novel Pris may be artistically gifted, and there is no doubt that she is (cf. Dillon 53–5), but she is undoubtedly not-wholly-human in her relations with Louis and others.

9. Dick admitted that *Androids* was written by cannibalizing previous works, and mentions *Confessions of a Crap Artist*, at that time another unpublished text he did not expect to see ever published (Rickman 1988, 133).

10. Another feature which may derive from crime fiction is the absence of the time-slips that characterize other works by Dick and that we have repeatedly mapped in this book: notwithstanding the abundance of coups de théâtre, the plot is extremely linear and compact, as all the events are told in chronological succession and take place in 24 hours.

11. There might be another interpretation of the name of the corporation, because it is based in Seattle, which was the city where Barrows lived in *Build*, not Louis. We might then imagine that Barrows eventually managed to take Louis and Maury's firm over — Eldon's devious manners (49) are more similar to Barrows' ways than Louis.'

12. Luba also tries to cheat Rick by explaining her systematic misunderstanding of the proverbs in the test with the fact that she is German, and takes literally what only a native speaker of English can perceive as metaphorical statements (80); it is another version of Polokov's ruse to pose as a stranger.

13. There is also the subplot about Buster Friendly, the TV emcee who exposes Mercerism as a hoax, which will be discussed in Chapter 10.

14. Peter Fitting is right when he says that Rachel is no more than "a grateful and subservient — and ageless!— sex doll" (Fitting 1987, 140) in the questionable ending of the first version (I am not sure this description fits her character in the rest of the movie); however, in the *Director's Cut* she is Deckard's peer (both are runaway replicants in the end) and his partner (thus mirroring or reintroducing the Roy-Pris couple), yet she is not amoral nor a destroyer of male strength. We might say that *Blade Runner* (both versions) is an anomalous noir because it lacks a veritable dark lady. Fitting already noticed the strong difference between Rachael and Rachel (Fitting 1987, 134).

15. Already noticed by Warrick (128).

16. That of undistinguishable androids looking all the same is an idea Dick had already exploited in one of his best short stories, "Second Variety" (1953).

17. I suspect Jameson may have had Vernet in mind when he characterized Deckard as a middle-class hero because the essay of the French critic was published in the same collection of essays, *Shades of Noir* (1993), where Jameson published his "Synoptic Chandler." Jameson explained in his essay on

"History and Salvation in Philip K. Dick" that he applied the same "synoptic" method he had used to explore Chandler's novels to Dick's fiction (Jameson 2005, 363–4).

18. The noir elements in the novel are also hidden by the simple fact that Rick, though endowed with one of the narrative foci, is not the narrating I of the novel. Both hard-boiled fiction and noir movies are strongly characterized by the voice of the protagonist/narrator which retrospectively comments on the events in the story with its unmistakable style unsurprisingly inserted in the final versio of *Blade Runner*.

19. One might wonder whether the idea to stage Luba Luft's "retirement" at an exhibition of paintings by Edvard Munch, including his celebrated *The Scream* (1893), does not hint at the plight of bounty hunters, as the description of the painting ends with "[t]he creature stood on a bridge and no one else was present; the creature screamed in isolation" (100); if bounty hunters must be isolate, and suffer for what they are required to do, Munch's scene of alienation is a perfect depiction of their distressing psychological condition.

Chapter 7

1. Interestingly Moylan analyzes one of Dick's short stories, the impressive "Faith of Our Fathers" (1967), and he reads it as a "supremely anti-utopian" narrative (Moylan 177), but one with a "closed mythic quality" which explains its lack of opposition, of a way out or forward of a utopian horizon (Moylan 177). Unfortunately the author of *Scraps of the Untainted Sky* did not tackle Dick's most classical dystopia, *Radio Free Albemuth*.

2. Of course I am well aware that condescension should be avoided even when talking about superheroes, be they Marvel or DC Comics or whatever, inasmuch as even in this genre there have been examples of artistic sophistication and excellence, such as Alan Moore's *V for Vendetta* and *Watchmen*, or Hugo Pratt's Corto Maltese stories.

3. Though it should be said that Winston Smith, the protagonist of *Nineteen Eighty-Four*, has a greater complexity than the characters of other "classical" dystopias.

4. In *Scanner* the repressive anti-drug apparatus is evidently a totalitarian system, inasmuch as the complex surveillance apparatus seem to have made the concept of privacy totally devoid of meaning; S.A. Fred, the undercover nark, spies on his fellow drug-addicts but also on himself as Bob Arctor, small-time pusher and junkie. In *Albemuth* the story is told by two ordinary men, Nicholas Brady and Phil Dick, who belong to the part of the nation which is oppressed by the police state set up by president Fremont; they try to resist the repressive political system depicted in the novel, but are crushed by it (Phil ends up in a concentration camp, Nicholas is executed).

5. Though Suvin changed his mind about the works of the 1970s, he did not revise his assessment of *Stigmata* in his 2002 article "Goodbye and Hello." In fact he chooses to "leave unresolved the stature" of *Stigmata*, but lets readers understand that it does not qualify as a member of Dick's creative plateau of the early 1960s, which should then only include *Castle*, *Bloodmoney* and *Time-Slip* (Suvin 2002, 373).

6. Carlo Pagetti read *Stigmata* as a sort of oedipal story where Barney has to deal with two equally overwhelming paternal figures, Eldritch and Bulero; Eldritch, "*the father of the father*" (Pagetti 1984, 204, translation mine) is then the ultimate patriarchal authority figure, resembling Saturn, the Greek god who ate his children.

7. We know that Dick used to recycle images he liked: in fact there is a minor character in an earlier novel, *The Simulacra*, who sports "stainless steel teeth" (83), Janet Raimer, the talent scout who works for the First Lady.

8. Once again readers should be warned that gnosis is not an organized Church whose articles of faith or dogmas are well defined and fixed (as it is in Roman Catholicism). Gnosis is a constellation of religious sects which thrived in the early Christian era, whose theological ideas we know only through fragmentary and incomplete sources.

9. The noun "translation" is however endowed with theological significations in some traditions; in the Church of Jesus Christ of Latter-Day Saints, for example, or in other branches of Mormonism, it indicates being physically changed by God from a mortal human being to an immortal human being—another transformation, and one which bears relation to the novel, as Eldritch boasts that "God … promises eternal life. I can do better; *I can deliver it*" (80).

10. The superimposition of Eldritch's face, especially his eyes and teeth, and his artificial arm on other characters takes place at pages 83–4, 98, 156, 158–9, 167, 170–1, 177, 200–1, and 204. It is not always a matter of accident superimposed on substance: in the final occurrence of this phenomenon,

Bulero asks Felix Blau "'Leo?' How come you keep calling me 'Leo'?" (204). Forgetting who you are may lead you to believe you are somebody else, possibly Eldritch himself.

11. Though Dick does not miss the opportunity to poke fun at Leo's triumph by means of Eldritch's apparition as a desecrating/defecating dog (97–8).

12. Another layer of meaning is the one that identifies the three stigmata with the original sin, or "original curse of God" (194). Religious references abound throughout the novel: among the books Barney takes to Mars there is Thomas à Kempis' *De Imitatione Christi* (127), whose title hints at Palmer's being a grim parody of Jesus Christ; on the other hand, Anne Hawthorne is reading an essay on Mars during her trip to the red planet, whose title, *Pilgrim Without Progress* (117) is both a pun on John Bunyan's famous Christian allegory and another hint at Palmer Eldritch, whose first name indicates a Medieval pilgrim who had visited the Holy Land.

13. BIP is the Black Iron Prison, a recurring phrase in Dick's writings of the 1970s and 1980s, indicating the dystopian alternate world where the Roman Empire still exists; it is a place where early Christians, among which Dick's alter ego, are jailed; but it is also an atemporal symbol of oppression and despair. Hence Dick's note means that *Tears* shows what is the actual world we all live in (the dystopian police state depicted in the novel is a sort of planetwide jailhouse), so that it is to the BIP what the *Acts of the Apostles* were to the Apostolic Age (from c. A.D. 26–36 to A.D. 100), the early "heroic" age of Christianity.

14. In the latter it only involves Ragle Gumm, but we may well surmise that after Ragle has left Earth the war will unavoidably end and the fake 1958 town will be dismantled, so that all its "prisoners" will be set free.

15. Though published in 1974, *Tears* was written in 1970, and is thematically close to such works written in the late 1960s as *Our Friends From Frolix 8* (which also features a totalitarian society) and *Maze* (featuring alternate worlds); I consider it part of a phase of Dick's literary activity beginning with *Eye* and ending with *Tears* itself.

16. Dick was not however totally wrong when he linked *Ubik* to *Eye* and *Joint*; also in this novel in an apparently normal — albeit futuristic — world a gradually unfolding chain of strange events (the regression of vehicles and appliances, mysterious messages appearing in the least likely places, the apparition of Runciter coins) makes the characters (and the readers) suspect that there must be something wrong. Nothing like that is found in *Stigmata*, where characters are abruptly thrown in a dismal, surrealistic wonderland.

17. Dick's doubts about the books written after 1964 is not just a matter of hindsight: he already declared his unhappiness about them in a May 1969 letter (Sutin 163). He was surprised by the critical interest about *Ubik*, for example, and in 1975 he could not understand yet why "Marxist critics" (under this definition he included Stanislaw Lem, unspecified French critics and those — like Suvin, Fitting and Jameson — who wrote on *Science-Fiction Studies*) "were so impressed" by this novel (*SL4* 25); he subsequently told a British critic that he "wrote the book and forgot how [he] came to write it" (*SL4* 41). His amazement at the critical enthusiasm about a novel he had probably written just to pay the bills led Dick to take literally Lem's thought experiment at the end of his essay "A Hopeless Case," the Appendix called "*Ubik* as Science Fiction" (Lem 1973, 96–104). While Lem wanted to prove that Dick's novel was sf, not fantasy — hence his examination of the "scientifically sensible notions" (Lem 1973, 97) the novel was arguably based on — Dick (possibly misled by the explanations of Lem's article provided by Claudia Bush, an Idaho State University student who was writing her MA thesis on Dick's fiction [*SL4* 41] and did not seem to be knowledgeable about genre theory) understood that Ubik was "a paradigm which applies to our own world" (*SL4* 42), that is a sf novel which accidentally explained what lies behind the apparent reality of our koinos kosmos. One more episode of Dick's uneasy and troublesome relation with the academia.

18. In a letter written well after the composition of the novel, Dick said: "I have a year of amnesia around the years 1968/70, which is about the time I wrote UBIK, MAZE OF DEATH and OUR FRIENDS FROM FROLIX EIGHT" (*SL5* 156). He may be exaggerating here, and his purportedly lost year may remind us of too many amnesiac characters in his novels, but this should be read as his quasi-fictional his way to express how difficult that period was.

19. These repeated reversals are instead read by Gallo in an epistemological perspective, suggesting that each new "discovery" compels characters to change their gnoseological paradigms, in a process of progressive disenchantment which resembles that of hard sciences (as outlined by Karl Popper); when Runciter finds the Chip coins, it means that "even the days of the new theory of reality are limited" (Gallo 1989, 78), translation mine.

20. As depicted, not without a certain amount of naivety, by Alexei and Cory Panshin in their history of Golden Age SF, *The World Beyond the Hill* (1989).

21. For a more detailed interpretation cf. Rossi 1996 and 2004.

22. The resemblance between the two novels did not escape a British critic like Andrew M. Butler (Butler 2007, 92). On the other hand, Christie's influence on Dick was suggested to me by Italian sf writer and expert Valerio Evangelisti in a personal e-mail, but he underscored the structural similarities between *Ten Little Niggers* and *Ubik*.

23. The influence of Alfred Jarry, the French proto-surrealist writer and inventor of pataphysics, the absurdist "the science of imaginary solutions," on Dick is attested by a 1978 letter where he admits he discovered Jarry through his former wife Nancy Hackett, who had studied at the Sorbonne for a year and belonged to a circle of pataphysicians (*SL5* 159–60); all this explains why the name of the ham actor who plays the part of Mercer in *Androids* is Al Jarry (*Androids* 157).

24. That milieu was optimistically depicted by Dick in his speech "The Android and the Human," delivered at the University of British Columbia in February 1972; there he proposed those streetwise kids as the real opponents of the "creatures who have ... become instruments, means, rather than ends" (*Shifting Realities* 187), that is, the alienated middle-class Americans of Nixon's years.

25. Dick claimed in another letter that he had completely rewritten the novel "adding all sorts of new touches" (*SL2* 151); he then declares "I had done 9 revisions and thought it to be perfect," and this might mean that the heavy revising of the manuscript had taken place in 1970, so that only the tenth and final revision was carried out in 1972. However, Dick's versions of the story in different letter are—as it often happens—not wholly consistent. I should add that while he was working on *Tears* he also wrote one of his most impressive short stories, "A Little Something for Us Tempunauts" (Ch. 5), which also shows better craftsmanship than his previous short fiction.

26. *Tears* may have also been influenced by Ursula K. Le Guin most Dickian novel, *The Lathe of Heaven* (Watson 66); though Dick had almost completed the novel in 1970, he rewrote part of it after the publication of *Lathe* in 1971. Le Guin's character of George Orr, a man who can change reality through his dreams, is an analogous of Dick's demiurges, though he is less threatening than Palmer Eldritch and Jory, and less devious than Alys Buckman.

27. The powerful musical subtext of this novel would deserve a detailed analysis. Suffice it to say that music does not only provide *Tears*'s title, part of which comes from a song by John Dowland published in 1600, whose lines Dick also used as epigraphs for the four parts of the novel; it is also a key element in the scene in chapter 18, when Jason meets Alys, and discovers that she is the only person who remembers him, and has two of his albums in her quibble; and in the climactic scene in Chapter 22, set in a coffee shop where the jukebox features Jason's songs, which are then played by Mary Ann Dominic and lead to Taverner's being recognized by the customers (158–9). Music then sanctions the return of Jason to his reality, to the primary text—or better, as we shall see, to what *looks like* the primary text.

28. Suvin seems to subscribe to this idea, but this brings him to brand *Tears* as a "broken-backed narrative" (Suvin 2002, 374). Besides, Suvin sees *Tears* as exemplifying one of Dick's sins of "political illiteracy," the fixation on the "Good Magnate or Ruler" (Suvin 2002, 393).

29. Or Dick's letters, whose reading might have prevented Robinson from writing that *Tears* has "a little protagonist, a TV star who one day wakes up in a world where no one has heard of him" (106). It is difficult to believe that Jason Taverner, rich, beautiful, famous, a celebrity whose show is followed by thirty million spectators, is a "little protagonist" at the beginning of the novel; he is then *turned into* a nobody who is however not an ordinary man like Dick's typical characters. Robinson may have been deceived by something said by Alys Buckman in chapter 18, "How now, little man?" (127), a rather ironical line, as Alys knows that Jason was a celebrity in the world he comes from. If Robinson had had access to the first volume of the *Selected Letters*, he could have discovered that Alys is actually quoting (or misquoting) one of Dick's favorite novels, Hans Fallada's *Little Man, What Now?* (*SL1* 64).

30. One more hint at the Zero Text: the character who manages to unravel Taverner's mystery in Chapter 27 is called Phil, like the author of the novel.

Chapter 8

1. Curiously he does not mention *The Transmigration of Timothy Archer*, and one might wonder whether this is due to the fact that it is not a sf novel.

2. Such an indirectly suggested continuity may be said to exist — albeit in an even less overt form — also for *We Can Build You* and *Do Androids Dream of Electric Sheep?* (Ch. 6).

3. Hence I find it at least surprising that Dick's VALIS Trilogy is absent from the chapter of the authoritative *Cambridge Companion to Science-Fiction* devoted to "Religion and science-fiction," written by Farah Mendlesohn.

4. There are also preternatural events which might induce to read *Archer* as a fantasy novel, but they are somewhat neutered in the text (Ch. 10).

5. This is also a possible reading of *Time Out of Joint* (Ch. 2).

6. Who is not incidentally one of the characters of the second novel in the Trilogy, *The Divine Invasion* (Ch. 10).

7. An example of a honest, albeit fragmentary attempt to read Dick in a religious, not literary, perspective being McKee's *Pink Beams of Light from the God in the Gutter*; a more organic effort could surely yield interesting results.

8. We should also take into account the fact that the novel Dick does not mention in that excerpt of the *Exegesis*, namely *Archer*, is the most skeptical part of the trilogy (Ch. 10).

9. Being based on Dick's own comments on the Trilogy, this interpretation could be undermined by other comments to be found in another letter, which Dick wrote to Ursula K. Le Guin on March 6, 1981, where he claims that *Invasion*, then just published, was part (and conclusion) of a "meta-novel" which also included *Flow*, *Scanner* and *VALIS* (*SL6* 137). One should however be suspicious of this claim, as it is meant to soothe Le Guin's "distress concerning the female characters" (*SL6* 137), by showing that *Invasion* should heal the wound of "the primordial death of the woman," i.e. Alys Buckman in *Flow* (Ch. 7). After this letter the purported fourfold "meta-novel" is never mentioned again, and there are several letters that describe the VALIS Trilogy as we know it today (Ch. 9).

10. First-person narrative was not the usual technique Dick resorted to, but he had already used a narrating-I in *Build*, *Confessions of a Crap Artist* and *Albemuth* (where the two protagonists, Nicholas Brady and Phil Dick, closely resemble those of *VALIS*).

11. Which are still undemonstrated hypotheses — like the one presented by Arthur Koestler in an article published on the July 1974 issue of *Harper's Magazine*, quoted by Dick in his letter (*SL3* 141). No experimental evidence for the existence of tachyon particles — which should travel faster than light — has been found yet.

12. Plus other problems about which Dick himself ironized, as when he wrote in a 1980 letter (hence written well after the 2–3–74 experiences) that people could easily think he "[t]ook drugs. Saw God. BFD" (*SL6* 27) i.e., drug abuse had permanently impaired his mental faculties.

13. It remains to understand whether Dick meant the scene to be convincing — or, if we take into account Frye's fallacy of premature teleology (Frye 17) — whether its position in the text, the role it plays in its architecture, aims at convincing readers of something specific: in *Albemuth* the scene is dramatic, because Nicholas lives in a totalitarian society where being aware of VALIS and its subversive messages is extremely dangerous; here it is the clandestine character of the act that is underscored. In *VALIS* this scene takes place *after* Phil has been healed by Sophia, when he is aware again that he and Fat are the same person, and it may well mark a recovery of his own past, as it refers to something happened at the time of the earliest pink beam phenomena — it is in fact part of an analepsis — and is not just related to the anamnesis of the Lord's Supper (209) — Dick's theological comments notwithstanding — but to a recovery of Phil's own memories. Like many other episodes of the novel, its tone oscillates between comedy and serious revelation.

14. This is what a superficial reader might understand when Palmer talks about "the blurring between fictional and historical" taking place in "low" postmodernism (Palmer 235n), and mentions as examples a few authors of fake memoirs/autobiographies, such as the male white Australian writer Leon Carmen who published a novel, *My Own Sweet Time* (1994), pretending to be an aboriginal woman, Wanda Koolmatrie; or the Swiss musician Bruno Dössekker who published a bogus Holocaust survivor memoir, *Fragments*, under the pen name of Binjamin Wilkomirski.

15. A rabbi being more a religious teacher than a priest.

16. One should compare Fat's predicament to that of Nicholas Brady in *Albemuth*, who is sure that VALIS (an alien communication satellite broadcasting precious subversive information) exists. Fat's situation is relatively closer to that of Herb Asher in *Invasion* (Ch. 9) who doubts about the reality of the world he is living in and suspects he is still in half-life; but in *Invasion* the multiple plot technique shows that God exists and is fighting on Herb's side, and readers are shown what is really going on when they read the parts about Emmanuel and Zina.

17. The Greek word this term derives from originally meant "to lead out"; exegesis being an interpretation or explanation of a text (usually a religious one) which should lead us out of the difficulties we may encounter while reading it.

18. Another autobiographical reference, as Dick attended group therapy sessions in that hospital in 1977 (Sutin 253).

19. Completed in 1978, four years after Nixon's resignation, most of the novel covers the period 1971–77, a time of conservative backlash, given Reagan's election as Governor of California in 1967 (an office he kept until 1975) and Nixon's election the following year.

20. This might seem offbeat in the early Eighties, but it does not sound insane in A.D. 2010 , after Negri and Hardt's *Empire* and all the talk about an American empire which preceded and followed 9–11.

21. It would be more correct to talk of a Nag Hammadi *library*: it is made up by thirteen leatherbound papyrus codices, together with pages torn from another book, which were found near the Nag Hammadi village in December 1945. The codices contained Coptic translations of 52 mostly Gnostic tractates dating back to the 2nd century A.D., including the famous *Gospel of Thomas*.

22. Therapy is, as we have already seen, one of the four corners of the semiotic square that Jameson has used to persuasively identify the fundamental semantic coordinates of Dick's works of the 1960s (Jameson 376, 382) — coordinates which are however still valid for Dick's later output.

23. This could be interpreted as another form of the paradox that we have met in *Androids* (Ch. 6): there we had a human being endowed with empathy (Rick Deckard) who is led by his own empathy to spare a creature (Rachael) who is totally deprived of that ability to understand and enter into another's feelings; here we have a man (Fat) who feels pity for another (Sherri) who has been rendered merciless by her terminal illness.

24. Jaynes' 1976 essay, *The Origin of Consciousness in the Breakdown of the Bicameral Mind*, is still controversial and contested by several psychiatrists; its theory of hallucinations being generated by the right hemisphere of the brain is however quite important for another novel written near the Nag, *Scanner*.

25. Once again the sf imagination shapes Dick's meditations on his mystical visions: this situation is similar to what we have in several sf novels and movies (such as Don Siegel's 1956 B-movie *The Invasion of the Body-Snatchers*), where those who have discovered a covert alien invasion are considered mad by other people, so that the invasion may continue undisturbed.

26. Kevin and David have been generally interpreted as portraits of Kevin Wayne Jeter and Tim Powers respectively, two of Dick's closest friends (both professional sf writers, by the way); but this identification should be taken *cum grano salis*. Robert Galbreath has suggested that Phil, Kevin, and David, whose initials spell PKD, might all actually be aspects of Dick's own (split?) personality (Galbreath 119). Besides, K.W. Jeter himself has said that he "wasn't a complete church-burning skeptic, … Phil wasn't this completely befuddled person," and Powers was not "a complete religious no-doubt fundamentalist" (Sutin 258); once again, reading *VALIS* as a barely disguised autobiography can be misleading. It is a fictionalized biography, similar to Carrère's *I Am Alive and You Are Dead*, which should not be read and used as a factual narration of Dick's life.

27. The autobiographical subtext is also important here: Mini's surname is the same of the man Kleo Apostolides married after divorcing Dick. Moreover, Mini is a sfinal portrait of the British musician Brian Eno, whose 1975 album *Discreet Music* Dick loved (Sutin 252). On the other hand, Eric Lampton is an avatar of David Bowie, whose acting in Nicholas Roeg's 1976 movie *The Man Who Fell to Earth* had greatly impressed Dick (Sutin 258).

28. Here Kevin interestingly suggests something quite different from Phil's first explanation of the "creation" of Horselover Fat: if Phil "believed" in Fat as a "separate person," that was not a deliberate narrative move, but a psychotic split caused by Phil's derangement. This reading is bolstered by a letter to Russell Galen where Dick defines Fat as the "psychotic self of the 'I' narrator" (*SL6* 18).

29. Kermode describes at length the scholarly dispute about where Mark's Gospel really ends; the usually questioned part, which many exegetes suspect of being a later addition, is Mark 16:9–20 (Kermode 65–73).

30. This idea is already present in Pierre Klossowski's labyrinthine novel-essay *La vocation suspendue*, which explores the complexities and contradictions of any novel which presents itself as a religious text.

31. Which unsurprisingly does not mention Dick, having been published in 1991, when Dick's canonization had just started.

32. Vonnegut describes the genesis of his "Dresden book" in the 1st-person Chapter One of the

novel, thus appearing as the author, and then as one of the many American soldiers in Europe in Chapter Five (Vonnegut 86).

33. If by these two terms we mean tales with a happy or sad ending, we have to admit that VALIS contains both: the comedy of Phil's healing, but also the tragedy of the Lampton family, which is a very dark variation on the theme of the Holy Family.

34. There may be an osmosis between modernism and postmodernism, especially in a writer like Dick who was under the influence of the high modernist classics (Kafka, Joyce, etc.) in his college years, when he befriended Robert Duncan (Sutin 56–7). But the osmosis between these two apparently conflicting seasons of Western literature may be something not at all incidental (Carravetta 482–3).

Chapter 9

1. Which will develop an embryonic idea I have found in Christopher Palmer's monograph (Palmer 38–9).

2. The image of the Holy Family is also present, in a more cryptic form, in *Time Out of Joint* (Rossi 1996). I have discussed its symbolic and political implications in more detail in a forthcoming article, "The Holy Family From Outer Space," to be published on *Extrapolation*.

3. Her figure is thus quite similar to Sherri, the dying and destructive friend of Horselover Fat in *VALIS* (Ch. 8).

4. Cf. the fictional portrait of Nixon as the evil president Ferris F. Fremont in *Radio Free Albemuth*. Dick's feelings about Nixon are briefly but effectively expressed in the May 2, 1974 letter he sent to the then President of the USA, which ends with this question: "If you feel such contempt for us, how can we feel anything good back for you?" (*SL3* 78). This letter is even more remarkable because if follows the April 20, 1974 letter where Dick sympathized with Nixon for the ordeal the President was going through due to the Watergate scandal (*SL3* 64–5).

5. Lorenzo DiTommaso also dealt with the religious subtext in *The World Jones Made* (DiTommaso 2001, 55–8).

6. Surely the plot is so complex and strewn with twists that also Suvin lost his bearings when he said that most of the first eight chapters are set on CY30-CY30B when actually only parts of chapters 1–5 take place there (Suvin 386).

7. Once again Dick is remarkably close to C.S. Lewis' *Out of the Silent Planet* (1938), where Earth is also isolated from the rest of the universe and under the domination of an evil spirit (or *oyarsa*), Thulcandra, who is actually Satan. Lewis is briefly mentioned in *VALIS* (Ch. 8) and this might be Dick's way to acknowledge his literary precursor, though the quotation is rather ironic.

8. The unsuccessful resistance of the Jews against the Roman Empire might well be a hint at the successful resistance of the Vietnamese against the American Empire; Dick wrote it in 1980, just five years after the Fall of Saigon.

9. Or in an essay like "Cosmology and Cosmogony" (1978), where the Demiurge becomes "an *artifact*, a computerlike teaching machine" (281) called Zebra (cf. Chapter VIII).

10. The Gnostic idea of our physical world as a Black Iron Prison is also present in *The Divine Invasion*, because Emmanuel realizes that "*This is a prison*, and few men have guessed" (123). In the same page Emmanuel opposes the world dominated by Belial (the B.I.P.) to the Palm Garden, which is the lost paradise where men originally dwelt.

11. Regardless of what Dick wrote in his letters and in the pages of the *Exegesis* that have been published so far. It is interesting to notice that most of what Dick wrote before February-March 1974 was reinterpreted by the writer in the late 1970s as containing a series of messages pertaining the real meaning of Dick's mystical experiences in early 1974. He wrote in the *Exegesis* that "[t]he vast overtheme could be extracted from the novels & stories" (*Pursuit* 167), but this extraction entails an interpretive work which can also be done in other ways, to extract other "over-themes" or local messages. Besides, Dick adds that the mystical truths to be extracted by his previous fiction (when he was not aware of it, of course) alone "would not prove it to be true" (*Pursuit* 167)—according to the writer, it was his 2-3-74 experiences proved it to be true. Hence our different experiences that compel us to extract other messages.

12. Surely in the essay—written by the two Marxist philosophers before 9-11 but often quoted by the media after the fall of the Twin Towers—the idea of Empire is not only tied to the domination of the USA after the dissolution of the USSR: their idea of Empire is more a postmodern network of

global organizations and institutions than a monolithic pyramid of power. Yet the USA are one of those insititutions; and we shall see that Dick's idea of Empire in *The Divine Invasion* is also more global than simply national.

13. USSR involvement in Afghanistan started on December 27, 1979 and the USA announced on March 21, 1980 that they would boycott the 1980 Summer Olympics to protest against the invasion; when Dick wrote the novel in May-June 1980, the issue of Afghanistan was undoubtedly hot on the media.

14. If the story of Emmanuel is a sfnal rewriting of the Gospel, we should realize that Dick changed the plotline in a highly meaningful way. Since Emmanuel should succeed where Christ failed, he will not die. Yet somebody else has to die, and that is Rybys, so that the moment in the Olive Garden where Christ accepts his destiny is present in Dick's novel, but with a woman, the new Mary, as the protagonist (63–6). This is not the only moment in which women play a key role in this sfnal story of the Second Coming, as we shall see.

15. That is a rectangle whose sides respect the Golden Ratio, mentioned in Chapter 11 as a feature of the doorways to Zina's Secret Commonwealth (144). The ratio itself, also known as Fibonacci Constant, is quoted in the novel, and it is interesting to notice that this proportion (lately made famous by Dan Brown's bestseller) had above all artistic applications, as it was used — among others — by Le Corbusier, Piet Mondrian and Salvador Dali. Hence the Secret Commonwealth is characterized by (artistic) beauty right from the start, from its very door.

16. His contention that "in *VALIS* and *The Divine Invasion*, the women characters are almost uniformly destructive personalities" (Robinson 123) is well-grounded as regards the former novel, but is completely off the mark in regard to *Invasion*. Neither Zina nor Linda can be labeled as "destructive"; as for Rybys, she may resemble the Dickian bitch wives in her second embodiment (in Zina's world), but her figure in the first part of the novel has a sort of tragic greatness, and the role she plays is absolutely not destructive, being the mother of the second Messiah.

17. Expressed in the notorious 1974 short story "The Pre–Persons," depicting a dystopian future society where abortion is legal well after the birth.

18. Interestingly, evil is here embodied in a domesticated animal, a kid, which resembles Rick Deckard unlucky sheep in *Androids*. The kid is killed on the roof of Linda's house, where Herb has landed with his flying car. The scene has striking similarities with the killing of the sheep (reported, not shown) in the twentieth chapter of *Androids* (Ch. 6). There is a symbolic inversion at work here, which has turned the innocent victim into the Prince of This World; such an inversion might be explained with Dick's comments about the "metal face" of the devil in "Man, Android, and Machine" (*Shifting Realities* 213), which seem to depict a generalized inversion in the meaning of certain symbols and images the writer had used in his works written before the 2-3-74 experiences (such as Palmer Eldritch's metallic features, or the evil metal face in the sky which purportedly inspired Dick to create Eldritch [Ch. 7]).

19. To follow this interpretive trail we should also take into account Dick's own life, and the complex relation to his twin sister Jane, who died less than a month after their birth, and remains an omnipresent shadow in his life and fictional world(s) (Sutin 17–9).

Chapter 10

1. For the dates of publication of the other five volumes, cf. the Bibliography. There is a remarkable asymmetry in the collection of letters, because 33 years of Dick's life are covered by a single volume, while the other parts of the collection cover periods of 2–3 years each (with the third volume only covering 1974, considered by the editors a particularly relevant moment because of the February-March experience). Since the texts of the letters in Volumes 2–6 have been prevalently taken from the carbon copies found in Dick's apartment after his death, and those that were typed before 1971 were presumably lost in the notorious November 17, 1971 burglary in Dick's house on Hacienda Way (Williams 1986, 26–46), the first volume was made only of those letters that the editors managed to retrieve from the addressees; hence the paradox that we are left with very few letters covering the most productive time in Dick's life (1952–1971). Since Dick often expressed different and contradictory opinions on the same issue in different letters, what we can or cannot find in Volume 1 of the *Selected Letters* should be taken with proper prudence (cf. also Butler 2007, 133–4).

2. I have found at least 5 letters where Dick says this: July 9, 1981 to Laura and Joe Coelho (*SL6*

178–9); July 25, 1981 to Glenn Ole Hellekjaer (*SL6* 195); July 28, 1981 to Ralph Vicinanza (*SL6* 196); August 30, 1981 to Cathy Workman (*SL6* 231); December 31, 1981 to Len Bales (*SL6* 300–1). To these we might add the June 7, 1981 letter to Lou and Cynthia Goldstone where Dick connects *Archer* with at least *The Divine Invasion* (*SL6* 163) because of the theme of Judaism.

3. Le Guin criticized Dick's portrayals of female characters in a famous letter sent to *Science Fiction Review* on February 26, 1981. It is a brief letter, which aimed at clarifying possible misunderstandings about the opinions she had previously expressed about Dick and his most recent production; Le Guin wrote that "it seems like you hate women now, and the part of you that is woman is denied and despised" and concludes "I can no longer follow your art, which has been such a joy & solace to me"— though she then adds "But I keep trying!" (Le Guin 1981). Robinson used this letter — which is definitely not as authoritative as a scholarly review — to bolster his contention that "in *VALIS* and *The Divine Invasion* the women characters are almost uniformly destructive personalities, and in the rest of his work the balance is not much better" (Robinson 123). Robinson thus questionably extended Le Guin's comments on *VALIS* (which were in any case not a meditated critical assessment) to the rest of Dick's oeuvre; this precipitous and superficial critical judgement was then — unfortunately — occasionally quoted by other commentators.

4. One might compare this letter to the one Dick sent Patricia Warrick on February 12, 1981, where he suggests a political interpretation of *VALIS*. Of course the writer was not unaware of his contradictions: in fact he tells Warrick "Once again my right hand did not know what my left hand was doing. I thought I was writing a theological, philosophical novel; but … VALIS can be interpreted as a call for political action against [the regime that has just now come to power here in the U.S.]" (*SL6* 103). Dick — who often re-read his novels in the last years of his life — was only dimly aware of the fact that a novel can tell more than one story at the same time — a truth critics should be well aware of.

5. An important sf editor and publisher who worked for the Timescape imprint of Simon and Schuster which had already published *Invasion* and *Archer*.

6. Judging from what Dick tells Russell Galen and others in the letters he wrote in the Autumn of 1981, he was prevented from starting *Owl* by a state of deep physical and psychological exhaustion which induced him to postpone the heavy work of writing a new novel (*SL6* 237–9, 243), even though he had been taking notes for some time. One might wonder whether Dick's dejection was a harbinger of the fatal heart attack which would kill him in March 1982; in any case he kept rather busy, projecting a trip to Metz, France which should also have brought him to New York and Germany in mid–1982; he also looked forward to the premiere of *Blade Runner*, also scheduled for that period (Sutin 286–9).

7. Warrick went so far as to propose the scheme of a "dynamic four-chambered metaphor" (Warrick 30) as a model to fully understand Dick's metaphorical method. Curiously Warrick does not seem to be aware that the literalization or materialization of tropes had already been proposed as one of the fundamental elements of fantastic literature by Tzvetan Todorov in 1970: "The supernatural often appears because we take a figurative sense literally" (Todorov 76–7). This idea is extensively developed (and applied) in the fifth chapter of Todorov's essay, "Discourse of the Fantastic."

8. Among the many literary quotations in this novel based on the recollection of things past, there is — unsurprisingly — Marcel Proust's masterpiece. Angel ironically complains: "I read *The Remembrance of Things Past* and I remember nothing" (9).

9. This is a remarkable inversion of what happens in Shakespeare's *Hamlet*— un-incidentally mentioned by Angel and Kirsten (161)—where it is Hamlet's father who only appears as a ghost. The Shakespearean subtext hints at the fact that this novel is pivoted upon the father-son relation; it also hints at the issue of revenge, because Hamlet must avenge his father, while Tim tries to avenge his son: he does not fight against a material usurper, but against tyrannous death (and fate, as we shall see).

10. *Archer* could also be read as a vindication of the historical character of Jim Pike, as Dick had been annoyed by Joan Didion's scathing portrait of the former bishop in her 1976 essay "James Pike, American" (later included in *The White Album*). Dick sent her a letter on February 13, 1981 (*SL6* 107–9), where he calmly describes Pike's personality (also quoting some episodes which are also present in the novel), implicitly rejecting Didion's depiction and her contention that Pike "shed women when they became difficult and allegiances when they became tedious" (Didion 57); Dick replied that his friend "was totally loyal to his friends. Those he never forgot" (*SL6* 109). The letter was then inserted in the second chapter of the novel, with Didion's name changed into "Jane Marion" (16–9), a choice that underscores its strong connection with the author's life.

11. Also Angel questions the cause-effect connection imprudently established by the Bishop between Jeff and the phenomena (described by Kirsten [106–7] but not directly witnessed by Angel), and it is interesting to see that while she needs the Indian philosophical concept of inference or *anumāna* (107–9), which is not exactly something familiar to Western readers, Bill manages to debunk the Bishop's inference by explaining that a pool of water under a parked car does not necessarily indicate that there is a leak in the radiator of that car. Dick here opposes Angel's scholarly, erudite and bookish frame of mind to Bill's eminently practical mentality.

12. The original Greek term *euangelion* means "good news," and the same may be said for the Old English phrase *gōd spell* which became "gospel" in Modern English — this is not something that could escape a writer like Dick, whose oeuvre is characterised, according to Suvin, by "messengers: from Juliana in *Man in the High Castle* and Walt in *Dr. Bloodmoney*, the theme grows omnipresent and mysterious in *Ubik*. In *A Scanner*, messages inside Arctor's brain get so confused that they break down. By the VALIS Cycle, almost everybody is a messenger and everything is a message" (Suvin 2002, 395). The message is more important, however, than the messenger; Mercer may be a fraud, the message of Mercerism is not.

13. Also a Berkeleyite like Angel uses illegal drugs, though she mostly smokes marijuana and only occasionally takes pills. However, she is starving, like her friends Tim and Kirsten, and like them is not shown eating bread or similar food.

14. Not an easy task, as Angel discovers when she is told by Dr. Greeby that she is a harmful influence on Bill (241–3). Greeby, Bill's psychiatrist, does not like Angel as a representative of the "Berkeley community" (242), yet he says something that may easily be overlooked when one reads their conversation: "We learn by erring" (241). This goes in the direction of that gradual — albeit painful and troubled — improvement which seems to be the message — or one of the many messages — of this novel. An improvement that Angel sets as her aim, countering the static, mechanical repetition which characterised her life before she met Barefoot (210–1).

15. For example in Angel's invective against Tim's involvement in the preternatural: "For this, Dr. Martin Luther King, Jr, died. For this you marched at Selma …" (111).

16. I take this concept from Frasca's discussion of Dick's fiction; he took it in turn from Yuri Lotman.

17. Dick had good reasons to choose Lennon in particular as an icon of the 1960s; it was from Lennon's suite that Timothy Leary phoned him in 1969 to announce that the British rock star had been fascinated by *Stigmata* and wanted to make a film out of it — another of those never materialised projects that are too often found in Dick's life (Sutin 129, 158).

Bibliography

Primary Literature

Novels

Clans of the Alphane Moon, 1964. Rpt. London: Granada, 1984.
Confessions of a Crap Artist, 1975. Rpt. New York: Vintage, 1991.
The Cosmic Puppets, 1957. Rpt. London: Granada, 1985.
Counter-Clock World. 1967. New York: Berkeley.
The Crack in Space. 1966. New York: ACE Books.
The Divine Invasion, 1981. Rpt. London: Corgi, 1982.
Deus Irae, 1976. With Roger Zelazny. Rpt. London: Sphere Books, 1982
Do Androids Dream of Electric Sheep? 1968. Rpt. London: Granada, 1984.
Dr. Bloodmoney, Or How We Got Along After the Bomb, 1965. Rpt. London: Arrow, 1987.
Dr. Futurity, 1960. Rpt. New York: ACE Books, 1972.
Eye in the Sky, 1957. Rpt. London: Arrow, 1987.
Flow My Tears, the Policeman Said, 1974. Rpt. London: Granada, 1984.
Galactic Pot-Healer, 1969. Rpt. London: Grafton, 1987.
The Game-Players of Titan, 1963. Rpt. New York: Vintage, 1991.
Humpty Dumpty in Oakland, 1986. Rpt. London: Paladin, 1988
In Minton Lunky Territory, 1985. Rpt. London: Paladin, 1987.
Lies, Inc., 1964. Rpt. London: Panther Books, 1985.
The Man in the High Castle, 1962. Rpt. Harmondsworth: Penguin, 1987.
The Man Whose Teeth Were All Exactly Alike, 1984. Rpt. London: Paladin, 1986.
Martian Time-Slip, 1964. Rpt. Ballantine: New York, 1981.
Mary and the Giant, 1987. Rpt. London: Paladin, 1989.
A Maze of Death, 1970. Rpt. London: Granada, 1984.
Now Wait for Last Year, 1966. Rpt. New York: DAW, 1981.
Our Friends from Frolix 8, 1970. Rpt. London: Granada, 1984.
The Penultimate Truth, 1964. Rpt. London: Granada, 1984.
Puttering About in a Small Land, 1985. Rpt. London: Paladin, 1987.
Radio Free Albemuth, 1985. Rpt. London: Grafton, 1987.
A Scanner Darkly, 1977. Rpt. London: Granada, 1985.
The Simulacra, 1964. Rpt. London: Methuen, 1983.
Solar Lottery, 1955. Rpt. London; Arrow, 1982.
The Three Stigmata of Palmer Eldritch, 1964. Rpt. London: Granada, 1984.
Time Out of Joint, 1959. Rpt. Harmondsworth: Penguin, 1984.
The Transmigration of Timothy Archer, 1982. Rpt. London: Granada, 1983.
Ubik, 1969. Rpt. London: Granada, 1984.
Ubik: The Screenplay, 1985. Rpt. Burton: Subterranean Press, 2008.
VALIS, 1980. Rpt. New York: Vintage, 1991.
The Variable Man, 1953. Rpt. New York: Ace Books, 1957.

We Can Build You, 1972. Rpt. London: Grafton, 1986.
The World Jones Made, 1956. Rpt. New York: Vintage, 1993.

Short Stories

Beyond Lies the Wub: Volume One of the Collected Stories, 1987. Rpt. London: Gollancz, 1999.
The Father Thing: The Collected Stories Volume 3, 1987. Rpt. London: HarperCollins, 1998.
The Minority Report: The Collected Stories of Philip K. Dick Volume 4, 1987. Rpt. New York: Citadel, 1991.
Second Variety: Volume 2 of the Collected Stories of Philip K. Dick, 1987. Rpt. London: HarperCollins, 1994.
We Can Remember It for You Wholesale: Volume 5 of the Collected Stories of Philip K. Dick, 1987. Rpt. London: HarperCollins, 1994.

Essays

The Dark Haired Girl. 1988. Willimantic: Mark V. Ziesing.
In Pursuit of VALIS: Selection from the Exegesis. 1991. Novato and Lancaster: Underwood-Miller.
The Shifting Realities of Philip K. Dick: Selected Literary and Philosophical Writings. 1995. Sutin, Lawrence, ed. New York: Vintage.

Letters

The Selected Letters of Philip K. Dick — Volume 1: 1938–1971. Novato: Underwood-Miller, 1996.
The Selected Letters of Philip K. Dick — Volume 2: 1972–1973 Novato: Underwood-Miller, 1993.
The Selected Letters of Philip K. Dick — Volume 3: 1974 Novato: Underwood-Miller, 1991.
The Selected Letters of Philip K. Dick — Volume 4: 1975–1976 Novato: Underwood-Miller, 1992
The Selected Letters of Philip K. Dick — Volume 5: 1977–1979 Novato: Underwood-Miller, 1992.
The Selected Letters of Philip K. Dick — Volume 6: 1980–1981. Ed. Heron, Don. Novato: Underwood-Miller, 2010.

Secondary Literature

Interviews

Boonstra, John. "Philip K. Dick's Final Interview, June 1982." *Philip K. Dick: The Official Site*. Online resource. <http://www.philipkdick.com/media_twilightzone.html> Retrieved on October 16, 2010.
Platt, Charles. 1980. "Philip K. Dick." *Dream Makers: The Uncommon People Who Write Science Fiction*. New York: Berkeley.
Rickman, Gregg. 1988. *Philip K. Dick: In His Own Words*. Long Beach: Fragments West/The Valentine Press.
_____. 1985. *Philip K. Dick: The Last Testament*. Long Beach: Fragments West.
Williams, Paul. 1986. *Only Apparently Real: The World of Philip K. Dick*. Encinitas: Entwhistle Books,

Monographs

Barlow, Aaron. 2005. *How Much Does Chaos Scare You? Politics, Religion and Philosophy in the Fiction of Philip K. Dick*. Brooklyn: Lulu.com.
Butler, Andrew M. 2000. *The Pocket Essential: Philip K. Dick*. Rpt. Harpenden: Pocket Essentials, 2007.
Caronia, Antonio, and Domenico Gallo. 2006. *La macchina della paranoia: Enciclopedia Dickiana*. Milano: X Book.
Frasca, Gabriele. 2007. *L'oscuro scrutare di Philip K. Dick*. Roma: Meltemi.
Gillespie, Bruce (ed.). 1975. *Philip K. Dick: Electric Shepherd*. Carlton, Victoria and Melbourne: Norstrilia.
Jameson, Fredric. 2005. *Archaeologies of the Future: The Desire Called Utopia and Other Science Fictions*. London: Verso.
Kucukalic, Lejla. 2008. *Philip K. Dick: Canonical Writer of the Digital Age*. London: Routledge.
Link, Eric Carl. 2010. *Understanding Philip K. Dick*. Columbia: The University of South Carolina Press.
Mackey, Douglas A. 1988. *Philip K. Dick*, Boston: Twayne.

McKee, Gabriel. 2004. *Pink Beams from the God in the Gutter: The Science-Fictional Religion of Philip K. Dick*. Lanham, MD: University Press of America.

Palmer, Christopher. 2003. *Philip K. Dick: Exhilaration and Terror of the Postmodern*. Liverpool: Liverpool University Press.

Rickman, Gregg. 1989. *To the High Castle — Philip K. Dick: A life 1928–1962*. Long Beach: Fragments West/The Valentine Press.

Rispoli, Francesca. 2001. *Universi che cadono a pezzi: La fantascienza di Philip K. Dick*. Milano: Bruno Mondadori.

Robinson, Kim Stanley. 1981. *The Novels of Philip K. Dick*. Ann Arbor: UMI Research Press.

Sutin, Lawrence. 1989. *Divine Invasions: A Life of Philip K. Dick*. New York: Harmony Books.

Vest, Jason P. 2009. *The Postmodern Humanism of Philip K. Dick*. Lanham: The Scarecrow Press.

Warrick, Patricia S. 1987. *Mind in Motion: The Fiction of Philip K. Dick*. Carbondale and Edwardsville: Southern Illinois University Press.

Essay Collections

De Angelis, Valerio Massimo and Umberto Rossi (eds.). 2006. *Trasmigrazioni: I mondi di Philip K. Dick*, Firenze: Le Monnier.

Kerman, Judith B. (ed.). 1991. *Retrofitting Blade Runner: Issues in Ridley Scott's* Blade Runner *and Philip K. Dick's* Do Androids Dream of Electric Sheep. Rpt. Madison: The University of Wisconsin Press, 1995.

Mullen, R.D., Istvan Csicsery-Ronay, Jr., Arthur B. Evans, and Veronica Hollinger (eds.). 1992. *On Philip K. Dick: 40 Articles from* Science-Fiction Studies. Terre Haute and Greencastle: SF-TH Inc.

Olander, Joseph D., and Martin Harry Greenberg (eds.). 1983. *Philip K. Dick*. New York: Taplinger.

Umland, Samuel J. (ed.). 1995. *Philip K. Dick: Contemporary Critical Interpretations*. Westport, Ct. and London: Greenwood.

Viviani, Gianfranco, and Carlo Pagetti (eds.). 1989 *Philip K. Dick: Il sogno dei simulacri*, Milan: Editrice Nord.

Essays Published on Collections, Conference Proceedings, or Academic Journals

Aldiss, Brian. 1975. "Dick's Maledictory Web: About and Around *Martian Time-Slip*." Rpt. Mullen et al., 1992, 37–41.

Barlow, Aaron. 1991. "Philip K. Dick's Androids: Victimized Victimizers." Kerman: 76–89.

Baudrillard, Jean. 1980. "Simulacra and Science-Fiction." Tr. Arthur B. Evans, *Science-Fiction Studies*, #55, 18:3, November 1991: 309–13.

Butler, Andrew M. July 2005. "LSD, Lying Ink and *Lies, Inc.*" *Science-Fiction Studies*, #96 32:2: pp. 265–80.

Campbell, Laura E. 1992. "Dickian Time in *The Man in the High Castle*." *Extrapolation*, 33:3: 190–201.

Carratello, Mattia. 2006. "Piccole città, piccoli uomini e un futuro possibile: i romanzi *mainstream* di Philip K. Dick." De Angelis and Rossi: 178–187.

Carter, Cassie. 1995. "The Metacolonization of Dick's *The Man in the High Castle*: Mimicry, Parasitism and Americanism in the PSA." *Science-Fiction Studies* #67, 22:3: 333–342.

De Angelis, Valerio Massimo. 2006. "Storiografie multiple in *L'uomo nell'alto castello*." De Angelis and Rossi: 168–77.

Desser, David. 1991. "The New Eve: The Influence of *Paradise Lost* and *Frankenstein* on *Blade Runner*." Kerman: 53–65.

Dillon, Grace L. 2006. "L'impulso divinatorio di Philip K. Dick: il ragno e l'ape." De Angelis and Rossi: 52–60.

Disch, Thomas M. 1982. "Toward the Transcendence: An Introduction to *Solar Lottery* and Other Works." Olander & Greenberg: 13–25.

DiTommaso, Lorenzo. March 2001. "Gnosticism and Dualism in the Early Fiction of Philip K. Dick." *Science-Fiction Studies* # 83, 28:1: 49–65.

_____. 1998. "A *logos* or Two Concerning the *logoz* of Umberto Rossi and Philip K. Dick's *Time Out of Joint*." *Extrapolation*. 39:4: 285–98.

_____. March 1999. "Redemption in Philip K. Dick's *The Man in the High Castle*." *Science-Fiction Studies* # 77, 26:1: 91–119.

Doll, Susan, and Greg Faller. 1986. "*Blade Runner* and Genre: Film Noir and Science Fiction." *Literature/Film Quarterly*, 14: 89–100.

Dossena, Giampaolo. 2000. "Postfazione." Philip K. Dick, *I giocatori di Titano*. Roma: Fanucci: 265-9.

Durham, Scott. 1988. "P. K. Dick: From the Death of the Subject to a Theology of Late Capitalism." Rpt. Mullen et al. 1992: 188–99.

Fitting, Peter. 2006. "Il mondo che sta dietro tutto questo: l'eredità di Philip K. Dick al cinema." De Angelis and Rossi: 263–74.

_____. "1989. Philip K. Dick Is Dead." Rpt. Mullen et al., 1992: 243–5.

_____. 1983. "Reality as Ideological Construct: A Reading of Five Novels by Philip K. Dick." Rpt. Mullen et al. 1992: 92–110.

Freedman, Carl. 1988. "Editorial Introduction: Philip K. Dick and Criticism," Rpt. Mullen et al. 1992: 145–53.

Galen, Russell. September 6, 2010. Email to the author.

Gallo, Domenico. 1989. "Il sogno di Galileo e l'incubo di Philip K. Dick." Viviani and Pagetti: 73–9.

Gopnik, Adam. August 20, 2007. "Blows Against the Empire: The Return of Philip K. Dick." *The New Yorker*: 79–83.

Hayles, N.B. 1982. "Metaphysics and Metafiction in *The Man in the High Castle*." Olander & Greenberg: 53–71.

Huntington, John. 1988. "Philip K. Dick: Authenticity and Insincerity." Rpt. Mullen et al. 1992: 170–7.

Jameson, Fredric. 1975. "After Armageddon: Character Systems in *Dr. Bloodmoney*." Rpt. *Archaeologies of the Future: The Desire Called Utopia and Other Science Fictions*. London: Verso, 2005: 349–62.

_____. 2005. "History and Salvation in Philip K. Dick." *Archaeologies of the Future*. cit. 363–84.

_____. 1989. "Nostalgia for the Present." Rpt. *Postmodernism, or The Cultural Logic of Late Capitalism*, Durham, Duke University Press, 1991: 279–96.

La Polla, Franco. 2006. "Dick a Hollywood: ovvero, la quadratura del cerchio." De Angelis and Rossi: 275–81.

Le Guin, Ursula. Summer 1981. "Letter. February 26, 1981" *Science Fiction Review*. No. 39, 32.

_____. 1975. "The Modest One." Rpt. *The Language of the Night*. Ed. Susan Wood. New York: Berkley, 1982: 165–68.

Lem, Stanislaw. 1975. "Philip K. Dick: A Visionary Among the Charlatans." Tr. Abernathy, Robert. *Microworlds*. London: Mandarin, 1991: 106–35.

_____. 1972. "Science Fiction: A Hopeless Case — With Exceptions." Tr. Koopmann, Werner. *Microworlds*. London: Mandarin, 1991: 45–105.

Lethem, Jonathan. 2002. "You Don't Know Dick." Rpt. *The Disappointment Artist*, New York: Doubleday, 2005: 77–83.

Pagetti, Carlo. 1977. "Introduzione a *La svastica sul sole*." Rpt. Viviani and Pagetti 1989: 132–49.

_____. 1984. "Introduzione a *Le tre stimmate di Palmer Eldritch*." Rpt. Viviani and Pagetti 1989: 199–205.

_____. 2002. "I procioni di Marte." Philip K. Dick. *Noi Marziani*. Roma: Fanucci: 7–21.

_____. 2002. "Un sinantropo di nome Bill Smith." Dick, Philip K. *Svegliatevi, dormienti*. Roma: Fanucci: 7–18.

_____. 2003. "Il tempo ritrovato di un piccolo Amleto americano." Philip K. Dick, *Tempo fuor di sesto*, Roma: Fanucci: 5–21.

_____. 2000. "Travestimenti da alieno." Dick, Philip K. *I giocatori di Titano*. Roma: Fanucci: 7–14.

Philmus, Robert M. 1991. "The Two Faces of Philip K. Dick." Rpt. Mullen et al, 1992: 246–56.

Pierce, Hazel. 1982. "Philip K. Dick's Political Dreams." Olander & Greenberg: 105–35.

Proietti, Salvatore. 2006. "Vuoti di potere e resistenza umana: Dick, *Ubik* e l'epica americana." De Angelis and Rossi: 204–15.

Rabkin, Eric. 1988. "Irrational Expectations: or, How Economics and the Post-Industrial World Failed Philip K. Dick." Rpt. Mullen et al.: 178–87.

Rieder, John. 1988. "The Metafictive World of *The Man in the High Castle*: Hermeneutics, Ethics, and Political Ideology." Rpt. Mullen et al. 1992: 223–32.

Rossi, Umberto. March 2009. "Acousmatic Presences: From DJs to Talk-Radio Hosts in American Fiction, Cinema, and Drama." *Mosaic*, 42:1: 83–98.

_____. 2000. "All Around the High Castle: Narrative Voices and Fictional Visions in Philip K. Dick's *The Man in the High Castle.*" *Telling the Stories of America — History, Literature and the Arts — Proceedings of the 14th AISNA Biennial conference (Pescara, 1997).* Eds. Clericuzio, A., A. Goldoni, and A. Mariani. Roma: Nuova Arnica: 474–83.

_____. 2006. "California/Marte," in Caronia and Gallo: 105–10.

_____. 1994. "Dick e la questione della tecnica (*o Della tecnologia*)." *Technology and the American Imagination: An Ongoing Challenge, Atti del XII Convegno biennale AISNA.* Eds. Mamoli Zorzi, Rosella, and Francesca Bisutti de Riz. Venezia: Supernova: 473–83.

_____. Winter 2002. "Fourfold Symmetry: The Interplay of Fictional Levels in Five More or Less Prestigious Novels by Philip K. Dick." *Extrapolation*, 43:4: 398–419.

_____. March 2002. "From Dick to Lethem: The Dickian Legacy, Postmodernism, and Avant-Pop in Jonathan Lethem's *Amnesia Moon.*" *Science-Fiction Studies* # 86, 29:1: 15–33.

_____. July 2004. "The Game of the Rat: A.E. Van Vogt's 800-Words Rule and P.K. Dick's *The Game-Players of Titan.*" *Science-Fiction Studies* #93, 31:2: 207–26.

_____. 2006. "Genealogie," in Caronia and Gallo: 147–52.

_____. 2002. "The Great National Disaster: The Destruction of Imperial America in P.K. Dick's *The Simulacra.*" *RSA: Rivista di Studi Nord Americani* #13: 22–39.

_____. Spring-Fall 2003. "The Harmless Yank Hobby: Maps, Games, Missiles and Sundry Paranoias in *Time Out of Joint* and *Gravity's Rainbow.*" *Pynchon Notes* #52–53: 106–23.

_____. Fall 1996. "Just a Bunch of Words: The Image of the Secluded Family and the Problem of λογοσ in P.K. Dick's *Time out of Joint.*" *Extrapolation.* Vol. 37 No. 3: 195–211.

_____. 2002. "Postfazione." in Philip K. Dick, *Svegliatevi dormienti,* Roma, Fanucci: 239–47.

_____. Summer 2009 [i.e. 2010]. "Radio Free PKD." *Foundation: The International Review of Science Fiction.* Vol. 37, No. 106: 10–28.

Schmid, Georg. 1987. "The Apocryphal Judaic Traditions as Historic Repertoire: An Analysis of *The Divine Invasion* by Philip K. Dick." *Degres: Revue de Synthèse à Orientation Semiologique* 51: F1-F11.

Stilling, Roger J. May, 1991. "Reading Philip K. Dick's *VALIS* and *The Divine Invasion* as Metapsychoanalytic Novels." *South Atlantic Review.* Vol. 56, No. 2: 91–106.

Suvin, Darko. Winter 2002. "Goodbye and Hello: Differentiating within the Later P.K. Dick." *Extrapolation* 43:4: 368–97.

_____. 1975. "The Opus: Artifice as Refuge and World View (Introductory Reflections)." Rpt. Mullen et al. 1992: 73–95.

Watson, Ian. 1975. "Le Guin's *Lathe of Heaven* and the Role of Dick: The False Reality as Mediator." Rpt. Mullen et al., 1992: 63–72.

Wolfe, Gary K. "1988. Not Quite Coming To Terms." Rpt. Mullen et al., 1992: 237–40.

Wolk, Tony. 1995. "The Swiss Connection: Psychological Systems in the Novels of Philip K. Dick." Umland: 101–26.

Other Texts Quoted in This Book

Badoglio, Pietro. 1946. *L'Italia nella seconda guerra mondiale.* Milano: Mondadori.

Barthes, Roland. 1957. *Mythologies.* Tr. Lavers, Annette. New York: Hill and Wang, 1972.

Benjamin, Walter. 1950. "Theses on the Philosophy of History." Tr. Zohn, Harry. *Illuminations.* London: Fontana, 1979: 255–69.

Boorstin, Daniel J. 1962. *The Image, or What Happened to the American Dream.* Rpt. Harmondsworth: Penguin, 1963.

Bukatman, Scott. 1993. *Terminal Identity: The Virtual Subject in Post-Modern Science Fiction.* Durham: Duke University Press.

Carell, Paul. 1960. *The Foxes of the Desert.* New York: Dutton.

Carravetta, Peter. 2009. *Del postmoderno: Critica e cultura in America all'alba del Duemila.* Milano: Bompiani.

Carrère, Emmanuel. 1993. *I Am Alive and You Are Dead: A Journey Inside the Mind of Philip K. Dick.* Tr. Bent, Timothy. New York: Metropolitan Books, Henry Holt, 2004.

Ceserani, Remo. 2002. *Treni di carta. L'immaginario in ferrovia: l'irruzione del treno nella letteratura moderna.* Torino: Bollati Boringhieri.

Christie, Agatha. 1939. *And Then There Were None.* Rpt. London: Harper, 2007.

Clute, John, and Peter Nicholls. 1995. *The Encyclopedia of Science-Fiction.* New York: St. Martin's Griffin.

Cowie, Elizabeth. 1993. "Film Noir and Women." Copjec: 1967-98
Copjec, Joan. 1993. *Shades of Noir*. London: Verso.
Damico, James. 1978. "Film Noir: A Modest Proposal." *Film Reader* no. 3.
Didion, Joan. 1976. "James Pike, American." Rpt. *The White Album*. New York: Farrar, Straus & Giroux, 2009: 51–8.
Domzalski, Shawn Michael. 2003. *Crash Course for the ACT: The Last-Minute Guide to Scoring High*. New York: Princeton Review Publishing.
Eco, Umberto. 1979. *Lector in fabula: La cooperazione interpretativa nei testi narrativi*. Milano: Bompiani.
Evangelisti, Valerio. March 15, 2000. "Ubik contro Eymerich." E-mail to the author.
Freedman, Carl. 2000. *Critical Theory and Science Fiction*. Hanover and London: Wesleyan UP.
Frye, Northrop. 1957. *Anatomy of Criticism: Four Essays*. Princeton: Princeton UP.
Gibson, William. 1982. "Burning Chrome." Rpt. *Burning Chrome*. London: Grafton, 1988: 195–220.
Hawthorne, Nathaniel. 1845. "P.'s Correspondence." Rpt. *Mosses From an Old Manse*. New York: The Modern Library, 2003: 287–301.
Hirsch, Foster. 1981. *Film Noir: The Dark Side of the Screen*. New York: A.S. Barnes.
Hite, Molly. 1991. "Postmodern Fiction." *The Columbia History of the American Novel*. Ed. Elliott, Emory. New York, Columbia UP: 697–725.
Hofstadter, Richard. November 1964. "The Paranoid Style in American Politics." *Harper's Magazine*: 77–86.
Hubbard, Ron L. n.d. *Typewriter in the Sky: An Adventure in Time*. London: Kemsley Newspapers Ltd.
Jameson, Fredric. 1996. "Longevity as Class Struggle." Rpt. *Archaeologies of the Future*. cit. 328–44.
_____. 1993. "The Synoptic Chandler." Copjec: 33–56.
Jones, Peter. 1976. *War and the Novelist: Appraising the American War Novel*. Columbia: University of Missouri Press.
Jung, Carl Gustav. 1941. "The Psychological Aspects of the Kore." Tr. Hull, R.F.C. Jung, C.G., Karoly Kerényi. *The Science of Mythology: Essays on the Myth of the Divine Child and the Mysteries of Eleusis*. London: Routledge, 1985: 184–208.
_____. 1941. "Transformation Symbolism and the Mass." Tr. Hull, R.F.C. *The Mysteries: Papers from the Eranos Yearbooks*. Ed. Campbell, Joseph. Princeton: Princeton UP, 1979: 274–336.
Kermode, Frank. 1979. *The Genesis of Secrecy: On the Interpretation of Narrative*. Cambridge, MA: The Harvard University Press.
Laing, Ronald David. 1965. *The Divided Self*. London: Pelican,
Lawrence, D.H. 1923. *Studies in Classic American Literature*. Rpt. London: Penguin, 1971.
Leiber, Fritz. 1958. *The Big Time*. Rpt. New York: ACE Books, 1961.
_____. December 1963. "No Great Magic." *Galaxy*: 150–94.
Luckhurst, Roger, 2005. *Science Fiction*, Cambridge: Polity.
May, Rollo (ed.). 1958. *Existence: A New Dimension in Psychiatry and Psychology*. New York: Basic Books.
McCaffery, Larry (ed.). 1995. *After Yesterday's Crash: The Avant-Pop Anthology*. New York: Penguin Books.
McHale, Brian. 1979. "Modernist Reading, Postmodernist Text: The Case of *Gravity's Rainbow*." Rpt. *Constructing Postmodernism*, London: Routledge, 1992: 61–86.
_____. 1991. "POSTcyberMODERNpunkISM." Rpt. McHale 1992: 225–42.
Mendlesohn, Farah. 2003. "Religion and Science-Fiction." *The Cambridge Companion to Science-Fiction*. Eds. James, Edward and Farah Mendlesohn. Cambridge: Cambridge UP: 264–75.
Muller, Gunter. 1948. "Erzahlzeit und erzahlte Zeit." Rpt. *Morphologische Poetik*. Ed. Muller, Elena. Tubingen: Niemeyer, 1968: 269–86.
Moore, Ward. 1952. *Bring The Jubilee*. Rpt. London: Gollancz, 2001.
Moylan, Tom. 2000. *Scraps of the Untainted Sky: Science Fiction, Utopia, Dystopia*. Boulder: Westview.
Negri, Toni, and Michael Hardt. 2000. *Empire*. Cambridge, Mass.: Harvard UP.
Orwell, George. 1949. *Nineteen Eighty-Four*. Rpt. Harmondsworth: Penguin, 1987.
Panshin, Alexei, and Cory Panshin. 1989. *The World Beyond the Hill: Science Fiction and the Quest for Transcendence*. Los Angeles: Jeremy P. Tarcher, Inc.
Rossi, Umberto. 2008. "Mind Is the Battlefield: Reading Ballard's 'Life Trilogy' as War Literature." *J.G. Ballard: Contemporary Critical Perspectives*. Ed. Baxter, Jeannette. London: Continuum: 66–77.

_____. 1995. *La prova del fuoco: storia, esperienza e romanzo nelle narrative della Grande Guerra.* Doctoral dissertation, Terza Università degli Studi di Roma.

_____. 2008. *Il secolo di fuoco: Introduzione alla letteratura di guerra del Novecento.* Bulzoni: Roma.

Scholes, Robert, and Eric S. Rabkin. 1977. *Science-Fiction: History — Science — Vision.* New York: Oxford University Press.

Sheckley, Robert. 1966. *Mindswap.* Rpt. London: Grafton, 1986.

Smith, Sidonie, and Julia Watson. 2001. *Reading Autobiography: A Guide for Interpreting Life Narratives,* Minneapolis, University of Minnesota Press.

Todorov, Tzvetan. 1970. *Introduction á la littérature fantastique.* Tr. Richard Howard. *The Fantastic.* Ithaca: Cornell Paperbacks, 1975.

Vernet, Marc. 1993. "Film Noir on the Edge of Doom." Copjec: 1–32

Vonnegut, Kurt. 1969. *Slaughterhouse-Five.* Rpt. London: Triad/Granada, 1983.

West, Nathanael. 1933. *Mrs. Lonelyhearts.* Rpt. New York, New Directions, 1969.

Index